Readings in
Psychological Tests
and
Measurements

THE DORSEY SERIES IN PSYCHOLOGY

EDITORIAL COMMITTEE

HOWARD F. HUNT

Columbia University

DONALD W. TAYLOR

Yale University

FLEISHMAN *Studies in Personnel and Industrial Psychology* rev. ed.

FISKE & MADDI *Functions of Varied Experience*

BARNETTE *Readings in Psychological Tests and Measurements* rev. ed.

BENNIS, SCHEIN, BERLEW, & STEELE *Interpersonal Dynamics: Essays and Readings on Human Interaction*

RATNER & DENNY *Comparative Psychology: Research in Animal Behavior*

COURTS *Psychological Statistics: An Introduction*

DEUTSCH & DEUTSCH *Physiological Psychology*

VON FIEANDT *The World of Perception*

ROZEBOOM *Foundations of the Theory of Prediction*

KLEINMUNTZ *Personality Measurement: An Introduction*

HAMMER & KAPLAN *The Practice of Psychotherapy with Children*

Readings in
PSYCHOLOGICAL
TESTS and
MEASUREMENTS

Edited by

W. Leslie Barnette, Jr., Ph.D.

Professor of Psychology and
Director, Vocational Counseling Center
State University of New York at Buffalo

Revised Edition • 1968
THE DORSEY PRESS, Homewood, Illinois
IRWIN–DORSEY LIMITED, Nobleton, Ontario

REVISED EDITION

First Printing, March, 1968

Library of Congress Catalog Card No. 68–17046

PRINTED IN THE UNITED STATES OF AMERICA

To the Reader

The present volume is based on the experience of the editor in teaching undergraduate courses in tests and measurements, which were largely populated by majors in the Department of Psychology. Experience has shown that it is desirable to use readings of recent origin to supplement the basic text used in the course. It is usually impractical to ask fairly large groups of students to read articles directly from journals in the periodical room of the campus library; it is also costly to have all such material reproduced for local use. For these reasons, the present selection of recent articles has been assembled.

This selection was also governed by another consideration—that the material so ably presented in the *Test Service Bulletins* (numbering 57 as of May of 1967), published by the Psychological Corporation in New York City, would not overlap. It is assumed that this collection of bulletins will be utilized in conjunction with the present collection of readings.

At the time that the first edition of this collection was printed, it was the sole such collection of readings then available. Since the first edition of this collection in 1964, several other volumes of readings dealing with tests and measurements have appeared. Apparently our first edition started a trend. Megargee's volume (1966) has essentially an advanced clinical psychology approach; the Chase and Ludlow collection (also 1966) is designed for use with a second-level measurements course, or a course offering even at the master's degree level. This Chase-Ludlow volume, while sharing more overlap with the present edition than does that of Megargee, will still be seen as very different from this current and second edition. The year 1967 saw the publication of two additional collections of readings: one by Flynn and Garber which is written largely for use by education students and has valuable sections on tests as used in schools; a second by Mehrens and Ebel which has been composed from a principles of measurement stance, thereby introducing more statistical and theoretical material which would be appropriate for an advanced measurements course. Anastasi (1966) has brought forth an excellent collection of papers originally presented at the Invitational Conferences on Testing Problems, sponsored each year since 1949 by the Educational Testing Service. The reader will find a few of these papers included in this present volume.

Taken as a unit, then, these five books, together with this second revision, will now constitute a very complete and concise shelf library of material dealing with psychological tests and measurements in its many phases. The editor finds it both surprising and pleasing that the content overlap among all of these six volumes is so slight.

The editorial job has been considerable. Only a few papers are here presented in their original form; most have been condensed or abbreviated in one way or another. The focus here has consistently been on the undergraduate psychology major whose knowledge of advanced statistics is modest. Articles presenting extensive tables and elaborate statistical analyses have been drastically edited from this point of view. The editor has frequently been irritated, while using other collections of readings in other undergraduate psychology courses, when such editing has not been done and, as a result, the beginning student meets up abruptly with F ratios, multivariate techniques, or complex Rorschach nomenclature. This second edition has not entirely eschewed such techniques—and here the instructor of the course will have to supplement—but the editor has attempted to keep them to an absolute minimum. The student reader, in the main, is expected to understand elementary statistical concepts such as correlation, various measures of central tendency and dispersion, and the simpler ways of expressing confidence limits. The general level of difficulty of this second edition, however, is at a more advanced level than the first since some new material on multivariate regression analysis and computerized programs has been included.

The bibliography at the end of the book lists all publications mentioned in the main body of the readings, including citations for the papers included in the collection itself. Unlike most collections of readings, the volume has been composed to conform with regular textbook format—tables and charts are numbered sequentially rather than in the manner of appearance in the original sources. Similarly, all references to other research cited by the authors of the articles have also been collected in one final bibliography at the end of the volume.

February, 1968   W. L. B.

Acknowledgments

The common attribution of credit to other persons for any merit a book may have is especially appropriate in regard to a book of readings such as this. It is to these authors, herein reprinted and edited with their permission, that the editor owes the first debt of gratitude; in the name of these contributors, a portion of the royalties from this volume has been assigned to the American Psychological Foundation.

In addition, the following journals and publishers and professional associations are to be thanked for their permission to use their copyrighted materials: American Association for the Advancement of Science, American Council on Education, *American Journal of Mental Deficiency,* American Personnel and Guidance Association, American Psychological Association, *Educational and Psychological Measurement,* Educational Testing Service, *Fortune, Harvard Educational Review,* Harcourt Brace and World, Inc., National Elementary Principals' Association, *Newsletter of Elementary School Principals' Association of Connecticut,* New York State Psychological Association, Penguin Books, *Review of Educational Research, Science,* Science Research Associates, *Scientific American,* Society for Psychological Study of Social Issues, and the U. S. Department of Labor.

The editor would also like to express sincere appreciation to Mrs. Bettye Berman for her work in connection with the initial typing of much of this manuscript.

W. L. B.

Table of Contents

PART ONE

General
Measurement
Problems

MEASUREMENT that purports to be scientific in any sense of the word has a logic of its own. Because of historical priority, this logic has largely been developed in the area of the physical scientists. The claims of social scientists, and especially workers in the field of psychometrics, must be evaluated against these same standards. It is well that the beginning student of psychological measurement know something of these principles. Writers such as Bridgman, Campbell, and Carnap have published treatises in this area from the vantage point of physics and mathematics. In the following article, Dr. Comrey, psychologist at the University of California in Los Angeles and well known for his research in psychometrics, spells out some of the fundamental facts of measurement as these relate to the mental testing movement. However, the reader is urged when he reads this article not to confine his thinking merely to "mental" tests but, rather, to generalize these arguments to the wider field of aptitude testing. The article originally appeared in *Educational & Psychological Measurement* in 1951.

Before attempting to understand all of Dr. Comrey's article, it would be wise for the student to be acquainted with the differences between and among nominal, ordinal, interval, and ratio scales.

MENTAL TESTING AND THE LOGIC OF MEASUREMENT

Andrew L. Comrey

By comparison with measurement in the physical sciences, psychological measurement has always enjoyed a somewhat unsavory reputation and has even been called by some the "queen of the inexact sciences." Many writers have pointed out deficiencies in the techniques employed in psychology; some have based their criticisms upon alleged violations of the traditional "laws of measurement." In a previous article (Comrey, 1950) certain implications of the logic behind measurement were given some attention. The traditional requirements were stated, criticisms of psychological measurement were discussed, and an interpretation of the position of psychological measurement with respect to these requirements was offered.

In the present paper, some of the general problems of psychological measurement will be discussed as they apply to the mental-test field. A brief review of the requirements of fundamental measurement will be given, together with a discussion of some difficulties in applying this model to mental testing. Some of the consequences to these difficulties for measurement practice will be mentioned and, finally, some suggestions regarding criteria for evaluating mental-test methods will be made which depart from the customary criteria of conformity to the pattern of fundamental measurement. The point of view will be expressed that the excellence of measurement methods in mental testing may be judged by the practical validity of those methods for the purposes at hand, in addition to comparing them with the model of measurement in the physical sciences. Reasons for giving greater emphasis to the former criterion will be offered.

CRITICISMS OF MENTAL TESTING

Perhaps the most comprehensive treatment of the requirements for fundamental measurement has been given by Campbell. Some of the more important requirements will be summarized with respect to ordinal characteristics, the relation of equality, and the operation of addition. The requirements for order specify that a class of elements must be defined unambiguously so that the elements vary with respect to some particular property. To be measurable with respect to that property, the elements must vary only in degree, not in kind. Furthermore, a relation "greater," which is transitive and asymmetrical, must be physically defined. That is, if Stimulus A is greater than Stimulus B, and B is greater than C, then A should be greater than C; also, if A is greater than B, B cannot be greater than A.

To satisfy the requirements for equality, a physical definition of the relation "equals" is needed. This definition must be such that physical equality is transitive and symmetrical, i.e., if $A = B$, and $B = C$, then $A = C$; also, if $A = B$, then $B = A$. And, finally, the requirements for addition state, among other things, that some experimental operation must be found whereby two elements possessing the measurable property can be added together to get an element containing an amount of this property greater than that of either element added. For properties which satisfy these requirements, a complete, or *fundamental* measurement is possible. Numbers assigned to elements of such classes of measurables can be manipulated in accordance with the rule of arithmetic. Furthermore, such measurements are made on scales with equal-unit and ratio properties. A few properties so measurable are weight, length, period of time, and electrical resistance.

It is fairly well known that certain difficulties are involved in trying to apply the model of fundamental measurement to the mental-test area. One of the first criticisms laid at the doorstep of mental testing is that classes of measurables are not even defined, i.e., the class of degrees of some property supposedly indicated by different scores on some test do not represent merely differences in degree but differences in kind as well. A Gestalt interpretation of mental organization would tend to contradict the notion that merely a quantitative difference is reflected by different test scores. Furthermore, the relation of equality does not meet the necessary conditions. It is stated that equal test scores do not mean identity with respect to some ability. Individuals may get the same test scores by solving correctly different combinations of items. Furthermore, by this line of reasoning, if $A = B$ (i.e., equal test scores), and $B = C$, there is no reason to suppose that the underlying ability organizations of A and C are the same, even though their numerical test scores are identical.

Interesting as these objections may be, the psychologist can minimize their importance on operational grounds. He can state that by the only measuring instrument available to him, i.e., the test, $A = B$ if they have the same test score. Aside from the question of differences in kind represented by different test scores, no contradiction in the actual numbers assigned can occur with respect to the relations "greater" and "equals." The fact that different combinations of items add up to the same score does not bother him too much because he feels that if the items themselves are of the same sort, the total score should be fairly indicative of the person's level of achievement.

That mental testing has no suitable operation of addition is quite apparent, and critics have not failed to mention this point. There seems to be no way to add physically one psychological magnitude to another to get a third even greater in amount. With fundamentally measurable variables, such as weight, length, resistance, and so on, this can be accomplished easily and, from such an operation, numbers can be assigned such that differences and ratios are endowed with the desired experimental meaning. The fact that the operation of addition is not defined in mental testing leads to considerable difficulty, since this operation is employed in fundamental measurement to endow measurement scales with equal-unit and ratio properties. Thus, it would appear that mental-test workers may not be able to develop test scales with equal units and ratio properties.

Let us consider, for a moment, two opposed points of view which might be adopted with respect to the nature of measurement involved in a mental test. First, it might be assumed that the human mind is composed of an undetermined number of abilities. A test may tap, so to speak, a few of these abilities which inhere basically in the physiological structure of the organism, but the test can be only an indirect measurement in terms of certain behavioral manifestations. A direct measurement is out of the question, at the present state of our knowledge of physiology, for there is no way that variations in these abilities can be directly observed. Behavioral products represent the only available indicators of such underlying variables at the present time.

Taking a simple case, suppose there were such an underlying ability and a test which measured this variable alone, plus some error variance. What is the functional relationship between the performance variable and the underlying ability? If a performance variable is to be used to yield a measure of ability in this sense, it is obvious that such functional relationships must either be determined experimentally, or assumed to follow a certain form. This functional relationship must be known before the task of securing equal-unit scales, with respect to the underlying variable, can be accomplished, for the equality of units must be in terms of the underlying ability, not the performance.

Unfortunately, it is not now possible to determine the nature of such functional relationships. An independent measure of the underlying ability would be necessary before the relationship of such measures to scores on the performance test could be found. Since no independent measurements (e.g., physiological determinations) for the underlying variable can be taken, this method of proceeding is impractical. It should be mentioned at this point that an approach to this problem can be made through the use of certain types of judgments. For example, one might employ fractionation and equal-appearing-interval methods for the scaling of the subjective difficulty of digit series and words in a vocabulary test. These methods do not comprise an experimental verification of unit equality on an underlying mental-ability variable, however. They do allow an operational meaning to be attached to unit differences on the subjective scale, but such units do not represent those of a fundamental type for the underlying variable.

From this analysis, it appears evident that one cannot prove that a performance or behavior test yields equal units along the scale of some basic underlying ability which in itself is not directly observable. It should be emphasized that the task of disproving an assumption of equal units in such cases is equally difficult, for this, too, would require experimental checks of the relationship between the performance variable and independent measurements of the underlying ability.

An opposite position which might be assumed by some persons with respect to the nature of measurement involved in a mental test is the point of view that a test measures a variable of some kind, or variables, and these behavioral products themselves are what concern us. It amounts to behavioristic approach, so to speak, which denies the necessity of dealing in terms of concepts which have no basis in observation. The extreme behaviorist might ask, "What is the point of assuming an underlying ability which cannot be measured, observed, or proved to exist?"

If the second approach is taken, what are the consequences? First, the matter of a functional relationship between the behavior variable and a hypothetical underlying variable is no longer of importance. The behavior itself is the variable, as determined by the performance on some test. The emphasis with this approach is switched from a consideration of whether the test measures the underlying variable properly to that of whether the variable measured is a useful one. It is assumed that the measures obtained from a test represent some variable in a one-to-one fashion. Since the variable is defined by the test scores, there can be no question as to whether the units on such a test are equal, because that is implicit in the assumptions. It follows from the general approach involved that the units of such tests are equal by definition. It is not the intention of the writer to advance either of these positions as his own. These points of view are considered as represented opposed positions which may flank most observers rather than represent them. The point of importance in this discussion is merely that, regardless of what systematic position one adopts, we do not have equal units of the fundamental type with any mental test and we will not have them until means are devised for direct observation of underlying physiological phenomena.

SOME POSSIBLE CONSEQUENCES OF THE DIFFICULTIES

It has already been suggested that the objections raised against mental-test methods with respect to the requirements for order and equality are crucial. The issues raised by the failure to achieve an operational definition of addition in mental testing are more serious, however. Since equal-unit and ratio properties of measurement scales are based upon addition, mental testing faces the task of evaluating the effects of this deficiency.

The most obvious conclusion which might be drawn is that measurement in this area is confined to the ordinal level. That is, numbers assigned by means of mental tests can indicate only the rank-order positions of performances to which those numbers have been given. This is the sort of conclusion which is often made by critics of psychological measurement.

Now, it is quite clear that many of the statistical procedures which are applied to mental-test results demand something in the way of a unit of measurement. Means, standard deviations, product-moment correlations, and all the statistical procedures based upon these must necessarily depend upon interval sizes along the scale of measurement. This is no less true of the rank-difference correlation method, which is derived from the product-moment formula, and hence involves the same concepts. (Ratio characteristics of measurement scales do not constitute as much of a loss to mental testing as the lack of equal units, for most purposes, since the typical statistical treatments need not involve such relations between test scores.)

These considerations suggest that one of two courses of action must be taken by those attempting to use mental tests for measurement purposes. First, they may show that using methods involving unit assumptions does not introduce serious errors or that certain procedures can be employed to minimize such error in spite of the absence of fundamentally equal units. Secondly, they may avoid the use of methods of analysis which depend upon interval interpretations. The multiple cutting-score methods, for example, do not demand such assumptions. Further, non-parametric methods may be used for statistical tests of hypotheses.

It is likely that further development of measurement techniques in mental testing will proceed along both these lines. Certainly, there is a vast unexplored territory in the area of the second procedure suggested above. With respect to the first program, it can be stated that insufficient attention has been given to the problem of determining the degree and kind of error introduced into the results of measurement by virtue of the fact that such measurements lack certain characteristics they are presumed to have. In the next section, criteria for judging the work of measurement methods will be treated in the light of the discussion to this point.

CRITERIA FOR EVALUATING MENTAL TEST METHODS

The fundamental-measurement model has typically been used as a criterion by which measurement procedures should be evaluated. Those procedures which fit this scheme are termed "good" methods, and procedures which fail to do so are held to be primitive and unsatisfactory as scientific instruments. Mental tests fall in this latter category, for they certainly fail to fit the fundamental-measurement model in at least one important respect, namely, in their defection with respect to the operation of addition. Are there other criteria by which mental tests can be evaluated which may be more useful? Under the first criterion mentioned above, all mental tests are unsatisfactory, and no discrimination among them is provided. Certainly, some tests are better and more useful than others.

The obvious answer to this question is that other criteria are available for judging the value of procedures in mental testing. These criteria are to be found in the validity of such instruments for the practical purposes of assessing and predicting status under a variety of conditions. Lest some misunderstanding on this point arise, it should be hastily added that the logic of fundamental measurement should not be forgotten or ignored. It is a good thing to know where one's methods fail to meet this more exacting pattern in order to avoid the errors which are likely to occur in the absence of this knowledge. The fact that mental-test methods do not satisfy such criteria need not blind us to the possibility and usefulness of evaluation in terms of these other more practical criteria.

Whereas many difficulties are involved in the use of mental tests for the purpose of establishing scientific laws, there seems to be little doubt as to their value for certain practical purposes. It seems reasonable to assert that mental testing is and will be for some time essentially an empirical science with certain rather well-defined practical objectives, rather than primarily a theoretical scientific enterprise. At least, in terms of relative proportion of activity in this area, such a position could scarcely be questioned. Some individuals may object to this point of view, since personal preferences in matters of emphasis are involved. Be that as it may, this position will be adopted with respect to the objectives of mental testing.

These considerations lead to certain conclusions regarding the attitude which practical mental-test workers should adopt toward the logic of measurement. In the first place, they should abandon attempts to manipulate their test scores for the purpose of making their measurements approximate fundamental measurement. It is quite clear that such objectives can never be attained in this manner; they can be attained only through experimental operations upon the underlying physiological determiners of behavior. The practical test worker is not in a position to engage in the type of research activity which might conceivably succeed in reaching such ends. This fact would be evident to anyone familiar with the logic of fundamental measurement, so mental-test workers should by all means be acquainted with measurement theory.

It should be pointed out in this connection that scaling procedures which are apparently designed for obtaining measurement properties beyond rank order are not necessarily bad. What is not defensible is to assume that such procedures can stand on their own because they appear to resemble, in the end result, measurement in the physical sciences. Whether such methods are good or bad can be assessed in terms of their capacity to help achieve the practical objectives of mental tests. Ultimately, methods may become available for checking the claims of such procedures with respect to measurement properties beyond rank-order but, for the present, such claims must rest upon assumptions for which there is insufficient experimental evidence.

Attempts to improve quantification techniques in mental testing should not be confined to the pattern of fundamental measurement but should be spread over a much wider area. Any and all techniques should be explored which might conceivably lead to better predictions or assessments of status, even though such techniques do not appear to have any possibility of making mental-test measurement more like fundamental measurement.

As a matter of fact, some such successful techniques may appear to be in contradiction to a goal in terms of the fundamental-measurement pattern. An article by Richardson (1936), for example, emphasizes the importance of considering the effects of test difficulty on validity. Richardson states that the validity of a test depends in large measure upon whether the test is properly tailored to the job with respect to difficulty. He states:

Suppose, for example, that a test of clerical aptitude is meant to sort out the best 15 per cent of all applicants. This is on the assumption that the labor market is such that one hundred persons will apply for 15 positions. It is then clear that the optimal difficulty of test elements should be in the neighborhood of plus 1 sigma and that easier tasks would give us discriminations beween individuals in whom we are not interested. . . . Under any circumstances involving educational or psychological measurement, the distribution of difficulty of the elements to tasks can be arranged to fulfill more accurately the purposes of measurement.

If, by some procedure, it were possible to develop a test of clerical aptitude which would represent truly a fundamental-measurement scale with a given number of items, the scale would be the same whether 15 percent or 85 percent of the applicants were being selected. Under conditions where error variance is not present in the test, success would probably be equal for any cutting score. However, under the conditions of testing existing, this fixed scale would not do the measuring job at a given level as well as a test tailored for that level, although this fixed scale might conceivably be the best general-purpose scale. Thus, the approach to better measurement through meeting the requirements for fundamental measurement, were it possible, would not necessarily give the best practical methods, since it ignores at least one of the important factors affecting test validity.

The methods to be employed in mental testing, then, have a definite purpose and they can be evaluated in terms of that purpose. From the standpoint of the ideas presented here, the primary value of item analysis and factor analysis, for example, lies in the possibility of using such techniques to increase predictive efficiency. Developing batteries of pure tests to predict some criterion through factor analysis of tests and criteria, constitutes a method the value of which can definitely be assessed in terms of higher validity coefficients. The same criteria can be applied to other methods introduced into the mental-test field. Where such good means are available for evaluating measurement methods it seems inappropriate to rely principally on comparisons with abstract logical criteria that were designed for a different context.

SUMMARY

1. Many difficulties lie in the path of securing for mental-test measurement the type of rigor found in the fundamental type of measurement. Among these, one of the most serious is the impossibility of obtaining equal units without independent physiological assessment of the variables under consideration.

2. This failure brings up many important problems with respect to the treatment of mental-test data by statistical methods, since many of these methods presume that a unit of measurement has been established. Some justification for the use of such methods should be offered.

3. It would be desirable to attain a fundamental type of measurement for mental testing but, at present, such a goal seems out of reach. If fundamental measurement is made the sole yardstick by which the excellence of measurement procedures is to be judged, mental-test methods are automatically classed as primitive and virtually without prospect of substantial improvement.

4. The objectives of mental testing are held to be primarily empirical in nature. Testing techniques are designed mainly for the prediction and assessment of status. These objectives provide additional criteria by which mental-test methods can be judged, namely, the practical validity determinations for the purposes at hand.

5. Mental-test workers should certainly be aware of what is involved in fundamental measurement, but they should devote their major efforts toward developing measurement techniques which give some hope for better satisfying the practical validity criteria rather than the fundamental-measurement criteria. This position is taken because *(a)* the fundamental-measurement criteria cannot be attained by the methods available to the mental-test worker, if at all, and *(b)* the practical-validity criteria and the fundamental-measurement criteria may sometimes be contradictory objectives in the practical situation.

▽ ▽ ▽

THE comments that follow represent a condensation of a book review by Dr. Dingle, published in the *Scientific American* (June, 1960). The author was writing about a volume that contained the contributions to a symposium on measurement held at the 1956 meetings of the American Association for the Advancement of Science. Dr. Dingle uses this occasion—which is the reason sections of the review are reproduced here—to write about the general operational approach to valid measurement, something that is applicable to physics as well as to psychology. The author takes issue with the first sentence of this book: "Measurement presupposes something to be measured, and, unless we know what that something is, no measurement can have any significance."

Dr. Dingle is an English astronomer and physicist. He is Professor Emeritus of History and Philosophy of Science at Univerity College, London.

BASIC PROBLEMS OF MEASUREMENT

Herbert Dingle

To understand what measurement means we must turn to the physical sciences as the field affording the potentialities of measurement their widest scope; there alone are all the known processes of measurement exemplified. Consequently a true conception of measurement must cover physical measurements in their widest generality. Such a conception shows that measurement is a self-contained process, a process that implies nothing beyond that of which it gives a numerical estimation.

It is perfectly legitimate to ask an astronomer to measure the area in the sky of the constellation Orion as defined by the International Astronomical Union. But what is the "something" that he measures? We no longer think in terms of a "sky," and from another viewpoint the constellation ceases to exist. There is no "something," but beyond question there is a measurement.

Pursuing the matter, we see not only that all physical measurements are of this kind, but also that, far from starting with a something and then measuring it, we start with a measure and then try to find something to which we can attach it. We measure the weight, W, of a body, and its height, h, above the ground, and form the product Wh. This we regard as significant because it is equal to the kinetic energy with which the body, having been released, reaches the ground. We therefore invent something that Wh measures and call it the potential energy of the body. When the body falls, and h becomes 0, it loses its potential energy. We are delighted, and think we have "discovered" potential energy. But we are now forced to say that when a body moves toward or away from the sun, it similarly loses or gains potential energy. Suppose, then, that our body falls to the earth when the sun is directly overhead. Has it gained or lost potential energy? We can take our choice, which means that potential energy is not "something to be measured," but a quantity devised after the measurement has shown its importance. In

11

its devising we are free to exercise our choice among various possibilities; and, if we do not devise it at all, the measurement has exactly the same status it had before.

Take another example. We make a measurement with a diffraction grating and call the result the "wave length" of light. But we do not first perceive the waves and then measure their length; we make a measurement and then invent "wave length" to attach to it. The invention is just as arbitrary as that of potential energy, and at present it is even less satisfactory. Another observer, moving away from us in the direction of the light, gets a different value. It is the same light. Which observer determines the "right" wave length? Clearly, at least one of our measurements does not imply a "wave length to be measured." But if the something is not wave length, what is it? We do not know, though there can be no doubt that this measurement is important.

So we could continue. For this reason I some years ago proposed the rudiments of a theory in which measurement was defined as "any precisely specified operation that yields a number; that is, measurement is related to the operation performed and not to the hypothetical "something" on which it is supposed to be performed. This theory appeared in *The British Journal for the Philosophy of Science* (Vol. 1, page 5), and as it seems not to have been noticed by any of the contributors to the present volume, I shall take the liberty of outlining its basic idea. But first of all I think it will be useful to take a step still further back and see how measurement came to be practiced at all. This point is not touched upon in the volume, yet it is of some relevance and is indeed essential if we are to understand fully what measurement signifies. The contributors to the volume take measurement for granted and then discuss—often admirably—what it is, but they do not ask why it must be taken for granted. They tacitly assume the strategy of the campaign, and concentrate on the tactics. Let us see why the strategy commits us to measurement.

The fundamental problem of philosophy is that of making sense of our experience. We are originally aware of a haphazard succession of experiences. After a while some regularities force themselves on our attention—night and day alternate, falling is followed by a pain, and so on. The first philosopher is the man who first conceives the possibility that other—perhaps all—experiences are related; that is, experiences form a rational system. Given a knowledge of some experiences, therefore, other experiences that seem quite independent can be predicted.

The earliest philosophers accepted the obvious relations and tried to supplement them—the alternation of night and day was associated with alternations of heat and cold, falling on grass hurt less than falling on stone—until in such a system as that of Aristotle, with its generalizations in terms of matter and form, a considerable area of experience became organized into a rational system. Two things characterized this approach: first, it was concerned entirely with involuntary experience; and second, progress in it was painfully slow.

By the 17th century the patience of philosophers was exhausted (I am of course describing not what consciously went on in their minds, but what we, knowing the outcome of their actions, can see to be the truest rationalization of them), and they said: "Look here; we aren't getting anywhere with ordinary experience; it is too difficult. Let us make some artificial experiences and find relations between them. Then perhaps ordinary experience will fit in later." So instead of studying the natural motions of birds and smoke and rivers, they made artificial motions—balls rolling down carefully prepared grooves. Thus was born scientific experiment: the deliberate production of artificial experiences more simply related to one another than those that come naturally.

The aspect of the artificial experiences that was examined was the metrical aspect. The rolling ball did not pass from potentiality to actuality; it merely gave readings on a measuring scale and a form of clock, readings represented by numbers. What was the advantage of this? Simply that, since rational relations were required, it brought into operation the most highly developed form of reasoning known: pure mathematics. The artificial experiences were reduced to experiences of numbers, and then metrical science was born. Thus the original aim of relating all natural experience was transformed to that of relating the numbers yielded by contrived operations.

But this was not at all understood. It was thought that each measurement represented a property of something in the "external world." The object of philosophy was conceived to be the study of this external world. Our experience—which is ultimately all that is of any importance to anybody— was simply a trivial effect of the casual impinging of the "world" on our bodies; the "world" would be exactly the same if this had never occurred. This idea could persist because there happened to be a pretty close correspondence between the other "things" that were thought to be measured and the "things" that we actually experience, but in fact this correspondence is illusory. Take mass, for instance. This is the name given to something conceived to be responsible for the recordings of certain measuring instruments. But mass was imagined to be "the quantity of matter in a body," and this was plausible, because when the instrument recorded a big number, a large body was usually seen. Hence it was believed that Newton's law of gravitation described the path of a planet around the sun. In reality it describes the path of a mass-point in a gravitational field, and both mass-point and gravitational field belong to an invented world that only in part corresponds to the common-sense world of material objects. If the earth should explode to smithereens through internal stresses, the mass-point (the "center of gravity") would continue on its orbit undisturbed, but there would be no matter where it was situated.

Every symbol in every physical equation stands for the result of a measurement or a combination of such results, and fundamentally for nothing else. In a simple case like that of mass, the correspondence between symbol and some element of ordinary experience is fairly close; usually matters are more complex. Take, for example, Avogadro's number, N—the number of molecules in a cubic centimeter of gas in a certain state. N actually stands for a combination of measurements with thermometers, pressure gauges, balances and so on. (There are various combinations that give the same result; that is why the "number" is important). But we describe N as "a number of molecules"—the name given to the result of the operation of counting. And we think of it as such. But in fact the operation of counting molecules is impossible. We can delude ourselves into believing that the operation of weighing is a discovery of the mass of a body, but no honest man can claim that when he is finding N he is counting anything. Yet such is our faith that each measurement is a measurement of "something" that we are ready to make such a claim in order to maintain that faith. Nor is that the worst. We even analyze the intricate concept that we call "the momentum of an electron" as though we had a particle of matter before us and were applying the process for measuring momentum to it; and then we imagine that we are learning something about the world of experience. God help us!

The whole world of physics is a set of relations between concepts that represent combinations of the results of measurements, i.e., of artificially created experiences. Nothing that this world contains would ever have happened if we had not made it happen. To verify any of the relations you must adjust the conditions with the greatest care; let experience come naturally, and their supposed requirements are always violated. Go on dropping an object to the ground, and it will come to rest at a different place every time. Go out one day, and you feel warm; do the same the next day, and you feel cold. The laws of falling bodies and of heat are obeyed only in laboratories. Physics tells us a tremendous amount about the world, but it is not the natural world; it is a world of our own making.

How is it, then, that we have turned the results of physical research to such significant account in ordinary life? Simply because of a purely empirical relation between the natural and the artificial worlds. Over a large part of experience they maintain a close parallelism. When a balance gives a big number, we usually do see a big object (but we have seen that a large value of M does not always mean that). When the thermometer has a high reading, we usually feel hot (but in outer space we should probably die instantly of cold, although astronomers tell us that the temperature there can be over 1,000 degrees centigrade). Why the sight of a big object is usually attended by a large $M,$ and feeling of heat by a large $O,$ we understand no more than Thales could have if he had known the facts. With all our science we have learned nothing about the relations existing in the world of natural experience. We have discovered how to create a world between the elements of which rational relations do exist, and we exploit the empirical fact of its close parallelism with the natural world.

This is of the greatest importance in regard to the function of measurement in other sciences such as psychology and sociology. Here exactly the same considerations hold good, but whereas in physics the parallelism between the metrical concepts and ordinary experiences is the rule and its breakdown the exception, in the other sciences the reverse is more nearly true; at least any supposed measurement of a psychological attribute is much less uniformly related to actual experience than is normally the case in physics. To take but a single example, the primary importance of Intelligence Quotient is not that it measures "intelligence," whatever that may be, but that it stands in simple relations to other measurements (in particular, a relation approaching identity with further determinations of the same quantity with the same person). We may expect that in time a considerable system of relations between psychological measurements will be built up, but woe betide us if we imagine that its relation to the world of experience is other than purely empirical. A large IQ may go with a good performance in other specified operations, but its possessor may well be a gambling addict, and so one of the most "unintelligent" of persons.

It is in view of such facts as these that measurement must be defined in terms of its origin in the operations we perform, without reference to anything external. Having so defined it, we can begin its analysis. Each measurement includes a manual and a mental part; for example, in measuring length we lay an object along a specified scale (the manual part) and subtract the smaller from the larger of the end-readings (the mental part). We deliberately relax the precision of the specification in two respects. In the manual part we allow one element of the operation to be changed ad lib.; in the example of length we can make "the object" anything we like, and we call the result (merely as a name) the length of that object. In the mental part we allow ourselves to multiply the result of any fundamental measurement (that is, a measurement that does not include another measurement as a part of its prescription) by any number; we call this (again merely as a name) "changing the unit of measurement." The whole process is thus described without wandering outside into a hypothetical "something to be measured."

AT the 23rd annual meeting of the New York State Psychological Association in 1961, the Division of Personnel Psychology sponsored a symposium on the reporting of test information. Dr. Dorothea McCarthy, professor of psychology at Fordham University, presented the main paper, in which she first summarized the significant questions any test user should ask about tests and then continued with the communication aspect of such results. In conjunction with this the student should also read *Test Service Bulletin #54*, by Dr. James R. Ricks, "On Telling Parents About Test Results."

ETHICAL AND PROFESSIONAL CONSIDERATIONS IN REPORTING OF TEST INFORMATION

Dorothea McCarthy

Mental test data of all sorts are coming into increasing use in schools, in mental health and community clinics, in employment agencies and in business and industry, as well as in the military services. For a long time tests were administered in schools, and the practice was considered generally desirable, but the information often remained in files on cumulative record cards and was not used or interpreted to the testee himself or to his parents, teachers, or counselors. Such testing programs are utterly useless and a waste of time and money unless the test results are to be made known and unless they are to be used in decision making about the individuals who have been tested. On the other hand, school administrators who are convinced of the potential value of testing programs sometimes make specific test results known in numerical terms without adequate interpretation to members of their staff who have very limited understanding of their meaning. In a school situation where every teacher can immediately associate each child's IQ with his name in her roll book one cannot help but feel that an overemphasis on test results has occurred somewhere along the line, without due recognition to the limitations of the instruments, the conditions of taking the tests, or of the importance of motivation and other personality characteristics in the makeup of the individual.

This discussion is limited to the communication of test results as distinct from all forms of confidential information which comes to the knowledge of the clinical psychologist. Yet as tests have spread more widely in the coverage they give, there are several areas of test information which must be recognized. The first is the area of general intelligence usually in the form of a verbal test of intelligence. Secondly, there is the measure of non-verbal intelligence or performance ability, which in most cases gives a comparison score. A third major area of test information concerns a person's level of academic achievement and his relative strengths and weaknesses in the various skills and subject matter areas. The fourth area in which fairly specific test information may become available is in the category of special aptitudes and interests. There is also the area of personality and adjustment in which there are two types of test results: the objective, quantitatively-scored inventory type of test, and the more subtle and less objectively-scored projective techniques. Finally, we have the important but nebulous area of test of impairment of mental functioning.

These seven types of test results from a series of criteria or gradients along which they should be evaluated prior to interpretation. The first gradient is that of *reliability*. How certain are we that the results in each of these areas really characterizes the client and is likely to characterize him in the near or distant future? What is the margin of error we are dealing with in each of the obtained scores? How much is the particular secured score on this occasion likely to change on retest due to chance alone? How much is the particular score likely to change and in which direction, due to anticipated growth or environmental changes in the life of the individual?

The second gradient is that of *validity*. How sure are we that the test in each of these areas really measures what we think it measures, or what the test designer intended it to measure? Is the test properly named, or is it a misnomer? It seems to me we are most certain of validity in the area of achievement and least certain in tests of mental impairment, or perhaps in the more subtle aspects of personality assessment.

The third gradient to be considered is evaluating the degree of confidence to be placed in the test results we are interpreting to others is that of the adequacy of the *norms* and the suitability or applicability of the norms in the particular case to which we wish to apply the instrument. Is it fair, right and proper to apply this instrument to the case at hand? Are there norms available for the group to which this client belongs or in which he will find himself competing?

The fourth and perhaps the most important gradient when it comes to matters of interpreting test results is the degree of *intimacy* of the information yielded by the test. How *sensitive* would most clients be about having these aspects of his total makeup known to others? How *personal* is this information usually conceded to be? In general, the more personal or intimate the information, the more conservative one must be about communicating it to others.

These remarks go back to some of the fundamentals of testing, but I think it is a healthy thing to remind ourselves, as practitioners and appliers of tests, of the limitations of our instruments. When we report experimental results of research we report the level of confidence with which the results or conclusions are presented. Often, we get in the habit of applying tests on a routine basis and forget to look at newer and perhaps better instruments, or sometimes we forget things we once learned about instruments we use habitually. Such matters as the fact that a certain test has a much smaller variability than another with which we constantly make mental comparisons, the fact that its standard deviation varies markedly from one age to another, or that it is based on very few cases at the upper and lower ends of the scale, even though it may be adequately standardized in the middle range, are points often forgotten by the psychometrician. If a test is designed to get at a pathological condition, how normal were the control cases from which the pathological cases were supposed to have been differentiated? Can we honestly answer all such questions about our instruments and answer them favorably? It seems to me that if we review these fundamental principles, we become rather humble with regard to our fallible instruments, and this humility can be our best guide in matters of test interpretation.

It is my observation and experience that the person who knows the *most* about the tests is likely to be most conservative and cautious in interpretation. When we hear of some horrible example of misuse of test results, it usually arises from ignorance, or from that little knowledge which can be such a dangerous thing.

When the knowledgeable and conscientious psychologist has applied the best tools at his command which are appropriate for the evaluation of the particular subject, and has given due consideration to the fallibility of the instruments employed in the light of the above-mentioned criteria, he must then ask himself a number of additional questions in deciding how much information to divulge, and *to whom* and *how* the information can best be communicated, so as to do the most good for the client and for society, and lead to the least possibility of harm or misinterpretation.

First should be considered the right of the person to the information. The client himself has a right to know the results of the tests he has taken if he is an adolescent or an adult who is not feebleminded or severely disturbed. Some limited interpretation can often be given to children, especially for reassurance. This is particularly true in cases where there is a severe feeling of inferiority or doubt as to one's competence and when the test results are normal or superior. Parents of normal or superior intelligence who are reasonably normally adjusted certainly have a right to information about the test results of their minor children, but here care must be exercised as to *how much* information is given and in *what terms* it is to be given. Opportunity must be afforded to confer about test results which may be unfavorable and difficult for the parents to accept emotionally, even though he or she may be fully capable of intellectual understanding of the material. Those who may have had a role in referring the case are entitled to a courteous note of acknowledgement. If they are in continuing contact with the client in school or in a medical or other professional capacity, they may be entitled to a general statement about the results of test findings. If such persons are professional people familiar with handling and interpreting test results, it may be appropriate to divulge actual test findings, but in such instances it is best to clear with the client or his deputy regarding the sending of a report to the school, the doctor or whoever the party may be. In addition, it is best not to assume too much psychological sophistication, even on the part of other professional people. A pediatrician may be amazingly ignorant when it comes to interpreting an IQ! When in doubt, it is best to make such reports conservative. A meager and conservative report can always be elaborated upon later should the need arise, if one later learns more about the competence of the person to whom the information is being given.

It is best to avoid giving information over the telephone to anyone who may ask for it. First of all, clients may have relatives who are busybodies who are fishing for information they have no right to know, and the client should be protected from such inquiries. Also there is great likelihood of being misunderstood and misquoted concerning information given over the telephone. If there is some degree of urgency it is always best to call the person back, so as to check on the identity of the inquirer, if he or she is not personally known.

Another important consideration in divulging test information is whether the person will be able to *understand* the information. Information given in conference is usually the best method, for one can usually tell from facial expression, accepting remarks, etc. whether the factual information is understood. The good psychologist can judge the intellectual level of the parent, teacher or principal, and couch his information in language which can be understood by the person to whom the information is being given. One would use very different words in explaining a test IQ of 75 to a bilingual parent with a fourth grade education and to a parent holding an MA degree in social work. A disturbed mother undergoing psychoanalysis can tolerate little information concerning the pseudo-mental retardation of her unloved child.

Mere intellectual understanding of test results is not, however, the only matter to be taken into consideration in deciding what and how to communciate test results. One must consider whether the test *results* are *favorable* or *unfavorable* or *likely to be regarded as such* by the person receiving the information. The relationship of the person to the client is important, for if the mother is pushing and overly ambitious for a child who is only average, her acceptance of his mediocrity may be very difficult. On the other hand a parent who has been told by a pediatrician that his child is "brain damaged," and who has been living with fear and panic, imagining imbecility and institutionalization ahead for the child, may be greatly reassured to learn that his child has mentality in the dull-normal range. It can readily be seen then that there is no ready rule of thumb to be followed in giving test results. We must ask ourselves what tests were used, how good are they, what level of rapport and effort were achieved, who should get the results, in how much detail and under what circumstances.

I shall conclude with a few thumbnail sketches of actual experiences which will illustrate the tremendous variety of discriminations the psychologist must make in his professional judgments concerning the communication of test results.

Two delinquent boys in a reformatory had similarly high IQs of 136 and 138. Quite different interpretations were given to them, however, because of their very different personalities and attitudes. To one who was extremely cocky and overconfident, the discrepancy between his high verbal and poorer performance score of 115 was stressed, and it was pointed out to him that he was not equally good in all kinds of skills and that perhaps there were areas in which he needed to improve. The other boy who suffered from a severe inferiority complex and feeling of utter worthlessness was given a very enthusiastic interpretation of his verbal IQ which raised his morale appreciably.

In another instance the Army Signal Corps inquired about our earlier clinical study of a recruit who was now in the service. We felt obligated to point out the finding that the boy was color-blind and should not be assigned to duty involving color discrimination.

A school principal was having difficulty trying to decide whether or not a child belonged in a class for gifted children. He was using a cutoff point of 130 IQ. The child in question had an Otis Group Test score of only 124 but his Stanford-Binet IQ was 138. When the differences in Standard deviation of the two tests were interpreted to the principal he realized that 124 on the Otis (SD: 12 pts.) would be equivalent to 132 on the Stanford-Binet (SD: 16 pts.) so that the two scores were really not so far apart, and the child really would meet the criterion for the special class when the scores were properly interpreted.

A mother of a retarded reader in fifth grade received a report that her child's reading level was 3.2. She was so impressed with the seriousness of the child's reading retardation that she thought he read at 3.2 years instead of a 3.2 grade level.

A clergyman learned that a young man who was about to be married had been known to a child guidance clinic because of non-reading. The clergyman thought only mental deficiency could account for such a difficulty. He merely wanted reassurance that the young man had sufficient intelligence to understand the nature of the marriage contract.

The mother of a nine-year-old in fourth grade referred the child to the clinic because she thought he was retarded in reading. The child was found, however, to be reading normally at the middle of the 4th grade and the mother was told his score of 4.5 grade level. She replied, "Oh, but is that good enough? He'll soon be going into fifth!"

My final example concerns a young intern who, while a medical student, chanced to see his score of 84 on a mental test. Since he thought all mental test scores were IQs, he found a book on mental testing and looked up to see what an IQ of 84 meant. He found it was in the "dull-normal" range. He decided that he had only been able to get through medical school because he had "a good memory," but he really wasn't very bright. When it was interpreted to him that results on college level mental tests were usually in percentiles, and a percentile score of 84 was interpreted to him, a great weight was lifted from his mind.

These are but a few illustrations of the confusions and difficulties which can arise when there is lack of proper communication concerning test results.

MUCH of psychological research, especially concerning personality traits, is limited because of the small range in the choice of subjects upon whom research results are based. Too often is the remark jokingly made that the science of psychology is a science based on only two population samples—white rats and college sophomores. Rather than merely settling for subjects that are conveniently available, we need to be more ingenious in our data gathering techniques and to approach measurement via multiple methods. It is to this point that Dr. Eugene Webb's article is addressed. The paper is also of interest because of its numerous examples of situational types of testing in which the researcher goes directly into the field for data, thereby using highly naturalistic situations, and in which the subjects are usually unaware of being tested at all.

Dr. Webb's paper, slightly condensed for this book, was originally presented at the 1966 Invitational Conference on Testing Problems, sponsored by the Educational Testing Service, the proceedings of which are now in print (ETS, 1967). Dr. Webb is director of research at the Medill School of Journalism, Northwestern University.

UNCONVENTIONALITY, TRIANGULATION, AND INFERENCE

Eugene J. Webb

All three of the nouns in this paper's title—unconventionality, triangulation, and inference—are imbedded in a more general concept: multiple operationalism as a way of knowing. With educational psychologists making significant contributions, the mistaken belief in the single operational definition of learning, of performance, or of values has been eroded.

Most students today would agree that it is appropriate to draw simultaneously on multiple measures of the same attribute or construct.

In 1953, E. G. Boring wrote:

As long as a new construct has only the single operational definition that it received at birth, it is just a construct. When it gets two alternative operational definitions, it is beginning to be validated. When the defining operations, because of proven correlations, are many, then it becomes reified.

But just as we ask if a correlated *x* and *y* are more highly correlated with *z*, it is also reasonable to ask if the components being converged or triangulated are truly complementary. Are we fully accounting for known sources of error variance? This is a serious question with most of the multimethod studies now available. "Multimethod" has usually been defined as multiple scales or behaviors collected under the condition in which the subject knew he was being tested. The multiple methods thus have tended to be multiple variants within a *single* measurement class such as the interview.

Every data-gathering class—interview, questionnaires, observation, performance records, physical evidence—is potentially biased and has specific to it certain validity threats. Ideally, we should like to converge data from several data classes, as well as converge with multiple variants from within a single class.

The methodological literature warned us early of certain recurrent validity threats, and the evidence has markedly accelerated in the last few years. It has been 30 years, for example, since Lorge (1937) published his paper on response set, and 20 years since Cronbach (1946) published his influential paper on the same topic in *Educational and Psychological Measurement*. Further, there is the more recent work of Orne (1962) on the demand characteristics of a known research setting and Rosenthal's stimulating work (1964) on the social psychology of the experiment. All these investigations suggest that reliance on data obtained only in "reactive" settings is equivocal.

As a guide to locating the strengths and weaknesses of individual data classes—to better work the convergent multiple-methods approach—my colleagues at Northwestern and I have tried to develop a list of sources of research invalidity to be considered with any data class. An outline of these sources of invalidity is contained in Table 1.

To bring under control some of the reactive measurement effect, we might employ data classes which do not require the cooperation of the student or respondent. By supplementing standard interview or pencil-and-paper measures, more dimensionality is introduced into triangulation.

TABLE 1

SOURCES OF RESEARCH INVALIDITY

I. Reactive Measurement Effect
1. Awareness of being tested
2. Role playing
3. Measurement as change
4. Response sets

II. Error from Investigator
5. Interviewer effects
6. Change—fatigue/practice

III. Varieties of Sampling Error
7. Population restriction
8. Population stability over time
9. Population stability over areas

IV. Access to Content
10. Restrictions on content
11. Stability of content over time
12. Stability of content over areas

V. Operating East and Validity Checks
13. Dross rate
14. Access to descriptive cues
15. Ability to replicate

In a recent paper which described the use of observation methods in the study of racial attitudes, Campbell, Kruskal, and Wallace (1966) studied seating aggregations by race. Two colleges were picked in the Chicago area —one noted for the liberal composition of its student body and the other more associated with a traditional point of view. Going into lecture halls, they observed seating patterns and the clustering of Negro and white students during class. With a new statistical test developed by Kruskal, they were able to demonstrate a greater racial mixture in the more "liberal" college. They also found, however, that the seating mix in the liberal college was significantly less than that expected by chance.

The linkage of secondary records is another way to develop control over reactivity. An example of this approach is DeCharms and Moeller's (1962) study of achievement imagery. They first gathered the number of patents issued by the United States Patent Office from 1800 to 1950. These data (controlled for population) were then matched to achievement imagery found in children's readers for the same period. There was a strong relationship between the level of achievement imagery in their sample of books and the number of patents per million population. Both data series are nonreactive, and although other rival, plausible hypotheses might explain the relationship, it remains as one piece in the inferential puzzle, uncontaminated by awareness of being tested.

For matching of other archival records, we can note Lewis Terman's (1917) study estimating Galton's IQ (not far from 200) and Galton's own early studies of hereditary genius (1870).

Another class of data comes from physical evidence, one example of which is Fredrick Mosteller's creative study (unpublished) of the degree to which different sections of the *International Encyclopedia of the Social Sciences* were read. He estimated usage by noting the wear and tear on separate sections: dirty edges of pages, frequency of dirt smudges, finger markings and underlinings on pages. He sampled different libraries and even used the *Encyclopaedia Britannica* as a control.

Thus far, the emphasis has been on data sources and overlapping classes of data. We might also profitably explore the possibility of using multiple samples. Again, this is different from the usual definition of multiple samples. In addition to sampling a number of different classrooms, or groups of students or cities, one may ask of there are different types or categories of samples available for the variable under study. Is there a group of natural outcroppings among occupations, already formed social and interest groups, or people who have common experiences? Can we economically exploit for research purposes the broad spectrum of already formed groups which may be organized along some principle of direct substantive applicability to the investigation?

Professor James Bryan of Northwestern and I have been interested in the use of these "outcropping" groups as a middle-level sampling strategy—one that straddles the elegant but cumbersome national probability sample and the more circumscribed "$N = 80$ volunteer males from the introductory psychology class" populations.

Because one sometimes doesn't know the universe for a study and because of cost restraints, subjects are most often selected because of proximity. Our subjects are typically drawn from the subject pool of the introductory class, from friends, friends of friends, or those unlucky enough to be members of the same institution as the investigator, be it the school, the hospital, or the prison.

Consider some convenience samples which may supplement conventional groups. Becker, Lerner, and Carroll (1964) used caddies loafing about a golf course waiting for jobs as a subject pool. E. E. Smith (1962) suggested firemen in a fire house. They have almost unlimited time available for questioning and offer the very happy situation of a naturally formed, real group, whose members know each other very well. This is a good setting in which to replicate findings derived from experimentally formed groups in laboratories or from natural groups.

Sometimes these convenient aggregates offer a special opportunity to get a high concentration of usable subjects. To study somatotyping among top athletes in different track and field events, Tanner (1964) went to the 1960 Olympic Village at Rome. In a study of proposed brand names for new products, in which one of the criteria was relative invulnerability to regional accents, MacNiven[1] sent interviewers to a nearby airport where they asked travellers to read off lists of names while the interviewers noted variable pronunciations.

In trait measurement, one may define altruism by one or by a series of self-report scales. But it may also be profitable to examine extant groups with some face-valid loading on altruism—say, volunteer blood donors, contributors to charitable causes, or even such groups as those who aided Jews in Nazi Germany.

Bryan and Test (1966) have recently reported on a provocative study of the influence of modeling behavior on altruism. Their objective in a field experiment was to see whether or not people stopped to help someone who had a flat tire. The experiment involved two women stranded with flat tires one quarter of a mile apart on a highway and a model, a man who had stopped to help one of them. In one part of the experiment, the traffic passed the women and the model and then, farther up the highway, passed the other woman. In the other part of the experiment, the traffic passed only one woman and no model (see pp. 209–11 for a full report of this study).

Other clusters of groups may help to define or locate a particular ability. Occupational categories may be particularly useful here. For studies of superior depth perception there are natural occupational outcroppings such as magnetic core threaders, jugglers, or grand prix automobile drivers.

Each of these groups possesses other attributes, and one might consider

---

[1] Personal communication.

the same group of automobile race drivers as a high risk-taking sample and link them with other high risk-taking groups such as sport and military parachute jumpers.

Or, for studies of deviance, there are the self-help deviant groups of Alcoholics Anonymous, Gamblers Anonymous, and prisoners who volunteer for therapy. All presumably share a common characteristic, but the setting of the phenomenon is varied.

As an expansion of this idea, consider Ernest Haggard's exemplary chapter on isolation and personality (1964). Haggard reviewed studies of isolation: How is personality affected by the restraint of habitual body movement in restricted, monotonous, or otherwise unfamiliar environments? Instead of limiting himself to the laboratory experimentation on sensory deprivation, he went abroad to the large literature of "naturally" occurring isolation. There are research findings on interstate truck drivers, pilots flying missions alone at night or at high altitudes, orthopedic patients in iron lungs, and anecdotal reports of prisoners in solitary confinement, shipwrecked sailors, and explorers. Haggard reports the commonalities among these widely *differing* groups, which overlapped on the isolation dimension, and which shared common sensory and personality phenomena. He compares, for example, the anecdotal reports of Admiral Byrd (1938) and the scientific investigation of Rohrer (1960) on International Geophysical Year personnel, both of whom found the individual cutting back on information input under isolated conditions—even when a mass of material was available to consume.

In another isolation investigation, Sells considered many of the same data in his applied study, "A model for the social system for the multiman extended duration space ship" (*NASA Report,* undated). Thinking of such long journeys as a Mars shot, Sells assembled data from many isolated groups, both natural and artificial. His analysis was careful and based on theory. He related the findings from different studies to a general model of an isolated social system—evaluating the degree to which results from the individual studies were likely to transfer to a space vehicle setting. Thus, data from submarine and exploration parties were most applicable, while the findings from shipwreck and disaster studies were least likely to transfer.

In this paper, I have stressed two main points. One is the utility of different data-gathering techniques applied concurrently to the same problem. The other is the laying of these techniques against multiple samples which are natural outcroppings of a phenomenon.

E. G. Boring, in a personal communication, wrote:

. . . The truth is something you get on toward and never to, and the way is filled with ingenuities and excitements. Don't take the straight and narrow path of the stodgy positivists; be gay and optimistic, like Galton, and you will find yourself more toward than you had ever expected.

▽ ▽ ▽

PART TWO

Test
Administration
Problems

TEST wise Americans often expect little difficulty with aptitude testing programs in other cultures, despite extensive anthropological and sociological evidence that culture and individual values are intertwined. In our easy adaptation to aptitude and achievement tests of all sorts, particularly in school situations, we are apt to forget that psychological testing is a very different sort of experience to foreigners, especially non-Westerners. Presumably, "culture free" tests (a clear misnomer, since no psychological tests can be constructed outside of any cultural value system) will minimize some of these difficulties; however, evidence that they can is sadly lacking. The following four articles deal with various aspects of test administration, both in "foreign" cultures and in U.S. subcultures.

The first article of this group relates some of the difficulties, as well as some very amusing sidelights that one psychologist met in his attempt to devise a selection battery for police officers in Vietnam. Dr. Wickert is professor of psychology at Michigan State University. During 1955–57, he was in Vietnam on a technical assistance mission to the Vietnamese government. The article is reproduced in its entirety from *American Psychologist*, 1957.

AN ADVENTURE IN PSYCHOLOGICAL
TESTING ABROAD

Frederic R. Wickert

In the room at the north end of the first floor of President Diem's Freedom Palace in Saigon, one day in September, 1955, several members of the "police team" and I were in a conference. We all belonged to the Michigan State University group sent to Vietnam to give technical aid to the government of that new country.

The police team members, one of several teams in the MSU group, had the mission of helping the Vietnam government improve the internal security of the country as rapidly as possible. In the States the police team members had all been engaged in professional police work. Normally, I am one of the regular teaching members of the MSU psychology department. Temporarily I had agreed to go to Vietnam as coordinator and deputy adviser for in-service training.

We MSU technical aides were conferring with Mr. Ro, something like a chief of staff to the Minister of the Interior, whose offices were in the palace. Mr. Ro, in addition to his many other duties, had been named to head the new police academy which our police team had been instrumental in establishing.

During the conference the subject of student selection arose. Mr. Ro asked whether we could give a test in order to make sure that only students who could benefit from the instruction would be included in the class. This request had a familiar ring to a psychologist. Further discussion indicated that the students should have completed the equivalent of sixth grade. From this it was concluded that an "intelligence" (educational achievement type) test, pitched at the level of students at the end of sixth grade, would be in order. We told Mr. Ro that we could, with help from him, prepare a suitable test in the short time remaining before the opening of the academy. Mr. Ro then arranged a visit to the Ministry of Education, where discussion with officials indicated that a test consisting partly of Vietnamese language items and partly of arithmetic items would be appropriate. Two "professors" who taught Vietnamese language and two who taught arithmetic, all at the sixth-grade level, were borrowed from the Ministry of Education. I spent some hours trying to explain to them how to construct objective items in language and arithmetic. The Far East edition of *Reader's Digest* fortunately contains a page of multiple-choice vocabulary items. These items provided a pattern for the language professors to follow. The idea of objective-type items came more readily to the arithmetic professors. It was most difficult to get both the language and arithmetic professors to prepare items of a wide enough range of difficulty. Specifically, they wanted to make difficult items only. Finally, some of the interpreter-translators around the office helped to construct items too. It got to be a game.

Vietnamese language is a tricky thing to work with. Basically it is mono-syllabic. Complex, abstract concepts are sometimes expressed by combining two or three monosyllables. Since, however, Vietnamese is basically a peasants' language (with, for example, about twelve different ways of ex-pressing the idea "to carry," a different word depending on what part of the body is doing the carrying), it is poor in abstractions, even when one tries putting Vietnamese monosyllables together to express more complex ideas. It borrows heavily from Chinese monosyllables, and combinations of mono-syllables, for abstractions. Vietnamese who would do well on Chinese-type language items were said to be overly pedantic and would not necessarily make too good policemen.

In addition, the Tonkinese or North Vietnam dialect is quite different from the South Vietnam dialect. Almost the only persons available to construct vocabulary items were North Vietnamese intellectuals who had fled from the North as the Communists took over following the Geneva confer-ence. But most of the persons who would take the test would know only the South Vietnamese dialect. Eventually these problems were largely over-come. A 60-item Vietnamese language and 60-item arithmetic test, including test booklet and a separate answer sheet, was finally prepared.

The Ministry of Education was asked to provide a large number of average boys, just beginning seventh grade, as a tryout group. After much negotiating, only one class of about 50 boys was made available. Instead of average boys, they turned out to be probably the best seventh-grade class in all Vietnam. The Vietnamese were out to show how well they could do. Naturally the items were too easy for this group. The item difficulty analyses did not show as much as would ordinarily have been expected.

Administering the test was an eye-opener for us Americans. It turned out to be necessary to give much supplemental instruction on the use of the separate answer sheet, on how to mark answers, etc. Boys would turn to each other for help, notwithstanding frequent instructions that they were not to talk to each other. Maintaining order was all the more difficult because of the Vietnamese habit of thinking out loud as they work problems or even study. How much neighbors listened to each other and benefited from this listening could not be determined. The test administrators and proctors could not be sure whether the students were communicating to each other or were merely doing the usual thinking out loud. The boys all seemed to try hard on the tests and remained in good spirits but looked very puzzled when we tried to keep them from talking. How to maintain "standardized" testing conditions under these circumstances?

Results showed that the arithmetic test took unnecessarily long, while the language test was too easy and too short. Odd–even reliabilities of the two-part scores were reasonably satisfactory, judging by the scatter diagrams of odd-versus-even scores.

In view of the above experiences, the test was reconstructed. The language test was expanded from 60 items to 100; the arithmetic was cut from 60 items to 40. The items were arranged in the order of their difficulty, as well as could be done from the data. Types of items thought to be difficult turned out to be relatively easy, and other types, thought to be easy, turned out to be difficult. Instructions were reworked in the light of specific difficulties encountered in the tryout testing.

The big day finally arrived when approximately 130 candidates, all policemen on the active force, appeared for testing. The two classrooms available for testing held but about 70 students each, so the group was split in two. Group 1 was started without much apparent difficulty. Its members were especially cautioned not to talk, and they stayed surprisingly quiet. We then went next door to Group 2. They had scarcely started when the slight rumble from the direction of Group 1 increased to a roar. We rushed back only to find that they had gone back to thinking out loud, each one trying to outshout his neighbor. In two hours practically all had finished and the papers were collected.

Results showed that we had guessed well on many things. Scatter diagrams showed odd–even reliabilities on both parts of the test to be about in the eighties or low nineties. The correlation between the two tests was probably in the low thirties. This time the items were fairly well arranged in the order of their difficulty. The test was rather easy, so that those subjects toward the lower end of the distribution were well spread out and discrimination among these persons was reasonably dependable. Incidentally, I had no time to work out any statistics. It was easy to teach Vietnamese assistants to score the tests, to make frequency distributions and scatter diagrams and to do simple item-difficulty analysis. In the rush of far more pressing matters, there was no time to teach them how to calculate correlation coefficients, and I had no time to do them myself.

Administratively the decision was made to send back to duty the 26 men with the lowest scores. A number of persons, both Vietnamese and American, objected to sending these men back on the grounds that they were the ones who most needed training. It was finally worked out that the low men from four or five classes would be accumulated and put through as a class for which the instruction would be especially adapted.

It developed that about three fifths of the group tested was made up of municipal police and the remaining two fifths were from the "Sureté," the plain-clothes, undercover men. Much to the surprise of the Americans, the Sureté men did no better on the test than the ordinary municipal police. To the Vietnamese this was no surprise. They did say that at least the test results would provide them with ammunition to try to convince the higher-ups that the Sureté should be given better men. The idea of using tests in selecting new men for the Sureté they have not yet been able or willing to grasp.

The staff of the Police Academy were most impressed by the speed with which test results were made available. They said that never before had they seriously considered using selection testing in a crash program like the present one. In the past, tests had always taken weeks and even months to score.

The speed-of-scoring feature of the tests had another by-product. The academy staff decided to give their classes weekly objective tests. Their first attempts to make true-false items were very crude, but they did better on multiple-choice items. In view of their obvious interest, I then gave the instructors some help on how to construct objective items. The students were much interested in the weekly achievement tests and demanded to have their scored papers returned to them quickly. Other parts of the government have begun to hear about the testing and have expressed an interest in learning more about how it is done. However, I have had no time to develop this field further.

Upon the graduation of the first class at the academy in late December, 1955, the candidates for the second class took the test. This time there was far less talking. According to some Vietnamese the word had gotten around with respect to how to behave during Western-style testing. This "word" was apparently far more potent than any test instructions. The volume of talking out loud during testing was down markedly.

A strongly worded request had gone out to all administrators sending candidates to the academy to refrain from sending any but good men in the future. A comparison of the first and second testings showed that in the first class 16 percent of 130 men made scores below 67, a kind of minimum passing score. In the second class, however, a little under 10 percent of the 165 candidates scored below 67. Although these results look as though either the statement to the administrators or other factors were operating to make the performance of the second group better, the difference is not significant.

Some other testing had been done in Vietnam. There is still a large sign over a courtyard leading to a government-type building which indicates that a psychotechnical center once existed there under the French occupation.

The Vietnamese military have developed two tests which were used in selecting men to technical military specialties. This little bit of testing, done in the past, had apparently made no imprint on the culture, judging from our experiences.

Testing in another culture, then, can have its surprises. It also can be useful in that culture. With more time and effort, testing in Vietnam could play an increasingly important role in an awakening movement to adopt improved personnel practices and to modernize educational procedures.

ALSO from Asia comes a second report of local testees' efforts to "beat the test." In Samoa, Navy tests were in English rather than in the native language, so a "mental" translation problem presented itself to the candidates. Not only was the local populace most enthusiastic about the arrival of the U.S. Navy Recruiting Team, since it opened up the possibility of lucrative jobs, but also their response to the U.S. testing situation was other than that many Americans would expect. Here, again, knowledge of cultural anthropology would have been most helpful to the team, and the troublesome problem of "culture-free" tests arises again.

Dr. Levine is psychological research adviser in the Navy Department. The following article is a condensation of the original report, which appeared in *American Psychologist*, 1957. Additional comments concerning the reported superiority of the Samoans on the Radio Code Aptitude Test have been taken from the rejoinder to the Levine article by J. B. Ford of Los Angeles State College. Ford's remarks appeared in the "Comment" columns of this same journal.

AFTER THE SAMOANS COME OF AGE

Abraham S. Levine

After the Samoans came of age—then what? They want to join the U.S. Navy!

The first Samoan recruiting mission arrived in 1954 and was enthusiastically greeted by all hands. The total stay on the islands of this popular team amounted to little more than a month. They were given a quota of 100 by the Chief of Naval Personnel in Washington. The first week was spent publicizing their mission and administering the Applicant Qualification Test which is the official Navy prescreening test made up of verbal, arithmetic, and mechanical items. This test was administered ostensibly to 1,410 applicants. However, it turned out that 1,410 did not represent the actual number. During this first week it did not occur to the Officer in Charge that a candidate would: *(a)* use any name but his true one, *(b)* take the examination more than once, *(c)* have someone else take the examination for him.

A bit of anthropology soon came to light. To "save face" is a trait of these people. Fictitious names were used so that in the event that names were published no one would know who had failed. This backfired: a successful candidate was unable to identify the examination as his paper. Also, many noneligibles took the examination hoping that either the fact that they were married, had dependents, or were underage would be overlooked or perhaps waived. Worse yet, some candidates took the examination more than once under different names or had friends take the examination for them. Taking an examination for someone else does not represent the kind of breach of ethics it would be in the United States. For the Samoans, it merely represents a bit of transfer of training from the well-established courtship custom reported on by Mead when a friend (if he doesn't speak for himself) serves as proxy.

When all the smoke had cleared away and the interviewers had completed their work, a total of 131 Samoans were considered eligible for the final screen—the medical examination. Of these, 84 were found physically acceptable and enlisted.

The 84 Samoans who successfully met all the requirements and became enlisted men in the U.S. Navy were subsequently administered a number of Navy aptitude and achievement tests for assignment purposes. The results of these psychometrics provide some interesting material for cross-cultural comparisons and represent the raison d'être of this article despite the rather discursive introduction. In view of the many limitations of these data, it would be presumptuous to regard them as being any more than suggestive, i.e., springboards for hypotheses and speculations which are perhaps better grounded than the well-meaning romanticizing which oft occurs in the absence of cold psychometric evidence.

It should be emphasized that these test data were obtained in connection with an operational mission rather than as part of a research project designed by psychologists or other competent social scientists. Also, it should be pointed out that the 84 Samoan males, selected out of an original pool of several hundred legitimate applicants, constitute those who achieved a passing score on a written test printed in English and devised for continental U.S. Navy applicants. The passing score for the Samoans was fixed at the same point as for applicants in the United States, i.e., the 10th percentile of a World War II Navy enlisted population. This selection standard was probably a good deal more rigorous for Samoans than for Americans. In other words, the Applicant Qualification Test was not a "culture-fair" test for the Samoans. This theme will be elaborated on when the test data are examined. Since the Recruiting Team was assigned a quota of 100 Samoans, it would not have been practicable to attempt to devise a specially tailored instrument for them. Besides it may be argued that, since the Samoans will have to adjust to the same complex subculture as will the recruits from the States, they should be selected and assigned on the basis of similar functional abilities as reflected in test scores. Even if this meant that in many instances a particular test score actually represented for the Samoans a greater potential to learn certain skills than would be the case for American recruits, this would be all to the good since it might serve to compensate for certain subtle cultural handicaps.

The battery of tests administered to the Samoans included:

1. General Classification Test: 100 completion and analogy items to measure verbal ability.
2. Arithmetic Test: 40 purely computational items and 60 problem-solving items.

3. Mechanical Test: pictorial items with a minimum of verbal descriptive material to measure basic mechanical and electrical knowledge and understanding of mechanical principles.
4. Clerical Aptitude Test: two sets of numbers to be rapidly and accurately checked as same or different.
5. Sonar Pitch Memory Test: items to measure ability to make fine pitch discriminations presented on phonograph records.
6. Radio Code Aptitude Test: a speed test to measure the ability to identify a few code characters at rapid rates of transmission. There is, first, a learning unit where examinees are taught three code characters; then a testing unit where examinees are tested at four different speeds on these learned characters.
7. Non-Verbal Classification Test: a general ability test, with items in pictorial or geometric form, designed for testing persons who can understand English but cannot read it.

Table 2 lists the mean scores obtained by the Samoans on this series of Navy aptitude and achievement tests. The screening test (Applicant Qualification Test) is also included. Several considerations should be kept in mind while examining these data:

TABLE 2

MEAN SCORES OBTAINED BY SAMOANS ON
U.S. APTITUDE TESTS

Test	N	Mean
Applicant Qualification Test	84	40.8
General Classification Test	84	33.6
Arithmetic Test	84	48.1
Mechanical Test	84	36.6
Clerical Aptitude Test	84	46.6
Sonar Pitch Memory Test	69	48.8
Radio Code Aptitude Test	80	63.2
Non-Verbal Classification Test	56	53.3

1. All of the test scores, with the exception of the Non-Verbal Classification Test, are expressed in standard score units. Mean standard score for Navy enlisted men is 50 and the standard deviation is 10. These statistics are based on a 1944, Navy enlisted, normative population. Actual means and standard deviations have fluctuated somewhat on both sides of these values, depending on a number of conditions, mostly of a supply-quota nature.
2. The Samoans in this sample represent a highly restricted segment of their population in education and ability variables. Moreover, they are rather difficult to characterize accurately in terms of psychometric referents generated in our culture. Consequently, it would not be too meaningful an enterprise to make comparisons on the basis of standard deviations and intercorrelations, since these statistics are particularly sensitive to the various kinds of influences which make for range restrictions in the specific test

variables under consideration. In view of all of these limitations, perhaps the most meaningful comparisons may be made between mean scores of the Samoans on the different tests. While making this intra-Samoan comparison, it should be remembered that Navy recruits in general tend to get about the same mean score on all the tests (except Non-Verbal Classification), i.e., 50.

On the General Classification Test, which may best be characterized as a verbal reasoning test, the Samoan sample mean is more than 1.5 standard deviations below the mean of American recruits; but on the Arithmetic Test, the Samoans fall just slightly short of this general mean (.2 of a standard deviation). Apparently, the Arithmetic Test represents more of a culture-fair test than the General Classification Test for reasons which are not hard to guess—most important of which is probably the higher vocabulary level of the General Classification Test.

Interestingly enough, the Mechanical Test is almost 1.5 standard deviations below the general mean. This, of course, may be attributed primarily to the relatively nonmechanical nature of the Samoan culture despite the impact on it of the gear-laden American Navy.

On the Clerical Aptitude Test, the Samoans score almost .5 of a standard deviation below the mean. There are no obvious cultural handicaps, except perhaps less opportunity for practice in related activities which may account for the slight, apparent depression in performance on the number-checking test. Any further speculation about such a thin disparity would be indefensible.

Results on the Sonar Pitch Memory Test provide nothing of special interest, since it corresponds closely to the general mean. However, as a group the Samoans perform exceptionally well on the Radio Code Aptitude Test (63.2—almost 1.5 standard deviations above the general mean). The reason for this is far from apparent but, if it could be successfully tested out, it is probable that it would be a significant nugget of information. However, one could hypothesize that these islanders living so close to nature have developed more acute sensoria and hence can more rapidly integrate auditory stimuli, which would account for superior performance on a test of ability to rapidly receive and decipher radio code. A corollary of this would be that our urban culture tends to restrict the development of certain of our perceptual skills, even as it stimulates the development of other types of cognitive abilities, e.g., verbal. Another kind of hypothesis with some plausibility is that, since the Radio Code Aptitude Test correlates about .50 with tests of either verbal or arithmetic reasoning (for American recruits), the superior performance of the Samoans on the code test derives from the fact that they represent a highly select group with respect to the kinds of potentialities measured by standard intelligence tests in our culture. However, this was not reflected in their scores on Navy tests which did not give them a fair shake.

The mean score on the Non-Verbal Classification Test is at about the same relative level for the Samoans as their Applicant Qualification Test score (about one standard deviation below the mean for a general Navy recruit population). The Non-Verbal Classification Test scores are expressed in raw score units. They were never converted into standard score units, as were most other Navy tests, since the test was devised for American illiterates, has a relatively low ceiling, and consequently was never administered to a general Navy population for standardization purposes. However, in a sample similar to those for the other tests, the mean raw score was determined to be 61 and the standard deviation about 9. The mean raw score of the Samoan sample under consideration is 53.3, which is almost a standard deviation below the general mean. This raises an interesting question regarding the difficulty of devising culture-free or culture-fair tests for use in other cultures. The Non-Verbal Classification test comprises a total of 75 items, 25 of which are made up of pictures of objects familiar to Americans and 50 of which are composed of abstract geometric designs that ostensibly give no advantage to individuals from any particular cultural background. In each item, the examinee is required to select the alternative which either does not belong with the other components or is in a similar analogical relationship to the third term as are the first two terms, i.e., the test is made up of classification and analogy type items. In view of the low scores obtained by the Samoans (substantially lower than on the Arithmetic Test, for example), it would seem that modes of thought as well as specific content are culturally conditioned. This would tend to make a test which is quite adequate for rank-ordering American illiterates in relation to some accepted ability criterion quite inappropriate for members of another culture, even those who have been exposed to more than a smattering of our cultural heritage. All of this points up some of the excruciating problems inherent in devising a satisfactory culture-free test.

(Note: To cope with American illiterates, the Navy has established Recruit Preparatory Training Units, which furnish a maximum of 13 weeks of special literacy and Naval orientation instruction, and has thus been able to enhance the usefulness of many of its marginal recruits. Groups of Samoan, Guamanian, and Filipino recruits, many with definite English language handicaps, were found to be unusually successful in this training—more so than the typical American recruit. It would appear that such groups as the Samoans evidence greater adaptability to the Navy situation than do Americans with similarly low test scores.)

Ford's comments on the superior test performance of the Samoans on the Radio Code Aptitude Test (*American Psychologist,* 1957, p. 751), setting down the reactions of a former governor of American Samoa to the Levine article, follow:

No one who spent any time in Samoa should find this surprising. The basic elements of Samoan music are percussive rhythm instruments, principally sticks, hollowed logs, rolled-up bundles of matting, and empty biscuit tins. Any group of Samoans engaged in group dancing will employ several of these rhythm instruments producing a total effect of very complex rhythmic patterns, against the background of which dancing and singing are performed. Consequently, from childhood the Samoan is accustomed to highly varied and rapid systems of rhythmic beats similar to that found in radio transmissions. So proficient do the Samoans become as radio operators that on the naval circuits between Samoa and Hawaii, which are in use to this day, it was customary to employ Samoans at the Hawaiian end because of the difficulty in obtaining any other kind of personnel who could receive messages sent from Samoa, so great was the rapidity of the Samoan operators in Pago. Since nearly everything in Samoa is done rhythmically, it is not at all surprising that the Samoan radio operators are among the finest transmitters of CW messages in the world.

ESPECIALLY with psychological tests that require individual administration, such as the Stanford-Binet or the Wechsler scales, to say nothing of projective tests, all test manuals exhort the test administrator to be neutral and objective, and to establish good rapport with the testee. Beyond general statements, such as the admonition to the examiner to remain interested and attentive, and in the instance of incomplete answers to ask for further information, little more is done with this general topic of rapport. A little reflection on the business of interaction between tester and testee, especially in an individual test situation when some area critical to the testee such as intelligence is being rated, would lead one to pay close attention to this aspect of test administration. Partly because the entire situation is supposed to be objective and because scoring instructions are so detailed, it is often assumed that this personal interaction phase of test administration can be minimized. The following report, one of the few in the research literature, shows that significant differences in test scores can result among testees (accomplices) who put on a warm or cold facade to the examiner, and that even in an objective situation of this type relatively experienced examiners can be adversely influenced.

Dr. Masling is professor of psychology at the State University of New York at Buffalo. A previous report by him, employing a projective test situation (1957), showed significant effects of such warm and cold facades. In the present report, condensed from the *Journal of Consulting Psychology,* 1959, the same effects are to be seen in a more objective and standardized test situation.

THE EFFECTS OF WARM AND COLD
INTERACTION ON THE ADMINISTRATION
AND SCORING OF AN INTELLIGENCE TEST

Joseph Masling

Several studies have examined the psychologist–subject relationship in projective test situations. The ambiguity which faces both examiner and subject here makes it probable that each will be influenced by the other in attempting to complete their respective tasks. In intelligence testing, however, the instructions are specific, the stimuli are clearly defined, and there are right and wrong answers. Here the examiner is required to read the questions as stated in the test and to evaluate the answers with the aid of a scoring manual.

The examiner–subject relationship in intelligence testing has not received a great deal of attention. During the course of their training most examiners are exhorted to establish "rapport" and admonished to be "objective." The "objective" examiner is charged with the responsibility of deriving as valid an estimate of the intelligence of the subject as can be obtained, without regard for his personal attitudes about the subject. He is thus expected to be standardized and depersonalized. The purpose of the present study was to investigate the extent to which an examiner could divest himself of personal bias in administering and scoring an intelligence test—in this case, three verbal subtests of the Wechsler-Bellevue I[1] (hereafter called the "W-B I") —when the subject acted in either a highly approving, interested (warm) manner or in a persistently rejecting, disinterested (cold) manner. The specific hypotheses which were tested were as follows:

1. When an examiner tests two subjects, one of whom acts warm to him and the other cold, he will be more generous in scoring the responses of the warm subject.

2. During the course of administration of an intelligence test to two subjects, one of whom is warm and the other cold, an examiner will: *(a)* make more reinforcing statements to the warm subject than the cold; *(b)* ask more questions of the warm subject, giving him the opportunity of clarifying or reformulating an answer.

METHOD

The Interaction. Manipulation of the interaction was effected through the use of attractive female accomplices, posing as test subjects (S's), who acted either warm or cold to the examiner. In the warm condition, the accomplice acted interested in the examiner and in the test; she responded freely to his questions and tried to communicate respect and liking for him. In the cold condition, the accomplice acted disinterested and bored with the test and the examiner; her attitude was that of fulfilling an unpleasant class assignment which she wanted to complete as soon as possible. She tended to answer pre-test interview questions in monosyllables and throughout avoided eye contact with the examiner. In the middle of each cold session the accomplice in a deliberate, calculated fashion put on sunglasses, thereby increasing the psychological distance between herself and the examiner.

Examiners and Procedure. These were 11 graduate students at Syracuse University, all of whom had completed at least one course in the administration of individual tests of intelligence. Six of these also had had further work with individual tests. The most experienced of the examiners had previously given over 200 W-B's. The median W-B administrations for the entire group was 21.

Each examiner was told that the author was interested in the comparability of various short forms of the W-B and that he would be asked to administer two or three subtests to subjects chosen at random. The subjects would be two undergraduates participating in the experiment as part of their Introductory Psychology course requirement.

Each examiner administered three subtests (Information, Comprehension, Similarities) to both subjects, one of whom acted warm to him and the other cold. Each accomplice had five cold and five warm roles. To insure uniformity in score, each examiner was directed to use the instructions in

---

[1] Listed incorrectly in the original report as "W-B II."

Wechsler's manual (third edition). The experimenter prepared a script for each accomplice to memorize and to repeat to each examiner, regardless of whether this was a warm or cold interaction. Fourteen of these responses were written to maximize difficulty in scoring. All test situations were tape-recorded.

RESULTS

There was no mistaking the impact of the warm and cold conditions on the examiners. All reported that one S seemed particularly disinterested in the test, with some emphasizing the notion that this represented "sick" behavior. One examiner correctly guessed that the S's were really accomplices, and he was therefore replaced and his data were not used.

Hypothesis I was tested by comparing the way in which each examiner scored the responses given him under the two conditions. Since the experimenter had intentionally written responses that gave a higher "true" IQ for one of the accomplices than for the other, the bias of the examiner scoring was determined from the mean of the 10 scores given each accomplice, rather than from the raw scores. Once a mean score for each accomplice had been obtained, the extent and direction of differences from each mean were derived for each examiner. A statistical test showed that the probability of obtaining such a distribution of differences by chance was remote ($p = .056$).

Hypothesis I can also be evaluated by looking at scores assigned above and below the subject's mean. Of the five examiners who tested Accomplice A under the warm condition, four gave her scores greater than the mean, while of the five examiners who tested her in the cold condition, four gave her scores smaller than the mean. The identical results were obtained for Accomplice B: four of the five examiners who interacted with her in a warm manner gave her scores greater than the mean, while four of the five examiners who interacted with her in the cold condition gave her scores smaller than the mean.

Hypothesis II was tested by having independent judges go through the tape recordings (all identifying data being removed) and rating examiner statements as reinforcing ("OK," "swell," etc.) or questioning ("Can you be more specific?"). There were 285 examiner remarks culled from the testing sections of the interviews. The judges independently agreed on the ratings of 89 percent of the remarks; the remainder were eventually agreed upon in conference. Once the number of reinforcing and questioning statements had been obtained, a comparison was made of each examiner's verbal behavior during the warm interaction and with his verbal behavior during the cold interaction. All examiners made more reinforcing statements to the warm subjects and they asked more questions of them. The sum of reinforcing and questioning statements was also greater for the warm condition than for the cold.

While the experimental hypotheses were substantiated, the differences between conditions seemed much smaller than the differences among examiners. For example, Examiner 1 made a total of only 14 remarks to his S's, while Examiner 7 made 64. Examiner 8's scoring favored the warm condition by 4.8 points, while Examiner 5's scoring was biased in favor of the cold condition by 1.8 points. Since it was possible that the more experienced examiners were least biased by the interaction, rank order correlations were computed between the number of W-B's previously given and the dependent variables. None of the *rho's* were significantly greater than zero.

DISCUSSION

The results of this study indicate that the examiner–subject interaction influenced the psychologist's behavior in the administration and scoring of the three subtests of the W-B I. When the instructions to the cold accomplice are considered, i.e., to answer in monosyllables, to appear disinterested, and the typescripts of the sessions studied, it becomes clear that the examiners tried to make contact with the Cold S and, in failing to do this, became silent. While the examiners were undoubtedly trained to encourage the S, this was difficult to do when friendly overtures elicited disinterest and rejection. The feelings which the interaction aroused in these examiners obviously influenced the manner in which they administered the tests. With warm, responsive S's they tended to encourage and question; with cold S's they tended to remain silent.

It is difficult to predict the extent to which this particular finding can be generalized to nonlaboratory situations. Probably few individuals taking intelligence tests act as hostile and nonparticipating as the cold accomplice. However, some S's, notably children, may become threatened by the testing situation, responding with belligerence or silence or other variations of avoidance.

The interaction also affected the examiners' "objective" judgment of the scoring of relatively "objective" material. Even though they had the Wechsler manual available, a response given in the warm condition tended to be given greater credit than the identical response given in the cold condition. This bias is even more striking when it is considered that the scoring occurred some time after the testing, allowing the examiners some perspective regarding the events of the session. Again, this study exaggerated the situation found in most clinic settings, since the examiners were given responses that were selected because they were difficult to evaluate. However, an examination of the scoring records indicated that there were systematic differences in scoring even for those responses which were cited as examples in the scoring manual.

The artificial nature of this study—the use of accomplices and relatively unsophisticated examiners, the exaggerated nature of the interjection, the use of ambiguous responses—together with the inadequate sampling of both the examiner and accomplice populations limits severely the generalization of these findings to nonlaboratory settings of psychologists and S's. What has been demonstrated is that in giving an intelligence test under these conditions, an advanced graduate student examiner will respond to the way S's interact with him and will act out his feelings about the interpersonal situation in administration and scoring.

SUMMARY

1. Eleven graduate students, each of whom had completed at least one course in the administration of individual intelligence tests, administered the Information, Comprehension, and Similarities subtests of the Wechsler-Bellevue I to two subjects. The test subjects were accomplices who acted in either a warm or cold role to the examiners, giving as their responses memorized answers, 14 of which were specifically devised to be difficult to score. One examiner became aware of the purposes of the experiment, and his data were not used. Each accomplice had five cold and five warm roles, and each examiner saw one subject who acted warm and one who acted cold.

2. From the typescripts prepared from these tapes, every examiner remark during the course of the testing part of the interview was rated. Of the 285 examiner statements, two judges independently agreed on the rating of 254 of them, for an agreement of 89 percent.

3. The results indicated that in scoring the responses, the examiners tended to be more lenient to the warm subject than the cold. The examiners also tended to use more reinforcing comments and to give more opportunity to clarify or correct responses to the warm subject. The magnitude of the differences in behavior to the two subjects was generally small, with individual differences more marked than differences due to the effect of the interaction.

Not only may client behavior influence test results and the interpretative comments derived from test protocols, but also client "stimulus input" may clearly influence an interviewer's or therapist's behavior. The behavior of the therapist, for example, may be very specifically determined by the stimulus characteristics of his client. Heller et al. (1963) decided to study these effects by using trained student actors who acted out hostile–friendly and dominant–dependent roles during a half-hour intake interview conducted by 34 graduate student trainees in clinical and counseling psychology. Clear results were obtained (with the exception of the client who portrayed the dependent–hostile role but was, in actuality, not very hostile) to show that clients could evoke reciprocal behaviors from therapists, even though these influences were not perceived. Experience of the interviewers or therapists used in this study, incidentally, varied from one semester's clinical practicum to several years of field experience.

In view of the widespread belief that testing conditions have significant effects on scores, Pierce (1963) was surprised to find little effect on scores for four WAIS subtests administered as part of a psychiatric screening process to several hundred patients over 60 years old. The test administrators rated the test conditions as good, fair, or poor (poor meant one or more disruptive events such as kibitzing of fellow patients). The mean WAIS summed scores did drop as one progressed from good to poor test conditions, but not significantly. Pierce admits that the rating of test conditions was crude, and that one could only conclude here that poor test conditions do not have the gross effects usually thought. He feels that perhaps a more homogeneous group, such as college sophomores, might be better suited to test these effects of noise and distraction. "But at least we have evidence that intelligence tests are more robust than test authors have thought" (p. 537).

The Masling report is one of a long series of studies in which experimenter and subject variables, rapport variations, and situational variables (such as discouragement) have been utilized in both intelligence and personality testing. Sattler and Theye (1967) have recently reviewed some 65 studies concerned with departures from what are usually seen as standardized procedures, all involving individual intelligence testing situations. They conclude that minor changes in test procedures are more likely to affect specialized groups (such as elderly, disturbed, or retarded individuals) than normals. Children, not surprisingly, are more susceptible to situational factors (as discouragement) than are older testees. Effects are greatest with test items or test responses that are ambiguous and less highly structured. Skin color of either the experimenter or the subject has rather unclear effects. Little is known, for example, about the effects of a Negro examiner with a white testee. Sattler and Theye report inadequate research designs in many of the studies they summarize. They conclude that a combination of man and machine test administration may solve some of the problems encountered but that, still, many questions will remain unanswered.

Experimenter–subject differences, especially when visible and obvious, may make for measurement distortions and invalid scores. Such experimenter–subject differences would be particularly significant in regard to intelligence testing, where so much of one's ego may be invested and where, say, the examiner is white and the subject is a southern Negro youngster. Masling's previous paper, describing warm and cold manipulations, can serve as a fitting introduction to the far more serious business of Negro-white interrelationships, especially when these concern test situations with ego-involving aspects.

So significant was this issue—especially since experience has shown that conventional instruments of mental testing were too often fashioned to fit the cultural ways of middle-class children, so that minority group children were being excluded from special training opportunities because of "cultural deprivation"—that the Society for the Psychological Study of Social Issues published a report (SPSSI, 1964) on how this unfortunate situation might be remedied.

Related to this broader issue is the following article by Dr. Irwin Katz and his collaborators, all of whom were associated at New York University at the time of this research, which was jointly supported by the university and the Office of Naval Research. The original report first appeared in the *Journal of Social Issues*, 1964, and is presented here in a slightly condensed form. Dr. Katz is now professor of psychology at the University of Michigan Center for Research on Conflict Resolution.

THE INFLUENCE OF RACE OF THE EXPERIMENTER AND INSTRUCTIONS UPON THE EXPRESSION OF HOSTILITY BY NEGRO BOYS

Irwin Katz, James M. Robinson,
Edgar G. Epps, and Patricia Waly

It was recently demonstrated that the efficiency of Southern Negro college students on a verbal task can be influenced by both the race of the experimenter and the evaluate significance of the task. Katz, Roberts and Robinson (1963) found that when digit-symbol substitution was presented as a test of eye-hand coordination, Negro subjects scored higher with a white administrator than they did with a Negro administrator. But when the same task was described as an intelligence test, there was marked impairment of performance with the white tester, while subjects who were tested by the Negro experimenter showed a slight improvement. The present study deals with the effect of these experimental conditions upon the arousal and expression of hostility.

There is reason to believe that emotional conflict involving the need to control hostility may have a disruptive influence on the performance of Negro students when their intelligence is evaluated by a white person. Sarason *et al.* (1960) have described the test-anxious child, whether Negro or white, as one who typically reacts with strong unconscious hostility to the adult tester, whom he believes will in some way pass judgment on his adequacy. The hostility is not openly expressed, but instead is turned inward against the self in the form of self-derogatory attitudes, which strengthen the child's expectation of failure and desire to escape from the situation. Thus, he is distracted from the task before him by fear of failure and an impulse to escape.

A number of studies support the view of blocking of aggressive impulses as detrimental to intellectual efficiency. Scholastic underachievement has been found to be associated with difficulty in expressing aggression openly. Rosenwald (1961) reported that students who give relatively few aggressive responses on a projective test suffered greater impairment in solving anagrams after a hostility induction than did students who had shown less inhibition on the projective test. Goldman, Horwitz and Lee (1954) demonstrated experimentally that the degree to which hostility against an instigator was blocked from expression determined the amount of disruption on three cognitive tasks.

With respect to Negroes, it is known that segregation engenders a feeling of intellectual inadequacy (for a review of empirical evidence, see Dreger & Miller, 1960), hence they should be prone to experience test situations as threatening. Hostility would tend to arise against the adult authority figure from whom an unfavorable evaluation was expected. The Negro student's hostility might perhaps be stronger against a white tester than against a Negro tester, since the former might be expected to compare him invidiously with members of the advantaged white group. However, previous research suggests that aggressive impulses against a white person will usually be strongly inhibited. There is also evidence (Berkowitz, 1962) that when there are strong restraints operating against openly aggressive behavior, even its expression on projective tests will be blocked to some extent.

In the present experiment, hostile expression was measured by means of a questionnaire that was disguised as a concept formation test. Negro students at a segregated high school in the South were given the questionnaire by either a Negro or a white experimenter, with instructions that described it either neutrally or as an intelligence test. Then scores were compared with those obtained previously by the same subjects in an informal, all-Negro setting. It was predicted that when neutral instructions were used, levels of hostile expression in the Negro-tester and white-tester groups would remain the same, but when intelligence test instructions were used, hostility scores would *increase* under a Negro experimenter and *decrease* when the experimenter was white.

METHOD

Subjects and Procedures.   The subjects were 72 male students at a Negro high school and junior high school in Nashville. They ranged in age from 13 to 18 years. Volunteers for the experiment were recruited in classrooms with an offer of one dollar for participating for an hour in a research project. The study was done on two successive days. The first day all subjects met after school in a large room and were administered the hostility scale by the assistant principal of the school. They were told that the purpose of the questionnaire was to aid in evaluation of a proposed new method for teaching vocabulary. Afterwards, they were given their assignments for the following day. For the second session the entire sample was divided into four groups of equal size. Each group was tested by either a white or a Negro adult stranger, with instructions that described the task as either an intelligence test or a research instrument. The two testers worked simultaneously in different rooms, and ran the two instructional conditions in quick succession, to prevent subject contamination. Both experimenters introduced themselves as psychologists from local universities (Fisk and Vanderbilt) and gave oral instructions.

The neutral instructions stated in part:

Yesterday you did some vocabulary items. Today you will do a slightly different version of this task for me. It is *not* a test. I am doing research on the meaning of certain words in American speech. To a psychologist, the meaning of a word refers to how it is used by people who speak the language. So I want you to show me how you use these words. Your answers will not be shown to your teachers. Yesterday you had a practice warm-up. It will not be scored. Today's answers are the ones that count. So answer what you think is correct today.

The intelligence test instructions were in part:

Yesterday you were given a vocabulary test. Today you will do a slightly different version of this test for me. I am interested in this vocabulary test because it will show me how intelligent you are. I am doing research on mental ability, and I want to see how bright you boys are at ———— School. This test will show your knowledge of words, your ability to recognize abstract concepts, and your general intelligence. It will show whether you could succeed in college, or in your chosen field of work. But your individual scores will *not* be shown to your teachers. They will be used only for research on intelligence. Yesterday you had a practice warm-up . . . (rest of instructions same as neutral conditions).

After the instructions were given, a hostility questionnaire was administered which was the same as the one used the previous day, except that the items were arranged differently.

The Hostility Scale.   The instrument used to measure hostile expression was based on a test that had been developed by Ehrlich (1961) to study the influence of aggressive dispositions on concept formation in Northern white adolescent boys. Our test had 58 items, each consisting of four words, with instructions to "circle the word that does not belong with the others." Twenty-nine items contained only nonaggressive concepts; elimination of a particular word resulted in a better concept than did elimination of any other word, e.g.: TUNNEL, BRIDGE, FERRY, TOLL. In the remaining 29 items, one word had an aggressive meaning, one was nonaggressive, and two were ambiguous, e.g.: HOMERUN, HIT, BASH, STRIKE. Here the subject could select an aggressive concept by eliminating HOMERUN, or a nonaggressive concept by dropping BASH. Out of a total of 58 items in our test, 47 were taken from Ehrlich's 84-item test. He found scores on his test to be related to ratings of overt aggression, as well as to hostility scores on a TAT-like projective test. The present version evolved from a preliminary tryout of the original instrument on a sample of Southern Negro college students, under neutral instructions. Items which did not appear to be suitable were dropped, and some new ones were added.

A subject's hostility score consisted of the total number of critical items in which he had included the aggression word, regardless of whether he had used the correct concept. In addition, a score indicative of the level of intellectual functioning was obtained by totalling the number of correct concepts attained on neutral items, and on aggression items. To study the effect of the experimental conditions, change scores were obtained by substracting each subject's scores on the pretest from his scores on the post test.

RESULTS AND DISCUSSION

The main findings of the experiment by analysis of variance, indicate that there was a significant interaction effect of the two variables, Race of Tester and Test vs. Neutral Instructions, on changes in hostility scores from the previous day ($p < .025$). The group means reveal that in the Neutral condition the change scores of subjects who had a white administrator were only slightly different from those of subjects who had a Negro administrator. But when test instructions were used, the White Tester group expressed *less* hostility than previously, while the Negro Tester group showed an *increase* in hostile expression. This difference between groups was significant ($p < .01$). Thus the experimental prediction was supported.

There were no significant effects of the experimental conditions on changes in the number of correct concepts attained on neutral items, on aggression items, or on all items combined. Within each of the four experimental groups, there were no correlations between the various measures of conceptual accuracy and hostility change scores. Finally, several items in a post-experimental questionnaire, which were intended to elicit information about the subject's emotional state and perception of the situation, failed to reveal any group differences.

Our interpretation of the results is that both task administrators instigated hostility in subjects when they announced that they were testing intelligence;

when the experimenter was Negro, students revealed their annoyance by forming aggressive concepts, but when he was white the need to control hostile feelings resulted in avoidance of aggressive words. This view of the data is of course inferential, since all that is actually known about the White Tester–Test Instructions group is that their hostility scores *declined* from pretest levels. There is no direct evidence of increased emotional conflict in this condition. Assuming that our interpretation is correct, the results suggest that inhibited hostility may have contributed to the behavioral impairment that Katz, Roberts and Robinson observed in Negroes who were tested intellectually by a white experimenter. Why then were there no effects in the present experiment on conceptual accuracy? Our belief is that the task was not an appropriate one for revealing the disruptive effects of emotional conflict. It has none of the usual features of tasks on which impairment has been found to occur under stress. For example, it was not speeded, and it did not involve complex learning, coordination of responses, or problem solving.

Finally, the results provide a methodological critique of previous research on Negro personality which did not take into account possible effects of the race of the investigator on subjects' responses. For example, the bulk of studies on Negro aggression that were reviewed by Dreger and Miller (1960) apparently were done entirely by whites.

PART THREE

Norms

WITH the troublesome concept of test norms, it cannot be stressed sufficiently that norm represents normal: if the average eight-year-old child correctly completes 15 arithmetic problems on Test X, then 15 is the norm. In fact, norms not only give the average; they also provide the relative frequency of the varying degrees of deviation from this norm—i.e., norm tables. There are, furthermore, many kinds of norms—local, class, grade, geographic area, and national norms, to mention only a few. Adequate normative data does not have to be based on millions of cases to insure accuracy and stability. The crux of this problem lies in the standardization procedures that were employed and, most important, the sampling procedures themselves.

In the history of psychological testing, the best sampling procedures have typically been with standardized mental ability scales for which national norm data are to be computed. In the United States, the prime example of this was the work of Terman and Merrill (1937), when they standardized Forms L and M of the Stanford-Binet and where they used a stratified sampling technique.

Random sampling, let alone 100 percent sampling, is rarely employed, but when it is carefully done very accurate results occur. Probably the best example of this sampling technique is the famous Scottish survey in 1939 (Macmeeken, 1940), very likely the most nearly complete testing on an entire population yet managed. All children born in Scotland on four days (February 1, May 1, August 1, November 1) were to be tested. As one might imagine, this meant a diligent, painstaking search to the remotest corners of Scotland in order to secure a final and complete sample. (There was a loss of only one case!) This search resulted in a total of 443 boys and 430 girls between the ages of 8 years, 11 months and 11 years, 9 months. All testees were administered the 1916 Stanford-Binet and eight of the performance measures devised by Pintner and Paterson. To illustrate one of the norm results: for the Stanford-Binet, the researchers secured a generally normal, but not perfect, curve. Here it should be remembered that all these tests were standardized on U.S. children.

With achievement tests, the sampling problems in regard to school and grade populations are no less difficult. Normative data from these types of tests are typically expressed in terms of grade placement indexes. Among the most widely used of such tests are the California Achievement Tests. Robert Dion, area director for the California Test Bureau, has written about the sampling procedures employed in standardizing the 1957 edition of these tests. His article, reproduced from the October, 1958, *Newsletter of the Elementary School Principals Association of Connecticut*, is here presented because he spells out so clearly what is involved in a stratified sampling technique.

NORMS ARE NOT GOALS

Robert Dion

After users have compared obtained results with the norms supplied with a test, the following reactions are not too uncommon: "The norms are too high."—"The norms are too low."—"The test must be off because our group is below the norm."—"The test is too easy because our group is above the norm."—"Our group is below the norm, but we'll work to bring it up to the norm."—"More cases should have been used in establishing norms." Searching for reasons for such reactions and other comparable reactions reveals that there is confusion and misunderstanding about norms; misuse of norms; and invariably no consideration is being given to a variety of factors that may account for deviations from test norms. Replies to the foregoing reactions embrace several concepts and procedures.

A test is merely a sampling from a broad area of knowledge, information and skill, and the preparation of a test involves two major aspects—(1) content (items, reliability, validity), and (2) assigning norms which will serve as reference points indicating the typical performance for described groups. This discussion concerns the latter aspect.

Although there are many ways of describing or recording performance on a test, numbers are the least cumbersome and complicated for practical use because they simplify communication, comparison and manipulation. Thus the raw score is an essential or fundamental piece of information. However, the raw score by itself is meaningless. Determining the total number of items in the test and expressing the score in terms of the percent of the total number of items in the test may have more meaning; however, the percent score may indicate a good or a poor score depending upon the difficulty of the items. To interpret raw scores it is necessary to know how others perform on the test. Raw scores have to be related to other types of information that may affect performance, so raw scores are converted into derived scores.

Derived scores can be expressed as grades, ages, percentiles, standard scores, etc., and the use of one type does not exclude the use of others. One of the most commonly used derived scores is the grade placement or grade equivalent, so let us examine what it means. If a pupil makes a raw score of 55 and 55 is the median score made by pupils tested at the sixth month of the fifth grade, he is said to have a grade placement of 5.6. This 5.6 grade placement is the norm and merely reflects or describes the typical performance of all tested in a described group who are at the sixth month of the fifth grade. Consequently, all examinees shouldn't be expected to reach or exceed a norm which has been established by a score achieved or exceeded by only 50 percent of the examinees in a group. Norms should not be considered standards of work, because standards are levels of performance or attainment fixed for an individual school or a pupil and expressed in terms of outcomes of instruction. It cannot be presumed that a given group is doing satisfactory work if the group is up to the norm without considering the objectives of the school and the background and ability of the pupils. For example, the standard of accuracy in arithmetic is 100 percent; however, the norms of sixth graders may indicate that only 85 percent of the computation has been done correctly.

The user of a test must understand the nature of the group upon which the test has been standardized, and he must determine that the norms yield meaning in terms of the particular purpose for which the testing is done. Large numbers of cases are no guarantee of an adequate sampling, and naming the localities (without additional information) where norms were obtained does not indicate the nature of the population. These two elements were established quite forcefully following the huge mail canvasses of ten million or more post-card ballots sent out by the *Literary Digest* back in 1936. Actually the number of cases required for an adequate sampling is a statistical problem, and in view of a number of criteria the amount required is relatively small. If the standardization group is not comparable to the group upon which the test is to be used then comparable results cannot be expected. If the norms are not based on groups with whom it is sensible to compare individuals we are testing, they are meaningless and misleading. Therefore, the main consideration is a definition of the standardization or normative group and the relevancy of the norms. Find the evidence in the manual.

Although standardization is complex and very often one procedure is preferred to some other procedure because of the philosophy of the test maker and the objectives underlying the test, it may be helpful to give an example of the procedures followed in the standardization of a series of achievement tests (Clark and Tiegs, 1958).

SAMPLING

1. Nation-wide Representation.   Students from 48 states and the District of Columbia were included in the overall standardization population. For selection and statistical purposes, eighteen geographical homogeneous areas were established. Data used in assigning states to an area were from the Biennial Survey of Education in the United States, 1952–54, published by the United States Office of Education and from other sources. Primary consideration was given to the following factors: average expenditures per student for instructional purposes; comparability of average scores on draft deferment examinations; length of school term; urban-rural characteristics; and type of school organization, attitudes and cultural characteristics. The areas were as follows:

Area 1.   Maine, New Hampshire, Vermont, Massachusetts, Connecticut and Rhode Island (5.04% of school population)
Area 2.   New York (7.40%)
Area 3.   New Jersey (2.53%)
Area 4.   Pennsylvania, Delaware and Maryland (7.63%)
Area 5.   West Virginia, Virginia and District of Columbia (4.61%)
Area 6.   Ohio (4.87%)
Area 7.   South Carolina, Alabama, Georgia and Mississippi (9.78%)
Area 8.   North Carolina and Florida (5.73%)
Area 9.   Tennessee, Arkansas and Kentucky (6.55%)
Area 10. Illinois and Indiana (7.38%)

Area 11. Michigan (4.00%)
Area 12. Minnesota and Wisconsin (3.77%)
Area 13. Iowa, North Dakota, South Dakota, Kansas, Nebraska and Colorado (5.92%)
Area 14. Missouri, Oklahoma and Louisiana (6.53%)
Area 15. Texas (5.75%)
Area 16. New Mexico, Idaho, Montana, Utah, Wyoming, Arizona and Nevada (3.20%)
Area 17. Oregon and Washington (2.78%)
Area 18. California (6.53%)

2. Population Density Categories. Within each area the schools were divided into the four population density categories from which the schools draw their pupils.

a) More than 100,000.
b) 10,000 to 99,999.
c) 2,500 to 9,999.
d) Less than 2,500.

3. Basic Sampling Pattern. For each grade level (Grades 1 through 12), representative classes were selected for each of the four population density categories in each of the eighteen geographical areas. Thus, the sampling procedure of the nationwide sample at each grade from 1 through 12 was identical. In computing the norms for the W-X-Y-Z series, the test statistics for each population density category and each geographical area were weighted in direct proportion to the percent the school children in these specific categories are to the school children in the United States as a whole.

4. Data from about 65,000 selected cases were utilized in the dual, two-stage standardization program. The first stage of sampling provided a large pool of subjects from which the second stage sampling drew stratified groups having statistically and educationally controlled characteristics. In addition to the sampling design, a number of other quality restrictions and controls are imposed on the standardization testing. Some of these were:

a) Only one grade per level was utilized in any one participating school. The rationale for this requirement was to avoid undue influence by any school system.

b) Special efforts were made to have the participating schools include only the designated normal or typical classes for the community. Neither accelerated nor retarded classes were included. Even mixed classes, i.e., those consisting of more than one grade level, were avoided. The purpose of this restriction was to maintain the normal homogeneity of classroom units in the standardization program.

c) No classes were included if they had recently been administered either a California Achievement Test Battery or the California Test of Mental Maturity. This restriction was imposed to avoid the possibility of spurious practice effects.

d) Most testing was done on Tuesdays, Wednesdays and Thursdays which did not immediately follow or precede holidays or athletic events. Any detrimental influences of fatigue after a holiday or the disturbance of anticipation of a special event or holiday were thus minimized.

e) Because the total testing required for both batteries was over two hours, testing was distributed over two or three days. The purpose of this was to avoid having examinees become test-weary and fatigued.

In their final form the norms for the California Achievement Tests have been based on a controlled (stratified), two-stage sampling which constituted a normal distribution of mental ability, typical age-grade relationships and other characteristics as follows: the median IQ for pupils in Grades 1 through 8 was 100 with a standard deviation of 16 points; for grades above the eighth, the median IQ for each grade was as follows: ninth—101.5, tenth—103, eleventh—104, twelfth—105; 70 percent were making normal progress through the grades; about 20 percent were retarded one-half year or more; 10 percent were accelerated one-half year or more; the norming sample contained various ethnic and cultural groups and pupils with bilingual problems. The two-stage national sampling design assumes a random sampling of examinees within the required cell design rather than the cluster sampling of total classes traditionally used which can give undue weight to some communities or regions. Weights were applied to obtain the number of sample cases proportional to the total of pupils enrolled in schools over the nation when classified with respect to population, geographic area and school grade.

Note that the above example defines the population, reflects a well-planned sample rather than data collected on the basis of availability, and reports the number of cases and details methods.

Differences in courses of study, materials of instruction, time allotments, emphasis on certain skill areas, differences in the quality of teaching, and age and intelligence of pupils are factors which may account for deviations from test norms. Among the foregoing let us consider three principal factors that influence test scores of pupils from a particular elementary school.

a) Curriculum. If, in a particular school, instructional materials tend to be taught earlier in the school program, then the test performance of that school at this grade will tend to be higher with respect to norms. Conversely, if materials are not taught until later than usual, the test performance of that school at this grade will tend to be lower with respect to norms. However, when all materials have been taught, it is expected (other things being equal) that the performance of the two groups will be about equal. Variations in curriculum primarily influence rate of growth and are detected by analyzing the test results in a longitudinal manner from Grades 1 to 8. The school introducing materials earlier and stressing the basic skills will have results that start out high at Grades 1, 2, and 3, but tend to drop somewhat at Grades 7 and 8. Those schools using a delayed approach start out lower, show more rapid growth, but end up at about the same level at Grades 7 and 8.

b) Age-grade relationship. Acceleration–retardation policies of a school influence test results. Consider a school system with a "no failure" policy. This policy will tend to lower the test results for a school in relation to the

norms which are based upon 70 percent of the pupils making normal progress through the grades with 20 percent being retarded and 10 percent being
accelerated by one-half year or more. Take a pupil in Grade 5 whose test
score is 4.0 grade placement units. Here his performance is 1.0 grade placement units below norms and he tends to pull the class average down. Now
assume that this same pupil has been in a school system that followed the
policy of retarding pupils low in achievement. In this school the pupil would
have been retarded and so would be in Grade 4 rather than Grade 5. At a
Grade 4 classification his performance would be the norm and he would
not tend to pull the class average down. Thus the more pupils are retarded
in a school system the higher will be the average performances of the various
grades. An analysis of the age-grade relationships is important in interpreting
test results.

c) Mental ability.   It is estimated that curriculum and age-grade factors
account on the average for about 30 percent of the variations from the
norms in test results of a particular school, and about 70 percent of the
variations may be attributed to variations in mental ability. Schools whose
pupils have an average IQ above 100 (median mental ability of the norm
group for Grades 1–8) would be expected to have achievement results above
the norm. There are several ways that the median IQ of a school may be
raised. In some schools all pupils with IQs below 80 or 70 are withdrawn
from regular classes and classified in opportunity rooms. This procedure will
raise the median IQ of the general classes. In independent schools entrance
requirements establish certain selective criteria. As a result it is found that
pupils in these schools usually have median IQs in excess of 100. Consequently, we would expect the median performance for such schools to exceed
the norms. Conversely, schools whose pupils have an average IQ below 100
would be expected to have achievement results below the norm.

Test norms should serve as the point of departure both in investigating
the reasons for obtained results and in determining the desirability of possible
modifications of the factors which account for the obtained results. The elements which constitute a norm provide somewhat of an average of all the
combined successes and failures of teachers and pupils ranging from the
poorest to the best. To use norms as goals, objectives or standards is to encourage mediocrity.

▽ ▽ ▽

REGARDING 100 percent sampling, reference has been made to the Scottish survey involving the 1916 Stanford-Binet test and certain of the Pintner-Paterson performance indexes. Perhaps at the other extreme would be when researchers are limited to only one subject and where measurements typically are obtained over extended periods of time. It is important to recognize that much valuable data may be obtained in this fashion. Studies of single persons or single events may also be very fruitful sources for hypotheses for further experimental testing. Too often in the field of measurement we insist on large numbers of cases, too easily taking comfort in that a large N ensures better sampling (which may be anything but the case). It is for this reason that Dr. Dukes's paper, summarizing researches involving only one subject, has been included here. An N of 1 is seen as also appropriate when, for the function considered, intersubject variability is low, when opportunities for observing a given class of events are limited, and when a supposed universal relationship is questioned and the obtained evidence is negative.

Dr. Dukes is associate professor of psychology and associate dean of the College of Letters and Science at the Davis campus of the Univerity of California. His paper originally appeared in a 1965 issue of the *Psychological Bulletin*.

$N = 1$

William F. Dukes

In the search for principles which govern behavior, psychologists generally confine their empirical observations to a relatively small sample of a defined population, using probability theory to help assess the generality of the findings obtained. Because this inductive process commonly entails some knowledge of individual differences in the behavior involved, studies employing only one subject ($N = 1$) seem somewhat anomalous. With no information about intersubject variability in performance, the general applicability of findings is indeterminate.

Although generalizations about behavior rest equally upon adequate sampling of both subjects and situations, questions about sampling most often refer to subjects. Accordingly, the term "$N = 1$" is used throughout the present discussion to designate the *reductio ad absurdum* in the sampling of subjects. It might, however, equally well (perhaps better, in terms of frequency of occurrence) refer to the limiting case in the sampling of situations —for example, the use of one maze in an investigation of learning, or a simple tapping task in a study of motivation.

As a corollary, the term $N = 1$ might also be appropriately applied to the sampling of experimenters. Long recognized as a potential source of variance in interview data, the investigator has recently been viewed as a variable which may also influence laboratory results (Rosenthal, 1963 and 1964).

Except to note these other possible usages of the term $N = 1$, the present paper is not concerned with one-experimenter or one-situation treatments, but is devoted, as indicated previously, to single-subject studies.

Despite the limitation stated in the first paragraph, $N = 1$ studies cannot be dismissed as inconsequential. A brief scanning of general and historical accounts of psychology will dispel any doubts about their importance, revealing, as it does, many instances of pivotal research in which the observations were confined to the behavior of only one person or animal.

SELECTIVE HISTORICAL REVIEW

Foremost among $N = 1$ studies is Ebbinghaus' investigation of memory published in 1885. Ebbinghaus' work established the pattern for much of the research on verbal learning during the past 80 years. His principal findings, gleaned from many self-administered learning situations consisting of some 2,000 lists of nonsense syllables and 42 stanzas of poetry, are still valid source material for the student of memory. In another well-known pioneering study of learning, Bryan and Harter's (1899) report on plateaus, certain crucial data were obtained from only one subject. Their letter-word-phrase analysis of learning to receive code was based on the record of only one student. Their notion of habit hierarchies derived in part from this analysis is, nevertheless, still useful in explaining why plateaus may occur.

Familiar even to beginning students of perception is Stratton's (1897) account of the confusion from and the adjustment to wearing inverting lenses. In this experiment according to Boring (1942), Stratton, with only himself as subject,

settled both Kepler's problem of erect vision with an inverted image, and Lotze's problem of the role of experience in space perception, by showing that the "absolute" localization of retinal positions—up-down and right-left—are learned and consist of bodily orientation as context to the place of visual excitation [p. 237].

The role of experience was also under scrutiny in the Kelloggs' (1933) project of raising one young chimpanzee, Gua, in their home. (Although observations of their son's behavior were also included in their report, the study is essentially of the $N = 1$ type, since the "experimental group" consisted of one.) This attempt to determine whether early experience may modify behavior traditionally regarded as instinctive was for years a standard reference in discussions of the learning-maturation question.

Focal in the area of motivation is the balloon-swallowing experiment of physiologists Cannon and Washburn (1912) in which kymographic recordings of Washburn's stomach contradictions were shown to coincide with his introspective reports of hunger pangs. Their findings were widely incorporated into psychology textbooks as providing an explanation of hunger. Even though in recent years greater importance has been attached to central factors in hunger, Cannon and Washburn's work continues to occupy a prominent place in textbook accounts of food-seeking behavior.

In the literature on emotion, Watson and Rayner's study (1920) of Albert's being conditioned to fear a white rat has been hailed as one of the most influential papers in the history of American psychology. Their experiment, Murphy (1949) observes,

immediately had a profound effect on American psychology; for it appeared to support the whole conception that not only simple motor habits, but important, enduring traits of personality, such as emotional tendencies, may in fact be "built into" the child by conditioning [p. 261].

Actually the Albert experiment was unfinished because he moved away from the laboratory area before the question of fear removal could be explored. But Jones (1924) provided the natural sequel in Peter, a child who, through a process of active reconditioning, overcame a nonlaboratory-produced fear of white furry objects.

In abnormal psychology few cases have attracted as much attention as Prince's (1905) Miss Beauchamp, for years the model case in accounts of multiple personality. Perhaps less familiar to the general student but more significant in the history of psychology is Breuer's case (Breuer & Freud, 1895) of Anna O., the analysis of which is credited with containing "the kernel of a new system of treatment, and indeed a new system of psychology" (Murphy, 1949, p. 307). In the process of examining Anna's hysterical symptoms, the occasions for their appearance, and their origin, Breuer claimed that with the aid of hypnosis these symptoms were "talked away." Breuer's young colleague was Sigmund Freud, who later publicly declared the importance of this case in the genesis of psychoanalysis.

There are other instances, maybe not so spectacular as the preceding, of influential $N = 1$ studies—for example, Yerkes' (1927) exploration of the gorilla Congo's mental activities; Jacobson's (1931) study of neuromuscular activity and thinking in an amputee; Culler and Mettler's (1934) demonstration of simple conditioning in a decorticate dog; and Burtt's (1932) striking illustration of his son's residual memory of early childhood.

Further documentation of the significant role of $N = 1$ research in psychological history seems unnecessary. A few studies, each in impact like the single pebble which starts an avalanche, have been the impetus for major developments in research and theory. Others, more like missing pieces from nearly finished jigsaw puzzles, have provided timely data on various controversies.

This historical recounting of "successful" cases is, of course, not an exhortation for restricted subject samplings, nor does it imply that their greatness is independent of subsequent related work.

FREQUENCY AND RANGE OF TOPICS

During the past 25 years (1939–1963) a total of 246 $N = 1$ studies, 35 of them in the last 5-year period, have appeared in the leading psychological periodicals. Although these 246 studies constitute only a small percent of the 1939–1963 journal articles, the absolute number is noteworthy and is sizable enough to discount any notion that $N = 1$ studies are a phenomenon of the past.

When, furthermore, these are distributed according to subject matter, they are seen to coextend fairly well with the range of topics in general psychology.

The breakdown is as follows:

	f
Maturation and development	29
Motivation	7
Emotion	12
Perception, sensory processes	25
Learning	27
Thinking and language	15
Intelligence	14
Personality	51
Mental health and psychotherapy	66
Total	246

As might be expected, a large proportion of them fall into the clinical and personality areas. One cannot, however, explain away $N = 1$ studies as case histories contributed by clinicians and personologists occupied less with establishing generalizations than with exploring the uniqueness of an individual and understanding his total personality. Only about 30% (74) are primarily oriented toward the individual, a figure which includes not only works in the "understanding" tradition, but also those treating the individual as a universe of responses and applying traditionally nomothetic techniques to describe and predict individual behavior (e.g., Yates, 1958).

In actual practice, of course, the two orientations—toward uniqueness or generality—are more a matter of degree than of mutual exclusion, with the result that in the literature surveyed purely idiographic research is extremely rare. Representative of that approach are Evans' (1950) novel-like account of Miller who "spontaneously" recovered his sight after more than 2 years of blindness, Rosen's (1949) "George X: A self-analysis by an avowed fascist," and McCurdy's (1944) profile of Keats.

RATIONALE FOR $N = 1$

The appropriateness of restricting an idiographic study to one individual is obvious from the meaning of the term. If uniqueness is involved, a sample of one exhausts the population. At the other extreme, an N of 1 is also appropriate if complete population generality exists (or can reasonably be assumed to exist). That is, when between-individual variability for the function under scrutiny is known to be negligible or the data from the single subject have a point-for-point congruence with those obtained from dependable collateral sources, results from a second subject may be considered redundant. Some $N = 1$ studies may be regarded as approximations of this ideal case, as for example, Heinemann's (1961) photographic measurement of retinal images.

A variant on this typicality theme occurs when the researcher, in order to preserve some kind of functional unity and perhaps to dramatize a point, reports in depth one case which exemplifies many. Thus Eisen's (1962) description of the effects of early sensory deprivation is an account of one quondam hard-of-hearing child, and Bettelheim's (1949) paper on rehabilitation a chronicle of one seriously delinquent child.

In other studies an N of 1 is adequate because of the dissonant character of the findings. In contrast to its limited usefulness in *establishing* generalizations from "positive" evidence, an N of 1 when the evidence is "negative," is as useful as an N of 1,000 in *rejecting* an asserted or assumed universal relationship. Thus Lenneberg's (1962) case of an 8-year-old boy who lacked the motor skills necessary for speaking but who could understand language makes it "clear that hearing oneself babble is not a necessary factor in the acquisition of understanding . . ." (p. 422). Similarly Teska's (1947) case of a congenital hydrocephalic, 6½ years old, with an IQ of 113, is sufficient evidence to discount the notion that prolonged congenital hydrocephaly results in some degree of feeblemindedness.

While scientists are in the long run more likely to be interested in knowing *what is* than *what is not* and more concerned with how many exist or in what proportion they exist than with the fact that at least one exists, one negative case can make it necessary to revise a traditionally accepted hypothesis.

Still other $N = 1$ investigations simply reflect a limited opportunity to observe. When the search for lawfulness is extended to infrequent "non-laboratory" behavior, individuals in the population under study may be so sparsely distributed spatially or temporally that the psychologist can observe only one case, a report of which may be useful as a part of a cumulative record. Examples of this include cases of multiple personality (Thigpen & Cleckly, 1954), congenital insensitivity to pain (Cohen *et al.,* 1955), and mental deterioration following carbon monoxide poisoning (Jensen, 1950). Situational complexity as well as subject sparsity may limit the opportunity to observe. When the situation is greatly extended in time, requires expensive or specialized training for the subject, or entails intricate and difficult-to-administer controls, the investigator may, aware of their exploratory character, restrict his observations to one subject. Projects involving home-raising a chimpanzee (Hayes & Hayes, 1952) or testing after 16 years for retention of material presented during infancy (Burtt, 1941) would seem to illustrate this use of an N of 1.

Not all $N = 1$ studies can be conveniently fitted into this rubric; nor is this necessary. Instead of being oriented either toward the person (uniqueness) or toward a global theory (universality), researchers may sometimes simply focus on a problem. Problem-centered research on only one subject may, by clarifying questions, defining variables, and indicating approaches, make substantial contributions to the study of behavior. Besides answering a specific question, it may (Ebbinghaus' work, 1885, being a classic example) provide important groundwork for the theorists.

Regardless of rationale and despite obvious limitations, the usefulness of $N = 1$ studies in psychological research seems, from the preceding historical and methodological considerations, to be fairly well established. Finally, their status in research is further secured by the statistician's assertion (McNemar, 1940) that:

The statistician who fails to see that important generalizations from research on a single case can ever be acceptable is on a par with the experimentalist who fails to appreciate the fact that some problems can never be solved without resort to numbers [p. 361].

PART FOUR

Response
Sets

A relatively recent development in test construction is the concern over response sets of one type or another. These are usually regarded as undesirable in the sense that they lower the validity of a particular test. In two significant articles (1946 and 1950), Cronbach has extensively discussed response sets, so that now most test constructors take pains, especially with personality measures, to minimize or delete these adverse influences. Cronbach's two papers summarize extensive evidence that response sets (such a bias in marking one particular alternative to a test item, tendency to guess, working for speed as against accuracy) also operate in the more conventional objective measuring devices. Such response sets can also be altered fairly easily by direct coaching or by suitable changes in directions to the testee. In his two papers, Cronbach has recommended the following: (a) response sets should be avoided, with the occasional exception of personality tests where traits such as carefulness are being measured, since such traits are psychologically similar to response sets; (b) the multiple-choice type of test in forced choice format, or utilizing paired comparisons or do-guess items, is to be preferred over other forms of test items. If, however, an item form is used where response sets do occur, the test constructor should take certain precautions to minimize these: (a) phrase the directions so as to reduce ambiguity and require every testee to respond with the same set; (b) avoid administering the particular test to a group for whom the test is quite difficult; (c) provide for a response-set score to be obtained, and use this to identify testees whose scores are probably invalid. Cronbach further believes that if test constructors adhere to these general guidelines future tests will increase their saturation with the particular factors these tests are attempting to measure.

Even standardized scoring keys for well-known psychological tests can be shown to be contaminated (unwittingly, it is assumed) by response bias. This has resulted from test makers' inattention to the general rule that correct answers to true–false or multiple–choice items should be randomized as to position. Metfessel and Sax (1958) have shown that this is fairly common, especially in older personality inventories where the true–false item form has been employed. Here follows a brief abstract of this report which originally appeared in *Educational & Psychological Measurement*.

SYSTEMATIC BIASES IN THE KEYING OF CORRECT RESPONSES ON CERTAIN STANDARDIZED TESTS

Newton S. Metfessel and Gilbert Sax

Inaccurate measurement results also because of the keying of the correct responses, by a test constructor, in certain alternative positions on multiple-choice and true–false tests according to a pattern not in harmony with randomization. For example, in a multiple-choice test consisting of 100 items and four alternative response positions, one would expect by chance randomization that approximately one fourth of the correct responses would be "keyed" by the test constructor to each of the four choice positions. If a statistically significant difference in the number of correct response placements at each of the alternative positions was in evidence, a bias on the part of the test constructor would be indicated.

There is evidence of the presence of response-set patterns on the part of subjects in responding to multiple-choice tests, and there is further evidence showing that subjects presented with true–false items tend to negate the false scores in favor of the affirmative ones. However, it should be explained that response sets for both multiple-choice and true–false tests operate only when the subject is in doubt or does not know the answer to a question. Cronbach reports in the case of true–false tests that this tendency (to mark items true rather than false) makes false items more valid and reliable than true items, reduces the range of test scores when the number of true and false items are equal, raises the mean score when a majority of the items are true, or lowers it when the majority are false, and causes the R–W formula to be inappropriate in many cases.

The purpose of our investigation is to determine which of a number of standardized tests have biases in their keying patterns. Instances where these biases were known to "test-wise" students or were in harmony with tendencies of compulsive subjects, results which are incongruous with "true" scores would be obtained. In this study, chi-squares were obtained for the distribution of correct responses on approximately twenty currently popular tests, all of them in wide use. Examples of the frequencies of keyed correct responses for each alternative position, some of which frequencies are clearly randomized and others not, are as follows:

	Response Alternative					X^2 Significant at .01 Level
	1	2	3	4	5	
Army General Classification Test	36	37	36	38	—	No
California Test Mental Maturity	13	42	37	26	—	Yes
Otis Quick-Scoring Test Mental Ability	5	14	24	13	10	Yes
Co-op Test Reading Comprehension	30	31	31	29	29	No
Bell Adjustment Inventory	133	27	—	—	—	Yes
California Test Personality	71	109	—	—	—	Yes
Thurstone Temperament Scale	109	31	—	—	—	Yes

Considering all the tests covered in this report, approximately 42 percent yielded chi-square values significant at the .01 level. There is a tendency for the authors of multiple-choice tests to place the correct response at the center of the response distribution. Also, test constructors tend to place the correct response at the "true" position on true–false tests. Thus, subjects who are test-wise or who have a compulsive tendency to avoid the "false" response have a greater-than-average chance of doing well on the test. It is suggested that test constructors become more aware of the bias which is involved in the tests themselves as well as the response-set of the subject.

IN other test situations, however, the presence of response sets is welcome, and a researcher, especially in the field of personality measurement, might hope to capitalize on these. Here, rather than try to remove such response sets, one would actively encourage and promote them but, again, always with their measurement in mind. Professor Berg, among others, has written a series of reports from just this point of view, his emphasis is not on item content but on the deviant responses that are obtained. The ubiquitous principle of individual differences again can be used here. Professor Berg would then make into an asset what, from another point of view, is often seen as a liability in psychological test construction.

The report of his Deviation Hypothesis is taken from an informal and what the author terms "a highly personal account," which appeared in the *Journal of Counseling Psychology* (1957). What appears here is a condensation of the original article. It is hoped that the student reader will also enjoy the highly informal writing style. Professor Berg is chairman of the department of psychology at Louisiana State University in Baton Rouge.

DEVIANT RESPONSES AND DEVIANT PEOPLE: THE FORMULATION OF THE DEVIATION HYPOTHESIS

Irwin A. Berg

This is a highly personal account of a research area and a concept which grew out of this research which has, during the past dozen years, held my interest with varying degrees of intensity. Conventionally, one does not write highly personal discourses dealing with research; at least, it isn't done more than once in a blue moon. Yet the haunch and the hoof, the bone and the gristle of the problem are for me intimately bound to the personal involvement.

This preamble sounds as if I am about to unveil something of heroic size and import, complete with final results. While the Deviation Hypothesis is perhaps ample in scope, I certainly have no final results to offer. What I have to offer is only a road that does have a few signposts, but makes its way like the River Meander and may end in a bog instead of leading to Rome. At times, I have been temporarily convinced that I was chasing a wild goose or the chimera of the ancients. When this conviction became strong, I turned to other studies, uttering sighs of relief between Anglo-Saxon expletives. But like a half-welcome suitor, I sooner or later returned to the object of my affections and received some encouragement in the form of small favors, only to be roundly spurned anew and left to repeat the cycle once again.

The problem I have been concerned with is an aspect of the old, old problem of "set" or einstellung, specifically, the problem of biased responses and what they mean. It has been known for a long time that when subjects respond to a stimulus pattern, the distribution of their responses often does not follow a normal probability pattern. A flipped coin, for example, is not a 50–50 "heads-tails" proposition insofar as human responses are concerned. On the first toss, 80 percent of the subjects will call out, "heads." When ascending to the balcony of some movie theaters, to consider another example, patrons may take either a stairway to the right or to the left and reach about the same point upstairs. Yet theater managers have noted with some exasperation that three times as many persons will use the right-hand stairway and the carpet wears out three times as fast.

RESPONSE BIAS IN TESTS

In psychological tests, similar biases often appear, and they are something of a headache to those who are aware of the problem. When subjects do not know the answer to certain items or when the test is otherwise unstructured for them, there is a demonstrable tendency for them to favor certain options which indicate aquiescence such as "true," "agree," or "like," as opposed to negative options as "false" or "disagree." Other biases may appear as preferences for "uncertain," "?," "cannot say," indicating evasiveness, when the test provides for such answers. Cronbach (in 1946) called such biases in tests "response sets," and he described a large number of them in detail. Incidentally, response sets are quite stable; and they affect test validity and reliability, often spuriously raising the latter. Curiously, although it is more than ten years since Cronbach published his excellent review of the significant role played by response sets in tests, a surprising number of psychologists appear to be unaware of what these response tendencies mean.

A number of writers have provided evidence that biased responses are related to personality characteristics. But while the evidence is clearly positive, it is not strong and, at best, indicates that only a moderate relationship exists. To take but one example: a reported correlation of —.43 between Bernreuter self-sufficiency scores and the number of noncommittal responses on a social attitudes test. That is what one usually finds: correlations in the .30's and .40's or, among groups, differences that just reach the 1 to 5 percent levels of statistical significance. Yet, to my mind, it seemed clear that anything highly stable and related to personality ought to be capable of being refined into a usefully valid instrument for measuring personality characteristics. Furthermore, there is something intriguing in the cloak-and-dagger sense of taking materials totally unrelated to personality, such as an algebra test, and from it deriving a valid scale for paranoid tendencies. Unfortunately, it didn't work out, at least for algebra tests and personality. The result was a few correlations around .10 and many Irish correlations, as John Darley once termed correlations of .02, .05, .06, and .08. For a history test, the correlations between response sets and scores on standardized personality tests were higher, but not much higher. There seemed to be several difficulties.

One was that response biases appear more frequently as the stimulus situation is unstructured, and I was using tests with a high degree of structure. Another difficulty was that the algebra test was entirely, and the history test partially, composed of multiple-choice items, and the multiple-choice form in structured tests is relatively free from response set influence.

I still hold firmly the conviction that it is possible to obtain useful personality measures from algebra or history tests by means of biased responses; however, appropriate items designed to elicit set will probably have to be inserted in the tests, because one cannot depend upon locating more than a few "response set" items in the usual standardized test. At any rate, since structure was a problem, I prepared a series of abstract designs of no particular significance and asked subjects to sort the designs, each of which were drawn on a 4″ x 6″ card, into one of four boxes labeled "like much," "like slightly," "dislike slightly," "dislike much." The idea was that with minimal structure and, with responses made on the basis of affect, bias would have ample opportunity to appear. When exploratory studies were made with small groups of subjects, it became immediately apparent that bias was present in the responses to virtually every item. This, of course, told nothing of any relationship to personality; so several groups which were operationally defined as "disparate" in personality were used for pilot studies. One group was composed of 12 accountants with five to ten years' experience, another was a group of 16 real estate salesmen, and the last group was composed of nine line supervisors of machine departments.

While the groups were small and the results could be regarded only as suggestive, the analysis of the responses to the abstract designs showed biases for all groups; and the pattern of bias was discernably different for each group. This was not much to crow about, but it was enough to get 60 designs privately published as "The Perceptual Reaction Test." This permitted large scale collection of data and the recording of test responses and other information on thousands of IBM cards. This step produced a variety of findings, all of them interesting and none of them conclusive. To mention a few, neurotics tended somewhat to prefer the "dislike" and psychotics the "like" responses, homosexuals showed a response pattern of their own, normal men revealed a significantly different pattern from normal women. Indeed, with respect to the latter, it was found possible to construct a reasonably valid scale for *mf* of interest. We were doing better than had ever done before in using response biases as measures of certain characteristics of behavior, but we weren't doing nearly well enough.

In mulling over these results, it occurred to me that I had been concentrating on the wrong thing. That is, the biases we have been talking about were, of course, only biases in the normal probability sense. They were not biased in the sense of responses made by the majority of people. Perhaps I had been stupidly floundering in some semantic quagmire of normal curves, normal people, and irrationally measuring bias first in terms of one and then the other. But whatever the reason, the key to the problem seemed to lie in the departures from any established pattern of bias, not in the bias itself. That is, on the basis of probability we should expect that 50 percent of the people should turn right and 50 percent left when they enter a branching hallway; the same is true of picking heads or tails when a coin is tossed or of circling "true" or "false" when responding to a question to which the subject does not know the answer. The fact that such is rarely the case with human responses does indicate bias; and as we have seen earlier, such biases, in the sense of being remote from normal probability, are reflections of personality variables.

But what of the people who deviate from the established pattern of bias? What about those who rather consistently say "false" when most people say "true," who turn left when most turn right or who say "like" when most people say "dislike"? These are the truly deviant responses. It seemed on this basis, that such deviant responses were the ones to be studied. Thus we could identify a pattern of bias and then examine those subjects who revealed deviant responses in the sense of departing from the common response pattern. E. K. Strong in his Vocation Interest Blank and Starke Hathaway in the Minnesota Multiphasic Personality Inventory years before had done much the same thing when constructing their tests. They were not, of course, concerned with set or bias per se; and they were concerned with item content. But the method they used was generally suited to my purposes. Accordingly, batches of IBM cards were sorted and the Perceptual Reaction Test (PRT) response patterns of various small groups such as schizophrenics, musicians, juvenile delinquents, were each compared with the patterns of normal persons or people-at-large. These groups were small, of course, but this time it really seemed that we had data which offered more than hope. There seemed to be obvious differences in the deviant response patterns for the various groups, at least insofar as one could judge from the scanty data available.

DEVIANT RESPONSES ARE GENERAL

As I examined these data and reviewed the various researches of other workers in this field, it seemed to me that there was something general about the deviant response tendencies among the small groups of deviant subjects for whom we had data. This, it may be noted, is one of the advantages of gathering your own data, namely, the opportunity to observe peripheral but sometimes meaningful aspects of the problem being attacked. But to take a specific example, we may note the behavior of schizophrenics. These patients, for the most part, experienced delusions and/or hallucinations, they were emotionally flat, and their thinking was bizarre. Such behavior, of course, explained why the schizophrenics were hospitalized, and such behavior is significant, in our society, for being placed under institutional custody. One simply does not go about talking of an alarm clock in his belly, nor asserting that an aged clergyman has been making sexual advances, etc., as these patients did. This, then, is critical deviant behavior.

Yet as I ruminated about these patients, it seemed obvious that they showed many other behavioral deviations which were essentially nonsignificant or noncritical in the sense that they would never be placed in a mental hospital if only these noncritical deviations were involved. Thus some schizophrenics grinned in a silly manner, others had a perpetual far-away look in their eyes; they used odd gestures or sat poker-faced and immobile. Most important in terms of my thinking, the schizophrenics also marked the Perceptual Reaction Test in a deviant pattern when compared to normal persons. It seemed, therefore, that deviant behavior might well be general; hence when noncritical behavior was measured, such as deviant patterns of response on a test, these noncritical deviant responses were indicative of deviant responses in a critical area of behavior, i.e., symptomatology indicating neurotic or psychotic reactions and the like.

So we could say that deviations in one area are associated with deviations in other areas. If so, we could draw together in a general statement the results of a wide variety of researches. We may mention a few of these to indicate the range of studies which could readily be included in our general statement. In a study of 845 mental patients and 423 normal subjects, Voth found differences in the amount of autokinetic movement for schizophrenic, epileptic, anxious, etc., patients when compared to normal persons. Wallen and Altus say that the number of food aversions is related to maladjustment. Guilford used the frequency of "?" responses on three tests as a measure of indecisiveness among foremen. Although the techniques and the behavior measured differed in these studies, each of them were measuring atypical behavior in a significant area by using responses obtained in a noncritical area of behavior. While he regarded similar response patterns as a nuisance and best eliminated from tests, Cronbach would not have been surprised at these results.

Now, thus far, we have been considering behavior on a continuum of adjustment–maladjustment and measuring responses in noncritical areas of behavior to predict maladjustment in critical areas of behavior. But do we need to confine our general statement to abnormality in the maladjustment sense? After all, "abnormal" means literally "away from the norm," or, broadly speaking, it means "different or uncommon." On this latter basis, we may say that brilliant or mentally retarded persons are abnormal; we may say that compared to men-in-general, salesmen or accountants or musicians, etc., are atypical since, after all, most men are not salesmen, etc. If this is true, and decades of experience with the Strong VIB indicates that it is certainly true for occupations, then we should be able to identify any atypical or "abnormal" group on the basis of deviant response patterns alone. We should be able to take any valid and operationally defined dimension of personality, of interest, of adjustment, and the like, and by using deviant response patterns, we should be able to measure these dimensions. Further, it seems that any type of stimulus pattern may be used for measuring noncritical behavior deviations (i.e. deviant test responses) to predict behavior deviations in the critical area under study (i.e.,

atypicalities, such as schizophrenia, anxiety states, creativity, mental retardation, interest in mathematics, etc.).

THE UNIMPORTANCE OF TEST ITEM CONTENT

In other words, the test item content isn't important; the deviant responses
are. As we have seen earlier, a number of relatively unstructured stimulus
patterns have been used, such as autokinetic movement, abstract designs,
lists of foods, sway responses to spoken words, etc.; and deviant response
patterns have been identified which are capable of identifying groups which
are atypical in a significant area of behavior.

What we are considering here is very serious business from the standpoint
of the theory of how certain tests are constructed and how they measure
whatever they are intended to measure. I am asserting that one could take
the MMPI items and, by using the same technique as Strong did, prepare a
Vocational Interest Blank. Conversely, one could use Hathaway's technique
to make an MMPI from Strong's items. Or, as far as I can see, one could
use a mixture of designs, nonsense syllables, pictures, sounds, smells, etc.
and produce either the MMPI or the Strong by using the same, painstaking
care in identifying the groups and in analyzing the data. In other words, E. K.
Strong need not have selected items related to recreations, amusements, occupations, etc. nor need Hathaway have troubled about his 26 categories of
MMPI items which ranged from general health to psychopathology. Indeed,
if valid external criteria are available, either Strong or Hathaway could have
used their techniques and their items to construct scales for such varied
facets of deviant behavior as accident proneness, rigidity, creativity, satyria-
sis, scholastic overachievement, etc.

In the paragraph immediately above, I have made some predictions of
what one aspect of the deviation hypothesis means. Candidly, I have run
ahead of the evidence, but this is not to say that there is no evidence. Let us
take the MMPI as a case in point, since we have some evidence which relates
to MMPI content. Also, this test is a good example to employ, because about
800 articles dealing with the MMPI have been published; and it is certainly
one of the most widely-used clinical tools. The MMPI scoring system provides that only those responses which are answered in the infrequent direction
are recorded. In other words deviant responses are recorded. Barnes (1956)
noticed this and reasoned that if MMPI item content were unimportant, he
should be able to take a heterogeneous group of 40 male patients and by
simply counting the total number of atypical responses (X's on the MMPI
record form) obtain a significant relationship between the total number of
deviant responses and some of the MMPI clinical scales. It should be
emphasized that Barnes merely counted all items answered in the infrequent
direction without any regard for content, and his group was a mixture of
diagnostic categories. He found, among other things, the total number of
deviant responses correlated .93 with the Schizophrenia scale and .87 with

the Psychosthenia scale of the MMPI. This is about as high as the reliability of these scales; hence correlations of greater magnitude are unlikely to occur.

In another study, Barnes (in 1955) used the results of some research which identified two major factors, neurotic and psychotic factors, in the MMPI scales. It occurred to Barnes, on the basis of the way psychotics and neurotics responded to the PRT, that atypical true answers without regard to item content of the MMPI should be essentially the psychotic factor and MMPI atypical false answers should be essentially the neurotic factor. Thus deviant sets, ignoring content, should account for the psychotic factor if they went in one direction, and for the neurotic factor if they went in the other. Barnes concluded that the simple count of atypical true answers represented a "pure factor test of the psychotic factor" and the total of atypical false answers had a heavy loading on the neurotic factor.

But while there seems to be some reason for disparaging the importance of item content per se, one may justifiably ask whether it is really possible to measure personality and the dimensions by using deviant responses alone. After all, it is reasonable to accept the results of exploratory studies described earlier and recognize that deviant response patterns could separate groups of 10 or 20 atypical subjects from "normal" or "people-in-general" on the basis of atypical responses. Yet this is considerably removed from demonstrating that valid measuring of particular facets of personality or the like could be constructed from responses to stimulus patterns such as, for example, a series of abstract designs drawn with ruler and compass.

Barnes became interested in what we were doing; he took as his Ph.D. dissertation the relationship of biased test responses of psychopathology, using the abstract designs of the PRT as his test. He tested 546 deviant subjects (360 males, 186 females) obtained from neuropsychiatric settings; and as his published article (1955) reveals, he was able to construct scales for several dimensions of psychopathology, using only deviant response patterns. Also, Barnes crossvalidated his scales, showed that they had adequate reliability and prepared a diagnostic "sharpener" scale to separate psychotic from character disorder patterns. When it is kept in mind that the PRT has only 60 items, all of which are abstract designs of no particular meaning, and that it takes only six or seven minutes to administer the PRT, I feel justified in saying that Barnes' scales are remarkable. Further, we have a clear demonstration that deviant responses alone can be used to measure psychopathology in several forms.

THE DEVIATION HYPOTHESIS STATED

As we review what has been said thus far, it is apparent that the Deviation Hypothesis has two aspects which are relatively independent of each other and which may stand or fall independently when subjected to empirical test. One aspect deals with the general pervasiveness of deviant response patterns, and the other deals with the unimportance of specific content for eliciting deviant responses. The formulation of the Deviation Hypothesis may be given as follows: Deviant response patterns tend to be general; hence those deviant behavior patterns which are significant for abnormality (atypicalness) and thus regarded as symptoms (earmarks or signs) are associated with other deviant response patterns which are in noncritical areas of behavior and which are not regarded as symptoms of personality aberration (nor as indicators, signs, earmarks). The material in parentheses is inserted in order to emphasize the feasibility of using deviant response patterns to identify occupational groups, interest patterns, morale level, accident proneness, etc. The remaining aspect of the Deviation Hypothesis may be stated as follows: Stimulus patterns of any type and of any sense modality may be used to elicit deviant response patterns; thus particular stimulus content is unimportant for measuring behaviors in terms of the Deviation Hypothesis. This means that, by the usual analysis, we should be able to produce a Bernreuter Personality Inventory, an MMPI, a Strong VIB, etc., by using sights, sounds, tastes, smells, etc., in any combination for item content.

The Deviation Hypothesis is regarded as rather broad in scope with respect to human behavior. The implications are myriad, and we have space to mention but a few of them. For example, when an emotionally disturbed client comes in for counseling, his behavior is deviant in a critical area and we should expect that his behavior would be deviant in noncritical areas, such as his speech, perhaps. He would be expected to talk slower or faster than normal, possibly with odd intonation and pitch; or he might, and this has been studied for one case, use many ego words such as *I, me, mine* and few emphatic words such as *you, we, our* as indicative of deviant speech output. Another implication and in another area is the relationship of the degree or extent of deviant responses in noncritical areas to the degree or extent of deviation in critical areas. Nothing much has been done on this problem; however, I should predict that the correspondence of deviant patterns in critical and noncritical areas is very close. Severe cases of schizophrenia should reveal more marked deviations in noncritical areas when compared to mild schizophrenics. Similarly, serious accident-prone persons should show greater frequency of noncritical deviant responses than those who were only mildly accident-prone. Yet another problem is the difficulty of measuring structure in stimulus patterns. Do nonsense syllables have more structure than interlaced triangles? This is not a silly question: for response sets are more readily elicited when structure is less definite. There are many other unresolved issues, such as the problem of drugs in relation to possible reduction of deviant responses in noncritical areas, the thorny question of psychological distance measurement for points of scales of affectivity, and a host of other specific problems.

There is some progress on other issues, however, which can be reported. Mentally retarded children, for example, show deviant response patterns in noncritical areas when compared to normal subjects, and their pattern is also different from psychotic patterns. A graduate student at Louisiana State University, Otho Hesterly, is studying PRT response biases in terms of several age groups with the eventual aim of constructing a maturity scale based upon deviant response patterns in noncritical areas. Thus far, he has hopes but no evidence one way or the other.

I wish I could close on the happy note that the Deviation Hypothesis was the center of an academic teapot tempest; for to my admittedly prejudiced mind, the Deviation Hypothesis contains some rather eyebrow-raising assertions and predictions, all of which are easy to test or, if tested, are not 100 percent substantiated. To date, no words have flown, all is calm, all is bright. The issue of whether particular content is essential for personality, interest, etc. tests, I wryly note, sleeps in heavenly peace.

For an interesting test of the Berg Deviation Hypothesis, using college freshmen, the reader should consult Grigg and Thorpe (1960). Deviation scores, obtained from an adjective checklist, were found to differentiate students seeking private psychiatric care or personal counseling for emotional problems as against students requesting vocational counseling or no help at all. McGee has published (1962) a valuable review and critique of this whole problem of response style.

In 1963, Sechrest and Jackson published a critical analysis and a review of issues raised by the studies of Berg and others concerning the Deviation Hypothesis in the hope of explicating certain issues clearly associated with this hypothesis (such as the problem of generality, response styles and deviation, measurement and interpretive problems). These authors feel the hypothesis is altogether too broad and lacking in clarity to permit differential predictions, especially when it is suggested that "psychotics, lawyers, cardiac patients, transvestites, young normal children, character disorders, the obese, the feebleminded, psychoneurotics and persons suffering from constipation, among others, represent deviant groups which might be expected to manifest their particular propensities toward deviation not only in a modality relevant to their particular symptoms and to items with relevant content, but also in response to one or more of the following: preference for abstract drawings, food aversion questionnaires, stimuli for conditioned responses, autokinetic and spiral aftereffect situations, vocabulary test items, figure drawings, musical sounds, and olfactory stimuli" (Sechrest & Jackson, 1963, p. 34). Regardless, these authors recognize that Berg has performed a valuable service in emphasizing the importance of studying these deviant response patterns.

Other writers are far more negatively critical. In a hard-hitting attack on the Deviation Hypothesis, Norman (1963) produces additional test data to show that different classes of test stimuli clearly do make a difference, and that test item content is relevant and crucial. His results, comparing test item content varying in relevance for the criterion groups used, rather clearly indicate that test item content is important when one is constructing valid empirical scoring keys. Norman feels that the *theoretical* or *explanatory value* which Berg ascribes to the Deviation Hypothesis is, at best, trivial; at worst, such a stand leads to an orientation concerning personality assessment of a most militantly theoretical variety.

In a recent and highly controversial book, which is critical of all objective testing, the Deviation Hypothesis (although unnamed) is treated to a witty exaggeration. In a hypothetical example, the statistics show that 90 percent of college freshmen earning high grades believe that Shakespeare wrote *Omelet* rather than *King Lear.* Under these conditions the author then says that the "best" answer will have to be *Omelet.* Surely this is "to condone the wedding of science and democracy where honor is done to neither" (Hoffmann, 1962, p. 85).

As a follow-up to the more general statement of the Deviation Hypothesis in the previous paper by Berg, we now present a research report designed to test certain of these formulations. Yea-saying and nay-saying here take the center of the stage in the study of personality.

Although the research presented here only concerns itself with nay-saying, Couch and Keniston (1960) have more recently presented an extensive summary of personality findings based on response sets measures intensively studied both by objective test items and by clinical methods, tracing these tendencies back to different resolutions of anality during the early socialization period. These authors feel that the importance of response sets in the area of psychological tests is very far-reaching and that the agreeing response tendency is based on a central personality syndrome. Their paper is far too long for reproduction here; therefore, a shorter research report has been selected for inclusion.

Asch's report is clearly an outgrowth from Berg's published statements. His report, of which this is a condensation, originally appeared in the *Journal of Counseling Psychology* in 1958. The report, in turn, was adapted from his Ph.D. dissertation at Syracuse University. At the time this research was done, Dr. Asch was with the VA Regional Office in Boston, Massachusetts. He is now a counseling and clinical psychologist on the staff of the Hines VA Hospital in Illinois.

NEGATIVE RESPONSE BIAS AND PERSONALITY ADJUSTMENT

Morton J. Asch

An approach to personality appraisal that has appealed to social scientists with diverse specializations is that which involves the yea-saying and nay-saying tendencies in man.

The American culture, in particular, is depicted as one which strives to "accentuate the positive and eliminate the negative." The citizens of Harold Laski's "American Democracy" value most highly the "booster" and shun the "knocker." David Riesman's "other-directed" man looks with suspicion at the nonconformist. The "neurotic personality of our time" as described by Karen Horney is basically hostile and negative in orientation.

More people turn to the right rather than the left on entering a museum; the probability is .80 that we will call the first toss of a coin "heads" rather than "tails"; most students, when in doubt, tend to judge statements to be true rather than false. These are illustrations of positive response sets, tendencies which have been shown to be fairly stable and possibly reflective of a more basic generalized life pattern.

The concern of this paper is with the less popular negative response sets. It represents an attempt to study Berg's deviation hypothesis utilizing the concept of negative response bias. For experimental purposes, negative response bias is defined as a type of response set whereby a person tends to answer "disagree" on test items when in doubt.

PROBLEM

In order to study whether this type of response set is related to more critical personality patterns, three hypotheses were framed for testing with a normal population. It was felt that negative response bias might be symptomatic of a more fundamental negativism. As individuals get older many find that the superficial positive reaction yields greater social rewards than the affective "no." In spite of this, or perhaps because of this, the seemingly acquiescent adult often harbors within himself intense hostility which shows itself in more subtle ways than it did when he was three years old. Conflict with the environment manifests itself readily, however, when conditions are such as to favor the safe expression of repressed impulses.

A technique was developed, The Speed of Decision Test, which would identify the quality of the underlying response pattern. This is a specially constructed preference inventory designed to assess response bias which is independent of content variables. In the present study, this test was administered to male veterans of World War II and the Korean conflict at Veterans Administration guidance centers in the Commonwealth of Massachusetts. Those men whose scores on the Speed of Decision Test indicated negative response bias and lack of response bias were compared on performance on the Rorschach, Minnesota Multiphasic Personality Inventory, and Draw-A-Person tests.

The first two hypotheses tested were a direct outgrowth of previous research studies. Item analyses and item counts of the MMPI suggest that neurotic-tending people have a tendency to respond negatively to personality inventory items; psychotic-tending persons have a tendency to respond in the acquiescing direction to these same items. In a recent article describing the formulation of the deviation hypothesis, Berg summarizes studies utilizing the Perceptual Reaction Test, an instrument requiring an affective response to abstract designs. The general findings indicate that individuals who do not demonstrate response bias tend to be less anxious and maladjusted than those who give deviant responses.

In an attempt to explore these questions further with a sample of young veterans, these hypotheses were developed:

1. Subjects who do not demonstrate response bias are judged, on psychological tests of personality, to be better adjusted than those who demonstrate negative response bias.

2. There is a significant relationship, in the positive direction, between neurotic-tendingness and negative response bias.

The third hypothesis of the present study stems from a consideration of psychoanalytic theory. The obsessive-compulsive personality is seen by the Freudians as one fixated at the anal retentive level. Such a person continues his battle against conformity by adult cantankerousness and petulance. Unlike the three-year-old, who responds to almost every request by a direct repetitive "no," the adult quibbles, begs to differ, and in still more subtle ways expresses his need for interpersonal conflict. The hysteric, on the other hand, is viewed as one regressing to the stage of avoiding the Oedipus conflict by a symbolic closing of the eyes. It was felt that the obsessive-compulsive, directing his psychic energy towards the environment, might be expected to demonstrate more negative bias than the conflict-avoiding hysteric whose energy is bound to his symptoms.

The third hypothesis therefore reads:

3. Subjects characterized by obsessive-compulsive trends demonstrate significantly more negative response bias than those whose predominant patterns of adjustment are hysteroid.

The primary concepts used in connection with this study were defined as follows:

Normal—a normal person is one who is not hospitalized and is not classified as a deviate in any available official record.

Maladjusted—a normal person who, on psychological tests of personality, performs similarly to individuals with established psychiatric disabilities.

Neurotic-tendingness—a tendency on the part of normal persons to demonstrate behavior on psychological tests of personality similar to that demonstrated by neurotics.

Obsessive-compulsive and hysteroid trends are defined operationally in terms of clinical judgment of personality test performance of normal persons.

THE SPEED OF DECISION TEST

The SDT had the advantage of being similar in appearance to many inventories in common usage. It could therefore be described to the subject as an attitude or interest or decision-making test. The items of the inventory could also be incorporated as part of a standard psychological test without the subject being aware of this. A new response bias instrument was also developed.

Three fundamental criteria were set up for the items to be included in the new inventory. They were to be subtle, neutral, and innocuous. Test items were considered to be subtle if their purpose was not apparent to the subject. A testee anxious to please an examiner or to create a favorable impression would experience difficulty in discerning what responses would accomplish such a purpose. They are neutral to the degree that each item tends to provoke a positive response as frequently as a negative response among the general population. They are innocous to the extent that they appear to be harmless and would not cause a pathological subject to respond differentially from a normal because of the content.

An exploratory tryout of a 75-item test was conducted with veterans and college students. On the basis of these trial runs the test was changed to isolate more effectively response bias as the factor being measured. (Example: "Forced to choose one, I would agree that Fillmore was a greater president than Buchanan.")

The directions given to the subject for taking the test and the fact that he is aware of his being timed encouraged the subject to think of this as a speed-of-decision test. Individuals whose score indicated that more than half of the items were checked in the "disagree" column might be assumed to be demonstrating negative response bias.

Three judges were used to establish that the items on the inventory met the criteria of being subtle, neutral, innocuous, and having reversal-paired statements. The final form consisted of 120 items. This form was tested on 100 college undergraduates, and a bell-shaped curve was obtained. Tentative limits, within which members of the experimental and control groups might be expected to fall, were set up as a result of an analysis of the pilot study.

Validity of the test had been established by expert judgment of test forms. Reliability was established by the split-half technique (.75 using the Spearman-Brown formula).

PROCEDURES

As part of the regular testing process at two VA guidance centers in Boston, Massachusetts, 500 normal male veterans were administered the SDT. None of these veterans had a history of any form of mental illness or a serious physical condition, such as tuberculosis or blindness, where significant psychological concomitants might be anticipated. Their mean average age was 23 years; their mean educational level was 12 years. Those men who received scores of 60 (i.e., no response bias) or scores of 54 or lower (i.e., negative response bias) were invited to participate in a study dealing with counseling techniques. There were very few men who expressed a reluctance to cooperate. This can be understood in view of their being predominantly veterans who had requested counseling and testing to help them in career planning.

The 50 men with the lowest scores on the Speed of Decision Test and the first 50 with scores of 60 were compared in terms of their performance on the three criterion instruments—the MMPI, the Rorschach, and Draw-A-Person test.

Three judges reviewed the MMPI profiles, three considered the Rorschach material, and one judge studied the D-A-P data. Only code numbers identified the subjects on these protocols. Each judge was asked to give three ratings for each of the 100 subjects on the factors of level of adjustment, presence or absence of obsessive-compulsive and hysteroid trends, and neurotic-tendingness. Judges were selected in terms of their special competency with the instrument used. They were encouraged to use whatever method was most meaningful to them in interpreting the test results to make the called-for ratings.

The majority or average opinion of the three judges on each rating for the Rorschach and MMPI was recorded as the Rorschach and MMPI diagnosis for each subject. With the D-A-P the opinion of the sole judge was accepted. Then a combined MMPI–Rorschach–D-A-P diagnosis was derived by finding the diagnosis based on maximal agreement at each level. It was recognized that this Composite Index, based upon evaluations of the individual tests, could very well differ from that which one might expect if the judges considered all of the tests together in acquiring a single diagnostic impression. The latter approach would have proved to be impracticable from the point of view of the time demands imposed upon the judges. Moreover, it is believed that the composite diagnosis which was used gave a more reliable impression, inasmuch as judges were dealing with the instrument with which they appeared to have most proficiency.

In testing the first hypothesis, the chi-square was used to examine the control and experimental groups in terms of the frequencies with which they were placed into the categories: "markedly maladjusted," "moderately maladjusted," and "not maladjusted." Hypothesis 2 was tested by using the chi-square to examine the relationship of the "no response bias" groups and the "negative response bias" group to the diagnostic categories of "highly similar to neurotic records," "moderately similar to neurotic records," and "not similar to neurotic records."

The third hypothesis was studied statistically through the use of a nonparametric method. Of the 100 subjects, the 29 who were judged to be clearly demonstrating obsessive-compulsive trends were compared with 13 who were judged as most clearly demonstrating hysteroid trends. It was predicted that the median score of the obsessive-compulsive group on the SDT would be significantly lower than the median score of the hysteroid group.

RESULTS AND DISCUSSION

The experimental findings may be summed up as follows:

1. Within the limitations imposed by the design of the study, the first hypothesis is confirmed. Negative response bias is associated with maladjustment. That this association is real and not a result of chance errors is attested to by the very significant chi-square values obtained with Rorschach, MMPI and Composite Index ratings. The D-A-P results approach statistical significance in the direction predicted by the first hypothesis.

2. Using the MMPI and Composite Index as criteria, the experimental results favor the second hypothesis. The Rorschach test and D-A-P ratings individually did not yield discriminations between experimental and control groups that were statistically significant.

3. Comparing the obsessive-compulsive and hysteroid subjects, differences

were found in the direction predicted by the hypothesis. But these differences did not establish themselves as significant at the one percent level set up for this study.

These experimental results tend to be consistent with those of similar and related studies on the negative response sets. They suggest the practical value of a subtle-items inventory, such as the SDT, as a group screening device for maladjustment. They underscore the importance of using several indices of emotional status in making individual diagnoses. Finally, they generally support what appears to this writer to be a most pregnant hypothesis for research in the fields of counseling and clinical psychology: "Deviant response patterns tend to be general; hence those deviant behavior patterns which are significant for abnormality and thus regarded as symptoms, are associated with other deviant response patterns which are in noncritical areas of behavior and which are not regarded as symptoms of personality aberration" (Berg).

SUMMARY

The aim of this study was to investigate certain aspects of the nature of negative response bias as it relates to personality adjustment. For experimental purposes, negative response bias was defined as a type of response set whereby a person tends to answer "disagree" on test items when in doubt.

A subtle items inventory, the Speed of Decision Test, was developed to measure the presence or absence of response bias in adults. This test was administered to 500 normal male veterans. The 50 men with the lowest scores constituted the experimental "negative response bias" group. The 50 men whose scores indicated lack of response bias were the control subjects. These 100 subjects were given three personality tests used as criterion instruments: the Rorschach, MMPI, and Draw-A-Person test.

The test protocols were examined by expert judges. They rated the material on three personality dimensions: adjustment, diagnosis, and dynamics. An analysis of the ratings indicated a definite association between negative response bias and maladjustment. The results also suggest that negative response bias is associated with personality traits defined as neurotic-tendingness and obsessive-compulsive trends.

The situation concerning response bias is still by no means clear. Some workers try to control or eliminate response sets, while others simply ignore. Some make the claim that personality inventories elicit responses so permeated by stylistic features that nothing substantive is thereby being measured. Others, such as Rorer (1965), hold the view that response styles do not even exist or, at best, account for only a small portion of response variation.

Rorer's extensive review article, "The Great Response-style Myth," was promptly countered by Rundquist (1966), who stated that response style is *not* a myth. Still others think of response styles as interesting personality variables in their own right and have set up research designs to locate behavioral correlates. On the other hand, might it not be reasonable to assume that the subject is telling the truth about himself, even though he is indicating a socially desirable response or characteristic?

The debate continues, most recently with the publication of Block's (1965) volume, which won the 1964 Century Psychology Series Award for excellence, and which deals exclusively with the MMPI. Block presents data for five different samples and finds that the acquiescence response set (yea-saying) is clearly inconsequential as far as the MMPI's factor structure is concerned. He feels that the impact of this response set is so small that often efforts to exclude its effect are not demanded. And a similar instance exists in Edward's notion concerning social desirability. "The final triumph of the MMPI against the challenge of a response-set reinterpretation may be seen to derive from (its) homely and homing concern with empirical anchor points" (Block, 1965, p. 129).

Not so, says Jackson (1967) in his review of Block's monograph. Block's conclusions are said to be false and the end product of "circuitous logical development." There were rejoinders and further rejoinders, with Jackson ending on the note that we should now attack the Herculean task of building an inventory based on a superior item pool. Here is where the work of Cattell, with his 21 Universal Index factors, and Gough, in developing his California Psychological Inventory, move away from the maladjustment emphasis in the MMPI items. Of the two, Cattell is really making a grand attempt to create a new inventory terrain. The wide scope and the sophistication of his research, together with the large amount of data that he has amassed, is conveniently summarized in his recent Penguin book (1965).

PART FIVE

Validity

OF all the topics concerning any kind of psychological measurement, but especially techniques that are applied to human beings and focus on subsequent decisions or plans—for example, aptitude or ability testing—that concerning overall validity of the measurements is paramount. (This point of view is reflected in this collection of readings in that the largest section is given over to validity.) As a general and succinct introduction to this topic, for the student there probably is no source better than the presentation contained in the revised edition of *Standards for Educational and Psychological Tests and Manuals*, prepared by a joint committee of the American Psychological Association, the American Educational Research Association, and the National Council on Measurement in Education. This is a technical manual concerned with general principles of test construction, together with specific recommendations about how these principles should be implemented. Every student of the field should be acquainted with it.

Introductory comments in this manual indicate that psychological and educational tests are frequently employed in arriving at decisions that may considerably affect the welfare of the individuals tested, decisions on educational points of view and practices, and even decisions on the development and utilization of human resources. Test users therefore need to apply high standards of professional judgment when selecting and interpreting tests; test producers, likewise, are obligated to produce tests that can then be of greatest possible service. Such a test author or publisher has the task of providing sufficient information concerning each test so that the test user can ascertain just how much reliance he can correctly place on it. The manual, therefore, in an important sourcebook or guide for both test authors and test publishers.

The following statements concerning general features of validity are taken verbatim from this manual (APA, 1966, pp. 12–14), wherein are outlined the three major types of validity—content, criterion-related, and construct. Of particular importance is the notion of construct validity, a concept that has recently come to assume a large place in the area of educational and psychological measurement. Following these remarks, specific recommendations, together with committee comments, are provided for both the test author and the test publisher.

VALIDITY

A.P.A. Standards for Educational
and Psychological Tests and Manuals

Validity information indicates the degree to which the test is capable of achieving certain aims. Tests are used for several types of judgment, and for each type of judgment, a different type of investigation is required to establish validity. For purposes of describing the uses for three kinds of validity coefficients, we may distinguish three of the rather numerous aims of testing:

1. *The test user wishes to determine how an individual performs at present in a universe of situations that the test situation is claimed to represent.* For example, most achievement tests used in schools measure the student's performance on a sample of questions intended to represent a certain phase of educational achievement or certain educational objectives.

2. *The test user wishes to forecast an individual's future standing or to estimate an individual's present standing on some variable of particular significance that is different from the test.* For example, an academic aptitude test may forecast grades, or a brief adjustment inventory may estimate what the outcome would be of a careful psychological examination.

3. *The test user wishes to infer the degree to which the individual possesses some hypothetical trait or quality (construct) presumed to be reflected in the test performance.* For example, he wants to know whether the individual stands high on some proposed abstract trait such as "intelligence" or "creativity" that cannot be observed directly. This may be done to learn something about the individual, or it may be done to study the test itself, to study its relationship to other tests, or to develop psychological theory.

Different types of tests are often used for each of the different aims, but this is not always the case. There is much overlap in types of tests and in the purposes for which they are used. Thus, a vocabulary test might be used (*a*) simply as a measure of present vocabulary, the universe being all the words in the language, (*b*) as a screening device to discriminate present or potential schizophrenics from organics, or (*c*) as a means of making inferences about "intellectual capacity."

To determine how suitable a test is for each of these uses, it is necessary to gather the appropriate sort of validity information. The kind of information to be gathered depends on the aim or aims of testing rather than on the type of test. The three aspects of validity corresponding to the three aims of testing may be named content validity, criterion-related validity, and construct validity.

Content validity is demonstrated by showing how well the content of the test samples the class situations or subject matter about which conclusions are to be drawn. Content validity is especially important for achievement and proficiency measures and for measures of adjustment or social behavior based on observation in selected situations. The manual should justify the claim that the test content represents the assumed universe of tasks, conditions, or processes. A useful way of looking at this universe of tasks or items is to consider it to comprise a *definition* of the achievement to be measured by the test. In the case of an educational achievement test, the content of the test may be regarded as a definition of (or a sampling from a population of) one or more educational objectives. The aptitudes, skills, and knowledges required of the student for successful test performance must be precisely the types of aptitudes, skills, and knowledges that the school wishes to develop in the students and to evaluate in terms of test scores. Thus evaluating the content validity of a test for a particular purpose is the same as subjectively recognizing the adequacy of a definition. This process is actually quite similar to the subjective evaluation of the criterion itself. Unless, however, the aim of an achievement test is specifically to forecast or substitute for some criterion, its correlation with a criterion is *not* a useful evaluation of the test.

Criterion-related validity is demonstrated by comparing the test scores with one or more external variables considered to provide a direct measure of the characteristic or behavior in question. This comparison may take the form of an expectancy table or, most commonly, a correlation relating to the test score to a criterion measure. Predictive uses of tests include long-range forecasts of one or more measures of academic achievement, prediction of vocational success, and prediction of reaction to therapy. For such predictive uses the criterion data are collected concurrently with the test; for example, when one wishes to know whether a testing procedure can take the place of more elaborate procedures for diagnosing personality disorders. A test that is related to one or more concurrent criteria will not necessarily predict status on the same criterion at some later date. Whether the criterion data should be collected concurrently with the testing or at a later time depends on whether the test is recommended for prediction or for assessment of present status.

Construct validity is evaluated by investigating what qualities a test measures, that is, by determining the degree to which certain explanatory concepts or constructs account for performance on the test. To examine construct validity requires a combination of logical and empirical attack. Essentially, studies of construct validity check on the theory underlying the test. The procedure involves three steps. First, the investigator inquires: From this theory, what hypotheses may we make regarding the behavior of persons with high and low scores? Second, he gathers data to test these hypotheses. Third, in light of the evidence, he makes an inference as to whether the theory is adequate to explain the data collected. If the theory fails to account for the data, he should revise the test interpretation, reformulate the theory, or reject the theory altogether. Fresh evidence would be required to demonstrate construct validity for the revised interpretation.

A simple procedure for investigating what a test measures is to correlate it with other tests. We would expect a valid test of numerical reasoning, for example, to correlate more highly with other numerical tests than with clerical perception tests. Another procedure is experimental. If it is hypothesized, for example, that form perception on a certain projective test indicates probable ability to function well under emotional stress, this inference may be checked by placing individuals in an experimental situation producing emotional stress and observing whether their behavior corresponds to the hypothesis.

Construct validity is ordinarily studied when the tester wishes to increase his understanding of the psychological qualities being measured by the test. A validity coefficient relating test to criterion, unless it is established in the context of some theory, yields no information about *why* the correlation is high or low, or about how one might improve the measurement. Construct validity is relevant when the tester accepts no existing measure as a definitive criterion of the quality with which he is concerned (e.g., in measuring a postulated drive such as need for achievement), or when a test will be used in so many diverse decisions that no single criterion applies (e.g., in identifying the ability of Peace Corps trainees to adapt to new cultures). Here the traits or qualities underlying test performance are of central importance. It must be remembered, however, that, without a study of criterion-related validity, a test developed for diagnosis or prediction can be regarded only as experimental.

These three aspects of validity are only conceptually independent, and only rarely is just one of them important in a particular situation. A complete study of a test would normally involve information about all types of validity. A first step in the preparation of a predictive *(criterion-related)* instrument may be to consider what *constructs* are likely to provide a basis for selecting or devising an effective test. Sampling from a *content* universe may also be an early step in producing a test whose use for *prediction* is the ultimate concern. Even after satisfactory *prediction* has been established, information regarding *construct* validity may make the test more useful; it may, for example, provide a basis for identifying situations other than the validating situation where the test is appropriate as a predictor. To analyze *construct* validity, all the knowledge regarding validity would be brought to bear.

The three concepts of validity are pertinent to all kinds of tests. It is the intended use of the test rather than its nature that determines what kind of evidence is required.

Intelligence or scholastic aptitude tests most often use criterion-related validity to show how well they are able to predict academic success in school or college, but the nature of the aptitudes measured is often judged from the content of the items, and the place of the aptitude within the array of human abilities is deduced from correlations with other tests.

For achievement tests, content validity is usually of first importance. For example, a testing agency has a group of subject-matter specialists devise and select test items that they judge to cover the topics and mental processes relevant to the field represented by the test. Similarly, a teacher judges whether the final test in his course covers the kinds of situations about which he has been trying to teach his students certain principles or understandings. The teacher also judges content when he uses a published test, but he can appropriately investigate criterion-related validity by correlating this test with tests he has prepared or with other direct measures of his chief instructional objectives. When the same published achievement test is used for admissions testing, it may reasonably be checked against a later criterion of performance. In any theoretical discussion of what is being measured by the achievement test, a consideration of construct validity is required. Whether the score on a science achievement test, for example, reflects reading ability to a significant degree, and whether it measures understanding of scientific method rather than mere recall of facts are both questions about construct validity.

Development of a personality inventory will usually start with the assembly of items covering content the developer considers meaningful. Such inventories are then likely to be interpreted with the aid of theory; any such interpretation calls for evidence of construct validity. In addition, a personality inventory must have criterion-related validity, if, for example, it is to be used in screening military recruits who may be maladjusted.

Interest measures are usually intended to predict vocational or educational criteria, but many of them are also characterized by logical content and constructs. This makes it more likely that they can provide at least a rough prediction for the very many occupations and activities that exist and for which specific evidence of criterion-related validity has not been obtained.

For projective techniques, construct validity is the most important, although criterion-related validity using criteria collected either concurrently with the testing or afterward may be pertinent if the instruments are to be used in making diagnostic classifications.

THE 1954 treatment of the notion of construct validity (A.P.A., 1954) generated a great deal of discussion. The revised edition of the A.P.A. publication (1966) expanded the treatment of construct validity and tightened the entire concept with specific illustrations. Prior to this revised edition of testing standards, Bechtoldt published an extended and negative critique of the entire concept in 1959, arguing from a position of the philosophy of science. Bechtoldt felt that the introduction of this concept into psychological theorizing created, at best, real confusion and, at worst, "a nonempirical, nonscientific approach to the study of behavior" (p. 628). Instead, he felt that the techniques of operational methodology were to be preferred.

This provided the springboard for a paper by Campbell (1960) who distinguished the philosophical problems posed by Bechtoldt from the more empirical business of test validation. This led him to suggest additional instances where the concept of construct validity needed to be considered. Campbell was, however, writing prior to the publication of the revised edition of the earlier *Technical Rcommendations*. This revision (A.P.A., 1966) did much to clarify the notion of construct validity further and it specifically mentions some of the examples or "additions" that Campbell wrote about.

Still another validity construct, as a sequel to Campbell's discussion, has been suggested by Sechrest (1963) for tests which are intended for applied predictive use. This he has termed incremental validity. Validity claimed for any particular test must be in terms of some increment in its predictive efficiency over and above information that is easily and inexpensively available. There are indications in the research literature where, in spite of better than chance validity, tests may not contribute to, or may even detract from, predictions made from easily obtainable interview or application blank information. Evidence produced for incremental validity would quickly spot this.

A fairly recent, promising development related to validity concerns what is termed "moderator or suppressor variables."

The English & English *Dictionary* (1958) defines a suppressor variable as a variable in a prediction battery that correlates zero with the criterion but high with another predictor in the battery. It has the effect of subtracting from the predictor variable that part of its variance that does not correlate with the criterion, and hence increases the predictive value of the battery (p. 537).

The validity of a certain psychological test or inventory of personality or interests is likely to vary among different population samples. We then must be able to predict these differences. In any distribution of scores that involve two variables, there are always some individuals who earn scores that place them close to the regression line (or the line of "best fit"). Other individuals fall quite wide of this mark, missing the regression line sometimes by large amounts. It might then be asked whether or not there is some special characteristic that might be pinpointed to differentiate between those persons far from or near the regression line. For example, it might be ascertained that a test worked better with middle-class boys or better with neurotics than with psychotics. Here, then, social class and degree of maladjustment are the moderator variables, since they function in ways to alter the predictive validity of the measures.

The following report, dealing with a much discussed student issue of academic motivation, is an illustration of both a study of construct validity and the workings of a suppressor variable. Dr. Drake, the senior author, is professor of psychology and director of the Student Counseling and Guidance Center at the University of Wisconsin; Dr. Oetting is now at Colorado State University, where he is associate professor of psychology. The study originally appeared in the *Journal of Counseling Psychology* in 1957.

AN MMPI PATTERN AND A SUPPRESSOR VARIABLE PREDICTiVE OF ACADEMIC ACHIEVEMENT

L. E. Drake and Eugene R. Oetting

In a previous study of MMPI profile patterns (Drake, 1956) it had been found that a group of profiles of male counselees characterized by their counselors as "lacking academic motivation" could be distinguished from profiles of other counselees by certain profile codings. Scales 8(Sc) and 9(Ma) paired among the three highest coded scales with Scale 0(Si) coded among the two lowest scales constituted a pattern. This pattern 89–0 was found significantly more frequently in the profiles of the "lacking academic motivation group" than would be expected from its frequency of occurrence in the total group of 2,634 profiles. Also, scale 5(Mf) coded among the highest three was found to occur significantly *less* frequently in the profiles of the "lacking academic motivation" group than would be expected from its frequency of occurrence in the total group.

It was concluded that a profile containing the pattern 89–0(Ma-Sc paired high with Si low) could therefore lead to a hypothesis of "lacking academic motivation," to be checked further in the counseling interviews. Also, since Scale 5(Mf) occurred less frequently in profiles for the above group, the above hypothesis might be modified when Scale 5 occurred coded high in profiles with the 89–0 pattern.

Partly on the basis of the above, two hypotheses were formulated which could be checked against an independent criterion. It was postulated that, if the profile pattern 89–0 was found more frequently in persons "lacking in academic motivation," then these individuals as a group would reflect that characteristic in terms of a lower grade point average in college studies. This, then, was the first hypothesis.

The second hypothesis has a more complex origin. It was noted above that Scale 5(Mf) occurred significantly *less* frequently coded high in the profiles for the nonmotivated group. In addition there are other indications that Scale 5(Mf) is in some manner associated with the ability to adjust socially and personally to situations where other MMPI patterns indicate difficulties. Hathaway and Monachesi (1953, pp. 133–34) point out in their study of delinquency, "Scale 5 also seems to be negatively related to the occurrence of delinquency in the boys. The frequency is low when 5 is the high point and also in most combinations with 5. Only scale 4 is clearly able to combine with 5 to produce a high rate."

It is hypothesized, then, that Scale 5(Mf) may act as a suppressor variable in some profile patterns. In this instance, individuals showing the profile pattern 89–0 should not obtain lower grades if Scale 5 is coded high.

The two hypotheses to be tested in this study, then, are: *Hypothesis 1*. Beginning freshmen whose MMPI profiles were coded 89–0(MaSc paired high with Si coded low) and whose profiles did not have Scale 5(Mf) coded high would obtain lower grades their first semester in college than the total group of freshmen. *Hypothesis 2*. Beginning freshmen whose MMPI profiles were coded 89–0 and whose Scale 5 was also coded high would *not* obtain lower grades than the total freshmen group.

PROCEDURE

The group form of the MMPI was administered to the entering freshmen during New Student Week in 1949, 1950, and 1951. There were 3,480 male students for whom there were profiles. The grade point averages were computed for the first semester's work for each individual. The MMPI profiles were then coded according to the Hathaway system. All those with the 89–0(MaSc paired high with Si low) pattern were separated from the total group. These were then divided into two subgroups: (*a*) those with the Scale 5 coded high and (*b*) those without Scale 5 coded high. The grade point average distributions were then tabulated for the two subgroups, and for the total group. These distributions were then tested for significance.

RESULTS

Table 3 shows the distribution of grade averages for each of the subgroups and the total group. As was hypothesized the subgroup with the pattern 89–0, the pattern which differentiated the group characterized as lacking academic motivation obtained a significantly lower grade point average than the total group as well as the group with the 89–0 pattern with 5 coded high. The X^2 was beyond the .001 level for both of these tests.

The second hypothesis, that the group with the same pattern (89–0), but with Mf coded high, would not have grades below average, also was supported. Not only did this group exceed the 89–0 group without 5, but it also exceeds to some extent the total group. The test for the latter was significant beyond the .05 but not beyond the .01 level of confidence.

Since Scale 5 appears to have such a strong influence on the code pattern one might raise the question as to whether or not Scale 5 could have been used alone to predict academic achievement. The scores on Scale 5 were correlated with the first semester grade point averages for the male students who entered the University in 1950. The resulting coefficient was $+.17$ for

TABLE 3

MMPI PATTERNS AND DISTRIBUTION OF FIRST SEMESTER
GRADES FOR MALE COLLEGE FRESHMEN

| | Percent with First Semester Averages of | | | |
MMPI Pattern	Below C	C to B	B or better	N
Total freshman group	41	39	20	3480
89–0, without 5 high	67	27	6	69
89–0 with 5 high	18	59	23	39
Between total freshman group and 89–0 without 5 high: $X^2 = 19^*$				
Between total freshman group and 89–0 with 5 high: $X^2 = 9\dagger$				
Between 89–0 without 5 high and 89–0 with 5 high: $X^2 = 24^*$				

* Significant at .001 level.
† Between .01 and .05 levels of confidence.

the 857 male students. The correlation between grades and the ACE for these same students was $+.46$. The coefficient of the multiple correlation, ACE, Mf with grades, was $+.47$. Scale 5 alone does not appear to be very efficient in forecasting scholarship.

DISCUSSION OF RESULTS

This study demonstrates several things that may be important in personality measurement. In the first place a rather complex pattern was necessary to predict the criterion. Analysis of the individual scales revealed no single scale in this pattern which differentiated the subgroup from the total group. Furthermore, although Scale 5 appeared to suppress the effects of this pattern, it, by itself, did not predict academic achievement to any great extent. It appears that, although the scores on a single personality scale may be related to some underlying construct, factorial or otherwise, the determination of behavior is unlikely to depend on a variable simple enough to be measured by a single scale. In order to predict behavior for a group, the group must be relatively homogenous for the behavior. Consequently the group must be selected on the basis of as many underlying traits as possible. In this study three scales were used to select the group and it was still necessary to include a fourth scale as a suppressor in order to predict the criterion. An important consideration in planning research of this type is to obtain a sufficient number of subjects from which to select subgroups sufficiently homogeneous for predictive purposes. Out of 3,480 profiles only 124 had the 89–0 coding for "lacking academic motivation." Of these 16 were for students who did not complete one semester (13 of the 16 did not have Mf coded high). This left 69 profiles for the subgroup without Mf and only 39 profiles with Mf coded high.

A second point is the demonstration of the effect of a suppressor scale. The prediction of lower grade point averages was made on the basis of pattern analysis of the original data. Scale 5 (Mf) was not used to predict the criterion directly, but rather to predict the errors, or false positives. Scale 5 identified those students who, although possessing the "lacking academic motivation" pattern, did not reflect this pattern in their grades. Whether these individuals were not lacking in academic motivation or whether their interests and emotional structure was such that they can perform in college in spite of a basic lack of motivation is not known. In the opinion of authors the latter is more likely. The original hypothesis was based in part on this interpretation of the action of Scale 5.

The third aspect of this study is that it is an example of Cronbach and Meehl's (1955) "construct validation." On the basis of previous studies and knowledge and experience with the test, an extension of the use of the test and the meanings of certain patterns was hypothesized. This extension was then tested and found to be significant. The fact that the extension could be made and validated not only demonstrates that this particular profile pattern on the MMPI may be used with a high degree of confidence in forming hypothesis in counseling about "lack of academic motivation," but also tends to add slightly to the feeling of confidence about all of the steps taken in making the extension. It suggests that the techniques of the original study of patterns on the MMPI were reasonable, that much further attention be paid to the action of suppressor variables in personality testing (particularly the Mf scale on the MMPI), and that the principles involved in extension of a "nomological net" and its construct validation may be highly useful tools in the difficult area of personality assessment.

A later study by Drake (1962) carried this research further, modifying these results somewhat but still testifying to the suppressor effect of scale 5 (Mf). Approximately 1,000 MMPI profiles for the entering male freshman students in the upper half of the distribution of scores obtained from scholastic aptitude tests were studied for peak scores and checked against grade-point averages. Findings from this large group were then cross-validated on about 1,800 similar profiles for the 1958–59 entering male freshmen. Scales 4 (Pd) and 9 (Ma), either alone or in combination, differentiated best in both the original and the cross-validation groups. In every case studied, however, the size of the differentiation increased when such profiles with scale 5 (Mf) coded high were eliminated from the distribution. Pattern 49 high gives the significant differentiation, and 5 acts as the suppressor variable.

In an industrial setting, Sorenson (1966) has reported the discovery of a suppressor variable where both useful levels of prediction and economics of testing were important. The problem investigated was the development and cross-validation of a test battery to be used in the selection of skilled industrial mechanics. An extensive test battery comprised of aptitude, interests, and personality measures (a total of 34 variables) was developed. The multiple R for these 34 variables against the criterion of job performance (supervisory ratings) for the 43 men used in the development sample was an exciting .92. However, when cross-validated, on the sample of 20 additional mechanics reserved for this purpose, this R shrunk to a vanishing .01! Various combinations of four and five different measures were tried, ending with a three-variable predictor that correlated .44 with the criterion for the development sample and .57 for the cross-validation group. It was here that inspection of the intercorrelations among the three predictors and their correlation with the criterion disclosed the presence of a suppressor variable (a near-zero correlation with the criterion and a relatively high correlation with one of the other predictors). This suppressor variable turned out to be scores on the Bennett Test of Mechanical Comprehension. High scores on this type of test, emphasizing knowledge of elementary physics, contributed negatively to the prediction, whereas high scores on a different type of mechanical aptitude measure (a nuts-and-bolts type of test) contributed positively. Thus, in this study, the ability to achieve a high score on the second type of mechanical aptitude test without benefit of a high score on the more academically oriented Bennett was associated with success on the job as industrial mechanic. For another study of a suppressor variable in an industrial assessment situation, see pp. 175–78.

In their extensive review of personality research, Klein, Barr, and Wolitsky (1967), succinctly summarize the role of moderator variables when they say that too often relations that "should have been" found are not because small notice has been paid to the possibility that relations between variables might differ in different subgroups of the larger population. The repeatedly reported differences in correlation matrices for the two sexes is one example. They select especially the Kogan-Wallach (1964) study of risk-taking as an excellent illustration. These researchers used defensiveness (measured by social desirability) and anxiety as moderator variables. They found that the most disturbed subjects—those high on both variables—were highly consistent in risk-taking, whether risky, cautious, or in between, which they interpreted as indicating a need to maintain a consistent self-image. The least disturbed subjects were moderately consistent, limiting their consistency to certain kinds of tasks. The least degree of consistency showed up in subjects whose degree of personality disturbance was intermediate.

THE research literature is replete with careful studies in which item analysis procedures have resulted in excellent measuring devices, but, as it turns out, only for the group on which the particular item analysis was done. Cross-validation here becomes all important. The following paper by Dr. Cureton is reprinted not only because he makes a strong point but also because of the humorous note in it all— something which is rather infrequent in professional psychological journals. Dr. Cureton is chairman of the department of psychology at the University of Tennessee, and has long been known for his work in test construction and test theory. The paper, reproduced in its entirety, originally appeared in *Educational & Psychological Measurement* (1950).

VALIDITY, RELIABILITY, AND BALONEY

Edward E. Cureton

It is a generally accepted principle that if a test has demonstrated validity for some given purpose, considerations of reliability are secondary. The statistical literature also informs us that a validity coefficient cannot exceed the square root of the reliability coefficient of either the predictor or the criterion. This paper describes the construction and validation of a new test which seems to call in question these accepted principles. Since the technique of validation is the crucial point, I shall discuss the validation procedures before describing the test in detail.

Briefly, the test uses a new type of projective technique which appears to reveal controllable variations in psychokinetic force as applied in certain particular situations. In the present study the criterion is college scholarship, as given by the usual grade-point average. The subjects were 29 senior and graduate students in a course in Psychological Measurements. These students took Forms Q and R of the Cooperative Vocabulary Test, Form R being administered about two weeks after Form Q. The correlation between grade-point average and the combined score on both forms of this test was .23. The reliability of the test, estimated by the Spearman-Brown formula from the correlation between the two forms, was .90.

The experimental form of the new test, which I have termed the "B-Projective Psychokinesis Test," or Test B, was also applied to the group. This experimental form contained 85 items, and there was a reaction to every item for every student. The items called for unequivocal "plus" or "minus" reactions, but in advance of data there is no way to tell which reaction to a given item may be valid for any particular purpose. In this respect, Test B is much like many well-known interest and personality inventories. Since there were no intermediate reactions, all scoring was based on the "plus" reactions alone.

I first obtained the mean grade-point average of all the students whose reaction to each item was "plus." Instead of using the usual technique of biserial correlation, however, I used an item-validity index based on the significance of the difference between the mean grade-point average of the whole group, and the mean grade-point average of those who gave the "plus" reaction to any particular item. This is a straightforward case of sampling from a finite universe. The mean and standard deviation of the grade-point averages of the entire group of 29 are the known parameters. The null hypothesis to be tested is the hypothesis that the subgroup giving the "plus" reaction to any item is a random sample from this population. The mean number giving the "plus" reaction to any item was 14.6. I therefore computed the standard error of the mean for independent samples of 14.6 drawn from a universe of 29, with replacement. If the mean grade-point average of those giving the "plus" reaction to any particular item was more than one standard error above the mean of the whole 69, the item was retained with a scoring weight of plus one. If it was more than one standard error below this general mean, the item was retained with a scoring weight of minus one.

By this procedure, 9 positively weighted items and 15 negatively weighted items were obtained. A scoring key for all 24 selected items was prepared, and the "plus" reactions for the 29 students were scored with this key. The correlations between the 29 scores on the revised Test B and the grade-point averages was found to be .82. In comparison with the Vocabulary Test, which correlated only .23 with the same criterion, Test B appears to possess considerable promise as a predictor of college scholarship. However, the authors of many interest and personality tests, who have used essentially similar validation techniques, have warned us to interpret high validity coefficients with caution when they are derived from the same data used in making the item analysis.

The correlation between Test B and the Vocabulary Test was .31, which is .08 higher than the correlation between the Vocabulary Test and the grade-point averages. On the other hand, the reliability of Test B by the Kuder-Richardson Formula 20, was —.06. hence it would appear that the accepted principles previously mentioned are called in question rather severely by the findings of this study. The difficulty may be explained, however, by a consideration of the structure of the B-Projective Psychokinesis Test.

The items of Test B consisted of 85 metal-rimmed labelling tags. Each tag bore an item number, from 1 to 85, on one side only. To derive a score for any given student, I first put the 85 tags in a cocktail shaker and shook them up thoroughly. Then I looked at the student's grade-point average. If it was B or above, I projected into the cocktail shaker a wish that the student should receive a high "plus" reaction score. If his grade-point average was below B, I projected a wish that he should receive a low score. Then I threw the tags on the table. To obtain the student's score, I counted as "plus" reactions all the tags which lit with the numbered side up. The derivation of the term "B-Projective Psychokinesis Test" should not be obvious.

The moral of this story, I think, is clear. When a validity coefficient is computed from the same data used in making an item analysis, this coefficient cannot be interpreted uncritically. And, contrary to many statements in the literature, it cannot be interpreted "with caution" either. There is one clear interpretation for all such validity coefficients. This interpretation is—

"BALONEY!"

▽ ▽ ▽

ALL textbooks, both in the area of aptitude testing and in statistics, talk of the lowering of validity coefficients when the range of talent of the group tested is restricted. One of the best known projects, involving large efforts to secure a heterogeneous experimental sample—despite the authorities' knowledge that most members of the experimental group would fail—was the Army Air Force's Aviation Psychology Research Program, directed by Dr. John C. Flanagan. Where such an original heterogeneous group is not available, the usual procedure is to make some sort of statistical correction for the restricted range of talent being dealt with. In a research project not likely to be equaled anywhere else, the AAF chose the harder way. It should be remembered, however, that all the failures involved (about 75 percent of the cases) were not entirely eliminated from the AAF, since these men could usually be shifted to many other useful AAF specialties and so were not lost to the service. But only with a huge and highly diversified organization, such as the AAF, can such personnel procedures work effectively.

As one example of how the size of the validity index drops when it is computed on a restricted (qualified) group, consider the instance of the Mechanical Principles Test, which is treated in the accompanying article. Here the biserial correlation for a small qualified group is a mere .18, whereas the corresponding statistic obtained from the total or more heterogeneous group is .44.

The AAF test battery was an extensive one, involving almost an entire day of paper-and-pencil tests followed by approximately two hours of apparatus testing. A final composite score on all these tests, after determination of best weights, was then converted into a pilot composite or stanine score—another form of a standard score—with a stanine of nine as top and one as bottom. Similar stanine composite scores were also computed to predict success in navigator and bombardier training and, later, for gunners. Thus the same test battery, but with different statistical weights for the individual tests, had multiple uses for the AAF.

The following article is an abstract, considerably reduced from the original report in *Educational & Psychological Measurement* in 1946.

THE EXPERIMENTAL EVALUATION OF A SELECTION PROCEDURE

John C. Flanagan

A common problem for research workers concerned with the development and improvement of procedures for the selection and training of personnel is the adequate evaluation of procedures after they have been established. Educational institutions, business and industrial concerns, and government organizations having once accepted certain procedures are generally opposed to suspending the use of these procedures for a large enough group to obtain an adequate evaluation of them. This makes it very difficult to refine and to further improve the procedures.

Because of the very large numbers of men involved and the great importance of the procedures for the selection of aircrew in the Army Air Forces, such an evaluation of these procedures appeared especially desirable. It was believed that a check on the value and interrelation of both the initial screening procedures and the procedures for qualifying men for pilot training on the more comprehensive Aircrew Classification Tests should be made. This could be accomplished by examining a large enough sample of applicants with these tests and by sending all of the men tested into training, regardless of the test results. Accordingly, a memorandum was prepared entitled "Experimental Study of Eligibility Requirements for Aviation Cadets" by the present writer in his position as Chief of the Psychological Branch in May, 1943.

A variety of objections to this proposal were eventually overcome and, in June of 1943, the argument that the procedures were not perfect and that further improvement depended on this type of evaluation won out. The only restriction was to require the regular physical examination of all recruits; no one was to be rejected from this experimental group except for purely physical reasons. Some forty boards, representing all nine service commands, were authorized to recruit the personnel, and each Board was given a definite quota. Total N was set at 1,450 men.

RECRUITING THE GROUP

To insure that the personnel of the boards should understand the general plan and the specific procedures to be followed, an officer from the Psychological Branch, Research Division, Office of the Air Surgeon, was sent during the month of July to each of the boards which had been given a quota. At the time these men were being recruited, the normal procedure was to be sent to basic training centers for six weeks' basic training, then to college for approximately five months pre-aviation cadet college training, and after that, to preflight school for about two months. Following this the individual was sent to primary flying or to one of the other aircrew specialty schools.

Since it was desired that the results of this experiment should be available as quickly as possible, it was decided that the pre-aviation cadet college course would be omitted for these men. Accordingly, beginning about August 1, 1943, all applicants at the authorized boards were given a statement to sign. This statement said, "I wish to enter pilot training. If I am found qualified by the Examining Board, I agree (1) to enter pilot training after a shortened period of basic military training without first taking the pre-aviation cadet college training course, and (2) to volunteer for induction within ten (10) days following the day on which I am found qualified by the Examining Board." For enlisted men a similar blank form was provided, except that it had no reference to basic military training or to volunteering. The examiner also read a statement to the men, pointing out the advantages to them of becoming aviation cadets five months earlier, of having the opportunity to earn pilot ratings and of becoming officers that much sooner.

All applicants who signed the waiver were given the AAF Qualifying Examination, and regardless of their score on this test were given a physical examination and an interview by the board. If they were found physically qualified and had no criminal record, they were qualified by the board for aircrew training. Records on these specially recruited men were sent directly to the War Department. In Washington special orders were written, sending a large group of them at one time to a basic-training center with special instructions for their disposition.

From the basic-training center they were sent to a classification center where the Aircrew Classification Tests were given them. If found physically qualified, they were sent into pilot preflight school, regardless of the scores made on the Aircrew Classification Tests. The orders assigning these men to classification centers indicated that they were members of the experimental group. Upon completing their classification processing, they were sent along with other aviation cadets to preflight schools with no designation as to which ones were members of the experimental group.

At the conclusion of this recruiting process, and after the physical examination and the psychological testing, plus inevitable losses and mistakes in such a large undertaking, a total of 1,143 men were assigned to pilot preflight schools. This constituted the primary sample on which the study was based.

DESCRIPTION OF THE SAMPLE

It is believed that the sample comprising the basic group for this experiment was thoroughly typical of applicants for aviation cadet training. The average was a little more than 21 years, with approximately 30 percent of the group 18 and 19 years old. By far the largest age group was 19, and 10 percent were more than 26. From the standpoint of education, 2 percent were college graduates, an additional 16 percent had had some college training, 58 percent were high school graduates, and the remaining 25 percent had not finished high school, including 1 percent who had never attended high school.

Approximately half of them were recruited from the Army and half from civilian status. With regard to previous flying experience, nearly 5 percent had flown solo and an additional 4 percent had had previous instruction. About 58 percent had been passengers in a plane but had received no instruction, and 33 percent had never been passengers in a plane. In this group, 25 percent were married, 74 percent single, and 1 percent widowed, divorced, or separated.

The average score on the Army General Classification test was 113.0, with a standard deviation for the group of 13.8. Approximately 10 percent of the group achieved Army General Classification Test scores above 130, which placed them in Category 1, and approximately 10 percent obtained scores below 95.

In this original group, 58 percent obtained scores which would have normally passed them on the AAF Qualifying Examination, and 42 percent made scores which would have caused their rejection. The average score was a few points higher than the passing marks, and the standard deviation was approximately that which had previously been found for unselected applicants.

It is clear from their educational background, their Army General Classification Test scores, and their scores on the AAF Qualifying Examination, that this group does not represent a random sample of men of Army age. Rather, it represents approximately the usual amount of self-selection which can be expected in a group of applicants who have chosen to compete for a highly desirable job for which the requirements are relatively high, both in terms of the examinations at the time of entrance and of the standards for retention in and graduation from the training schools.

THE RESULTS

In total, 1,143 men were assigned to pilot preflight schools, but, eventually, only 265 graduated from advanced flight training and were rated as pilots. Of the 878 men eliminated, 99 were eliminated for academic deficiencies in preflight school, 591 were eliminated for flying deficiency at one of the three phases of flight training, and 65 were eliminated at their own request or because of their fear of flying. The remaining 123 men were eliminated for administrative reasons, including physical disqualification. Approximately half of these were eliminated during preflight training.

Thus in this group of applicants who were allowed to enter pilot training without any screening for aptitudes, interests, or ability, only 23 percent were successful in completing the course of pilot training and becoming rated pilots. The question which the experiment was designed to answer was, "How well did the initial screening test results, the various classification test scores, and the pilot stanine predict which one of this group would succeed?"

Figure 1 shows the success of the pilot stanine in predicting which of these applicants would be successful. Very few of the 8's and 9's were eliminated in the training schools, and of those that were, many were eliminated for physical or administrative reasons which the tests were not designed to predict. Nearly half of the 7's were successful in completing training, but only a quarter of the 4's and 5's and only a very small percentage of the 2's and 3's. None of the 1's were successful in completing pilot training.

Figure 2 presents a similar study. It includes only those cases with no

FIGURE 1

EXPERIMENTAL GROUP
VALUE OF AUGMENTED PILOT STANINE FOR PREDICTING GRADUATION OR
ELIMINATION FOR ALL REASONS FROM PILOT TRAINING—
PREFLIGHT THROUGH ADVANCED

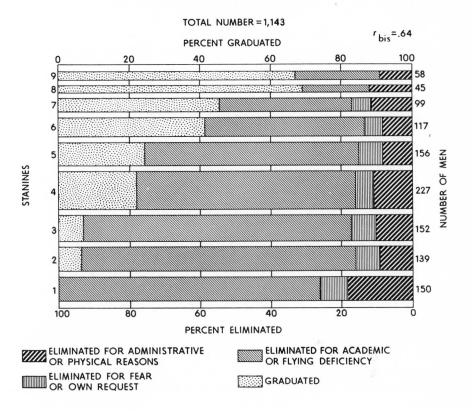

TOTAL NUMBER = 1,143

$r_{bis} = .64$

ELIMINATED FOR ADMINISTRATIVE
OR PHYSICAL REASONS

ELIMINATED FOR ACADEMIC
OR FLYING DEFICIENCY

ELIMINATED FOR FEAR
OR OWN REQUEST

GRADUATED

previous flying experience (no pilot credit) who graduated from preflight school and entered elementary flying schools. It also excludes from consideration men who were eliminated for any reason other than flying deficiency or fear of flying. This chart also indicates the marked success of the pilot stanine in predicting which men would graduate from flying training.

When one evaluates the validity of the individual tests, it is of interest to note that the two best tests, by quite a large margin, were the General Information Test and the Instrument Comprehension Test II (biserial r, respectively, of .50 and .48 against a pass-fail criterion). These two printed tests were also found to be superior to any of the apparatus tests in predictive value. Both of these tests represented novel ideas developed within the Aviation Psychology Program. The other printed tests also showed substantial predictive validity: Mechanical Principles ($r_{bis} = .43$) and Spatial Orientation Test II (.40).

FIGURE 2

VALUE OF PILOT STANINE FOR PREDICTING GRADUATION OR ELIMINATION
FOR FLYING DEFICIENCY, FEAR, OR OWN REQUEST FROM FLYING TRAINING,
PRIMARY THROUGH ADVANCED, EXCLUDING CASES WITH CREDIT FOR
PREVIOUS FLYING EXPERIENCE

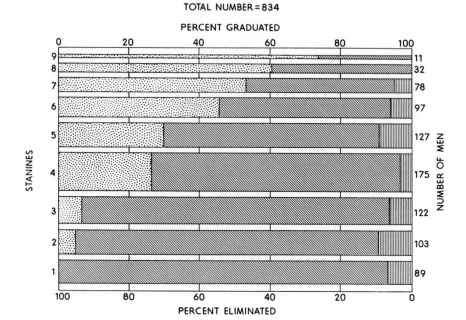

TOTAL NUMBER = 834

THE SPATIAL ORIENTATION TESTS

The predictive value of the six apparatus tests at the time the experimental group was tested is shown in Table 4. These are biserial correlations against a pass-fail criterion in pilot training. Elimination from the group was for flying deficiency, fear, or at the individual cadet's own request; the time span involves preflight through advanced pilot training.

TABLE 4

PREDICTIVE VALUE OF APPARATUS TESTS FOR SUCCESS IN PILOT TRAINING

Discrimination Reaction Time	.42
Rudder Control	.40
Complex Coordination	.41
Two-Hand Coordination	.36
Rotary Pursuit	.31
Finger Dexterity	.18

It is seen that the Discrimination Reaction Time Test, the Rudder Control Test, and the Complex Coordination Test all have substantial predictive value for pilot training. The Two-Hand Coordination Test had somewhat less predictive value and the Rotary Pursuit Test still less for this sample. The Finger Dexterity Test was not weighted for prediction of success in pilot training (but it did help in the prediction of success in other AAF specialties such as navigator, and so was retained in the battery).

A number of statistical studies were made to evaluate the effectiveness of this test battery. Intercorrelations among all variables were computed and best weights for individual tests were studied. In calculating these coefficients, men eliminated for physical and administrative reasons were excluded from consideration. The two categories consisted of 262 men who graduated from advanced training and 755 who were eliminated in preflight, primary, basic, or advanced schools because of academic failure, flying deficiency, or fear of flying. The results of these analyses are reproduced in Table 5.

TABLE 5

Predictive Value of Various Combinations of Tests for
Success in Pilot Training as Determined from an
Experimental Group of 1017 Men

Combination of Predictions Used	Correlation Coefficient with Pilot Training Graduates—Eliminees (academic and flying deficiency and fear of flying)
Pilot stanine	.660
Best-weighted combination of aircrew classification tests for this sample	.690
Best-weighted combination of printed tests in aircrew classification battery for this sample	.641
Best-weighted combination of apparatus tests in aircrew classification battery for this sample	.578

As it is indicated in the table, it is also possible to predict success in pilot training with printed tests alone with an accuracy only moderately diminished, a correlation efficiency .05 smaller, than with the complete battery. Using the apparatus tests alone, the corresponding reduction in the coefficient is .11.

A type of problem frequently encountered in selection research is the question of the effect of selection on the basis of one variable on the predictive value found for a second set of scores. To make an empirical check on this, biserial correlation coefficients were computed excluding all of those individuals who would have normally been rejected on the basis of the AAF Qualifying Examination score. The correlation coefficients obtained for this group of 540 men were compared with those obtained for the uncurtailed group of 1,036 in predicting success in preflight and primary training schools. It was found that the average coefficient was approximately .05 lower in the restricted group. The validity of the pilot stanine was also .05 lower in this curtailed group.

A special study was made of the aircraft accident records of this group. Of the total group of about a thousand men, twenty had aircraft accidents in training planes in the AAF Training Command. There were five accidents that involved pilots with pilot stanines of 7, 8, or 9. These higher stanine groups produced approximately a hundred of the graduates from pilot training. The lower stanine groups, which produced 150 graduates, had a total of 15 accidents.

Four of the accidents were fatal, and these all involved individuals in the lower stanine groups. For the four men involved in fatal accidents, the stanines for bombardier, navigator, and pilot training were, in that order, 324, 636, 445, and 996. The first three were all violating flying regulations at the time of the accidents. The fourth individual overshot his turn from baseleg to final approach in lining up with the runway. In trying to bring the plane back, he stalled out and went into a half-snap. The instructor then took over but the plane hit on the left wing and cartwheeled.

IMPLICATIONS

This study of 1,000 applicants and their success in pilot training in relation to their scores on the selection and classification tests has clearly demonstrated the effectiveness of these procedures when applied to groups of men recruited from civilian life or from the Army. Of 405 men who failed on the AAF Qualifying Examination and were subsequently sent into pilot training, only 12 achieved pilot stanines of 7, 8, or 9, and only 4 of these and 41 others of the more than 500 men who failed the Qualifying Examination were graduated from pilot training.

The value of the second screening by the Aircrew Classification Tests was dramatically demonstrated by the graduation of only 16 men out of 442 with pilot stanines of 1, 2, and 3 sent into preflight training. At the same time, 113 men graduated of the 199 with pilot stanines of 7, 8, and 9 sent into preflight training.

The correlation coefficient of .66 obtained between pilot stanine and success in pilot training compares favorably with the best predictions which have been obtained in educational and industrial work. It now appears that further improvement of instructional techniques and procedures for passing and failing students needs to be made before a substantial amount of further refinement in the selection and classification procedures can be expected.

▽ ▽ ▽

IN Dr. Flanagan's paper concerning AAF aptitude test batteries for Air Force technical occupations, he noted that attention should probably be given to instructors and their ratings of pass and fail—that possibly predictions might be increased still more if training were given in the assignment of grades. The following report analyzes one aspect of this situation with pilot instructors.

Dr. Krumboltz served with the AAF as research psychologist in 1955–57, and is now associate professor of education and psychology at Stanford University. Dr. Christal is chief of the Occupational Structures Research Division, Air Force Research Laboratory, in San Antonio. This study was conducted at the Lackland Air Force Base in Texas under ARDC Project No. 7719, Task No. 17009. Reproduced here is a condensation of an article that appeared in the *Journal of Applied Psychology*, 1957.

RELATIVE PILOT APTITUDE AND SUCCESS IN PRIMARY PILOT TRAINING

John D. Krumboltz and Raymond E. Christal

If a cadet with medium aptitude for flying is placed in a group of high aptitude cadets, would he be more likely to fail than if he had been placed in a group of low aptitude cadets? The question may be put another way. Does a flying instructor have an absolute frame of reference in judging which cadets pass and which fail, or does he have a relative frame of reference so that his standard of what is acceptable varies with the quality of students he is instructing? It might be that an instructor would fail the worst student in his group, even though the worst student in his group might have been the best student in some other group had the groups been formed differently. This problem is especially acute in pilot training, since each instructor usually has only four students. If the four students are randomly assigned to instructors, and if a relative frame of reference operates, then chance factors would contribute to the probability of passing. One student grouped with highly talented fellow students might fail while another student of equal or even less ability might pass because he had happened to be placed with students of low ability. If such a condition prevails, the Air Force is not getting the best possible pilots; deserving men are failing; and the true validity of the pilot stanine is not being estimated accurately. The present study was designed to determine whether such a phenomenon exists.

It seems reasonable to suppose that one's frame of reference shifts in accordance with the quality of the material to be judged. Such a supposition has been confirmed by psychological research dealing with adaptation levels and frames of reference. The generalized result of a number of studies is that individuals tend to form their standards of judgment from the nature of the objects to be judged. The beauty of a picture, the wickedness of a crime, the pleasantness of a color, and the loudness of a sound are just a few examples of how judgments are subject to the frame of reference of the observer.

There is already some evidence that instructors in primary pilot training do not possess an absolute frame of reference in judging the quality of student pilots. Boyle and Hagin (1953) found that 70 percent of the students with no previous flying training passed when they were grouped with each other, but only 49 percent passed when they were in groups with students who had prior light plane training.

PROCEDURE

The records of one primary pilot training school over a six-year period of time were utilized to obtain cases for the present study. To achieve a relatively homogeneous sample, the only cases included in the study were aviation cadets in instructional groups of four. Any group containing a cadet held over to a later class was excluded from the study. Instructional groups containing one or more student officers (AFROTC graduates) were not analyzed because of a possible instructor bias for or against student officers. Groups containing student officers only were not numerous enough to justify extensive study. A total of 54 instructional groups containing 216 aviation cadets met the requirements for this study.

The criterion of success consisted of the dichotomy of "pass" or "fail" in primary pilot training. All men eliminated from training and not held over to a later class were classified in the "fail" category, regardless of the stated reason for their elimination.

Each student's relative pilot aptitude (RPA) score was determined in the following manner. Students' names and their pilot stanine scores were first arranged in accordance with the actual instructional grouping that had occurred during primary pilot training. Then for each man the mean pilot stanine of the other men in his group was calculated. Each man's own pilot stanine minus the mean stanine of the other men in his group, plus a constant of ten (to eliminate negative members) constituted his RPA score. A high score, therefore, indicated that a man had relatively more aptitude than the average of the other men in his group. A low score indicated that he had relatively less aptitude than others in his group.

Within each stanine level the men were ranked by RPA scores and divided according to whether they passed or failed in pilot training. The distribution of RPA scores was split approximately at the median for each stanine level. Therefore, the men of each stanine level were divided into four categories: high RPA and "pass," high RPA and "fail," low RPA and "pass," low RPA and "fail."

It was hypothesized that within each stanine level, cadets with high RPA scores would be more likely to pass than cadets with low RPA scores. Furthermore, it was hypothesized that this would be more true in the middle range of talent than at the extremes. For purposes of statistical analysis, these hypotheses were translated to statistical null hypotheses as indicated below.

The primary null hypothesis was that within each stanine level the proportion of passing cadets in the high RPA group is the same as the proportion of passing cadets in the low RPA group.

The second null hypothesis was that there is no difference in the proportion of passing cadets among stanines. This hypothesis, as stated, was not basic to the study but was included to provide for a test of an interaction effect—the third hypothesis.

The third hypothesis was that there is no interaction between stanine level and RPA scores. That is, the proportion of passing cadets in the high and low RPA categories is the same for each stanine level.

In 1956, Wilson described a method for computing tests of analysis of variance hypotheses with nonparametric data. This technique was utilized for testing each of the above hypotheses. The .05 level of confidence was chosen for rejection of the null hypotheses.[1]

RESULTS

The number of cases falling in each RPA and "pass-fail" category by stanine is presented in Table 6.

TABLE 6

NUMBER OF AVIATION CADETS FALLING IN EACH RPA AND PASS-FAIL CATEGORY BY STANINE

	Stanine														
RPA	9		8		7		6		5		4		3		Total	
Score	Pass	Fail	Pass	Fail	Pass	Fail	Pass	Fail	Pass	Fail	Pass	Fail	Pass	Fail	Pass	Fail
High ...	6	1	7	3	13	3	14	2	19	5	10	5	6	5	75	24
Low ...	5	1	9	2	11	5	14	7	14	10	7	10	8	9	68	44
Total ..	11	2	16	5	24	8	28	9	33	15	17	15	14	14	143	68

Note: Three cadets with stanine 2 scores and two cadets with stanine 1 scores are not included in this table because of the low frequencies involved. All five failed in primary pilot training.

The relative pilot aptitude of a man within his instructional group was found to be significantly related to his chances for success in primary pilot training. In general, a cadet had a better chance of success if he was grouped with cadets of relatively lower aptitude than himself rather than with cadets of relatively higher aptitude. The first hypothesis is therefore rejected.

---

[1] Dr. Krumboltz, in a personal communication to the editor, comments that even though this Wilson test lacks "power" (McNemar, 1958), the findings of this study, significant in spite of this inefficient test, remain unaltered.

The second hypothesis was accepted, since the proportion of cadets passing in each stanine did not differ sufficiently to reach the required significance level. It should be noted that the test of this second hypothesis was not a sensitive one: It failed to take into account the linear trend for higher stanine levels to be associated with greater proportions of passing cadets. The validity of the pilot stanine itself is revealed by the biserial correlation of the stanine with the pass-fail criterion which is reported in Table 6. The second hypothesis was included in the analysis to isolate the source of variation due to stanine level and to provide for a test of the interaction between RPA categories and stanine levels.

No significant interaction was observed. It was originally hypothesized that a cadet's relative pilot aptitude would have more effect on cadets in the middle range of aptitude scores than on cadets toward either extreme. A tendency in this direction can be noted. Inspection of Table 6 reveals that the effect of RPA standing on success is more pronounced in stanines 4, 5, 6, and 7 than it is in stanines 3, 8, and 9. In fact, there is a slight reversal in direction in stanine 8. However, such differences in the effect of RPA standing at different stanine levels were too slight to produce a significant interaction effect.

The biserial validity of the RPA scores against the pass-fail criterion was .412 while the validity of the pilot stanine was only .348. It is obvious that the validity of the pilot stanine was attenuated by the instructors' relative frames of reference which introduced irrelevant variance into the criterion. Without this attenuation, the validity of the pilot stanine would be identical to the validity of the RPA scores. This is true since the RPA scores are in reality nothing more than pilot stanines adjusted for differences in group means.

The RPA score can be analyzed in another manner by breaking it into its components: (a) the pilot stanine score, and (b) the mean pilot stanine of the other three men in the group. Table 7 reports the intercorrelation of these two components, along with their validity for the pilot training pass-fail criterion. Although the second component has a validity of only —.134, it raises the validity of the pilot stanine from .348 to .414 when the two components are combined in a multiple correlation formula. It may be

TABLE 7

INTERCORRELATIONS OF RPA WITH PASS-FAIL IN PRIMARY PILOT TRAINING
(N = 216)

	Variable				
Variable	1	2	3	Mean	SD
1. Pilot stanine		.240	.348[a]	5.51	1.81
2. Mean of other three men	.240		—.134[a]	5.50	1.22
3. Pass-Fail	.348[a]	—.134[a]		.66[b]	.47[b]

a Biserial correlations
b Pass = 1, Fail = 0

observed that this multiple correlation is identical to the validity of the RPA score itself.

There is some evidence of homogeneous grouping by aptitude in this sample. A simple analysis of variance revealed that the mean pilot stanines of the instructional groups varied more than might be expected if there had been no homogeneous grouping. Inspection of the groupings revealed that most of the groups were arranged alphabetically, but that a few groups did have considerable restriction in variability. To the extent that homogeneous grouping did occur, one would expect attenuation in the validity of RPA scores. If no homogeneous grouping had occurred in any of the groups, the effect of RPA standing on success in pilot training would have been even more pronounced than it was found to be here.

IMPLICATIONS

Results of previous research studies have been confirmed in a practical situation. An instructor does not have a constant frame of reference for evaluating the performance of pilot trainees, just as subjects in other experiments lack a constant frame of reference for judging the beauty of a picture or the magnitude of a weight. To the extent that these results are generalizable to other training situations in civilian as well as military life, certain implications are apparent.

First, the true validities of aptitude tests are being underestimated when this phenomenon operates. The criterion is contaminated by irrelevant variance which is unrelated to the predictors.

Secondly, many students are being graded unfairly. Some students are given low grades or are eliminated from pilot training, not because their performance is below some absolute standard, but rather because it is below the average of the particular group in which they happen to find themselves. When this happens, the nation does not get optimal utilization of the available qualified manpower. In the Air Force, the likelihood of grading bias can be reduced by assigning cadets to instructional groups in such a way that each group would have the same mean on the pilot stanine. When the means of all groups have been made equal, then the pilot stanine would correlate perfectly with RPA scores. In civilian institutions it might be possible to assign students to sections of an undergraduate course in such a manner as to equate section means on some related aptitude score. When this is not desirable or convenient, an alternative might be to inform each instructor of the general level of aptitude in his section. He could use this information to guide his evaluations. In certain cases it might be possible to set up objective tests for measuring proficiency. In other instances, as in the pilot training program, for example, the instructors could be furnished a standardized set of case studies which contain objective and observable characteristics of persons judged to be making satisfactory or unsatisfactory progress.

A related problem has to do with the changes in grading practices over time. Grades and attrition rates in any civilian or military training program are not likely to be sensitive to fluctuations in the level of incoming talent. The standard for satisfactory performance tends to slide up and down with the ability of the group. Any method of standardizing grading practices would help alleviate this problem. Where objective and valid selection tests are employed, administrative action could be taken to vary grades and the attrition rate inversely with the level of talent selected.

SUMMARY

Does a flying instructor have an absolute frame of reference in judging which cadets pass and which fail, or does he have a relative frame of reference so that his standard of what is acceptable varies with the quality of students he is currently instructing? Based on a sample of 216 aviation cadets sampled from one primary training base over a six-year period of time, the analysis revealed that a cadet has a better chance of success if he is grouped with cadets of relatively lower aptitude than himself, rather than with cadets of relatively higher aptitude. Thus, instructors in this study tended to have a relative frame of reference. To the extent that this phenomenon operates in other training situations, the nation is denied the services of the most highly-qualified trained personnel, and the true validity of aptitude tests is under-estimated. (Methods of minimizing these dangers have been discussed.)

THE General Aptitude Test Battery (GATB), the product of years of research by the U.S. Employment Service, is possibly the most successful of the various multi-aptitude test batteries currently in use. Its origins go back to the work of the Minnesota Employment Stabilization Research Institute during the depression years (Dvorak, 1935). Extensive validity data, both concurrent and predictive, are available, and this research is a continuing process. For a general description of these tests, consult Dvorak (1956). Research with these tests is especially significant since aptitude patterns have been developed, which has resulted in a psychological classification of occupation groups into "families." Recently, the test norms have been extended downward to ninth-grade groups (U.S. Department of Labor, 1959) so that now this battery covers a very wide range of talent.

Dr. Dvorak is chief of the Testing Division, U.S. Employment Service, Department of Labor, and it is she who has been largely responsible for the general direction of GATB research. The following material has been abstracted and condensed from Section III of the GATB Manual (U.S. Department of Labor, 1958). This manual, together with that of the Differential Aptitude Test Battery, is a model of completeness, especially in regard to the presentation of extensive validity data.

DEVELOPMENT OF OCCUPATIONAL NORMS

Beatrice J. Dvorak

The basic assumption underlying the GATB is that a large variety of tests can be reduced to several factors, and that a large variety of occupations can also be clustered into groups according to similarities in the abilities required. It is assumed that occupations differ from each other in varying degrees and that occupations can be grouped into families on the basis of similarities in the abilities required. One of the major efforts of this research has been to show that these are differential ability patterns among workers in various types of occupations, and that these patterns have validity. The GATB may then be accurately described as a "multipotential" test battery.

Since the GATB has been designed for use primarily in everyday employment situations, the emphasis has been placed on empirical and predictive validity (although other types of validity have not been ignored). The GATB is the only multi-aptitude test battery currently available which is based on such extensive "working population" norms. For this reason, the GATB treatment of validity is all-important. The discussion of validity has, therefore, a thoroughly realistic base in the world of occupations.

Since a suitable criterion is essential to the successful conduct of a test development study, the determination of the availability of the needed criterion, or measure of job performance, is made early in the process. It is important here that the criterion be a measure of an important phase of the job which involves the essential job performance abilities, rather than a measure of general job success. For example, although factors such as co-operativeness, dependability and diligence are important determinants of general job success, these factors are not measured by aptitude tests and should not be reflected in a criterion to be used for test development purposes. A suitable criterion for aptitude test development purposes should be a reliable and valid measure of each worker's job proficiency with respect to quantity and quality of production; it should be a good measure of the performance that we wish to predict with the aptitude tests.

TYPES OF CRITERIA

In broad terms, criteria can be classified into two main categories: objective and subjective. An objective criterion is a quantitative measure of quantity and/or quality of production. "Production records" is a general term used to denote a variety of objective criteria. The actual records may be expressed as "units produced," "percent of production standard achieved," "piece-rate earnings," or some other comparable measure to reflect quantity of production; or they may be expressed in terms of the number of errors made or the number of items rejected to reflect quality of production. Sometimes the two types of records may be combined statistically to obtain a single measure of both the quality and quantity of production for each worker. In addition to production records, work samples, such as proficiency tests in typing and stenography, may be used as objective criteria. It is possible to obtain separate or combined measures of speed and accuracy with work-sample criteria.

Subjective criteria involve a judgment of performance, usually made by somebody who is in a good position to rate the performance of each individual in the sample, such as a foreman, supervisor, or instructor. The rating technique might involve one of a variety of procedures, such as broad category or group ratings, rank-order ratings, paired comparison ratings which yield a rank-order distribution, or the use of a descriptive rating scale. Regardless of the type of rating procedure employed, the objective is to place each individual in the experimental sample in the correct relative position with respect to his job performance ability.

School grades are also used as criteria for test development studies. These may be primarily objective, or to a large extent subjective, depending upon the grading system used in the school. For example, school grades would be considered as objective if the final grades for each course were based solely upon examination marks made by the students. However, school grades become relatively subjective when an instructor uses the examination marks as a guide and assigns final grades in accordance with his judgment of each student's total performance.

Even though traditionally it has been customary to classify criteria as either "objective" or "subjective," it should be borne in mind that there seldom is a clear-cut line between these two types of criteria. There often is an element of subjectivity in a criterion that is expressed in units which appear to be completely objective. For example, when records of the number of rejects are employed to evaluate the quality of workers' performance, the criterion appears to be completely objective. However, there must necessarily be subjective factors involved in setting the standards of acceptability for the items being produced, as well as in the evaluation of finished products in terms of the established standards to determine if they should be accepted or rejected. Similarly, there are subjective elements involved in criteria based on quantity of production. Subjective determinations are made of factors, such as the method of measuring quantity of production and the rate of production considered to be satisfactory.

At one time objective criteria were generally regarded as more dependable measures of job performance than subjective criteria. In the early years of the Employment Service test development program, attempts were made to use only objective criteria for test development purposes. However, objective criteria were just not available for many occupations, and for many jobs for which objective criteria were available, it was not possible to obtain comparable measures on samples of sufficient size for test development purposes. It was also found that objective criteria usually covered only one facet of job performance, such as quantity of production. These factors led to the employment of objective criteria in test development studies. Experience has since shown that it is often advisable to obtain both objective and subjective criterion data for the same sample. Each criterion correlated separately with the test scores can contribute data for meaningful interpretation. In a test development study on the occupation of tile paster, a job in the production of ceramic products, both production records and supervisory ratings were obtained as criteria. The production records showed significant correlation with measures of manual dexterity and motor speed, whereas the supervisory ratings showed significant correlation with measures of form perception as well as with measures of manual dexterity and motor speed. Further study showed that the production records were based solely on quantity of production, whereas the supervisory ratings reflected both quantity and quality of production. The job analysis data indicated that although form perception was involved in quality of production it was not a determinant of quantity. In this instance the subjective criterion data not only served to substantiate the findings of the objective criterion, but also revealed a significant relationship between job performance and measures of form perception that could not have been made evident through use of the objective criterion alone. On the basis of experiences similar to the one cited immediately above, it is believed that we should not generalize with respect to the superiority of one type of criterion over another. Both objective and subjective criteria have their specific uses. When both types of criterion data are available, the choice to lean more heavily on either one or to make equal use of both for purposes of test validation must necessarily vary in accordance with the pertinent factors to be considered in each specific situation.

QUALITY OF CRITERION

The success or failure of a test development study can be determined by the quality of the criterion that is obtained. Therefore, it is of extreme importance to evaluate the criterion data in every way possible. As already stated, it is important that the criterion employed for a test development study be primarily a measure of each worker's job proficiency and that other determinants of general job success, such as cooperativeness and dependability, be excluded from this criterion. Data should be collected which enable a statistical evaluation of the reliability and validity of the criterion. The reliability of a criterion can be measured by obtaining two or more sets of criterion data covering different periods of time and correlating them, or by correlating the ratings on the same people made by different supervisors or foremen.

The validity of the criterion is extremely difficult to measure and usually can be measured only indirectly. For example, we can determine the extent to which factors other than job performance might be influencing the criterion. Significant correlation between the criterion and variables such as experience, age, and education are sometimes indicative that the criterion is not a true measure of job performance. In some instances, it might be possible to apply a statistical correction to nullify the effects of these extraneous factors. Or this objective might be achieved by applying some type of experimental control, such as excluding from the sample those individuals at the extremes of the distribution of the variable that is unduly influencing the criterion. For example, if an analysis of the data has revealed that length of experience on the job has biased the job performance ratings assigned to workers, the experience factor can be held relatively constant by excluding from the sample those workers who have either extremely high or low amounts of experience relative to the other workers in the sample. Sometimes, however, no statistical correction or experimental control technique is applicable and we either have to discard the criterion, or use it with caution and interpret our results with reservations.

It should also be pointed out that in some instances, a criterion may be a valid measure of job performance even though it does exhibit significant correlation with variables such as age, experience, and education. It is difficult to determine when these correlations are indicative of spurious relationships which call for some correction to be made or for the data to be discarded, or when job performance really does have a true relationship to these other variables. Every effort should be made to obtain as much information as possible which might enable a meaningful interpretation of the obtained relationships. For example, in a particular experimental sample the workers who have been on the job longer may actually be the best performers or they may have been given the higher ratings only because the supervisor is better acquainted with them. Sometimes a thorough examination of the experience and criterion data may yield some meaningful clues. The observation that none or very few of the less experienced workers have been placed in the high part of the criterion distribution might be indicative that the ratings are unduly biased. If all workers in the sample have completed the training period, and there has been no significant change in the labor market or company hiring procedures between the time that the more and less experienced workers were hired, then it is unlikely that there would really be a marked preponderance of proficiency among the more experienced workers.

It is important to make certain that objective criterion data are comparable for all workers and are not influenced by working conditions rather than by each worker's job performance ability. Production records as a measure of proficiency are considered a good criterion if each worker has an equal opportunity to produce as many units as he can and production is measured uniformly for all workers. If because of the nature of the job, the flow of work is subject to fluctuations, or if a machine controls the speed of production, production records would not make a suitable criterion. Factors such as lighting, age of machines, availability of materials and additional duties performed by workers must be taken into consideration when the use of production records as a criterion is contemplated in order to insure comparability.

TREATMENT OF CRITERION DATA

In order to make use of the criterion for purposes of statistical analysis, it is necessary for the data to be in a form which enables us to determine the relationships between the criterion and test performance. Usually objective criteria are expressed in units already forming continuous distributions which can be readily correlated with the test results. Sometimes, for the sake of convenience of computation, some conversion of the units might be desirable.

Subjective criterion data usually require conversion to form which enables correlation with the test results. For example, rank-order ratings, which place each individual in his correct relative position, space each person an equal distance from the next, which tends to indicate that the job performance of each individual in the sample varies by an equal amount from the next better and poorer workers. This, we know, is not the case, because job performance tends to be normally distributed. Therefore, before using rank-order ratings to compute product-moment correlations, we convert the ranks to linear scores, which are a better representation of the true differences in job performance between each worker and the next. Items on a descriptive rating scale are usually weighted and summed to obtain a numerical score for each person in the experimental sample. Broad category or group ratings, which might merely designate each worker in the sample as either above average, average, or below average, are converted to quantitative values on the basis of the normal distribution curve. These data can then be used to compute product-moment correlation coefficients corrected for broad categories. When ratings are expressed in two categories, such as satisfactory or unsatisfactory, biserial correlation coefficients can be computed.

Since norms on Employment Service test batteries are established for use with the multiple cutoff method, and scores are regarded as either "qualifying" or "nonqualifying," a technique which enables the correlation of a dichotomously expressed variable is employed to evaluate the norms. The criterion, regardless of its original units, is also dichotomized and tetrachoric correlation coefficients are computed. The question arises with respect to the point at which the criterion should be dichotomized, or where should the criterion cutting score be set?

When the criterion is to be dichotomized, it is desirable to find the "true" point of demarcation between the high and low criterion groups whenever possible. This point is not constant for all groups but varies from one study to another. Experience in conducting test development studies and consultation with foremen and supervisors have indicated that, in general, a valid division is obtained by placing approximately one-third of the experimental sample in the low criterion group and approximately two-thirds in the high criterion group. However, this does not mean that the criterion should always be dichotomized with approximately one-third of the sample placed in the low criterion group. To make the best determination of the division point, it is necessary to consult with the foremen, supervisors, or instructors who are familiar with the performance of everybody in the sample and who are in the best position to specify where the line of demarcation between satisfactory and marginal performance falls. It is often difficult for this determination to be made even by foremen or supervisors who are thoroughly familiar with the performance of everybody in the experimental sample. Greater difficulty in making this determination is experienced when there are no established quantitative standards available. On the other hand, if production records are available and it is known that production below a specified level is regarded as unsatisfactory by the company, then determining the criterion critical score is not a difficult matter; or if school grades are the criterion and it is known that the passing grade is at a certain point, there is not much difficulty.

It should be recognized that in some samples, where there has already been some restriction in the range of ability, there may not be a "true" unsatisfactory or low criterion group. This would be particularly true for groups of college seniors or samples of experienced workers which include only those individuals who have demonstrated satisfactory performance, and from which those people who have not performed satisfactorily have dropped out. For samples of this type, in which everybody exhibits satisfactory performance, even though some people are better than others, it is necessary to establish high and low criterion groups on a relative basis by setting a criterion critical score at some arbitrary point which divides the most proficient from the less proficient people in the sample.

EXPERIMENTAL BATTERY

After a suitable and reliable criterion has been obtained, the next step is to select the experimental battery. When the United States Employment Service (USES) first began its test research program in 1935, about 15 suitable tests were selected for tryout in a particular study by inspecting the job analysis information to see what abilities might be involved, and by considering the results of previous studies of the same or a similar occupation. Over a period of time a large number of tests were constructed, and by a process of factor analysis, it was found that they grouped themselves into ten families or groups of tests. These were measuring ten significant vocational abilities. Fifteen tests were selected which provided a good measure of all ten of these abilities. These constitute the first edition of the USES GATB, B–1001. From 1945 to 1952 this battery has been used as the standard experimental battery in every test development study that has been undertaken to develop occupational norms. However, in the fall of 1952 another edition of the GATB, the "Separate-Answer-Sheet Form," B–1002, was introduced to the State Employment Services for use also in operational activities and in test development studies. The entire General Aptitude Test Battery is usually administered to every experimental sample.

EXPERIMENTAL SAMPLE

In the USES test development studies, the sample may consist of applicants, employees, trainees, apprentices, or students. The objective is to have the sample large enough to be truly representative of the population from which it is drawn, and to be chosen without bias in regard to the proficiency of the good, mediocre, and poor individuals comprising the sample. It is desirable to include in the experimental sample all the people in the occupation being studied who meet the requirements with respect to factors such as job duties performed, age, education, experience, criterion of job performance, and availability for testing. As the size of the sample increases, the dependability of the statistics computed on the basis of the sample increases.

When a sample of employed workers is tested for test development purposes, it is desirable for the final sample to include at least 50 workers, preferably more, who are all performing the same kind of work and who have survived the training period on the job. It is recognized that some plants may not have as many as 50 workers all performing the same job duties, or perhaps, the management cannot see its way clear to make all the workers on a particular job available for experimental testing, because this would interfere too much with the plant's production. In such instances the study is conducted on a sample of fewer than 50 but no less than 30 workers. Experience in conducting experimental studies has shown that after the data are collected, some workers are excluded because of the incompleteness or inadequacy of the data, or because they are not representative of the workers generally found in the occupation being studied. Thus to have at least 50 workers remaining in the final sample, it is sometimes necessary to include 70 or more workers in the sample initially selected for testing.

When a sample of students, trainees, or apprentices is tested for test-development purposes, the size of the experimental sample depends upon the objective of the study and the time when testing occurs. If the objective is to develop norms for a vocational course, such as machine shop or radio, or for a college or university area of specialization, it is desirable for the final sample to include at least 50 students. If the testing is done at the beginning of a course, it is desirable to include a much larger number of students, since some will drop out before the completion of the course.

When a sample of students, trainees, applicants, or apprentices is tested, the "longitudinal" experimental design is often used. A criticism frequently made by people interested in test research is that little, if any, follow-up work is done to evaluate the operational efficiency of test norms resulting from test development studies based on experimental samples of employed workers. It is generally conceded that ideally it would be preferable to establish occupational norms based on samples as similar as possible in respect to age, education, and experience to the group on which it is expected the test norms will be used; that such samples should be tested prior to hiring; and that such hiring should be done without regard to test results. However, in fact, it is not often possible to achieve this ideal in practice. Similarly, it is difficult to obtain follow-up data showing the predictive value of the estab-lished norms in terms of data which readily lend themselves to statistical interpretation. Notwithstanding these difficulties, the USES has obtained data from a number of studies using the longitudinal experimental design in the development of occupational norms. In this type of design the tests are administered to all applicants for a job rather than to those who are already employed in the job. This experimental design is particularly apropos when a new plant is being staffed and hence no workers are available for study. In this design the entire GATB is administered to all applicants that are referred to an employer, but the test scores are not used in making selections. Only regular interviewing methods are used. After the workers have been on the job a sufficient length of time to reach normal production, criterion data are obtained. Criterion data are also obtained on those individuals who did not complete the training period because of inability to perform the job duties satisfactorily. Studies of this type have the advantage of sampling a relatively wide range of ability with respect to both test and job performance. The longitudinal design has the advantage also of using test scores that have not been influenced by training.

The Employment Service makes it a point to utilize the longitudinal design for test development purposes whenever possible. However, all too often it is not feasible to use this type of experimental design because a waiting period which may vary from several weeks to several years is required before test norms can become available for operating purposes. In instances where test norms are required as soon as possible for a particular occupation, the concurrent validation experimental design must be used. The correlations obtained between test results and the criterion in studies of this type are regarded as measures of descriptive or concurrent validity. When studies which yield measures of descriptive or concurrent validity have been conducted, an effort is made to conduct check studies by using the longitudinal design in order to obtain correlations between test results and the criterion that can be regarded as measures of predictive validity.

ANALYSIS OF DATA

After the tests have been administered to an experimental sample and the criterion data have been collected, the data are analyzed to determine the group of tests having maximum validity for the occupation. Various methods for analyzing such data have been used. In the early years of the test research program, when the USES was interested merely in developing one specific battery at a time, the Wherry-Doolittle Multiple Correlation Technique was used to arrive at the combination of tests with maximum validity for the occupation. When the use of the General Aptitude Test Battery was inaugurated, however, the methods of analyzing the data were changed somewhat because the objective became somewhat different. The USES is now interested not only in establishing test norms for a single occupation but also in relating a given set of occupational norms to the norm structure for groups of occupations, so that a single battery of tests can be scored for a large variety of occupations. This means an interest in occupational differentiation as well as in differentiating good from poor workers within an occupation. A shift was made to the multiple cutting-score method. All the aptitudes regarded as significant are considered for inclusion in the final test norms. The data are further analyzed to determine which combination of significant aptitudes and cutting scores will yield the best selective efficiency in terms of the criterion of the experimental sample.

ESTABLISHMENT OF TEST NORMS

Norms on Employment Service test batteries are established for use with the multiple cutoff method, and scores are regarded as either "qualifying" or "nonqualifying." A critical or minimum qualifying score is set on each aptitude included in the final battery for subsequent use in the selection of new workers or the counseling of applicants by means of the multiple hurdle method. In other words, an individual is considered qualified only if he meets the minimum score on *each* of the key aptitudes. There is no total weighted score to be obtained.

Since Employment Service test norms indicate whether an individual is "qualified" or "nonqualified," a technique which enables the correlation of a dichotomously expressed variable is employed to evaluate the norms. Therefore, the criterion is dichotomized and tetrachoric correlation coefficients are computed between trial set of norms and the criterion. The trial norms consist of various combinations of significant aptitudes and minimum scores; the combination which yields the best selective efficiency is established as the final norms or test battery for the specific occupation being studied.

Minimum scores on Employment Service test norms are set so that the proportion of the experimental sample in the nonqualifying test score group approximates the proportion in the low or unsatisfactory criterion group. This usually tends to maximize the tetrachoric correlation coefficient and results in the test norms qualifying the maximum number of satisfactory individuals and screening out the maximum number of unsatisfactory individuals. Of course, factors such as the composition of an experimental sample, labor market conditions, production requirements of a particular plant, caliber or supervisory personnel, training techniques and production methods are determinants of the proportion of a sample placed in the low criterion group as well as the proportion that it is expedient to screen out on the basis of test results. Since it has been found that these proportions frequently approximate one-third of the sample, setting the minimum score on each significant aptitude approximately one standard deviation unit below the mean obtained for the experimental sample usually screens out the desired number and results in good selective efficiency. The number of aptitudes included in the final norms also affects the points at which minimum scores are set, because as the number of aptitudes included in the norms is increased, it is usually necessary to lower the points at which minimum scores are set in order to screen out the desired proportion. In general, if the final test norms include only two aptitudes, minimum scores are usually set at 5-point score levels slightly higher than one standard deviation unit below the sample mean on each aptitude; if the norms include three aptitudes, minimum scores are usually set at 5-point score levels close to one sigma below the mean; and if the norms include four aptitudes, minimum scores are usually set at a 5-point score levels slightly lower than one sigma below the mean. Minimum scores are set at 5-point score levels in order to avoid taking undue advantage of chance fluctuations, to effect greater comparability of the results of various studies, and to facilitate use of the norms for operating purposes.

We noted that often there seemed to be a relationship between test scores and job proficiency only to an optimum point. Since there was not a straight-line relationship throughout the entire range, the Wherry-Doolittle Multiple Correlation Technique did not yield that ability in the final norms. For example, finger dexterity might be a crucial ability for some jobs; without a minimum amount of it, persons would not be able to perform successfully on the job; but, beyond a certain point, additional increments of finger dexterity would not be associated with additional production on the job.

Even when a crucial ability does show a straight-line relationship between test scores and success, the method of multiple regression weights permits the possession of other abilities to compensate for a low amount of a crucial ability. In our experience, an employer is not satisfied with a worker who is awkward with his fingers in a certain job, even though he may have an unusually high amount of other abilities required by the job. Hence we use the multiple cutoff method which does not permit such compensation of some abilities for others required by the job.

DETERMINATION OF VALIDITY OF BATTERY

The validity of the test battery composed of the key aptitudes and cutting scores is determined by means of a correlation coefficient showing the relationship between the norms and the criterion. Usually the tetrachoric correlation coefficient is used to indicate this relationship. In the USES studies, a tetrachoric correlation coefficient is not regarded as significant unless it is at least twice its standard error.

The following are two examples of test-development studies. That for mounter is an illustration of the concurrent validation experimental design in which the minimum qualifying scores eliminate approximately one-third of the experimental sample. The study for file clerk is an illustration of the longitudinal design in which the minimum qualifying scores eliminate approximately 30 percent of the experimental sample.

Study of Mounter I (DOT code 7–00.016).   Assembles radio tube mounts and stems of cathode grids and plate by positioning and connecting very small and medium sized parts and wires either manually or with tweezers; spot welds parts in place. Experimental sample of 65 workers with criterion of piece-rate earnings. Statistical results: Table 8 shows that the aptitudes with high mean scores relative to the general population and to each other aptitude are spatial, form perception, aiming, and finger dexterity; the aptitudes with low standard deviation relative to the general population and to each other aptitude are numerical and aiming; aptitudes with correlations significant at the .01 level are finger dexterity and manual dexterity.

TABLE 8

STATISTICAL DATA FOR 65 MOUNTERS AND GATB SCORES

Aptitude	Mean	σ	r	σ_r
G—Intelligence	106.9	15.3	—.075	.123
V—Verbal Aptitude	102.2	14.7	—.061	.124
N—Numerical Aptitude	105.8	13.3	.064	.124
S—Spatial Aptitude	109.3	16.6	—.009	.124
P—Form Perception	111.8	15.6	.015	.124
Q—Clerical Perception	106.2	15.9	.097	.123
A—Aiming	107.1	13.9	.229	.118
T—Motor Speed	103.6	15.5	.191	.120
F—Finger Dexterity	109.5	18.4	.437	.100
M—Manual Dexterity	98.7	20.7	.353	.109

The job analysis data for this occupation showed that the aptitudes of form perception, aiming, finger dexterity, and manual dexterity appeared to warrant consideration for inclusion in the test norms. Considering this together with the statistical results, the aptitudes of form perception, aiming, finger dexterity, and manual dexterity were selected. The critical scores were set at 85, 85, 90, and 85, respectively.

To check on the effectiveness of these norms, analysis showed that 14 of the 26 poorer workers (54 percent) failed to achieve the minimum scores established as cutting scores for these norms. Of the 42 workers who made qualifying test scores, 30 (71 percent) proved to be good workers. This indicated that if the norms had been used for selection, 54 percent of the poorer workers would not have been hired and 71 percent of those hired would have been good workers. In statistical terms, this represents an r_{tet} of .49 with standard error of .20.

Study of File Clerk (1–17.02). Experimental sample here involved 50 workers, tested before they were hired, and who were selected without regard to test scores. Criterion: supervisory ratings (group ratings in fifths). Test results showed aptitudes with high mean scores relative to the general population and to each other aptitude were: $G. V, S, Q, A,$ and F (see Table 8 for identification of these symbols). Aptitude with low standard deviations relative to the general population and to each other aptitude were $G, P,$ and Q. Aptitudes with r's at the .01 level are $G, V,$ and Q. In the determination of occupational norms, the job analysis showed that $G, V, Q,$ and F warranted consideration for inclusion in the test norms. Taking this into consideration, together with the other statistical results, G and Q were selected, and the critical scores were set at 100 and 95 respectively.

Regarding the effectiveness of these norms, one study showed that 12 of 17 poorer workers (71 percent) failed to achieve these minimum standards. Of the 36 workers who made qualifying test scores, 31 (86 percent) proved to be good workers. This indicated that, if test norms had been used for selection, 71 percent of the poorer workers would not have been hired and 86 percent of those hired would have been good workers. Statistically these data can be summarized by an r_{tet} of .90 with a standard error of .24.

CHECK STUDIES

The USES people are well aware of the necessity of cross-validation studies. It is always unwise to accept the results of any one study as "true" or "final." Whenever possible such studies are conducted, typically with good results. The interested reader may refer to the GATB Manual (U.S. Dept. of Labor, 1958, Sect. III).

It would perhaps be wise to conclude this section on validity with a cautionary note and a specific reference to the indispensable monograph of Ghiselli (1966), which summarizes an enormous literature on personnel testing and the prediction of occupational success. His review was restricted to aptitude tests, and validity is discussed only in connection with prediction of success in training and in level of job proficiency achieved. Only studies involving adults were surveyed, and only investigations in the United States and with American workers were used. The published professional literature from 1919 to the middle of 1964 was canvassed; in addition, Ghiselli reports that numerous unpublished studies, obtained from sources such as industrial and governmental offices, were included. Occupations were grouped, first, in a broad general occupational classification scheme and then, second, according to the codes in the *Dictionary of Occupational Titles* of the U.S. Department of Labor.

Taking individual tests singly, i.e., not reporting results for an entire battery, the conclusions are sobering. For example, Ghiselli states (pp. 120–21) that the grand average of validity coefficients for training criteria is of the order of .30, and for the proficiency criteria around .20. At their worst, these grand average validity coefficients are quite low (at least they are *not* zero), and at their highest they are at least moderate. "It is apparent that even the most optimistic supporter of tests cannot claim that they predict occupational success with what might be termed a high degree of accuracy. Nevertheless, in most situations tests can have a sufficiently high degree of predictive power to be of considerable practical value in the selection of personnel" (p. 127).

PART SIX

Ability
Testing

IT should be no surprise that test administrators also meet situations in which testees are motivated to beat the test. This is especially obvious in selection testing where personality inventories are employed, and there have been many studies to demonstrate faking both "good" and "bad" in these situations. What may not be so obvious is that motivation can make large differences in performance on a mental ability measure, even with testees that would be presumed to be rather unsophisticated about phychological tests.

Dr. Jennings is a member of the staff of the Wharton School of Finance and Commerce at the University of Pennsylvania. The test referred to (Wonderlic Personnel Test) is an industrial version of the Otis Higher Mental Examination. Both tests are widely used mental ability measures, which may be administered in groups and which provide IQ ratings. The article originally appeared in the *Journal of Applied Psychology* in 1953.

THE MOTIVATION FACTOR IN TESTING SUPERVISORS

Eugene E. Jennings

Effectively using psychological testing to aid in selecting supervisory personnel presents an extremely important problem in motivation. The question is whether there are differences in motivation in taking tests for research or for actual promotion purposes. If there are motivational differences between taking tests for research and for keeps, which basis of motivation will elicit test responses that more clearly reflect the individual's actual aptitude?

METHOD

The writer had an opportunity to check this with a sample of 40 supervisors who volunteered initially to participate in a testing program aimed at obtaining for research purposes a measure of the qualities and characteristics identifying the group as a whole. The supervisors were randomly divided into two groups of 20 each. Rough comparability was obtained in age, education, and experience, since differences between these means and sigmas did not exceed the .05 level of significance. The two groups identified as 1 and 2 were given the Wonderlic Personnel Test, Form A.

Three months later the same two groups were given Form B, but supervisors in Control Group 1 were encouraged to cooperate for purely research purposes while supervisors in Experimental Group 2 were asked to cooperate for the purpose of giving management additional information for determining whom among them to promote to higher supervisory levels.

In order to determine which basis of motivation elicited test scores more nearly representative of actual aptitude, a criterion of overall performance was obtained. Superiors knowing each supervisor in Group 1 ranked them from best to poorest on overall performance as defined in a training session. The same procedure was followed in evaluating supervisors in Group 2. A reranking of each supervisor in both groups three months later showed the criterion to have an estimated + .89 reliability. Correlations between test scores and criterion for Groups 1 and 2 for both testing situations were obtained by the rank-difference method.

RESULTS

Table 9 shows the mean scores and sigmas for Groups 1 and 2 with respect to Forms A and B of the Wonderlic Personnel Test.

TABLE 9

SCORES OF THE WONDERLIC TESTS

	Group 1 (N = 20)	Group 2 (N = 20)	d
Form A			
Means	19.1	19.9	.78
Sigmas	5.5	5.0	.44
Form B—3 Months later			
Means	20.0	26.6	6.63*
Sigmas	5.7	6.4	.63

* Indicates significant difference beyond .05 level of confidence.

Whereas the differences in means and sigmas were not significant between the first and second testing for Control Group 1, Experimental Group 2, believing their performance at the second testing would affect their opportunity for promotion, increased their mean score almost seven points.

However, did supervisors in both Group 1 and 2 maintain comparable scores in the two testing situations? The correlations by the rank-differences method between first and second testings were +.76 and +.39, respectively, for Groups 1 and 2. The former but not the latter is significantly greater than zero, since it exceeds the .05 level of confidence.

Generally, supervisors in Group 1 maintained comparable absolute and relative scores in both testing situations. Supervisors in Group 2 did not maintain absolute and relative scores when advised that promotions would be based on test performance. Inspection revealed that several supervisors changed rank-positions from highest to lowest, and in two cases rank values changed while numerical scores did not.

The correlations between test scores and criterion for Groups 1 and 2 were, respectively, +.41 and +.34 for the first testing and +.37 and +.67 for the second testing. Only the last correlation is significantly greater than zero, since it exceeds the .05 level of confidence.

These data tend to indicate that an insignificant relationship existed between test scores and criterion of overall performance when the tests were administered for purely research purposes. However, changing the basis of motivation from that of research to that of promotion purposes brought about a highly significant relationship between test scores and criterion.

It might be interesting to mention that two men from Group 2 were actually promoted since the several supervisors up for consideration were just by chance in Group 2. However, their test scores were not helpful in deciding which of the several to promote since all of their scores on the second test were fairly high. But had scores on the first test, given for purely research purposes, been used to aid management in promoting two supervisors, it is doubtful that the two actually selected would have been, since they had two of the lowest scores in their group.

SUMMARY

The problem of whether there are differences in motivation in taking tests for research or for promotion purposes was studied by giving to a group of supervisors two forms of the Wonderlic Personnel Test with a time interval between for research purposes. A second group took the same two forms but the second administration was with reference to possible promotion. The following results were obtained:

1. The promotion motivation produced significant increases in the mean score whereas the control group showed no such increases.

2. The promotion changed the individual's relative standing in the experimental group as shown by the lower correlations between the two tests than occurred in the control group.

3. Scores motivated by promotion purposes had greater validity, as indicated by correlations with a criterion based on ratings of overall performance.

Although it is very difficult to draw general conclusions, the implications of this study should serve to sound a note of caution to others doing research on aptitude tests in industry to take special pains to control the factor of motivation.

▽ ▽ ▽

THE IQ has come in for a great deal of criticism. An anonymous but facetious critic labeled it "that new tool of infant damnation." This literally becomes very serious business when the IQ score is rigidly used to classify individuals for placement in slow-learner groups in school or, more significantly, when it is used as a basis for commitment to institutions. It is comforting to think that today test users are more sophisticated in IQ interpretation and, in the main, they are. Some school systems, however, still insist that a child's IQ be 74 (and not 75) in order to gain admission to a retarded group. Even more serious are errors that result in commitment to state institutions.

The following report, based on data obtained from the State Home in Beatrice, Nebraska, is by no means a survey of the whole problem. It is to the credit of the professional staff at Beatrice that this study was completed and also that these reexaminations meant the subsequent discharge of the cases reported here. This report is a condensation of the original, which appeared in the *American Journal of Mental Deficiency* in 1960. Drs. Garfield and Affleck are psychologists on the staff of the Nebraska Psychiatric Institute of the University of Nebraska College of Medicine.

A STUDY OF INDIVIDUALS COMMITTED TO A STATE HOME FOR THE RETARDED WHO WERE LATER RELEASED AS NOT MENTALLY DEFECTIVE

S. L. Garfield and D. C. Affleck

The diagnosis of mental deficiency with its concomitant problems is not always as simple a matter as it sometimes appears to be on the surface. Not only are these difficulties in differentiating a mentally retarded person from persons with other types of conditions, but an erroneous diagnosis is one which has very serious consequences for the individual concerned and in many cases for the family as well.

Although problems pertaining to the diagnosis and definition of mental retardation have received some attention, comparatively few research studies have been reported on the occurrence of incorrect diagnosis. The concept of "pseudofeeblemindedness," however, has been one evidence of difficulties in this area. More recently, concern has been expressed over problems in the diagnostic differentiation of mental deficiency from childhood autism and childhood schizophrenia. Obviously, the matter of diagnosis is important for proper treatment and disposition.

We became interested in this problem as a result of coming into contact with some cases diagnosed previously as mentally retarded, but who were found on later examination not to be retarded. On a superficial inspection these cases presented a pattern of factors which had led to institutionalization for mental deficiency or to consideration of such action. Usually the individual displayed some behavioral or social difficulty, there was an inadequate home situation, and an intellectual examination had reported an IQ below 75. In several instances, because of behavioral or personality disturbance, such individuals were studied more intensively in our setting and gave indications that they were intellectually above the retarded level. Sometimes the total score on intellectual tests was not too high, but the variability of intellectual performance suggested a state of emotional disturbance which precluded optimal functioning. We were impressed also with the tendency of some psychological examiners to report psychometric data and IQ scores with little sensitivity to other non-cognitive factors which may affect intellectual performance.

THE PRESENT STUDY

As a consequence we were interested in the problem of individuals incorrectly diagnosed as mentally retarded and in the factors that contribute to such problems in diagnosis. In contacts and visits with the staff of the Beatrice State Home, we were informed of 24 individuals who had been reexamined and found not to be mentally retarded. We decided, therefore, to make a study of these 24 cases. We were interested primarily in seeing what types of cases these were, the factors leading to their institutionalization, and the events responsible for their being judged not mentally retarded with subsequent discharge from the institution.

Fourteen of the group were males and ten were females. The group was predominantly white, with only one Negro. The age of institutionalization varied markedly for the subjects in the present investigation. The youngest was four months of age and oldest was 64 years of age at the time of admission. The period of institutionalization ranged widely—from 1 year 8 months to almost 58 years. Seventeen of the patients had some sort of psychological examination prior to admission and, as might be expected, it was the older cases which had no such examination. While the psychological examinations played a role in the initial admission of most cases, psychological reexaminations at a later time also were instrumental in contributing to the revised judgment concerning the lack of mental retardation.

FACTORS ASSOCIATED WITH COMMITMENT

Although some similarity in patterns was noted among the cases relative to the apparent reasons for admission, there were also unique features which are not too easily categorized. One of the more frequent reasons for being institutionalized appeared to be a combination of social difficulty and lack of an adequate home situation. While this was not always the case, it seemed to be reflected in the comparatively large number who were committed to the

State Home from other types of institutions—training schools, orphanages, state hospitals. The largest single group of individuals in this study were those who came to the State Home from another type of institution—11 of the current group of 24 were in this category. Various factors appeared to play a role in the eventual transfer or commitment of these patients to the State Home. These included behavioral difficulties, poor educational progress, and patterns of behavior judged to be unusual or indicative of mental disability. Generally, the individual was seen as having some type of personality or behavioral disturbance, and in most instances a psychological or psychiatric examination was then requested. If the latter indicated a low IQ or clinical judgment of mental deficiency, plans for a transfer to the State Home were instituted. This appeared to be the pattern for this group of individuals, but, of course, one cannot state on the basis of our data how frequently such a pattern occurs.

In the other cases listed, a variety of factors seemed to be responsible, including physical disability, a disturbed home situation, death of parents, and behavior judged unsatisfactory by others in the community. In several of these cases definite pressures were exerted to have the individual removed from the home or community. In one case, for example, the individual and his brother were abandoned by their mother while the father was in the service. After the father remarried there was continued bickering in the home. The boy began to act out his difficulties by stealing, setting fires, and fighting. During this period he received psychiatric treatment with somewhat variable results. The stepmother insisted on his removal from the home and he was eventually institutionalized in the State Home. In another case, that of a 15-year-old illegitimate girl, institutionalization was requested by a relative with whom she was living and who was unable to control her. In another instance, a 27-year-old woman living with a man in a common law relationship was committed because of complaints of abuse filed by a domestic relations worker.

Thus, while the specific situations varied somewhat, in most instances there were serious difficulties or problems in the current life situation of the individual. External stresses were particularly notable in the case histories of the 14 individuals who were committed prior to their 18th birthday. Very atypical environmental situations are seen in the fact that eight of these persons were transferred from state or private institutions and three others came directly from a disrupted or inadequate home situation.

PSYCHOLOGICAL TEST RESULTS

Because the results of the psychological examination played a significant role in the commitment or eventual discharge of a number of these persons, it is of some importance to make a separate analysis of these findings.[1] Seven

---

[1] Table III in the original report should be consulted for details.

of the subjects had no psychological examination prior to commitment, and these tended to be those institutionalized some years ago. In some instances the name of the test was not indicated in the reports in the case records. In a few cases also, the individual received an extensive battery of tests including special and less-known instruments, and these results are not included.

The range of scores and the variation in findings are of considerable interest, even though a competent clinical psychologist today would not base his diagnostic impression on the IQ alone. Without question, however, the IQ played an important role in the commitment of the majority of these cases. Where a low IQ was obtained prior to commitment it was apparently seized upon or utilized as a means of committing the individual to the State Home. At least from the material available for some cases, one received a feeling that the individual was viewed as a problem and the opportunity to dispose of the problem was not to be slighted. For example, in one case when the re-examination at the State School revealed the individual was not retarded and this was communicated to the original institution, the latter stated the IQ didn't matter, since the person was a difficult problem. In this instance and in a few others there was decided reluctance to take the individual back.

A few comments can be offered with regard to psychological examinations performed prior to commitment. While most of the IQs obtained were low, little allowance was made in the psychological reports for possible emotional factors which conceivably might have contributed to the lowered level of performance. If a number of these individuals were experiencing difficulties, were away from their home and family, or conceivably were anxious about the test situation, little was said about this and apparently it was not deemed to be of much significance. This was so, even though other data available on the cases, including psychiatric appraisals, made mention of personality difficulties, frequently of severe degree. It is of interest that seven of the 17 cases examined psychologically prior to commitment had been examined psychiatrically or received psychiatric treatment. Nevertheless, little mention was made in the psychological report of the possible influence of such disturbance on test performance. In some instances mention was made of the negativeness or inadequate cooperation of the subject, but this did not seem to influence the interpretation of the test scores. In general, the emphasis was placed on the IQ score and the interpretation of mental deficiency was followed by a prognostic statement to the effect that the individual would never progress beyond a limited level of mental development. Commitment was also recommended in most instances. By and large, these reports were quite positive in terms of the definiteness and conclusiveness of findings. In most instances, they were performed by psychologists who had not received any extensive training in clinical psychology.

In two cases, IQs in the 80's were reported, but the individual still was committed or retained in the institution. In one of these cases an IQ of 88 by a qualified psychologist was followed by three lower IQs reported by psychologists with limited clinical training. Even though the report containing the 88 IQ mentioned the possibility of significant emotional disturbance in the child, the later IQs carried the day and the child was institutionalized by order of the court. In the other such case, institutionalization occurred prior to the psychological examination. This took place 40 years ago and the data are meager. However, the individual remained in the institution approximately 35 years after an IQ of 87 was obtained.

The IQs secured at a later date in the State Home average considerably higher than those secured earlier. Unfortunately, in not all cases was a psychological examination performed prior to institutionalization, nor was the same test always used in the later examination. This makes the matter of evaluation and interpretation of the data somewhat more complicated. Obviously, different factors might be involved in the various cases, and perhaps no definitive conclusions can be drawn. After reviewing all the available data, however, the present authors believe that the most apparent explanation, at least in a large percentage of those cases tested prior to commitment, concerns the inadequacy of the original examination and the failure to evaluate the importance of emotional factors on intelligence test scores. In over half of these cases, there were data already available pointing to the existence of personality and behavioral disturbance at the time of testing. Secondly, even the brief reports by the examiners made mention of some resistiveness, peculiarity, or other unusual behavior on the part of the subject which was not considered in the evaluation of the test data. To the experienced clinician, this appeared to be definite disregard of personality variables as they affect test scores. Thirdly, in four cases which were examined at our institute, the pattern of test scores and the behavior evident during the testing situation led the clinical psychologist to consider personality disturbance as a significant variable affecting test scores. In these instances, the psychologists felt the patients' intellectual potentials were above that of the mental defective level. Other factors which seemed to play a role in the original test scores were that the individuals were examined at a time when they were experiencing some type of adjustment difficulty, were separated from home and family, were anxious or lacked motivation. It is a time honored colloquialism in mental testing that the examiner must secure rapport and cooperation with the subject in order to secure optimum results. If there seem to be factors interfering with this, the results probably cannot be viewed as valid. This view seemed to be disregarded completely in some of the cases.

While the authors were most impressed with the lack of concern on the part of previous examiners for variables which affect test scores, other explanations are also possible for some of the cases. In two cases (5 and 9), an additional explanation seems obvious. In these two instances, examinations were performed at or before age two, with IQs in the neighborhood of 50. The IQs at later ages on the 1937 Stanford-Binet and WISC were in the 80's. This is in line with other studies indicating the relatively poor predictive ability of infant testing. In the third case tested originally at age two, the differences between the early scores and the later ones were not as marked.

Obviously, the findings discussed do not lead automatically to definite interpretations or conclusions. The writers, in going through the case material, were struck with the very inadequate job of psychological examination in a majority of cases, the lack of sensitivity to the importance of personality factors on test scores, and the almost exclusive reliance on the IQ. To us, this was a disturbing finding with very important social consequences. However, other problems also appear to be raised by our data, even though the latter are limited. One concerns the dangers of relying on the results of tests at or before age two. The other, concerning lack of comparability between tests, also has significant practical implications, since most individuals outside of professional psychology tend to react to all IQs as equivalent, regardless of the test used. When differences occur, which IQ's shall be considered as a basis for practical decisions? While it is certainly true that important decisions should be based on more than the IQ, our data strongly suggest that the IQ carries tremendous weight in such decisions.

FACTORS LEADING TO DISCHARGE

The majority of individuals discharged were identified primarily by two means. One of these was a retesting program instituted relatively recently. The other was the result of someone on the staff noting that an individual functioned better than expected. In these instances the individual was given a psychological examination, and if it appeared to indicate that the individual was not mentally retarded, attempts were made to have the individual discharged. Although various staff members were involved with some of these individuals, it appeared that the staff social workers were those most frequently requesting a re-evaluation because certain individuals impressed them as not being retarded. In one instance, a re-evaluation was requested by an outside agency. The psychologist's findings indicated the individual was not mentally deficient, and a recommendation for discharge was made. In three instances, various patterns of acting out or related problems led to evaluation at our own institution. It can be noted also that generally it was more difficult to get an individual out of the institution than it was to get him in. Not only are there numerous problems to consider in getting a person back into the community at large, but in some instances there was definite opposition from the community organizations which played a role in the original institutionalization. This is another reason why errors in diagnosis leading to unnecessary or inappropriate institutionalization have unhappy consequences.

DISCUSSION

Our data appear to lend support for the need to evaluate the influence of emotional and environmental factors on tests of intelligence. Such considerations were rarely suggested in pre-commitment reports in this sample. Apparently in the desire to appear "objective," great reliance was placed on test scores alone. This reliance was not only evident in the reports, but in the reaction of social agencies and the courts to the evaluation. Credence is readily granted a reported test score because of its ease of statement and seeming objectivity. When argument did occur initially in some pre-commitment cases, it was largely over discrepant IQ scores. The misuse of IQ scores is very evident in subsequent correspondence about the cases. In some instances, the scores are cited as authoritative estimates of intellectual potential or as positive indications of how much ability the person has, e.g., "This boy has 50 percent intelligence." "This girl has an IQ of 66 percent; and since feeblemindedness may be quantitatively defined as any score below 70 percent, she may be considered definitely feebleminded and classified as a moron."

In the light of these misuses, one may question the advisability of report-ing IQs. Very few persons who use psychological reports appear to under-stand that any IQ is only a means of ranking a person relative to a standardi-zation group, and that when emotional disturbance is present, such ranking may not be reliable. For such reasons, it seems preferable to have a qualita-tive evaluation of intellectual functioning where the clinical psychologist translates his test findings into language which is meaningful to laymen and not as subject to misinterpretation.

Somewhat related to these considerations are the problems concerning the limitations of test results secured at very early ages and the matter of comparability of scores on different tests. Undoubtedly more careful re-search on these problems is needed, particularly in terms of which tests ap-pear to correlate most with other criteria of social adjustment.

The high percentage (46 percent) of cases in this sample of patients who came from other institutions is also a finding of considerable interest. It would appear that in these cases also, too great attention was given to intel-lectual factors and test scores when these were in great part symptoms of broader emotional disturbance. The basis for this may rest on the historical availability of institutional care for the mentally retarded and a failure to be adequately sensitive to the total functioning of the person. Where below average (or dull normal) intelligence is combined with anti-social behavior, inadequate home situation or emotional disturbance, institutionalization in a home for the retarded may be viewed as a solution to the problem, partic-ularly if under stress the IQ falls close to the mentally retarded range. It is also possible that unless a child shows grossly psychotic behavior, emotional factors do not receive primary consideration. Related to this may be the fact that institutional facilities for emotionally-disturbed children are relatively scarce and perhaps reserved for those of higher intelligence and grosser dis-turbance. Outpatient treatment probably is not considered when the home situation is unstable. The net result is that the individual is incorrectly diag-nosed and inappropriately institutionalized.

Finally, it should be stated that we have no precise estimate of the extent of the problem reported on here. The current sample is not the result of a statistical survey, and there are undoubtedly variations from setting to setting. Nevertheless, it does emphasize a problem which, though small in number, is important in terms of the welfare of the individual. Periodic re-appraisals of the institutionalized individuals in the higher ranges of the mentally retarded would appear justified.

IN any cross-cultural setting, one of the real difficulties is to find adequate or fair mental ability measures. Usually, nonverbal materials have been applied, but these also can be easily loaded with specific cultural referents. The problem has usually been "solved" by employing matrices of varying degrees of complexity. Cattell and Raven are two British researchers who have prepared such tests. Cattell has produced evidence that these types of tests are loaded with "g," and that this "g" may be separated into "fluid" and "crystallized" intelligence. It is his belief that a culture-fair test should be loaded with the "fluid" kind of "g."

Culture-fair tests would appear to have great utility in testing the various under-privileged groups that elicit so much interest now. It would be helpful here to be able to compare such individuals with this kind of test score as against the more conventional measures of mental ability known to have a built-in cultural bias.

Not all test specialists are so enthusiastic about this possibility. Critics point out the problem has two aspects—measurement of general intelligence and elimination of cultural influences. Simultaneously accomplishing both of these objectives may be impossible. Probably nobody has as yet produced a really satisfactory culture-fair test. Cattell's success in this area is, however, at least partial, and the topic is introduced here as an interesting variant in the area of intelligence testing.

Professor Cattell is research professor of psychology at the University of Illinois, and is widely known for his ingenious and diverse tests of aptitudes and abilities and the like. The following remarks about the culture-fair test (labeled "culture-free" when first published) are taken, with some deletions, from his 1965 book (pp. 301–9).

SOME PRACTICAL IMPLICATIONS OF THE THEORY OF FLUID AND CRYSTALLIZED GENERAL ABILITY

Raymond B. Cattell

The new theory claims that there are actually *two* general ability factors which, from their properties, have been called *fluid* and *crystallized* general ability. In intelligence test practice the quickest way of designating these two is by pointing to the culture-fair and the traditional (verbal and numerical) tests, respectively. Culture-fair tests were implicit in the work of Spearman's students, Fortes, Line, and Cattell, in the late twenties, demonstrating his argument that it does not matter what subject matter is used among the elements between which one asks the subject to perceive relations. Provided the relations are complex enough one can, for instance, generate an analogies test among shades of colour. The systematical application of this to producing tests which would be comparatively free of cultural influences did not begin, however, for nearly another decade, when the present writer, with his students Sarason and Feingold, and Raven in Britain, developed tests which have since been called the I.P.A.T. Culture-Fair Intelligence Scales and the

Progressive Matrices. (The Culture-Fair tests include Matrices as one of four sub-tests.)

The present writer first sought to generate sufficiently complex relations among "fundaments" which are common to people all over the earth and which would not, of course, be presented in verbal symbols, but as pictures. (Intelligence tests given pictorially are, of course, far from culture-free.) It seemed that parts of the human body, sun, moon, and stars were about the only things common to cultures. But, additionally, any shapes on paper, or in plastic, that do not represent objects peculiar to a culture, or have names, proved effective. Figure 3 shows two examples of such material. Such "per-

FIGURE 3

A Series Test in a Culture-Fair Intelligence Test

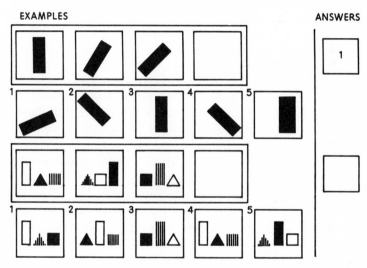

ceptual" tests were shown by Feingold, Sarason, and other researchers with the present writer, as well as by Raven, (*a*) to correlate very well with general intelligence estimates and the general factor—much better than "performance tests" with form boards, etc., and (*b*) to show no cultural effects. For example, Feingold compared immigrants to the U.S. on these and traditional tests (1) on entering, and (2) a year or more after acclimatizing. The traditional tests were woefully misleading but the culture-fair stood firm. The C. F. tests have since been shown to be effective in China, Africa, India, and across most culture varieties.

What is called the *fluid* general ability factor (because it is free of particular investments) shows itself particularly in the culture-fair tests but also by other characteristics. First, it separates as a distinct but correlated factor from crystallized ability. Secondly, as an ability to perceive relationships in any material, new or old, it reaches its maximum level at about fourteen or fifteen years, as the brain finishes its growth. But crystallized ability may go on being deposited with further investments in training, education, and experience beyond this age and in college populations the test performance curve does not "flatten out" till twenty-one or so. Age or brain injury may bring a general reduction of the fluid ability level, but the crystallized ability retains the "shape" which fluid ability and experience have given to it—just as the coral rock formation retains the form reached by the once living coral organism, so that only quite special areas, such as verbal facility, may be damaged.

This metaphor of a coral growth brings us to the crux of the meaning of "two general abilities" and requires that we take stock of our understanding of the statistical pattern which we have all along been calling a "factor." Fluid ability appears as a general factor because it is some sort of active mental capacity or energy, which is thrown now into this problem and now into that. The different performances correlate, i.e. a person high in one tends to be high in all, because people differ in their endowment in it, and it is the same force now exerted here and now there. But the correlation found among the parts of the crystallized general ability, e.g. between judgment in English, in mathematics, in history, etc., is of a different origin. It springs largely from the uniformity of our school curriculum, whereby a person who has been twice as long at school as another will simultaneously know *more* of all these things. If this is the case, one may ask: "What then is the difference between crystallized intelligence and what we simply call general school achievement?" General school achievement includes much that is known merely by rote, i.e. by good memory and school interest, and which required no great fluid intelligence for its acquisition. What we call crystallized intelligence is the collection of *skilled judgments* a person has acquired by applying his fluid intelligence to his school opportunities. It is a sort of "holding company" for what fluid intelligence and school experience have jointly produced, and as such it has a life of its own in that its skills tend to generate more skills like them.

The difference of fluid and crystallized ability is brought out most clearly if we consider persons raised in two different cultures, say in Britain and France. It would be unfair to make any precise inference about an English seventeen-year-old's intelligence from his decisions on the correctness of synonyms in French or the shrewdness of his comment on the domestic policies of Louis Quinze. Within any culture the differences are not so great, but social status, locality, and opportunity differences still make the correlation between fluid and crystallized ability only about $+0.6$, not the $+1.0$ which would justify deriving an estimate of a child's natural, fluid intelligence by the traditional intelligence test (crystallized ability) rather than by the fluid intelligence factor (as in a culture-fair intelligence test). Again, this can be sharply brought home by the fact that one simply cannot compare, say, American and Chinese children on an intelligence test by an American or Chinese intelligence test. Yet, when the I.P.A.T. Culture-Fair test is used, the Chinese in Taiwan and the Americans in Illinois have been demonstrated to possess almost exactly the same average score and scatter. Naturally, the mere fact that the identical test gives the same score in these two circumstances does not alone prove that the test is getting at native ability. A good culture-fair test should *sometimes* decline to show differences between people in different cultures because the cultures may alone distinguish them, but at other times it should even show differences when both groups are within one culture. Such tests, in fact, show lower scores from the north island of Japan than from the south (a fact which Japanese understand), and lower scores in southern Italy than the north (a fact which Italians understand). The finding that Chinese in China score the same as Americans fits other indications of Chinese intelligence, such as the equal performance of their descendants in America in traditional intelligence tests in English. (The prize for Gaelic poetry has recently been given to a Chinese girl brought up in Ireland.) Whether the lower scores found on these tests by anthropologists working in the Congo is to be explained by temporary conditions is something for science to investigate.

Within one country the discrepancy between individual intelligence levels as measured respectively by traditional "crystallized" intelligence factor measures and culture-fair measures of the fluid ability factor is not great *during the growth period*. But after school there is increasing divergence. One person may begin investing his fluid ability in entirely new fields—say mining engineering—while another becomes a school-teacher and another concentrates on the verbal skills of a journalist. Because skilled habits in any field get dusty with disuse, the traditional intelligence test, like the Terman-Binet, the Wechsler, W.A.I.S., etc., will deal rather unfairly with the cowboy, the farmer, or mining engineer, compared with the teacher or journalist, if they are retested at, say, forty years of age. This has been noted in the selection problems of Mensa, a society in England and America, entry to which depends democratically upon the individual, no matter what his background, scoring above a stipulated high I.Q. level on an adult intelligence test. The selections made by traditional tests (the Cattell Scale III, for superior adults) and culture-fair tests have only a moderate degree of consensus. In Figure 4 the two coordinates represent scores on the two types of test, the angle between them being adjusted to give the correlation of about 0.7, which is approximately correct for such tests among *general adults*. (Among students, having the same educational background, the agreement would be much higher than 0.7.) It will be seen that the same cut-off points—the top 5 percent and the top 10 percent on the two tests—garners a different crop, and that the number in common to the two crops gets lower as the selection point is made higher. In one survey made by the writer the highest score on the I.P.A.T. Culture-Fair was made by a young sailor—a very intelligent man who, through an adventurous and easy-going temperament, had become a deck-hand—and the highest score in the Cattell Scale III traditional test by a classics student at Oxford. Each was pretty high on the other test too, but if we accept fluid ability as "native intelligence" the sailor was the

FIGURE 4

DIFFERENCES EXPECTED IN SELECTION OF BRIGHT PEOPLE ON CULTURE-
FAIR AND TRADITIONAL INTELLIGENCE TESTS

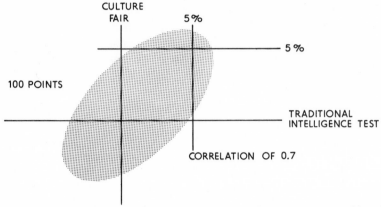

1 percent are in common to the groups formed by the top 5 percent by culture-fair and traditional intelligence tests.

brighter man. The difference in membership of such a society, according to whether it adopted the fluid or a crystallized intelligence factor as its definition of intelligence, illustrates the general importance of the choice of test in the social application of intelligence tests.

However, the greater discrepancy between fluid and crystallized scores among adults arises not only from the fact that crystallized ability is no longer being "pushed along," just ahead of, and by the growing fluid ability in the common learning environment of the school. For a gap between them develops also from the fact that fluid ability can *sink down* below its late adolescent level. To take an extreme case, a brain injury to the parietal area of Broca may cause some *general* loss of fluid, adaptive ability, but in the crystallized ability measurements it will affect only one of the circle of skills commonly measured in such an intelligence test, in that it will cause specifically some verbal aphasia, i.e. a loss of skilled use of words. Thus if the traditional test used happens to measure the individual on crystallized abilities *not* affected by the locality of injury a wrong impression of his general mental capacity is obtained.

In adult life particularly, when a prediction is required of how intelligently a person will operate in some entirely new field, e.g. in wartime induction testing, assigning new job areas, a fluid ability measure by a culture-fair test is the wiser measure to use. But even at the school age where the two measures are usually in closer agreement, injustices can be done by a test which looks backward to past opportunities rather than forward to potential performance in a new type of school. The word of Dr. Douglas and his colleagues at the London School of Economics brings this out clearly by showing that on traditional intelligence tests the average IQ of children from lower social status homes drops relative to that of more environmentally favoured children when retested over the age range from eight to eleven plus. For if the alleged intelligence test is actually contaminated with school achievement and home cultural background, the obtained apparent I.Q. will deviate from its proper constancy in the one case in an upward and in the other in a downward direction.

In the coming decade, with increasing interest of the general public in effective and fair application of mental tests, we are likely to see considerable debate on the proper roles respectively of traditional and culture-fair tests. Against the advantages of the latter, two arguments are likely to appear. First, they do not have "face validity." That is to say it is hard to see from looking at them why they test intelligence. For example, a frequent comment is "This test involves no word skills whatever. How can it possibly predict capacity to succeed in English?" The professional psychologist, but not the general public, has long given up face validity (or "faith validity" as the specialist calls it), recognizing that the first reaction of the general public to the automobile was "How can it possibly go without a horse?" In one group in which varied students were subsequently subjected to intensive English training the culture-fair actually predicted English achievement better than an ordinary verbal intelligence test.

A second criticism is that *within the same year* and among students *all in the same kind of school,* the culture-fair does not correlate with ("predict") achievement quite so highly as the traditional test. This is not only admitted, but treasured by the exponent of the newer tests. The reason that the traditional test gives a better immediate "prediction" is that it already contains an appreciable admixture of the school achievement it is supposed to predict. If all we want to do is predict, in March, children's school achievement in, say, July, we can do better than any intelligence test by predicting from their school achievement scores in March. The very object of an intelligence test, however, is to be *analytical.* As we study any individual child we are terested in the *discrepancy* between his native intelligence and his school achievement, and the more clearly and reliably this is brought out the better the test. The claim of the culture-fair tests is that it will make a more fair selection for future performance when the passage of some years has given a chance for the present accidental inequalities of achievement opportunity to be ironed out.

Beyond two such apparently real criticisms it has been said by shrewd observers that since the professional interest of educators and sociologists is specifically in culture they are not likely to be enthusiastic about a measurement which aims to ignore it. Indeed, it is less than a generation since the majority of sociologists taught their students that there are no innate differences in intelligence, and that "native intelligence" must be a figment of the imagination. The researcher's position is that it is possible to infer the relative contribution of genetic and environment variation to the observed population variance in any trait. What fresh light does this newer analysis of intelligence into two general factors throw on the old and vexed question of how far intelligence is inborn? With tests in use before the advent of culture-fair scales an 80/20 percent ratio in favour of heredity has commonly been found, but recent results suggest that the hereditary determination is higher than this for fluid ability and possibly lower for crystallized ability. However, one must insist that the constitutional determination is still well short of 100 percent for fluid ability, i.e. it is not properly labelled the individual's innate ability level. For its level is affected by accidents of gestation and birth, and thereafter by physiological environment, head injuries, etc., if not by the school environment of the individual. Thus this issue, like many others, is likely to become more understandable as research clarifies the new theory of two general ability factors, fluid and crystallized.

Ability testing historically began with global measures such as *general* intelligence but with the advent of factor analysis, test batteries sampling not one but several types of aptitudes have been constructed. Such factorially pure test batteries, typically known as "multifactor" batteries, logically would have the advantage since they so economically could measure a wide sampling of different abilities and aptitudes. Research has shown, however, that these multifactor tests tend to be less predictive of school or occupational success than do batteries which have been specifically developed or "tailor-made" for that purpose. But for the purposes of guidance and counseling—as against the more specific personnel goal of selection whether for medical school or success on the job—the multifactor test battery has the advantage.

The following article by Dr. Super, reproduced here with only minor editorial changes, served as the introduction to a series of seven specific reviews of multifactor tests which appeared in the *Personnel & Guidance Journal* and beginning in the September, 1956 issue. The batteries later discussed are the Differential Aptitude Tests, the General Aptitude Test Battery,[1] the Guilford-Zimmerman Aptitude Survey, the Crowder Unifactor Tests, the Primary Mental Ability Tests, the Factored Aptitude Series (by King), the Multiple Aptitude Test (by Segal), and last, the Flanagan Aptitude Classification Test. The idea for this series grew out of the Conference on Using Multifactor Aptitude Tests in Educational and Vocational Counseling and Prediction, held in June, 1953, at the University of California.

Dr. Super is professor of psychology and education at Teachers College, Columbia University, and currently is perhaps best known for his longitudinal Career Pattern Study tracing the vocational development of approximately 275 8th and 9th grade boys from a single New York State community. Data collection for the study was begun in 1951 (Super *et al.*, 1957).

THE USE OF MULTIFACTOR
TEST BATTERIES IN GUIDANCE

Donald E. Super

In recent years a number of batteries of tests based on factor analysis have been offered to the public for use in guidance. This represents something new, for in earlier years factor analysis had served solely as a tool for researchers interested in the structure of mental abilities and human traits. Its practical use has only been recent.

Such being the case, it is desirable to take stock, to see just what is the current state of development of these instruments. It is important to understand the structure of mental abilities, but for the practicing counselor or admissions officer the vital question is the educational and vocational significance of these mental abilities or factors. Counselors need to know what the

---

[1] See pp. 117–28 for a discussion of this test battery.

scientific-appearing batteries of tests indicate as to an individual's prospects of success and satisfaction in various fields of study and of work.

A dim view of multifactor test batteries is taken by Cronbach in the 1956 issues of *Annual Review of Psychology* (pp. 177–178). He writes: "We conclude that while factorial scores may be useful for a theory of abilities, as soon as testors make inferences to behavior in significant situations," *e.g.,* predict success in school subjects, "they encounter the same troubles as personality assessors" who attempt to forecast behavior in unknown situations on the basis of data on personality structure. "Group factors serve only when regression equations are constructed about the criterion in a single institution." Cronbach goes on to cite the withdrawal of the *American Council on Education Psychological Examination* from the market, and its replacement by a measure of verbal and quantitative achievement (the *Cooperative School and College Ability Test*), as further evidence of the dubious status of differential aptitude testing.

This is in sharp contrast with the more optimistic views taken by both Cronbach (1949, p. 234) and the present author (1949, p. 358) in 1949, when the latter wrote: "The days of the publication of isolated tests of single aptitudes will no doubt soon be past," and Cronbach wrote: "In due time we may anticipate that pure, psychologically valid tests can be developed which will have empirical validity adequate for vocational and educational guidance."

How justifiable is Cronbach's pessimism concerning multifactor test batteries for guidance? To what extent have they lived, or failed to live, up to the great promise of the 1940's?

THE DESIDERATA OF GUIDANCE TESTS

What are the desirable characteristics of a test or battery of tests to be used in guidance? One could, of course, give an elementary textbookish answer to such a question, but let us take reliability for granted, and talk in terms which are more concrete and operational than the usual language of reliability and validity.

Tests for use in counseling should *describe* a person so that we can see him as he is at the time of testing; they should *predict* what he will be like and what he will do at some future date; they should be relatively *timeless;* and they should, like the people they test, be *multipotential.* Let me elaborate on each of these points.

Tests Should Describe. They should tell something of the make-up of the student or client at the time of testing, how he compares in intelligence, in perceptual speed, in finger dexterity, in computational interest, or in social dominance with other students at the same educational level or of the same age. They should tell what curricular and occupational groups he resembles, and how closely he resembles them. One of the purposes of testing is to get a picture of the person with whom one is dealing, to see to what degree he has a variety of psychological characteristics, where his relative strengths and weaknesses are, and how he compares in each of these characteristics with others who have had comparable experiences and have reached a comparable stage of development, or who are engaged in activities in which he might engage. Having a picture of the stage of development attained by the individual, and of his make-up at that stage, one has a basis for understanding better his recent and present performances, and for setting up reasonable hypotheses concerning the nature of his future development and behavior.

Tests Should Predict.   Tests should have some value as indicators of probable status, behavior, achievement, and satisfaction in the future. There are two aspects to this kind of prediction, one being the prediction of what the individual *will be like,* the other the prediction of *what he will do* or how he will react, in the future. Both are important, for in guidance one needs to understand what the student or client will be like, and even more to understand what he will be able to do and how he will like doing it. Predictions of achievement need to be educational and occupational: they need to clarify the would-be medical student's prospects of success in medical school, and to provide evidence as to his probable success and satisfaction in the practice of medicine. Too often, in the case of the professions which require long periods of training, only the former type of validity data are available; but it is in these very same occupations that the size of the investment in training makes it especially important that the investment pays dividends in the long run in the vocational success and satisfaction of the person who obtained the training. And as Ghiselli has pointed out (1966, pp. 118–119), the much used training criteria have little relationship to job criteria.

For example, Strong and Tucker's work with physicians (1952) showed that men who completed medical training, but who lacked the interests which are typical of physicians, tended to shift from medical practice to administrative work in which their medical training was not essential. A good instrument such as Strong's could have been used to help these men see that they would in due course find more satisfaction in administrative work than in the practice of medicine. Had this fact been known when they were thinking of entering medicine, and had other opportunities which were equally attractive in income and prestige been made obvious to them, they might have made more economical choices.

Tests Should Be Timeless.   Tests can, of course, be timeless only in a relative sense, but differences in the timelessness of aptitude tests are well illustrated by the Meier and McAdory Art Tests, which were first published in 1929. By 1940 the latter test was quite unusable, because many of the items included in the test smacked strongly of the 1920's and looked absurd two decades later, particularly the hats and skirts of the flapper years and the angular automobiles which went with them. The Meier Test, on the other hand, was in this respect as usable in 1940 as in the mid-twenties, for the art forms used in its pictures were good in the Renaissance and are good today, and the forms used in the vases and other items pictured in the test have been good at least since the days of ancient Greece. In such instances, norms collected at some time past, and validities established in longitudinal studies covering a period of years, are not likely to be outdated so soon as to make the test useless. That is, they will not be outdated if the occupation in question has not undergone substantial change, and if the population from which it draws is still substantially the same. Thus Stewart (1947) has shown that, in general, occupational intelligence requirements changed little from 1918 to 1945.

Tests Should Be Multipotential.   People are, occupationally speaking, multipotential. They are not square pegs, able to fit only into square holes, nor are they round pegs able to fit only into the round holes. If they were, all one would need would be one test to measure squareness, another to measure roundness, and counseling and selection would be simple. People are polygonal, and so are jobs; in both instances the polygons have so many sides that each person fits more or less easily into a great variety of holes. Test batteries and the tests which make them up, therefore, need to be so constructed that they can be applied to people in a great variety of occupations, and, once normed and validated, used with each person tested for the evaluation of his promise for a number of different fields.

Suppose, for example, that tests useful for predicting success in engineering were useful only for that one occupation, and that the same were true also of medicine, dentistry, and chemistry. In counseling a college bound high school senior who is thinking about all four of these possibilities, one would have to find time for four different batteries of tests, of some three to six hours each—an impossible demand both on the time of the student and on that of the counselor. But this is exactly what develops from the construction of one test or battery for the selection or counseling of engineering students, another for use with medical students, and so on. From the point of view of a school or organization selecting students or employees, this may be the most economical procedure, but it does not result in instruments which are economical or useful for counseling individuals concerning educational and vocational choices.

THE PECULIARITIES OF MULTIFACTOR TEST BATTERIES

Factorial Purity.   While batteries of tests such as the Differential Aptitude Tests and the General Aptitude Test Battery have not uniformly striven for factorial purity, they have tended to aim at measuring either pure factors or constellations of closely related factors. Thus the GATB is based on one of the most extensive factor analysis studies so far completed, and the test scores are combined to give scores based on the factor loading of tests. While the DAT includes such impure tests as the Mechanical Reasoning Test, with its loadings of heavy spatial, reasoning, and information factors, this was done as an exception to a rule which was observed in the case of less complex tests such as those of spatial reasoning, verbal reasoning, and perceptual speed and accuracy. Other batteries such as Guilford's, Flanagan's, Holzinger's, and King's have striven for factorial purity.

This is, of course, well known. But the fact bears stressing because of what it means in terms of the desiderata of guidance tests. It means that multi-factor test batteries *are* likely to be *descriptive, multipotential,* and *timeless;* it also means that they are *likely not to be as predictive* as certain other types of tests. Let me justify each of these brief statements.

The tendency of developers of multifactor test batteries to strive for factorial purity in their tests, resulting as it does in minimal overlapping of the tests, provides scores for traits or aptitudes which, as data accumulate, have a maximum of psychological meaning. While it is true that factor names such as "Factor Q" do not convey much to the user, that even somewhat more descripive labels such as "Memory I" and Memory II" tell little, and that there is often room for disagreement in naming factors, in due course the study of such factors results in agreement on meaningful names. The terms "spatial visualization," "perceptual speed," "numerical reasoning," all of them derived from or further developed by factorial studies, have come to have considerable psychological meaning, even though at first they were used only as descriptions of what seemed to be the process underlying a particular task with a particular type of test item. These terms have proved to be much more meaningful than terms such as "mechanical aptitude" applied to the scores derived from such diverse tests as the O'Rourke and McQuarrie, useful though these tests have been.

Multipotentiality has, of course, been one of the prime objectives of the developers of multifactor tests, and has been invitable in view of the emphasis on measuring basic psychological characteristics. For if each of the aptitudes measured is important in a variety of occupations and if it is measured in relatively pure form, its true role in each occupation can be ascertained, unobscured by other factors which are specific to one or to a few occupations but are not always associated with the basic factor being measured. For example, a test of spatial visualization will contribute to a prediction of success both in engineering and in art, whereas a test of mechanical aptitude can be used only for the former. This is because the latter is heavily enough weighted with the mechanical information factor that its spatial factor is rendered inoperative in the prediction of artistic success. A battery of tests measuring relatively pure factors can thus be normed and validated for a great variety of occupations and for a great variety of curricula, and a given student's promise for a large number of fields can be appraised in a relatively brief testing session, at least in the institution in which the validity (regression) data are obtained.

The emphasis on factorial purity has meant, also, an emphasis on relatively simple, abstract types of items. Often these are geometric, numerical, or verbal, of a type which lacks easily dated content and which is therefore relatively timeless. The items are, for instance, more likely to resemble those of the undateable Likert-Quasha Revision of the Minnesota

Paper Form Board, or the relatively timeless names and numbers of the Minnesota Clerical Test, than the Model-T Ford parts which appear in one form of the O'Rourke Mechanical Aptitude Test.

All of these outcomes of the tendency to aim at factorial purity are good; one other is not so beneficial. This is the unfortunate tendency of factorially pure tests to be less predictive of success in a given subject or occupation than tests which are developed specifically for that purpose. The factorially pure test, we have seen, tends to be abstract and general in its content. It is the direct opposite of the miniature situation test, which attempts to reproduce in a small way the complexity of the subject or job itself. The miniature situation test, and work sample, copying as it does the tasks of processes of the activity or occupation, taps a great variety of abilities called for in the work. Some of these are measured fairly well by the factor-tests of the battery, but some are specific enough not to be included in the battery. Even the aptitudes common to both tests are, in the miniature situation test, measured in a form more like that in which they are tapped by the job than they are in the more abstract multifactor battery. The specificity of the miniature situation test gives it a validity which is greater than that of the more generally applicable but hence less specific multifactor test. In this way the multifactor test battery is truly a guidance test battery, whereas the miniature situation test is more truly a selection test, and a custom-built test at that.

This lessened predictive value of the multifactor test is the price of versatility. Apparently one cannot eat one's cake and have it too, at least not in aptitude testing. Custom-built tests for the selection of employees for a given job, in a given organization, are better than standard tests even when the latter are locally standardized for the same purpose. But they are not as good for counseling possible entrants into that occupation in any of a number of companies as are tests which have been standardized on a more varied sample of members of that occupation. Specific factors which make the custom-built test the best for its peculiar situation make it only second best for a variety of situations. Similarly, extraneous factors in the miniature situation test contribute to its validity for some purposes even though they minimize its validity for others. Hence the battery of tests which aim at versatility tends to miss some relatively specific factors and to lose some specific validity. It has been demonstrated that batteries of multifactor tests can have extremely high validities, if those reported in the revised manual for the GATB can be taken at face value. This is, however, made somewhat difficult by the fact that, as Cronbach puts it (1956, p. 177): "Striking variation is found in concurrent correlations with different achievement measures in the same field and with different samples. The tests often do not correlate where they are expected to correlate."

THE CHARACTERISTICS OF AVAILABLE MULTIFACTOR BATTERIES

Initial concern with factorial purity in the development of multifactor batteries led to an emphasis on the internal validity of the tests, on questions, that is, of internal consistency and of the independence of the various scores. The work of Thurstone well illustrates this emphasis. The Guilford-Zimmerman Aptitude Survey is another illustration of the primary concern with establishing the factorial purity of the tests, and of the tendency to minimize the importance of external validity.

This emphasis has been rather frustrating to those who use tests in guidance, because factorial purity does not help much unless one knows the practical significance of the factors which are being measured. But it has been an essential first stage in the development of multifactor test batteries; the tool has to be shaped before it can be put to use. The expectation is that the theoretical preoccupations of the test constructors result in better instruments once they are ready for use.

How ready are they for use? The answer varies, of course, with the battery. One of the functions of test manuals is to give the potential test user the information necessary for judging the readiness of a test or battery for a particular use. The two most widely used multifactor batteries are among the oldest of their types, and are also the two which have been most studied from the point of view of external validity. One of them, the differential Aptitude Test Battery, has been used primarily in studies of educational success; the other, the General Aptitude Test Battery, has been validated largely for occupational success. In both cases a large number of studies have been completed, and in both cases the results of these studies have been incorporated in revised manuals. Thus users may judge the validity of the tests for their particular purposes and be guided by the known relationships of the tests to success in various types of endeavor when counseling students and clients. It is no exaggeration to state that no *aptitude* tests have ever been accompanied by such a mass and variety of validity data as are these two batteries; in fact, probably only the Stanford-Binet and Strong's Vocational Interest Blank, both of them considerably older than these batteries, can compete with them in this respect.

It has been shown that even tests which strive for factorial purity generally do not approach it very closely. For example, Thurstone's Primary Mental Ability Tests have moderately high intercorrelations; the median intercorrelations of the tests and of the factors in the GATB are, respectively, 0.35 and 0.30; and the Differential Aptitude Tests intercorrelate somewhat more highly than this, as might be anticipated from their lesser emphasis on factorial purity. The intercorrelations of the tests in the batteries result, as the Differential Aptitude Tests manual shows, in a somewhat distressing uniformity of validity, i.e., in a somewhat discouraging lack of differential validity, in the tests and aptitudes measured. By this it is meant that one finds that some tests are *generally* rather good predictors, verbal reasoning for example. Similarly, others are generally rather poor predictors, for instance perceptual speed and finger dexterity. This is true no matter what the type of achievement being predicted. Perhaps this makes the situation seem worse than it actually is, and certainly this is less true of some batteries than of others, but there is a tendency of this type in the validity data. Cronbach thus points out that, according to the FACTS manual, the only difference between printers and professors of humanities is that the latter have good memories (1956, p. 178)!

IMPLICATIONS FOR COUNSELING

If the extensive norms and validity data of multifactor test batteries such as the DAT and the GATB prove them to be adequate, the use of singly developed and validated aptitude tests in counseling will in due course be virtually a thing of the past: the multipotentiality of the multifactor test battery gives it too many advantages. The large-scale validation programs which must inevitably be undertaken by the authors and publishers of such batteries, if they are to live up to their ambitious plans, and meet professional standards, give these batteries another great advantage over the singly developed tests.

It would be easy, however, to have too much faith in the general usefulness and comprehensiveness of the batteries which are available, to be over-impressed by large numbers, well-written arguments, or large validity coefficients, and to rely too heavily on these batteries. As technical standards improve, writers of test manuals increase their skill in giving tests the appearance of validity. Sometimes the counselor will deal with special problems or with special occupations on which more light could be thrown by other tests or batteries; he will therefore need to continue to be alert for the development of new tests of special aptitudes not covered by the standard batteries, and for normative data on occupations not adequately included in those sampled by them.

In particular, he should be aware of the fact that the grouping of occupations into broad families, as has been done in the occupational norming of the GATB, obscures differences in occupations which may be of vital significance for some students or clients, even though unimportant for most. Engineers and physicians have much in common, and hence have the same GATB occupational ability pattern, but also differentiating characteristics not brought out by the GATB data; the same is true of tobacco-wrappers and turret-lathe operators.

The test batteries which are considered here still impress me as the most significant developments in the field of aptitude testing since the work of the Minnesota Employment Stabilization Research Institute. The tools which they make available are potentially the most useful, but also the most complex, which we have had. They deserve careful study, before using them, as they are used, and after they have been used. Their special advantages, and their present defects, need to be known if they are to be made maximally useful in guidance.

Dr. Super's previous article on multifactor tests had a generally encouraging and hopeful tone despite the reservations indicated. The article was written some ten years ago when there was some occasion for optimism for factor analytically derived test batteries. For a recent and negative view of these matters, the student should consult a 1964 article by McNemar who is anything but optimistic. Taking the one multifactor test battery for which there is a very large array of validity data (the DAT of the Psychological Corporation), McNemar comes to the conclusion that such tests are not good differential predictors of school achievement. "The concept of general intelligence," he writes, "despite being maligned by a few, regarded as a second-order function by some, and discarded or ignored by others, still has a rightful place in the science of psychology and in the practical affairs of man" (McNemar, 1964, p. 880).

PART SEVEN

Personality

PSYCHOLOGICAL tests are frequently described as either objective or subjective, and typically, this labeling is in terms of the type of item. When most students ask an instructor about a scheduled examination, one inevitable question is whether or not the test is to be objective. By this students mean whether it is to be an essay-type examination or, say, an examination composed of multiple-choice items. A little reflection will show that the form of the item has little to do with whether the test is truly objective. It would be possible—and this is rather frequent with teacher-made achievement tests—to compose a multiple-choice or true–false item that was 100 percent subjective.

In the following article, condensed from the original that appeared in a 1958 issue of the *Journal of Counseling Psychology*, Professor Cattell has carefully spelled out the distinctions between objective and subjective, and, furthermore, has indicated that there are two degrees of objectivity.

Professor Cattell, a British psychologist, has spent most of his professional life in the United States. He describes himself as an exponent of multivariate experimental psychology, and he is famous for his work in the area of psychometrics, particularly factor analytic or multivariate analyses. He has brilliantly carried on the British psychometric approach here in the United States. He is the author of many books and articles, as well as of batteries of psychological tests, in the area of personality and motivation. Cattell's 1957 volume, *Personality and Motivation Structure and Measurement,* brought into a single book an integrated account of his massive investigations of these problems. His 1965 book, *The Scientific Analysis of Personality,* is the clearest and fullest account to date of his distinctive system. Another advantage of this 1965 volume is that the style is aimed at the general reader rather than at the specialist.

Cattell has said that his major purpose is to speed "the coming revolution in clinical practice" by providing clinical psychologists with a definitive taxonomy of human personality and motivation, plus a rational and efficient technology of measurement related to this. The approach is factor analytic; the results are applicable to the normal personality, since most of his data are based on normal adult samples. All factors are identified by factor code letters and index numbers in his Universal Index (a total of 33). For a summary and critique after publication of the 1957 volume, see Sells (1959).

WHAT IS "OBJECTIVE" IN "OBJECTIVE PERSONALITY TESTS"?

Raymond B. Cattell

This note to practical psychologists in the mental testing area concerns itself purely with the clarifying of test nomenclature. There is no doubt that much confusion arises in the communications of practical test users, through failure of descriptive precision in the matter here to be discussed.

TWO MEANINGS OF "OBJECTIVE"

The sense in which "objective" has been increasingly used by the present writer and his co-workers is clearly distinct from the older use still appearing in many text books. This older and more trivial sense has mainly been employed by those concerned with teaching teachers the difference between essay examinations and multiple-choice achievement tests, or those preoccupied with biographical inventories and other "itemetric" approaches. It is still given equal weight with other meanings in the texts of well-known educational statisticians.

These meanings, as we shall see, are in a sense two degrees of objectivity. The term "objective," in the first degree, has been used by educational psychologists to indicate a test which requires something different from essay-type appraisal, and involves, instead, an agreed key for selective (multiple-choice) or inventive (open-ended) responses, such that all psychometrists scoring the test will get the same numerical result. However, it happens historically that the pioneers in structured personality research used the term "objective" in a more fundamental sense. In this higher degree of objectivtiy it was required not only that the test result should be scored similarly by two different psychologists, but that the test stimulus situation, and the whole mode of response, should be such that the subject himself could not fake the response, or distort it to fit his subjective desires for a particular kind of "good or bad" score. That is to say, there could be no "motivational distortion" such as is systematically involved in the questionnaire, i.e., the self-appraisal inventory. Incidentally, these objective tests have been far more varied in type than the pencil and paper inventories, for they have frequently not even broken down into items, but have been measures of global behavior, and have thus not been susceptible to the restricted rules of that branch of psychometrics which we may call "itemetrics." They include miniature situational tests, stylistic tests, misperception tests (projective tests), psychophysiological measures, etc., and are perhaps best illustrated by the 100 or more varieties of scores shown in my own Objective Analytic Personality Factor Test Battery. These tests are, in fact, designed to eliminate the systematic distortion through poor self-knowledge, strong motivation to make a good impression, or dishonesty, which normally reduce both the reliability and the validity of data. In general, the pioneers in this field have tacitly agreed (and the present writer concurs) in assuming that the first degree of objectivity, i.e., mere scoring objectivity, shall always be present as a prerequisite in such tests, much as one assumes that scores will not have clerical errors, or private manipulations by the examiner. There are, indeed, a considerable number of hard-headed psychometrists who are not even willing to consider that a procedure constitutes a "test" until this initial objectivity of scoring exists.

THREE MEDIA FOR PERSONALITY MEASUREMENT

It is this more radical sense of objectivity which has been consistently employed by the present writer, through 20 years of systematic personality structure investigation. This sense has been implicit in the notion that there are three, and only three, fundamental media through which measured or unmeasured data on personality can be collected, as a basis for research and theory. These three media of observation, which it is important to distinguish, both for theoretical research purposes and for efficiency of practical routine testing work, are:

1. Observations of individual behavior made in the individual's actual life situation, e.g., the behavior embedded in occupation, family relations, social life, etc., unplanned and unaffected by the observations being made. Such data can be obtained by behavior ratings, made by a sufficient number of observers, or by numerical recordings of actual events, e.g., time sampling of specific behaviors, actual records of achievements, automobile accidents, salary, human relations (sociometry). This procedure is more accurately called "life record observation," and has been systematically referred to as "L-data."

2. Observations of personality which come to the psychologist in terms of introspective, verbal, self-record and self-evaluation, typically in inventories, questionnaires, opinionnaires and all the evidence of the consulting room. This gives "mental interiors"—a view of the external behavior constituting L-data, as seen from the unique position of the subject. As just stated, such test data is naturally more subject to faking and self deception, and does not, in any case, permit the psychometrist to calculate a conspect reliability coefficient, i.e., a correlation between two independent observers (as in L-data) or experimenters as in T-data below, since only one person— the subject—can observe from this particular vantage point. Such observations are symbolized as Q'-data (Q for questionnaire, in the broadest sense). One should distinguish between such Q'-data, in which the subject's statements about himself are accepted as descriptions, and Q-data, in which the questionnaire response itself is merely taken as "behavior," the meaning of which has still to be established by correlation with L-data behavior factors.

3. Observations on personality made by measuring actual behavior in a miniature situation—a test. The person reacts to a standard stimulus situation, and his behavior is measured in ways of which he may not be aware and with interpretations of which he will certainly not be cognizant. This child is called an objective test, or T-data. Some questionnaire response, namely, Q-data but not Q'-data, by virtue of being recorded only as behavior and not as accepted true self-evaluation, can come under the rubric of T-data, but most T-data comes from far more varied miniature situations, as indicated above.

TEST VERSUS CRITERION

It will be noted that both Q- and Q'-data and T-data come from tests, thus contrasting with L-data which comes from everyday life and is, therefore, the realm of criterion data. In calling questionnaire (Q'-data) and objective test (T-data) both test data—in contrast to L-data—we should perhaps stop to define a test as such (self-evaluative or objective). In this most general form, therefore a test may be defined as: an artificial, transportable, standardized situation, which the subject recognizes and voluntarily enters, agreeing to respond within specified forms, and the responses to which are measured or classified according to rules agreed upon by psychologists. Although Q'- and T-data contrast with L-data in that both the former are tests, L- and T-data contrast, alternately, with Q'-data in that the two first are concerned with objectively measured behavior; while a third grouping would place L- and Q'-data over against T-data in that the two former are concerned with everyday behavior, whereas T-data can be, and commonly is, exotic or artificial.

OTHER DIMENSIONS OF PERSONALITY TESTING

Focusing attention now, within the above trio, only on the test forms of behavior measurement—in order more fully to bring out the properties defined as objective—we should note that tests, like anything else, can in general be defined in terms of either "types" or "dimensions." The division just made between objective and self-evaluative tests is really a dichotomy on a dimension, and permits recognition of other ways of "cutting the cake" to be simultaneously recognized. Indeed, in order not to fall into any confusion about the objective-vs.-self-evaluative dimension, it is desirable to work out two or three other important dimensions, including that of objectivity of scoring, referred to at the beginning. It is necessary at the outset to realize that objectivity of test, as defined here, is quite distinct from reliability and validity. However, objectivity should increase the probability of good validity (by reducing faking), of good reliability (by reducing systematic shifts in the mode of distortion from one test-motivation situation to another) and of certainty of interpretation of the test, e.g., determining the meaning of a factor found in test response.

The most important second dimension, after objective-vs.-evaluative (or self-appraising), is what can most aptly be called rative-vs.-conspective, corresponding to part of that total difference which exists in educational psychology between essay and multiple choice, and in clinical psychology between open-ended projective (or down-right crystal ball, e.g., reading character in handwriting, devices) and tests objectively scored by a key. A more precise terminology than the old "objective-vs.-subjective" is deserved by this dichotomy, and is required to distinguish it from the first and more basic dimension of objectivity just described.

Let us look more closely at what is involved. The essay or rating requires interpretation by the private judgment of the individual psychologist, and the resulting numerical value is a function of the subject's and the psychologist's personalities. (The multiple choice may also rest on no more than one unaided judgment, but it is an explicit, agreed and subsequently common judgment of all the psychologists concerned.) This difference is shown operationally in an index which the present writer, in his survey of reliability coefficients, has called the "conspect reliability coefficient," i.e., the correlation between two examiners or raters to determine how far they "see together" (conspect) in scoring tests. When the conspect reliability coefficient reaches unity, we have what has sometimes been called an objectively scored test, or what we might now, to avoid confusion, better call a conspective test.

A conspective test might synonymously be named a "key-scored" test, were it not that this is too concrete and awkward a term, since, conceivably, perfectly conspective tests may yet be found that are not key-scored. Besides, conspective brings out the operational relation to the conspect reliability coefficient. The opposite of a conspective test one thinks of by such terms as "equivocal," "examiner-biased," "privately rated," "double-personality-determined," etc., which, though usefully descriptive, are too cumbersome. A correct Latin-derived expression would be "disspective" but since, for psychologists, the meaning of "personal viewpoints introducing" is now well tied up with the verb "to rate," perhaps "rative" would more briefly and accurately designate the nonconspective scoring of a test.

It should be noted at once that conspective-vs.-rative is not the same dimension in the test world as "selective (fixed choice) vs.-inventive (open-ended)." For an open-ended, inventive-answer, projective test, for example, can have definite scores assigned, for all free responses, by prior agreement among psychologists. This is a third, essentially independent dimension of test design and construction. However, there will be a high prevalence of rative scoring among inventive-answer tests.

THE ESSENTIAL MEANING OF "OBJECTIVE"

Before concluding it is desirable to define more sharply the dichotomy of "objective-vs.-self-appraising" (or "taking self-evaluation at face value") tests, now that it has been sorted out from its confusion with "conspective-vs.-rative." Elsewhere the writer has defined this sense of an objective test as "A test in which the subject's behavior is measured, for inferring personality, without his being aware in what ways his behavior is likely to affect the interpretation." If he is told, as in an inventory, to evaluate himself, and the examiner accepts these descriptions, the test is obviously not meeting these conditions, for the subject knows in what sense to misrepresent in order favorably to affect the score. Only the test defined in this sense as objective escapes the motivated distortion, fakability and situation-sensitivity of the self-appraising test. In an examination of test properties in relation to L-, Q'-, and T-data, the nonobjective, self-appraising form does not connote that faking must occur, while absence of self-appraisal design does not guarantee that faking cannot be effective, unless the subject does not know how his behavior is being measured or what inferences are being drawn from it. The Objective-Analytic Test Batteries illustrate the way in which test design can thus leave the subject pretty completely in the dark. He can, of course, still refuse to cooperate, and thus introduce error into his score or give no answers at all; but he cannot fake his behavior successfully to convey some impressions which he falsely (consciously or unconsciously) wishes to make.

To sum up, there are three essentially independent dimensions of test description:

1. Objective-vs.-Self-appraising. This defines the kind of stimulus response situation, and instruction, given to the subject, in terms of the degree of his ignorance of the behavior upon which he will actually be scored.

2. Selective-vs.-Inventive (open-ended), defining the kind of response situation limitations to which the subject agrees to be restricted.

3. Conspective-vs.-Rative, defining the kind of scoring situation in which the examiner is placed, and therefore the magnitude of the conspect reliability among examiners.

These three dichotomous dimensions will yield (except for incompatibilities) eight (2^3) types of test, for which eight nouns might be used. But it would probably be simpler to depend on use of the present three-fold adjectival description. For example (a) use of the Rorschach with previously assigned scores for free responses constitutes an objective, inventive, conspective test; (b) certain standardized interview tests give self-appraising, inventive, rative measures; while (c) Scheier's anxiety scale is an objective, selective, conspective test. There may be other dimensions of test description needed for special purposes, but this definition of (1) stimulus situation, (2) response opportunity, and (3) scoring basis, should suffice in general to "place" a test beyond misunderstanding.

▽ ▽ ▽

IT all started with Meehl's little volume, *Clinical versus Statistical Prediction* (1954). Meehl reluctantly came to the conclusion that clinical judgment, frequently involved with his favorite test (the MMPI), showed up poorly. He reviewed 20 studies which he thought were relevant to this issue and in which clinical and actuarial methods could be contrasted. In all but one of these, the predictions made actuarially were either approximately equal or superior to those made by a clinician. Meehl did admit, however, that none of these studies had been planned to "test" this issue specifically. This sad report started a host of other studies by hopeful clinicians. Meehl himself returned to the issue in a 1957 report, "When Shall We Use Our Heads Instead of the Formula?" Here he reported on 27 empirical studies: 17 showed the superiority of the actuarial approach, and the remaining 10 showed no difference. None showed a clinical superiority. The cookbook approach again won out.

An example of this type of study is the following report (a 1964 M.A. thesis at the University of Minnesota) by Burton Danet, utilizing the MMPI scaled scores and the prediction of future mental illness in a college sample. Clinicians with varying amounts of experience (up to 21 years) were employed, and their ratings or judgments compared against seven inexperienced graduate students. Correct number of hits were then checked for the two groups against the more straightforward and simple actuarial prediction.

Dr. Danet is presently a member of the staff of the University of Minnesota Mental Hygiene Clinic, which is part of the university health service.

PREDICTION OF MENTAL ILLNESS IN COLLEGE STUDENTS ON THE BASIS OF "NONPSYCHIATRIC" MMPI PROFILES

Burton N. Danet

The literature on the Minnesota Multiphasic Personality Inventory (MMPI) contains numerous studies in which more or less successful discrimination between groups of individuals having different characteristics is made on the basis of their inventory profiles. Many fewer reports have been published describing an attempt to predict characteristics of individuals which develop over a span of time. In the present study, the following question was raised. Could clinical judgments be made on the basis of MMPI profiles obtained during college enrollment as to whether college students would be treated for a mental illness within approximately two years following their matriculation? Recent evidence has suggested that in similar prediction problems, statistical methods may ultimately replace much of the clinician's art (Meehl, 1954, 1957). It was, therefore, of interest to devise a simple statistical method of prediction. A comparison could then be made between actuarial prediction and the performance of clinicians.

The contribution of clinicians' or students' experience to the accuracy of the clinical predictions was also studied. Here the question was: Are clinicians with more experience or education more accurate in their predictions than others of relatively less experience and education? Similarly, are clinicians more accurate than a group of inexperienced graduate students who have just completed their first 30-hour course on the MMPI?

METHOD

Samples.   Each year prior to entering the University of Minnesota, freshmen take the MMPI as part of their orientation program. From this population of tests obtained during enrollment, 70 were selected from the files of the Student Counseling Bureau. These were all of freshmen and sophomores whose mean age at the time of orientation was 18 years, 2 months. Included were 36 male subjects and 34 female subjects. Among these were three preselected subsamples. One, the *clinic sample,* consisted of 10 male subjects and 14 female subjects who had received 10 or more psychotherapeutic hours at the Mental Hygiene Clinic, University of Minnesota Health Services. The mean number of months between the enrollment MMPI and the time subjects were evaluated at the clinic was 6.4, with a range from 0 to 31 months ($SD = 7.8$). The second, the *hospital sample,* included 10 male subjects and 6 female subjects who had been admitted to the psychopathic unit of the University of Minnesota Hospitals. The mean time lapse between orientation profile and hospital admission was 18.2 months, with a range from 3 to 54 months ($SD = 12.8$). The third, the *normal sample,* consisted of 30 college students who had indicated some interest in participating in psychological experiments and had become part of the Psychology Subject Pool at the University. All in the latter sample denied having ever received psychiatric care. They did so within a mean of 18.8 months from the date of the orientation MMPIs, the range being from 7 to 31 months ($SD = 11.5$). None had been admitted to the psychiatric service of University Hospitals nor were their names on record at the Mental Hygiene Clinic. There were 16 male subjects and 14 female subjects, 26 sophomores and 4 juniors. They listed 18 different majors, suggesting they represented a wide sampling of students at the University.

Procedure.   The profiles of students who had been treated for an emotional disturbance (hospital and clinic samples: $N = 40$) were randomly intermixed with those of students who showed no official record of having received psychiatric treatment (normal sample: $N = 30$). These 70 MMPI profiles were presented to 41 judges, 34 clinicians, and 7 students just completing a course on the MMPI, who were all asked to make the predictions. The judges were told that the profiles were orientation results for students at the University of Minnesota. The mean age and age range of the sample were given. In addition, the judges were told that some of the subjects, independently of their MMPI testing, had sought out or been referred for psychiatric treatment. The number of subjects in the sample who had received such care was *not* disclosed. The clinicians were also told that other subjects in the sample showed no official record of having received help for emotional problems. On the profile sheet for each subject, the only identifying information presented was age, sex, and marital status at the time of orientation, and the raw scores (K corrected) and standard scores for the 3 validity and 10 clinical scales. The profiles were all coded according to the Hathaway (1947) system.

Judges were asked to sort the profiles into 12 categories. Categories 0 through 5 represented a decision that the subject probably *will* develop a mental disorder later on in his college career. Categories 6 through 11 represented the judgment that the subject probably will *not* develop a mental disorder. Within these subgroups, the category of choice depended upon the extent the judge felt it was likely that the subject would develop a mental illness *and* seek out or be referred for psychiatric treatment. No stipulation was made regarding the number of subjects to be placed in each category.

Judges. Among the 34 "experienced" judges, the area of specialization most heavily represented was adult clinical psychology ($N = 21$). There were also seven child clinical psychologists, five counseling psychologists, and one school psychologist. Of these clinicians, 16 held the Ph.D.; 7 others had the equivalent of the doctorate. There were also 11 graduate students in the clinical and counseling psychology training programs at the University of Minnesota. All of these students were at least at the M.A. level and had 1 or 2 years' clinical experience behind them. The numbers of years' experience for the 34 ranged from 1 to 21, with a mean of 7.6 years. Three levels of experience (1–2 years, 3–10 years, 11–21 years) were eventually divided among the judges, with about one-third of the group in each category.

The seven "inexperienced" judges were students without clinical training who had just completed a 30-hour course on the MMPI. Of these, four were in the adult clinical psychology program, two were in sociology, while one was in social psychology.

RESULTS

Simple Actuarial Prediction. Table 10 presents the results of predictions made on the basis of the following simple statistical procedure. Profiles were called "likely to develop a mental illness" if at least *one* clinical scale was at or above a T score of 70. In this table, the number of "hits" (valid positives and valid negatives) and "misses" (false positives and false negatives) are presented. A contingency analysis showed that these actuarial predictions were more accurate than chance expectation ($p < .005$).[1] The hit rate was 70% which also reliably exceeded chance expectation of 50% ($p \leq .008$).[2]

Performance of the Judges. When the number of hits and misses of the

---

[1] For the contingency analyses, "chance expectation" was defined as the frequency of "mentally ill" cases in the sample of students whose profiles were given to the clinicians. Since actual base rates in the college population were estimated to be extremely low, between 5% and 10%, it was feasible to include only a small group of students in this study with the sample base rate for mental illness considerably higher than in the student population. Thus, it was of interest to determine how well judges could predict the base rate in this sample, when not considering population base rates as level of expectation.

[2] For the analysis of percentage of "hits," a chance level of 50% was assumed. The reason for this procedure stemmed from the fact that judges were *not* informed of the frequency of "mentally ill" cases in the sample of subjects and were asked to make their predictions based on MMPI profile data alone. Thus, for each subject for whom the judgment was made there was a 50% chance the judge would be correct.

TABLE 10

NUMBER OF HITS AND MISSES BY SIMPLE
ACTUARIAL PREDICTION

Hits		Misses	
Valid positives	29	False positives	10
Valid negatives	20	False negatives	11
Total	49	Total	21

34 experienced clinicians were submitted to contingency analyses, for all but 4, the judges were significant at or beyond the .05 level of significance (chi-square). The four clinicians whose predictions were not significantly different from the expected chance values stated they had had 1, 2, 12, and 21 years' experience.

The mean percentage of hits for the 34 experienced clinicians was 63%, reliably different from chance or 50% ($p < .06$). The hit rate was significantly in excess of chance ($p \leq .06$) for 20 of the 34 judges.

Experience and Accuracy of Prediction. Table 11 presents the mean percentage of hits for inexperienced students and for clinicians having different amounts of experience, as well as for judges of various educational levels. Apparently accuracy of prediction is not different at the various levels of experience and education.

Despite the small size of the sample of inexperienced student judges who had completed the MMPI course, their results were strikingly similar to those of the 34 experienced clinicians. As shown in Table 11 the mean

TABLE 11

MEAN PERCENTAGE OF HITS FOR INEXPERIENCED STUDENTS AND CLINICIANS OF
VARIOUS LEVELS OF EXPERIENCE AND EDUCATION

Years of Experience	N	Percentage of Hits	Educational Level	N	Percentage of Hits
0	7	65.1	Student	7	65.1
1–2	11	62.3	M.A. equivalent	7	62.8
3–9	11	62.4	M.A.	4	60.7
10–21	12	65.3	Ph.D. equivalent	7	62.2
			Ph.D.	16	64.1

percentage of hits of the seven students was 65.1%, reliably different from chance (50%) at the .04 level of significance. This figure is remarkably comparable to the mean percentage of hits for all other judges (63%). The contingency analysis for each of these individuals showed that all but one of the chi-square values were significant ($p \leq .05$). Similarly, all but two of the students achieved percentages of hits which were significant ($p \leq .05$).

DISCUSSION

The results of this study support the proposition that individual clinicians are able to predict which college students will be treated for a mental illness on the basis of "nonpsychiatric" MMPI profiles better than the chance level of expectation. However, statistical confirmation of this fact does not necessarily demonstrate the applicability of the procedure to any clinical decision-making process. The significance of the clinical predictions is further reduced when it is noted that the method of simple actuarial prediction, that is, calling mentally ill those student with profiles having at least one clinical scale at or above $T = 70$, yielded a hit rate of 70%, which was reliably better ($p < .02$) than the mean percentage of hits of the clinicians (63%). It may be concluded that this study once more lends support to the actuarial mode of prediction. Of 34 experienced clinicians, only 4 achieved a hit rate the same as or better than that of the simple statistical procedure (the best clinician's hit rate was 74.38%). Since this conclusion is in agreement with evidence accumulating in recent years, it seems that a natural step would be to turn from the clinical to the actuarial mode of prediction in the use of MMPI data. Kleinmuntz's (1963) study is an excellent example, as he used a digital computer to aid in "shuttling back and forth" to arrive at the most successful set of decision rules.

No evidence was found in this study that experience aids the clinician in making the predictions. It cannot be said that those who performed least well were also least experienced. Further, amount of experience and level of education had no relationship to the ability of expert judges to make the judgments. Students who had no clinical experience were able, *as well as* clinicians with experience, to predict mental illness from MMPI profiles beyond chance expectation. Of these seven inexperienced students, five performed at a level equal or superior to 74% of the 34 experienced clinicians.

It should be noted that the failure of experience to aid the clinician in making the predictions may be an artifact of the procedure employed in this study. Since the frequency of treated versus not-treated subjects in the sample was not disclosed, some sophisticated judges may have made the false assumption that subjects were drawn at random from the college population. They may then have concluded that only approximately 1 in 20 would be likely to receive treatment. Their performance, therefore, would be hindered to the extent that consideration of the population base rates influenced their judgments. A tentative conclusion that may be drawn is that a certain fundamental knowledge of the MMPI in and of itself seems sufficient to make the predictions in question under the present procedure. If provided with the base rate of "mental illness" in the sample of college students in this study, more experienced clinicians may then improve their predictions relative to less experienced individuals.

Cooke and Kiesler (1967) have replicated and extended Danet's study by determining whether differences can be seen between the MMPI clinical scales with students who applied for psychological counseling five or more months after entering the University of Iowa. When compared to a randomly selected nonclient group, counseling clients had significantly higher total MMPI mean scores and a significantly higher neurotic traid mean. Danet's specific result that a T-score of 70 or more for an individual on one or more of the clinical scales would spot those who received therapy in the future (in contrast to those that did not) was not replicated here. However, since, his data were based on both a clinic and hospital sample there probably would be more individuals with elevated scores, especially with the hospital sample.

At one of the Invitational Conferences on Testing Problems, Zubin (1955) noted that this whole issue is a pseudo problem. The dilemma is nonexistent. Despite Meehl's book, he feels the distinction between clinical and actuarial prediction is heuristic rather than basic. The business of predicting for a group is quite different from predicting for the individual case. And it is the group prediction that can be entirely statistical. Here the prediction might be that there is a .70 probability of "success," but then a decision must be made on this. The two types of prediction supplement each other, and the discrepancies between the two ought to be studied reciprocally to improve each other.

Sawyer (1966) has pointed out that the issue of clinical versus statistical prediction is only half the problem. The prior problem—clinical versus statistical measurement—has been largely neglected. He reviewed a total of 45 studies involving 75 comparisons of the two methods, and concluded that the problem remains unresolved. Improvement along methodological lines is what is badly needed.

In his review of research in personnel selection for the *Annual Review of Psychology* (1967), Guion comments that the clinical versus statistical prediction issue seems to have quieted down, and that no special skill, brilliance, or even prejudice is required to admit that some efforts at so-called clinical prediction are in reality "nothing more than arrogance put up as the facade of ignorance." He states that it is obvious that "careful, competent clinical prediction works, and the fact is particularly valuable where statistical methods cannot even be tried as in executive selection and the Peace Corps" (Guion, 1967, p. 206). It may be remarked, however, that the Peace Corps makes use of the MMPI plus extensive field observation of trainees by clinical psychologists over a period of many weeks. For a negative note on executive selection, see the comments by Whyte (pp. 344–53).

$\triangledown \; \triangledown \; \triangledown$

A perennial problem with all self-report devices is faking—conscious or unconscious. Not only is there the unexpected situation of a testee's desire to "fake
good," but also there is the distinct problem of detection of the "fake bad." The
second is, for obvious reasons, not encountered so frequently as the first, but it
does exist—for example, draftees "faking bad" in order to avoid military service.
Earlier psychometricians paid little attention to this problem, other than resorting
to exhortations for honesty, not requiring testees to sign names, and the like. In
recent years, more sophisticated attempts have been made to cope with faking.
These generally are based on giving the testee a real chance to distort answers and
then deriving an empirical "fake key" from this. Ruch (1942) was probably the
originator of this technique when he first had college students fill out the Ben-
reuter Personality Inventory under normal conditions and, for a second time, as if
they were applying for the job of salesman, which they sincerely wanted and for
which they knew the test scores would be used.

With the appearance of the Minnesota Multiphasic Personality Inventory
(MMPI), much attention was given to the problem of conscious and unconscious
faking. Of all the paper-and-pencil personality inventories, the MMPI has been the
subject of the largest amount of research on this issue. Four validity scales were
developed by the test authors; other psychologists have continued work toward
further refinement. By necessity, most such work has involved college students who
are asked to take the MMPI on repeated occasions but under different psychological
sets.

In the following report, Drs. Drasgow and Barnette were able to secure a non-
student group—candidates in industrial assessments by means of psychological
tests for upgrading—for which the application of the $F - K$ index (Gough, 1950)
brought promising results. The study was done while both authors were serving as
counseling psychologists at the University of Buffalo's Vocational Counseling Center
(now State University of New York at Buffalo). The report is a condensation of the
original article, which appeared in the *Journal of Consulting Psychology,* 1957.

The F scale of the MMPI is composed of items answered true or false by very
few normals; any testee that had several of these was probably careless or inatten-
tive in taking the test. The K scale is the "suppressor scale" of the MMPI. High
scores are secured when the testee wants to place himself in a good light; low scores
are earned when the testee is either unusually frank or is adopting a highly defen-
sive attitude. Since K is the longer of the two scales, the arithmetical result of
$F - K$ is typically a negative number.

$F - K$ IN A MOTIVATED GROUP

James Drasgow and W. Leslie Barnette, Jr.

A recurring problem in the use of any personality test is the question of
dissembling. The Minnesota Multiphasic Personality Inventory (MMPI)
contains at least four separate scales ($?, L, K, F$) which directly contribute

to evaluating the validity of the scores in the profile. Each one of these four scales assesses validity from a somewhat different approach, but apparently the only promising combination of scales to date is Gough's F minus K.

Several empirical studies have reported on the meaningfulness of the values obtained by subtracting the K raw score from the F raw score. These studies have been especially concerned with establishing optimum cutoff points in the $F - K$ distributions. The distributions that have been studied and reported were obtained from subjects under different conditions, e.g., (a) "normal" subjects who were given no particular instructions designed to affect $F - K$, (b) normal subjects who were instructed to feign abnormality, (c) normals who were instructed to act more normal, and (d) patients who were given instructions designed to be analogous to those given to the first three "normal" groups. The most rewarding results have been obtained with condition (b). These studies have been well replicated and cutoff scores corroborated. The present study focuses on the unsolved reverse problem of detecting profiles which have been faked to make a "good impression."

In an attempt to discover what precise range of $F - K$ values might be used to discriminate the subjects who were instructed to fake a "good" normal profile, earlier studies have merely concluded that more research was needed.

Why is it that the faked-good profiles have been so difficult to detect? In previous studies with subjects working under fake-good instructions, their motivation is open to question. The choice of motivated subjects by previous researchers appears to have been unfortunate since the probability of finding real differences has been minimized by supplying only instructions to stimulate motivation. The present brief report has therefore focused on this aspect and supplies a group with higher motivation.

SUBJECTS

The University's Vocational Counseling Center provides a job applicant screening service to business and industry. The job applicants from this service formed the group with which we worked. Some of the applicants were applying for jobs with companies without having been previously associated with the company, while others were old-line company employees competing for promotion to a choice spot. All Ss were employed males on their "old" jobs at the time of testing. The jobs for which they were being tested included such titles as foreman, salesman, supervisor, superintendent, and vice-president. The jobs can be seen in a framework of advancement and betterment, so that in this society we can reasonably infer an appreciable degree of motivation to get the better job. Many of the men said that they had been working years for the job in question, and that it was not merely a matter of money.

The total number of "industrial cases" with MMPIs available for use in the present study was 92. Within this total pool, 66 profiles had scores within the normal range ($T = 30$ to 70), and 26 profiles had one or more scores outside. The normal sample of 66 cases is utilized here.

The modal person in the sample was a 34-year-old white married male with two children and two years of college. He was currently employed, but trying to get a "better" job.

RESULTS AND DISCUSSION

All scores on all MMPI scales on the profile were within the accepted normal range as stated earlier. The mean raw F was 1.6 and the SD was 1.5; the mean raw K was 17.6 with an SD of 3.2. The difference of -16 for $F - K$ is well beyond the .01 level.

Hunt (1948) reported a mean $F - K$ of -11 for the group of Navy prisoners who were asked to make a good impression, but he was dissatisfied with this statistic because too many normals also gave this value. One might then expect an $F - K$ of this size as an indication of a "normal" amount of hypocrisy which may be associated with making a good impression in this society. Gough (1950) gives -7 to -10 as a modal range within which the majority of normals would fall.

A corroborating factor and potential source of explanation for the obtained results appeared in the relationship between a job applicant's $F - K$ and his number of dependents. Because of the restriction in the range of the number of dependents and the non-normal nature of the distribution, a non-parametric correlation technique was used to estimate the association. The correlation was .61 and significant beyond the .01 level. Concomitantly, it is of interest to report that the correlation between $F - K$ and age was zero, while that between $F - K$ and education was $-.18$ (Pearsonian r's in both instances).

The relatively high relationship indicated by the .61 could probably be interpreted in a variety of ways. The writers would relate it to the American middle class value of upward social mobility. We postulate that the more dependents the client has, the greater will be his felt personal responsibility and that, as a partial consequence, the more motivated he will be to make a good impression so as to secure the proposed upgrading on the job.

SUMMARY

Other MMPI studies involving $F - K$ samples where testees have been requested to fake good are criticized on the ground of inadequate motivation or felt responsibility. Results are presented, utilizing 66 normal MMPI profiles obtained from clients tested for upgrading where evidence was available for high motivation. The mean $F - K$ index for this group was -16. Age and years of education had little or no effect; number of dependents, however, was significantly related to this index. It is proposed that the felt responsibility and upward motivation of these clients are the important factors in producing such elevated $F - K$ indices.

Ruch and Ruch (1967) have reported a study in which MMPI scales without K corrections were used with success. Involved were 182 sales representatives from about 9 companies, ranging from beverage sales to business forms. With each sample, the salesmen were divided into upper- and lower-criterion groups. The classifications were based on sales managers' ratings. The five uncorrected MMPI scales, which are normally subjected to K correction, differentiated significantly between the criterion groups in the expected directions. The K suppressor variable, when applied according to the manual's directions, surprisingly decreased validity to almost zero. The uncorrected scales were then better correlated with selling effectiveness.

THE usual admonition to the respondent, especially when administering personality and interest inventories, is that he record his first impressions and avoid excessive mulling over of individual test or inventory items. This is one of the means by which the test administrator hopes to minimize social desirability effects or faking good and the like. The result is an expected increase in the validity of the final reporting on the answer sheet. There is also, of course, the matter of avoiding over-long testing sessions that would enormously increase the cost of test administration.

The following report by Oseas, a condensed version of the original which appeared in a 1966 issue of the *Journal of Counseling Psychology,* is of interest because the respondent (who was also the test administrator in this instance) did just the opposite and took, overall, about 9 months to complete a personality inventory that consisted of a mere 187 items. He managed this by attempting to devote exclusive attention to one item per day and by letting his introspections flow as freely as possible. His report is interesting since he then compares this extended administration with the standard administration he began with. Dr. Oseas currently is professor of psychology and director of the Psychological Services Center at the University of Cincinnati.

"GIVE THE FIRST NATURAL ANSWER"

Leonard Oseas

In a famous James Thurber cartoon, a colossal, house-engirdling female dominates an entire domestic landscape, including an obviously intimidated little man. The cartoon requires no caption since the look of stern disapproval on the face of the female speaks volumes. It is curious how like Thurber's portrayal of the war between the sexes is the relationship between the principals in the test-taking encounter.

The main actors in both the testing and domestic situations are natural adversaries whose needs for each other somehow manage to overcome apparently instinctive mutual distrust. The dominant partner, especially, attributes to the weaker a certain readiness to equivocate and lie and takes pains to let it be known that this weasel-like penchant does not go unnoticed. Consider, for example, the usual instructions on a personality questionnaire. Almost invariably they include an appeal to the examinee to give honest answers to test questions. At the same time, the ingenuity with which the test-maker provides against lapses from truthfulness, e.g., by presenting the examinee with questions whose intentions are artfully oblique and by building into his instrument subtly contrived (but cynically labeled) "lie" scales, indicates that the test-maker's faith in the efficacy of appeals to reason and fair play is not boundless.

It was in the context of such melancholy reflections that disturbing doubts about the real purpose behind another common innocent-appearing instruction crept into my thoughts. I refer to the caution to "avoid pondering over individual questions." On the surface this appears to be a reasonable condition. But why should the examiner actually prefer ill-considered, superficial answers over those arrived at after careful deliberation? Time considerations excepted, might it not make good sense, and contribute to the development of mutual trust and respect, to permit the examinee to spend as much time as *he* thinks necessary to select an answer *he* could feel confident was truly descriptive of his personality?

Since I was both examiner and examinee in the exercise I am about to describe, time considerations could be managed without prejudice to either party. Moreover, as examiner I would be privy to the innermost thoughts of the examinee, and this arrangement admirably suited the larger purpose of the present undertaking.

THE EXERCISE

The 16 P.F. Test (Cattell, Saunders, & Stic, 1957) was selected for the exercise for practical reasons, the main one being my previous unfamiliarity with it. The test is a product of Cattell and his associates at the Institute for Personality and Ability Testing (IPAT) and is based on his source trait conceptions of personality structure (Cattell, 1957). The instructions to the testee are standard for this type of paper-and-pencil personality inventory. One is urged to give first "natural" answers, to avoid as much as possible resorting to the middle of three possible choices, to answer every question "somehow," and to resist the temptation to impress the examiner by merely marking what seems the "right thing to say."

The first step in the present investigation was to be a good subject: I took the test under standard conditions.

Then, in a second administration, I chose to ignore the admonition against spending too much time on a given item. I pondered each question exhaustively, associating freely to its stimulus, dredging up all pertinent memories, and weighing all the evidence before committing myself to an answer. To do justice to all of the 187 items of Form A at one sitting would be a physical and psychological impossibility, so I decided instead to consider only one item a day. The same time each working day (ten minutes before the morning coffee break) was set aside for undivided attention to the task. One obvious consequence of the one-a-day format was that I exceeded the suggested 30 minutes to complete the entire test. My delinquency extended roughly nine months. During the one-a-day administration, I taped the responses to several widely separated and arbitrarily selected questions.

I repeated the standard administration approximately six weeks after finishing the 187th question. Form A was used for all three administrations, and all were scored after completion of the third test administration.

RESULTS

If the arrangement of being both examiner and examinee nicely circumvents the troublesome matter of confidentiality, there is still the problem of selecting the material to report. In the account which follows, I am not unmindful of the danger of a breach of good taste. Still, the occasion calls for candor if it is to have any relevance at all for a psychology of test-taking.

My suspicions that the task I had set for myself would be a difficult one were quickly and repeatedly confirmed. The expected discomfort of any prolonged introspection was intensified by the effort to stay within the cramped confines of a particular item at a particular time. The flow of associations was anything but smooth. The exhilarating sense of embarking on an adventure (where who knows what undreamed-of treasures might be unearthed) with which each new item was greeted dissipated with disheartening regularity in an arid associational wasteland. Promising trains of thought got derailed or hung-up on maddening broken-record repetitions.

There was a distressingly high proportion of static to substance in the typical response. Distractions came mainly from two sources: from an overseeing ego which, while observing itself functioning, did not hesitate to make passing comments on these observations; and from the nagging reminders of a hyper-alert superego—I had answered affirmatively question 2, *viz.,* "I am ready to answer each question as truthfully as possible."

No amount of conscious effort succeeded entirely in preventing recollections from prior responses from intruding on ongoing ones. Once admitted to the associational process, these memory traces exerted a definite influence in one of two ways: as an impetus toward response consistency or as a temptation to compensate for response excesses; i.e., to bank deviation credits. ("If I am deliberately deviant now, I will not need to reveal myself in some more damaging way later.") Thus, it proved exceedingly difficult to be indifferent to the personality picture being etched item by item and to resist influencing this process in a favorable way.

Certain answers did indeed seem to be the "natural" ones which the test authors mention in their instructions. These responses seemed so instantaneously right, and they exerted such a strong pull, that it represents no great distortion of the subjective experience of responding to them to note the similarity of this process to tropisms in lower species. The impulse to retreat to these compellingly right answers before the other alternatives were given full consideration had to be opposed with an effort of the will.

The whole range of emotions entered, and in some subtle ways no doubt, influenced the associational process. However, it would be less than candid to fail to note the prevalence of peevish feelings. Most often my annoyance was aimed in a vague and impersonal way at the unknown test-makers who, in my extremity, I was tempted to hold responsible for (*a*) using unclear language, (b) my failure to arrive at satisfactory choices and (c) subjecting me to an arduous, disagreeable experience! It will come as no surprise that impatience to be done with a question, regardless of the correctness of the answer, was among the more urgent sentiments.

The disagreeable aspects of the exercise were quickly overshadowed by the surge of relief upon completing it and by the quieter satisfaction I found in the conviction that the personality picture that would emerge must be a valid one. How does this "real me" born of nine months labor compare with its 30 minute (or instant) counterpart?

As the profiles in Figure 5 testify, the resemblance is a close one. Compar-

FIGURE 5

PROFILES FROM STANDARD AND EXTENDED ADMINISTRATIONS OF THE 16 P.F. TEST

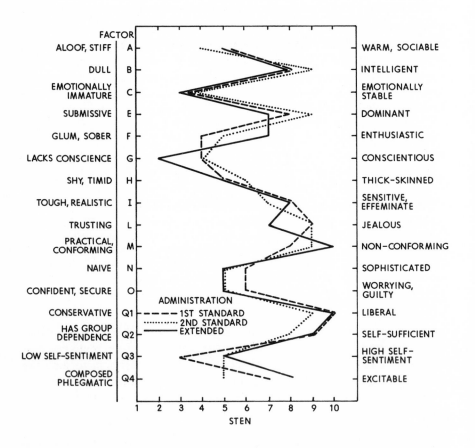

ing the responses on the extended administration with those of the first standard administration, and disregarding the direction of any changes, 138 answers were identical, 38 shifted one position and 11 shifted two positions. The comparable figures for the two standard administrations were 141, 41 and 5. There was somewhat less reliance on noncommittal "b" answers in the extended case: 50, compared with 55 on the first and 61 on the second standard administrations.

On only three factors, F ("Surgency"), G ("Superego strength") and L ("Pretension," or paranoid orientation) does the difference between the extended and *both* of the standard administration scores equal or exceed two stens. (Stens are ten-step equivalents of the more familiar stanines.) The higher F in the extended case indicates a greater degree of happy-go-lucky optimism, the lower G suggests less perseverence and more indolence, and the lower L depicts a more trusting outlook! Thus, the very qualities demanded by the task were the ones to diminish in the personality portrait that is the end product of that task, as though they were somehow depleted in the process.

That such anguish as characterized the experience apparently could father a picture of light-hearted optimism is one of the darker mysteries and ironies of the undertaking. It is all the more mystifying in view of the fact that I am confident my mood was elevated on the day I took the test the first time. Consider the following verbatim extracts from notes made just prior to the first administration: "Spirits good . . . slight undercurrent of apprehension (anticipation?) . . . F's visit stirring up some excitement . . . Kids doing well . . . Health fine, beat C. at handball . . ." It appears that either (a) I was deluding myself about the true quality of affect I was experiencing on both the standard and extended administrations, or (b) the choice of answers to questions pertaining to feelings is not positively related to the actual emotional state while responding, and may, in fact, be inversely related to it.

The result that most tempts me to self-justification, however, is the reduction in G, the superego factor. The test authors say of G:

This factor . . . is characterized most by energy and persistence. The hypothesis may be set up that (G) corresponds to the super-ego in psychoanalysis. On the whole, it best depicts the regard for moral sandards, the tendency to drive the ego and to restrain the id, which are most frequently regarded as marks of the super-ego (Cattell *et al.*, 1957, p. 13).

Since I consider myself to be not less well endowed in these qualities than the next man, I indignantly reviewed my responses to the ten items listed by the test authors as high scoring for G for a clue to where I might have incriminated myself. The three sample items below are quite representative of the ten. In each, the "a" answer is the high contributor; my responses are in italics:

Item 134: I think the police can be trusted not to ill-treat innocent people. (a) yes, (*b*) in between, (c) no.
Item 160: I always make a point, in deciding anything, to refer to basic principles of right conduct. (a) yes, (*b*) in between, (c) no.
Item 184: Everyone could make a success of his life with reasonable effort and perseverance. (a) yes, (b) in between, (*c*) no.

In my judgment, the *G* items are of the kind most likely to elicit socially desirable answers where such a set exists (and I would argue that it exists to some extent in the vast majority of persons). More to the point, however, is the fact that *G* was higher under the rushed conditions of the standard administrations. Thus, the succession of rapid, ill-considered decisions called for by the standard instructions appear to have encouraged the development of a response habit, even in the context of a personality not especially predisposed to it (if I interpret the entire test profile correctly). The "me" of the orthodox administrations is admittedly somewhat "nicer" by conventional standards, but I retain a strong personal preference for the more painfully arrived-at soul-searching *G* answers of the extended administration, incriminating though they may be.

The 16 P.F. Handbook provides 28 occupational and six clinical profiles against which an individual test profile may be compared by a simple goodness-of-fit procedure. The handbook gives no profile for the occupation of clinical psychologist, though the test authors suggest that the high *H* ("parmia") persons among them are likely to be the better group therapists. Similarly, they judge that sensitive clinicians may be distinguishable from ordinary psychometrists, and presumably from the tougher-minded actuarial-leaning clinicians, by their greater "premsia" or high *I*. High *I* persons are said to be demanding, impatient and subjective, but these liabilities are apparently offset by the imaginativeness of their inner life and their ability to act on intuition.

CONCLUSIONS

I remember an almost off-hand comment made many years ago by a senior professor to a student who had cavalierly dismissed the meaning of a pure *C* Rorschach response. It was to the effect that the solutions to many of the fundamental riddles of human psychology were imbedded in that response if we had the wisdom and techniques for extricating them. The remark has equal cogency for the process of responding to a personality questionnaire item. Even allowing for the artifacts introduced by amplifying the response process in the manner of the present exercise, the subtlety, richness and complexity of that process was made abundantly evident. Any significant improvement in the efficiency of personality measurement devices might well depend upon our success in unravelling this inherent complexity. Concepts such as response set, focused as they must be on the end products of a process rather than on the process itself, may be inadequate to the task. Perhaps what is needed now is an imaginative assault on the intricacies of the examinee's interactions with the test parameters that stimulate and provoke him.

This experience has had its rewards on a purely personal level. It permitted me to become familiar with a sophisticated instrument and opened new possibilities for empathy with fellow examinees. I believe I know myself better for having gone through the experience; having done so, I would summarize it in the way that 15 million veterans are prone to speak of their army experiences: I would never willingly go through it again, but I would not have missed it for the world.

THE personal interview still remains probably the principal technique of assessing personality despite all that is known concerning its unreliability. The employment interview, in particular, is an example where the interview is used as a basis for decision (for example: to hire or not to hire). In an interesting series of studies in this type of interview situation conducted at McGill University, the focus was entirely on how judgments, both good and bad, were reached (Webster, 1964). Many of these studies reported were Ph.D. theses with, in the main, personnel officers of the Canadian army cooperating as interviewers who talked with young men who wanted to enlist. (Enlistment in the Canadian army differs from civilian employment only in that the recruit signs up for three years; the military competes in the open labor market with civilian employers who also see people who want to change jobs.)

The Webster summary of these researches is largely a mournful one. A bias is clearly established early in the interviews, and it tends to be followed either by a favorable or unfavorable decision about the candidate. The stereotype is not unique to the individual interviewer but is common to all such persons who have a modest amount of experience. Unfavorable impressions carry far more weight than do favorable ones. One of the McGill studies reported that even one unfavorable impression is followed by rejection in 90 percent of the cases (Webster, 1964, p. 87). The summary section of this volume begins: "This chapter would have been easier to write had the experiments reported not been undertaken. Furthermore, it would have been written differently and with more assurance. The studies reported have shaken the principal investigator's faith in the interview as an appraisal technique" (p. 101).

An example of these McGill studies, the research report by Dr. Rowe, utilizing the concept of "category width" derived from the cognition studies of Bruner at Harvard, is included. The original research constituted her Ph.D. dissertation at McGill and appeared in the *Journal of Applied Psychology* in 1963. Dr. Rowe is at present a member of the department of psychology at the University of Waterloo, Waterloo, Ontario, Canada.

INDIVIDUAL DIFFERENCES IN SELECTION DECISIONS

Patricia M. Rowe

It is a well-documented observation that when several personnel interviewers separately assess the same applicant they arrive at very dissimilar decisions. One conclusion frequently drawn from this finding is that personnel selection decisions based on interviews are extremely unreliable and, consequently, that selection procedures should be drastically modified. However, the observed individual differences among personnel interviewers should be of intrinsic interest to psychologists, and their study might eventually make it possible to control interview unreliability at its source—in the interviewer himself. In the closely related area of categorization of simple, inanimate objects, investigators have taken the approach of regarding unreliability as an individual difference problem. These investigators have been successful in isolating a number of "response styles" underlying individual differences in categorization or judgment.

One of these response styles has been termed "category width" by Bruner and his co-workers. A typical category-width study is that by Bruner and Tajfel (1961). Subjects first viewed a slide containing a cluster of 20 dots. Subsequently, they were presented with slides containing clusters of 20–30 dots and asked to judge for each stimulus whether or not it contained 20 dots. Category width was defined by the number of stimuli judged "20 dots," and subjects were classified as broad or narrow categorizers depending on whether they made many or few such judgments. In another paper Bruner (1957) suggested that the accessibility of a category (and thus category width) is determined by two factors—the learned probabilities of occurrence of events in the individual's world, and the search requirements that are dictated by his need states.

If the principle of category width applies to decisions about persons, it may be that much of the "unreliability" of selection decisions could be accounted for in terms of individual differences in the width of the category "acceptable applicants" among the interviewers. The present investigation was designed to test this notion, and, further, to examine the role of Bruner's two factors of past learning and present motivational state in determining category width.

METHOD

Subjects. Because previous studies (Webster, 1964) indicate that selection standards vary as a function of company employment practices and job requirements, it was necessary to use as subjects interviewers employed by the same company and regularly selecting employees for the same position. The most readily available group meeting these requirements was the Personnel Selection Service of the Canadian Army. Of the 263 Personnel Selection Officers (PSOs) first approached for this study, 146 completed all tests and constituted the sample of subjects.

Two characteristics of the Canadian Army should be mentioned here because of their relevance to the analysis of the data: (*a*) All Canadian servicemen are volunteers; in recent years there have been many more applications than openings. Consequently, the PSO must *select* some applicants and reject many more on other than medical grounds. (*b*) The PSOs in this study are of two types: Regular Force PSOs are those employed in the Army on a full-time basis; Militia PSOs are roughly equivalent to members of the Active Reserve in the United States, and serve in the Army for approximately one-half day per week.

Test Materials. Pilot studies had indicated that applicants themselves change as a function of being interviewed several times; therefore, written descriptions of applicants were chosen as stimuli. One hundred fictitious "applicant" descriptions were constructed from 60 characteristics, 30 favorable and 30 unfavorable. Each applicant description was composed of 6 of the 60 characteristics. Three of the characteristics were favorable, the other three unfavorable, arranged in random order. By using an equal number of favorable and unfavorable characteristics, individual differences were probably exaggerated, but on the other hand, the likelihood of obtaining spurious agreement among the subjects was reduced. The following is a sample item:

This applicant has no commitments: he is completely independent. He seems cocky, a bit of a smart aleck, ready to tell anybody off. He tends to be an active participant in outdoor activities. The applicant makes a good impression; his appearance, language, all round ability and bearing make him stand out in a group. He has often left jobs following disagreements with superiors. The applicant seems to be an argumentative person.

All descriptions were presented to the subjects as applicants for the Regular Force, Canadian Army, who had met minimum Infantry standards on all criteria. The task for the subject was to accept or reject each applicant. In addition to the 100 descriptions, a Characteristic Rating Scale was included in the test material. The subjects rated each of 119 characteristics, which included the 60 used in constructing the applicants, on a 7-point scale from 1 (very unfavorable) to 7 (very favorable). Thus the more favorably a characteristic was rated, the higher was its score.

Procedure.   All test materials were mailed to the subjects, who returned the completed forms to the investigator. In order to get a better estimate of the reliability of the decisions, the applicant descriptions were mailed in three groups (consisting of 35, 35, and 30 descriptions, respectively). The Characteristic Rating Scale was mailed separately after the judgments had been received.

RESULTS

The mean number of applicants (descriptions) accepted by the 146 subjects was 34.86 out of 100, with a standard deviation of 20.02, and with a range from 0 to 92 applicants accepted. An analysis of variance, in which the variation between subjects was compared to the variation within subjects from one mailing of the test to another, yielded an F of 17.00 ($p < .01$), and thus demonstrated significant individual differences in the number of applicants accepted. Moreover, the correlations between the numbers of applicants accepted in the three mailings of the descriptions showed a high degree of within-individual consistency. The correlation between Parts 1 and 2 was .849; between Parts 2 and 3, .863; and between Parts 1 and 3, .828. It may be concluded, therefore, that there are both significant between-individual differences and within-individual consistencies in the width of the category acceptable applicants.

Not only do the subjects vary in the number of applicants accepted, but also, the applicants themselves differ in their likelihood of being accepted. The mean number of acceptances received by the 100 applicants was 50.89 out of 146, with a standard deviation of 26.51, and with a range of 8–116 acceptances received. Because of these differences in applicant acceptability we may raise the question of whether the differences in the category widths of the subjects are nonrandom—that is, do the subjects, regardless of the number of applicants they accept, tend to select those applicants most frequently accepted by the group as a whole? Such an analysis is equivalent to determining the scalability of the subjects.

In the present study subject scalability was determined with Bryden's (1960) rank-biserial correlation. In all, 142 coefficients were calculated (in four cases the statistic was not applicable) of which the mean coefficient was .569, the standard deviation was .141, and the range was from .179 to .873. Of these coefficients, 132 were significant beyond the .01 level, 7 were significant at the .05 level, and 3 were not significant. It is clear that the subjects in this study are scalar—almost all PSOs, regardless of the number of applicants they accepted, tended to select those applicant descriptions most acceptable to the group as a whole.

Is the dimension of acceptability of the applicants related to any other properties of the applicants? The mean rating of each characteristic making up the applicant descriptions was determined from the Characteristic Rating Scale. These scores were then combined appropriately to yield two scores for each applicant description: the mean rating assigned the three favorable characteristics, and the mean rating assigned the three unfavorable characteristics. The correlations of the number of acceptances received with these two scores were .471 and .616, respectively; with the total of the two scores, .713; the multiple correlation was .801. Correlations of such magnitude indicate that the more favorably an applicant's characteristics were rated, the more frequently was he accepted by the subjects.

Now let us turn to a consideration of the sources of individual differences in category width. Table 12 presents the findings of an analysis of number of applicants accepted as a function of kind of service (Regular Force or

TABLE 12

ANALYSIS OF NUMBER OF APPLICANT DESCRIPTIONS
ACCEPTED BY KIND OF SERVICE AND RANK

Group	N	M	SD	t or F
Regular Force				
Majors	8	27.38	4.18	
Captains	28	28.78	20.04	$F = .06$
Lieutenants	5	31.00	10.22	
Militia				
Majors	31	26.29	15.29	
Captains	58	41.83	20.33	$F = 7.09†$
Lieutenants	16	41.81	21.38	
Regular Force	41	28.76	17.95	
Militia	105	37.24	20.28	$t = 2.33*$
Total Group	146	34.86	20.02	

* $p < .05$.
† $p < .01$.

Militia) and rank (Major, Captain, or Lieutenant). The difference between the Regular Force and Militia PSOs was determined by a *t* test; differences between ranks were tested by one-way analyses of variance and the means compared two at a time. Regular Force PSOs accepted fewer applicants than did Militia PSOs, thus reflecting the different standards of acceptance in the ordinary duties of the two kinds of officers. Moreover, Militia Majors accepted fewer applicants than did Captains or Lieutenants, which suggests that with increasing experience in personnel selection the interviewer learns that not all men make good soldiers, and consequently reduces his number of acceptances.

The number of applicants accepted was also found to be related to the manner in which the subjects responded on the rating scale. For purposes of the present study the Characteristic Rating Scale consists of four types of characteristics: favorable ($N = 30$) and unfavorable ($N = 30$) characteristics used in constructing the applicants, and favorable ($N = 26$) and unfavorable ($N = 33$) characteristics not used in the descriptions. For each subject the mean rating assigned to each of these four subgroups of characteristics was computed. (The higher the mean, the more favorably were the characteristics of any type rated.) The correlations between the number of applicants accepted and the mean ratings of the characteristics used in the applicant descriptions were .308 (favorable) and .608 (unfavorable); for the characteristics not used in the descriptions they were .348 (favorable) and .495 (unfavorable); all correlations are significant beyond the .01 level. These correlations show that both favorable and unfavorable characteristics are rated more favorably by subjects who accepted many applicants than by those who accepted few.

DISCUSSION

To the extent that between-individual differences and within-individual consistencies in the width of the category acceptable applicants have been demonstrated, the present investigation has shown that the concept of category width is applicable to decisions in personnel selection. Although written descriptions were used as applicants in this study, this conclusion is at least warranted in the area of selection decisions (e.g., those concerning applicants for graduate studies) made on the basis of letters of recommendation to which the present descriptions bear much resemblance. It is not unreasonable to expect that similar, large individual differences may be found in other decision-making areas. For example, we might find that dentists vary in their judgments about "enough decay to necessitate extraction of the tooth," that judges differ regarding "seriousness of a particular crime," and that baseball umpires disagree on decisions of "within the strike zone."

Interviewers differ in the number of applicants they accept, but agree as to the relative acceptability of the various applicant descriptions. That is, regardless of the number of applicants a subject may accept, he tends to select those who are most acceptable to the group as a whole. It follows from this finding that in most cases a fairly accurate prediction of whether or not a particular subject will accept a particular applicant can be made from the knowledge of two variables: the rank order of that applicant in the whole group and the category width of that subject. Moreover, applicant rank order is not necessarily an ad hoc measure, but may be determined from how favorable his characteristics are. The importance of applicant rank order in decision making is not surprising; what the present study contributes is the fact that, because the interviewers are scalar, category width also plays a significant role in accounting for differences associated with selection decisions.

Several characteristics of the subjects were found to be indicative of the sources of individual differences in category width. Kind of service, rank, and ratings assigned to applicant characteristics were all related to the number of applicants accepted. Differences as a function of kind of service and rank are evidence for the importance of Bruner's (1957) two factors of motivational states and past learning in determining category width. The finding that subjects show closely related differences in their standards of acceptance of both applicants and single characteristics is further support for the notion that category width is a general trait displayed in a variety of decision situations.

To summarize, then, this study has emphasized certain characteristics of the interviewer in producing individual differences in selection decisions. Apparently, applicants can be meaningfully ordered along a dimension which is defined by how favorable their characteristics are. Whether a particular applicant will be accepted is a joint function of his position on this dimension and the category width of the interviewer he sees. Future investigations should be directed towards the relation between individual differences in category width and such variables as the accuracy of decisions, prescribed numbers of applicants to be accepted, and personality and motivational characteristics of the interviewer.

Interviews may also be studied for their effectiveness in the selection process, probably the most frequent use to which the interview is put. Mayfield's (1964) recently published a review of all the relevant studies concerning selection interviewing goes back to the early 20th century. He concludes that structured interviews are to be preferred, especially because of their greater reliability; nonstructured interviews, where the dialogue is allowed to flow without much direction, simply do not adequately cover the necessary topics. Regardless, the validities are usually of low magnitude. A characteristic prominent in all such studies is the paucity of replication. The McGill studies (Webster, 1964) are cited as an example of productive and promising research on the interview, which if pursued further will pay off dividends.

▽ ▽ ▽

ESPECIALLY in the area of personality measurement, one is often forced to rely on trait ratings for criterion data simply because few, if any, objective standards of performance are available. Ratings by supervisors are certainly the most frequently used device for learning about an individual's merit, temperamental characteristics, research competence, and a host of other traits in which an organization or immediate supervisor is interested. Writers of letters of recommendation frequently are asked to fill out some form of graphic rating scale on a candidate about whom they are writing; this scale may determine, in the last analysis, whether the candidate gets the post or gains admission to a graduate school or passes through the selection screen. It should then be obvious that the reliability and validity of the ratings given should be known, and that the rating scales used should be true psychological scales. However, the usual trend is to employ merely intuitive scales where large halo effects are typically demonstrated.

In the following research paper, Smith and Kendall have described a technique by which rating scales—in this case to be used in the evaluation of nursing performance—are anchored to examples of expected behavior. The scales they finally produce, while obviously fakeable, call for the voluntary cooperation of the rater and ask the rater questions he can honestly answer, rather than attempting to trick him in the manner of a forced-choice situation. And the reliabilities are impressive.

The Smith-Kendall technique has recently been successfully implemented at Cornell with approximately 900 short interviews for various student position (Maas, 1965). The usual adjective rating scales were originally tried; each candidate was interviewed twice, but only very modest reliabilities resulted. Significant improvement on this score was observed when the scaled expectation technique was introduced.

Dr. Smith, at Cornell University when this research was done, is now professor of psychology at Bowling Green University, Ohio. She is also an industrial consultant to Cain-Smith Associates, where her work is largely concerned with management assessment.

Dr. Kendall is chairman of the department of psychology at Simon Fraser University in British Columbia.

RETRANSLATION OF EXPECTATIONS:
AN APPROACH TO THE CONSTRUCTION
OF UNAMBIGUOUS ANCHORS
FOR RATING SCALES

Patricia Cain Smith and L. M. Kendall

In many situations, the use of ratings as criteria for validation of tests and as indices of effectiveness of educational, motivational, and situational changes involves extreme demands upon the quality of the ratings. Ratings from different raters in different situations should be really equivalent since they are almost always treated as if they were so. This demand for comparability means that interpretation of the rating must not deviate too widely from rater to rater or occasion to occasion, either in level (evaluation) or in dimension (trait, situational characteristic, job demand, temporal requirement, etc.). The present report covers the development of a rationale for a series of scales with such characteristics, and the testing of a procedure for their construction.

Psychologists seeking to establish reliable and valid rating systems have tended to impose their own values, interpretations, and beliefs about behavior upon the raters. Those who believe in trait theory construct scales based on presumably orthogonal dimensions established by factor analysis or by their own clinical intuitions. Those who believe that evaluation is either one general summary judgment or a composite of a large number of specific observations set up undifferentiated lists of good and bad statements, perhaps item-analyzed against some summary rating. In neither case is the rater consulted about the interpretation he would make of his own report.

This imposition of psychologists' values presupposes both understanding among psychologists concerning the organization of traits, and agreement among raters about the interpretations of various forms of behavior in relation to these traits. Without agreement, at least among a plurality of psychologists, impositions of their interpretations upon others seems presumptuous to say the least. Without consensus among the raters, more importantly, the raters cannot be expected to utilize the scales offered to them with any conviction or agreement.

This kind of consensus can be achieved only if the persons who will be rating indicate, in their own terms, what kind of behavior represents each level of each discriminably different characteristic, and which trait is illustrated by each kind of behavior.

Moreover, the rater must be "sold" upon the desirability of completing the ratings honestly and carefully, which means that the rating scales must have face validity for the purposes of the rater (which include guidance and counseling) as well as those of the reasearcher. Participation in the rating program must be elicited by virtue of the apparent usefulness of the procedure. These requirements are superimposed upon such essential measurement requirements as interrater reliability and independence of scales.

The present scales were constructed to meet the needs of raters in extremely diverse situations—head nurses rating the performance of staff nurses in a variety of hospitals, under a wide range of working loads, and with a diversity of previous training of both raters and ratees. Despite the differences in raters, they can be reasonably expected to share some common core of experience and of values concerning behavior on the jobs they will rate. The situation is similar to that in most executive, administrative, and technical positions, in which jobs with a single title are seldom comparable in either level of performance required or dimensions of performance considered important. In many of these situations, moreover, participation in the rating program cannot be demanded or even "persuasively encouraged" by higher echelon personnel, but must be voluntary.

The format proposed for the rating scales is a series of continuous graphic rating scales, arranged vertically, in a manner similar to that of the Fels scales. Behavioral descriptions, exemplifying various degrees of each dimension, are printed beside the line at different heights according to their scale positions as determined by judgments of head nurses similar to those who will be expected to use the scales. The examples are intended as anchors to define levels of the characteristic, and as operational definitions of the dimension being rated. Ratings are to be made by checking at any position along the line. Provision is made in the format for support of each check by notes concerning actual observed behavior.

This format was chosen as a means of combining the relevance to direct observation of critical incidents and similar techniques with the acceptability to raters of graphic rating scales. Rating errors associated with lack of definition of either dimensions or levels militated against the use of any of the traditionally used rating scales. Use of critical incidents, although extremely desirable because of reference to observed behavior, was eliminated since pretests had indicated that because of variations in the nursing situation a specific critical behavior often could not occur and hence could not serve as a basis for rating; and since most critical incidents cited tend to be too extreme for good psychometric policy which requires most accurate rating near the mean, rather than at the extremes. Use of forced choice was eliminated because of potential fakeability despite format and lack of validity in some important field tests (Kay, 1959).

The unacceptability to the rater of the forced-choice format was the most crucial deciding factor. The experience of the Army with this system led to its abandonment in 1950. Raters found it so unacceptable to rate without knowledge of the final outcome that they concentrated on finding ways to beat the system. In addition, forced-choice scales and home-office-scored checklists were both rejected because, in our experience, these scales include items almost as vague as those in the traditional rating scales.

The examples we used, therefore, represent not actual observed behaviors but inferences or predictions from observations. Raters are asked to decide whether a given behavior they have observed would lead them to expect behavior like that in the description. Instead of statements such as "shows interest in patients' description of symptoms," the anchors consist of expectations such as "If this nurse were admitting a patient who talks rapidly and continuously of her symptoms and past medical history, could be expected to look interested and listen." Calling for the rater to make such predictions implies that he is willing to infer from observations of behavior, that he has his own—at least implicit—belief about the intercorrelation of behaviors. The present procedure gambles that among a relatively homogeneous group of judges such as head nurses, these beliefs will be reasonably well standardized. It demands that such predictions be organized into areas not by theoretical similarity, but by judged similarity as indicated by the raters, and that the areas represent dimensions meaningful to the raters. It also provides checks in that each rater records briefly the behavior on which his prediction was based.

The use of an open, obviously fakeable format assumes that raters will, under proper circumstances, give conscientious estimates of the level of performance of ratees.

We believe that most rating errors are not due to deliberate faking. Moreover, no rating scale is really proof against distortion by a rater who really wants to do so. Better ratings can be obtained, in our opinion, not by trying to trick the rater (as in forced-choice scales) but by helping him to rate. We should ask him questions which he can honestly answer about behaviors which he can observe. We should reassure him that his answers will not be misinterpreted, and we should provide a basis by which he and others can check his answers.

The use of expected behaviors is intended to encourage such conscientiousness by making the predictions (a) so concrete that, in view of previous agreement by the peer (head nurse) group, central tendency or hedging effects will be minimized; and (b) so verifiable that the insight, judgment, values, etc., of the rater are potentially challenged if later behavior of the ratee should fail to confirm the prediction.

The basic procedure for scale construction resembles that employed to ensure that translations from one language to another adhere to the connotations as well as to the denotations of the original. Material is translated into a foreign language, and then, by an independent translator, retranslated into the original. Where "slippage" occurs, translations are corrected. Similarly, we required that examples, or expectations, be classified as indicative of a given dimension of nursing performance, and that independent judges indicate what dimension is illustrated by each. In addition, we defined the dimensions in the judges' own terminology and scaled the examples along these dimensions.

The submission of examples and subsequent reallocation by the raters' peers seems to ensure a high degree of content validity for the items and the scales.

PROCEDURES

Four groups of head nurses were sent by their hospitals to participate in conferences concerned with the use of evaluation in improving nursing performance. Data were gathered by mail from the remaining head nurses from the same hospitals from which two of the conference groups were drawn. One sample was held out for an independent replication. The samples are diversified and probably representative of head nurses who would be likely to use such a rating instrument.

The procedure used was essentially an iterative one, work performed by one group being checked and revised by others, so that the number of judges differs for different parts of the data. The content area was restricted to that of medical-surgical nursing.

1. First, qualities or characteristics to be evaluated were listed by each group; the most frequent dimensions were selected for further analysis. The nurses' own terminology was retained. Coverage of important aspects was further insured by gathering and classifying critical incidents in the customary way (for one sample only).

2. The groups formulated general statements representing definitions of high, low, and acceptable performance for each quality.

3. The groups submitted examples of behavior in each quality, and these were edited into the form of expectations of specific behavior.

4. Judges indicated, independently, what quality was illustrated by each example. *Examples* were eliminated if there was not clear modal agreement as to the quality to which each belonged. *Qualities* were eliminated if examples were not consistently reassigned to the quality for which they were originally designed.

5. Other judges used the examples to describe a specific nurse with outstandingly good nursing performance and another nurse with unsatisfactory performance. The difference between the outstanding and unsatisfactory nurse was computed for each pair of ratings to determine the discrimination value for each example.

6. Each vertical scale, together with the general definitions, was presented with a list of items previously judged by other raters as belonging to that quality. Judges rated each item from 0 to 2.0 according to the desirability of the behavior illustrated. Items were eliminated if the dispersion of judgments was large, or if the distribution was multimodal. All of the items which met these criteria were assembled for each scale, and the mean scale positions assigned to them for each group of judges were intercorrelated to give estimates of scale reliabilities. It was recognized that mean values were distorted somewhat by skewness in the distributions of judgments at the extremes, but it was felt that since the effect of skewness would be to reduce the stability of the means as estimates of central tendency, correlations using means would give at least a minimal estimate of agreement among groups of judges as to the relative position of items on a scale.

In addition, a comparison among samples of means and variances for all items in each scale indicates the similarity in the absolute location of the items by the various groups of judges.

RESULTS

The qualities which were most frequently considered important are listed in the first column of Table 13. An attempt was made to construct a scale and it proved possible to write general difinitions about which there was considerable agreement in each of these areas. Examples of expected behavior were submitted which met the standards of group agreement for each.

The retranslation procedure, however, eliminated many items and several qualities. Table 14 shows the number of items surviving for each. Some of the eliminations are interesting in themselves; items designed to illustrate Reaction under Pressure, for example, were frequently allocated to Organizational Ability or Knowledge and Judgment, on the grounds that a certain

TABLE 13

AGREEMENT CONCERNING ALLOCATION OF ITEMS TO CHARACTERISTICS

Characteristic	High Agreement (above 59%)	Lower Agreement (40%– 59%)
Knowledge and judgment	16	7
Conscientiousness	11	8
Skill in human relationships	21	9
Organizational ability	16	4
Communication skills	1	4
Objectivity	2	8
Flexibility	5	1
Reaction under pressure	1	1
Observational ability	7	4
Total number of items	80	46
Percentage of 141 items presented	57%	33%

TABLE 14

AGREEMENT BETWEEN ONE SAMPLE AND ALL OTHERS
ON ASSIGNMENT TO MODAL QUALITY

Quality	Number of Items Assigned by Both Groups	Geisser's Concomitance Measure R
Knowledge and judgment	16	.52*
Conscientiousness	12	.55*
Skill in human relationships	23	.84*
Organizational ability	18	.90*
Objectivity	9	.71*
Observational ability	11	.83*

* $p \leq .01$.

degree of crisis is normal in nursing and ability to meet it involves primarily establishing priorities and knowing what to do. Communication Skills items were allocated to Skill in Human Relationships or Conscientiousness because the items involved, to a large extent, either explaining to patients or keeping records. Both Reaction under Pressure and Communication Skills were eliminated at this step. Flexibility was also considered unpromising, although attempts were made to retrieve it in later institutes not reported here.

The significance of agreement of judges in assigning items to the same modal classification was tested for six scales (see Table 14) by a test of concomitance (Geisser, 1958) for all items which, after editing, had been presented for allocation to areas or qualities. This coefficient showed agreement to be significantly above chance when the judgments of one sample were compared with judgments of previous groups. It should be noted that this agreement was tested for examples presented in a scrambled order and judged one at a time; much better agreement can be expected when several examples of the same quality are grouped together on a single page as in the proposed rating scale format. A separate test of allocation of a few pairs and triads of items showed very high agreement.

Discrimination of items was checked by comparing average ratings assigned to outstanding and unsatisfactory nurses. For all items passing the previous criteria the differences were significant by the chi-square test. Also, virtually all differences for individual judges were positive. Therefore all retained items were clearly relevant in discriminating extreme levels of performance.

Scale reliabilities for the first four samples of judges for all retained items were ascertained. The mean evaluation of each of these items for four samples was correlated with that given to it by the holdout sample. The lowest scale reliability is .972. Grand means and variances for all items in each scale were calculated for each sample. Differences among the grand means within each scale were not significant by F tests.

Parenthetically, there are no consistent or significant differences in intercorrelations, means, or variances between Conference and Mail groups.

DISCUSSION

In general, the procedure seems satisfactory, with adequate agreement concerning allocation of examples, excellent discrimination, and high scale reliability. The potential advantages of scales based on such procedures are obvious; they are rooted in, and referable to, actual observed behavior; evaluations of the behavior have been made by judges at least reasonably comparable to those who will eventually use the scales; whatever we think of the terminology, the traits of qualities covered are operationally defined and are distinguishable one from another by the raters. Both dimension and level have been agreed upon, so that there is a fair chance of treating ratings by different raters as comparable just so long as they agree with the interpretations of the expectations. Even though different specific behaviors may be observed in different situations, they are referred to the common set of expectations which serves as a mutual frame of reference. Moreover, the chance to supplement predictions with documentation of the actual observed behavior upon which the predictions are based (as is provided by the scale format) permits checking and revision of examples and scales. Also, the use of these supporting anecdotal records, as well as the ease with which predictions can later be checked, favors honest and conscientious rating.

The disadvantages are equally obvious. The decision to use the raters' own theory of traits, and retranslation as a method of checking items, implied that raters would eventually be able to make decisions concerning what characteristics were involved in a given observed behavior. Most behavior is complex, and certainly not attributable to a single cause in the makeup of the individual, without regard to interaction of needs or to the influence of the situation. The use of trait names, and of general statements concerning levels of performance, in addition to the behavioral anchors may make for ambiguity in ratings, especially if one set of raters is less critical than another and displaces the items in relation to the general standards. One set of raters may also be more likely to attribute complex behavior to one cause while another set may prefer another. There are also too many scales for easy handling.

We hape that the number of qualities can be reduced after actual field use permits computation of scale intercorrelations and interrater reliabilities under normal rating conditions. We expect that experience and training with the scales will enable the rater to evaluate complex items of behavior on several relevant scales (and that this evaluation may serve some useful function in improving the rater's ability to interpret, diagnose, and improve the behavior of the person rated). We further hope that the general trait names, with their accompanying general definitions, will "wither away" and be replaced in use by the operational definitions provided by the behavioral expectations. Grouping the expectations on a single page will improve agreement as to qualities also. We expect, moreover, that as higher standards of performance become generally accepted, examples may appear that may be placed even higher in the vertical scales than the present items.

Weights for combining scales in order to give a summary rating, where needed, should be determined empirically by the use of multiple regression against a reliable rating of overall performance obtained in the field and probably separately for each nursing situation.

The consistency of judgments renders tenable the hypothesis that homogeneous groups of judges do share a common belief about the manner in which behaviors are intercorrelated and can extrapolate from observed to predicted behavior.

The procedure seems promising not only for nursing, but also for other complex tasks. Parenthetically, we should point out that reliabilities are so high that procedures similar to this one could certainly be attempted with smaller numbers of judges, and that sampling differences seem to be a relatively trivial source of error. Wherever behaviors may be expected to be reasonably comparable or interpretable from one situation to another, as in many professional and administrative jobs, and in research settings where observations can be made under fairly uniform conditions, the procedure seems applicable. We hope that it will prove useful in industrial, educational, and social areas of research.

Ratings have been traditionally employed to summarize personality data or interview impressions or actual performance. A new and rather unusual use of ratings is to be found in the work of Carkhuff and Berenson (1967, Ch. 1) and their colleagues. These authors have developed a series of five-point rating scales to measure counselor-therapist effectiveness with clients where a rating of 3 is the minimally facilitative level of interpersonal functioning. One of the scales measures counselor empathic understanding of the client's frame of reference; others measure genuineness and self-disclosure on the part of the counselor (i.e., lack of facade or how fully the counselor is himself to the client); still others deal with the counselor's respect and concern for client feelings and the degree to which the counselor enables the client to deal concretely and specifically with client feelings. Finally, other scales deal with the extent to which the client, in turn, is able to explore himself and experience himself with immediacy. Research has shown these to be reliable scales which can succinctly measure necessary conditions for therapeutic change. This research has shown to a distressing degree that few individuals— professionals included—cast in a helping role attain an average rating of even 2 of these scales; furthermore, graduate students in traditional clinical training programs tend to show declines in overall ratings as their graduate training proceeds!

PART EIGHT

Situational
Testing

A topic always of great interest to students in courses devoted to psychological testing is performance measures of personality, or situational testing. Typically, in such situations either the subject is quite unaware that he is being observed at all —as illustrated by the first article in this section, dealing with the pecuniary honesty of the public—or else the subject is unclear about the purpose of the test situation in which he has been placed. More often, when situational tests are devised it is the second type that can be laboratory based. With the first, of course, the test administrator must go directly into the field.

The designs for such tests often are very ingenious. Understandably, it is easier to design these performance measures for children than for adults, but good results have been achieved with both such groups. Perhaps the earliest large-scale studies using performance measures with children are the monumental reports of Hartshorne and May (1928–30), whose intensive and detailed studies for the Character Education Inquiry included tests of traits such as honesty, money handling, truthfulness, persistence, cooperativeness, and generosity. A famous and well-publicized World War II situational testing program was one for the Office of Strategic Services, the predecessor of today's Central Intelligence Agency. This testing program, of which performance measures of personality were only a part, extended over some three and one-half days, and was conducted on an estate outside Washington, D.C. The psychologists hoped that they could successfully measure, by situational testing, such complex traits as emotional stability, reaction to stress, frustration tolerance, and creative problem-solving ability. For details about this ambitious program consult the volume published by the OSS Assessment staff (1948).

The reader's attention is called to the Webb Paper (see pp. 22–26), wherein many examples of ingenious situational testing were presented.

The first article deals with a public, or field, situation where individual testing was not the focus. The study involves imaginative and entertaining observations about the pecuniary honesty of the public. The study was published in 1948 in the *Journal of Abnormal & Social Psychology,* and is reproduced here in its entirety. Dr. Merritt is associate dean of the Graduate College at the University of Arizona; Dr. Fowler is a physicist at the University of Oklahoma.

THE PECUNIARY HONESTY OF THE PUBLIC AT LARGE

Curtis B. Merritt and Richard G. Fowler

INTRODUCTION

Honesty has been described by some investigators as a general characteristic or trait and by others as an aggregation of specific habits. While the question of the existence or nonexistence of some traits cannot be regarded as finally settled, the authors incline to the view that there are fundamental dispositions which influence human behavior. Without attempting to identify honesty itself as a basic human characteristic, the purpose of this study is to sample the trustworthiness of the public in a situation involving financial honesty and to provide some measure of the trait underlying the obliging acts which were manifested during the course of the experiments.

Human honesty is unusually difficult to investigate because of the influence of surveillance on the results. It is believed that the technique to be described largely obviates this criticism. How many human beings will remain honest when there will never be any judge of their dishonesty other than themselves? How many will be sufficiently tempted by the suggestion of a small financial gain to react dishonestly? Within the limits of a particular situation this study proposes to answer these questions as completely as possible. By extension of the experimental method it was found possible to answer other questions as well.

METHOD

The necessary conditions for an objective test of honesty were achieved by use of the United States Postal Service. Nearly everyone has had the experience of recovering lost articles or mail through the grace of the public. If stamped and addressed letters seemingly containing money were judiciously distributed, the number returned should give some indication of the honesty of the finders as a group. The success of the tests depended upon the reliability of the mails. This was found to be perfect in a score of checks made on it, and is known to be excellent in general knowledge.

If the result is to be the completely undisturbed reaction of the individual it must be assured that he is alone when he finds the article. This could not always be guaranteed, and so the experimental data are perturbed by the gregariousness of human beings. It is our impression that a large majority of the letters were found by single pedestrians, but group morality must certainly have influenced a number of the cases. This could have been eliminated by observing the discovery of each lost article but time did not permit this. An estimate of the departure of the result obtained by random tests from individual morality could be made at any time by a study of the frequency of groups of pedestrians as a function of number in a group.

The actual method of procedure in these experiments was generally as follows. Stamped, self-addressed, and sealed letters of two types were "lost" by depositing them prominently but discreetly on the sidewalks of various cities in the East and Midwest. Type A contained only a trivial message, while type B contained, besides a message, a lead slug of the dimensions of a fifty-cent piece. The accompanying message indicated that the lead disc as such was of value to the addressee. Care was taken to drop the letters in locations sufficiently removed from one another to preclude the possibility of any one person finding more than one of the letters. All were put down in clear weather so that the envelopes would not become soiled and hence lose their appearance of value. Tests were made by night and day in both business and residential districts. The technique of dropping the letters was to let them fall to the ground through a hole in the experimenter's trouser pocket. It was possible to drop letters in this manner, even on crowded streets, without establishing ownership by attracting the attention of passers-by.

The envelopes used were standard 3½-by-6½-inch size. They were addressed in ink and stamped. No return address was given, nor was there any clue as to the owner, other than the potential owner, the addressee. The moneyless (type A) letters contained a simple message on a single sheet of paper to keep their general appearance normal in every respect. The loaded (type B) letters were similar except that they contained a lead disc the exact size and thickness of a fifty-cent piece. The disc was roughened to enhance as much as possible the impression that it was an actual coin. Also the lead disc was enclosed in a smaller envelope to prevent its breaking through and being lost.

The letters were dropped on many different days and in many different cities to insure a representative sampling of the public at large. No attempt was made to watch the pickup of all the letters. However, in order to eliminate the possibility of any selective factor operating to affect the random sampling, the places where the letters had been dropped were checked in about a third of the cases, from fifteen minutes to an hour afterward. This check revealed the pickup to be 100 percent. About twenty specimens were watched until picked up. This brought out that in 90 percent of the cases the first person who noticed the letter picked it up, whether walking alone or in a group. To obtain preliminary information on the reliability of the public at returning lost mail before investing money and effort in the main research problem a test was made by distributing postcards. Here, in spite of the difficulties attending because light cards were blown around by the wind and defaced by rain, three quarters of the one hundred cards were returned. This made it certain that some information would be obtained from the experiment and accordingly it was carried out.

DATA AND DISCUSSION

A summary of the data obtained is given in Table 15. The table is self-explanatory.

TABLE 15

Article	Number Dropped	Number Returned	Returned Opened	Percentage Returned
Type A (blanks)	33	28	0	85
Type B (test letters)	158	86	11	54
Type C (postcards)	100	72	0	72

Eighty-five percent of the control type letters were returned. This is roughly comparable with the result of the postcard test in which 72 percent were returned. The difference between the two figures probably represents the number of postcards dispersed and lost by natural forces, together with those judged by the finder to be not worth mailing because of the triviality of the message. In the 15 percent of these control letters lost we see very little reason for random losses except in the case of those which may have fallen into the hands of small children. Times of day and locations were in general chosen to minimize the effect of children on the experiments. Of perhaps twenty cases in which the pickup was observed, only one was by children, and they gleefully hurried to the nearest box and posted the letter. The factors which seem most important in the missing 15 percent of controls are dishonesty, curiosity, forgetfulness, and carelessness. Procrastination and forgetfulness probably combined to lose a few letters. This does not seem likely to be very important in view of the experimental fact that, out of the many tests made, no missives were postmarked more than forty-eight hours beyond the time of distribution, and only one showed the folding marks which would be present from being carried in a pocket for any length of time. Curiosity over the nature of the message and the sender probably stimulated several finders to open controls. Subsequent disappointment and chagrin at the triviality of the message then operated to cause the destruction of the letter. No doubt the ancient human principle of salvage rights was next invoked, although illegally, to acquire the stamp. In some cases it is possible that the finders may have applied this principle to the stamp *ab initio*. The factor of curiosity, with or without accompanying dishonesty, seems satisfactory to account for these losses.

The type-A letters cannot be regarded as acting as a perfectly effective control on the type-B letters. Their failure to do so derives from two factors, the first of which is curiosity. Fewer type-B letters should be lost from curiosity than those of type-A, since the presence of a specious fifty-cent piece in the letter should act as a deterrent for most of the curious but intrinsically honest, while honest individuals, whose curiosity still carried them away, could be expected to mail the opened letters. Seven percent of such previously opened slug-bearing letters were received. This figure of course must also include people whose dishonesty applies only to money and who, on finding the slug to be worthless to them, but valuable to the addressee, mail it. It can be said of them that their honesty undergoes a transition between the postage stamp fee and fifty cents. The second factor which tends to invalidate the controls as such is the probable lower random loss of the slug-bearing letters. These remained in place more satisfactorily and, once found, it seems unlikely that they would have been neglected as the blank letters may have been. Since the blank letters could not be regarded as a good control, we were compelled to establish the degree of certainty that a given letter is picked up by someone.

To attain this information it was customary to make the distribution in circuits, going over the same course after an interval of time had elapsed. This was done in at least half of the tests made, and in every case it was found that the missive was gone within an hour. It seems likely, therefore, that the honesty coefficient is more nearly related to the actual percentage of slug-bearing letters returned than to the control.

Losses among the slug-bearing letters can be attributed to dishonesty, salvage, and random loss. It is doubtful that the random loss was very large, and on the basis of the sampling previously described it seems unlikely that it extended to more than one or two letters. Even one letter which was found by a paper-picker was not deposited in his waste basket, but in his pocket, and later mailed. Loss occasioned by forgetfulness, carrying the letter home, mislaying it, etc., does not seem to be important, for certainly no one is likely to throw a stamped envelope apparently containing fifty cents into the discard without examination. The chief distribution of losses must therefore be between dishonesty and salvage.

By salvage we mean the ancient law that lost articles are the property of the finder. Legally, this is the case with unidentifiable articles only. The potential owner of the pseudo-fifty-cent piece was clearly indicated. Although it does not seem likely that many of those who actually opened these letters did so as an assertion of right, it must be conceded that cases may have occurred in which the finder erroneously believed the property to be legally his.

The eleven letters which were returned opened were especially interesting. Each contained the imitation fifty-cent piece and three had even been placed in new envelopes with another stamp. The remaining eight had been patched up in various ways before being mailed. Because of the factor of curiosity mentioned before, it cannot be said how many of these cases are human obligingness combined with dishonesty or financial need. These eleven letters seem to support the contention of previous investigations that there are varying types and degrees of honesty. It would be worthwhile to perform a similar experiment with coins of a different denomination in order to throw additional light upon this point. It would be most interesting if actual bills could be included conspicuously in glassine windowed envelopes to determine the irreducible minimum of honest people.

Watching the pickup of the letters proved to be a most entertaining pastime. Some were picked up and immediately posted at the nearest mailbox. Others were examined minutely, evidently precipitating quite a struggle between the finder and his conscience, before being pocketed or mailed. Some were carried a number of blocks before being posted, one person carrying a letter openly for nine blocks before mailing it. A lady in Ann Arbor, Michigan found a letter and carried it six miles in her car to deliver it personally, although she was not acquainted with the addressee. One letter, picked up in Harrisburg, Pennsylvania was mailed from York, Pennsylvania. Another, picked up in Toledo, Ohio was mailed in Cleveland. Still another from the Toledo streets was mailed from Monroe, Michigan. Two missives left on the steps of the cradle of liberty in Philadelphia failed to find their way into a mailbox. Two of five letters left on church steps during Sunday services failed to return.

INTERPRETATION

The first human quality which we believe that the tests begin to measure is that trait underlying the obliging acts, consideration, and altruistic responsibility. We believe that this is the case because the letters were placed carefully and conspicuously with their stamp side up so that they were easily recognizable for what they were as they lay. The observations of actual pickups clearly demonstrated that, in the majority of cases, the first person to see the missive accepted the responsibility for its care. In only one case observed was a letter passed over by a man who had seen it. This man stopped, bent down and glanced at it, and passed on. He may have concluded that the owner would come back after it. On this basis we feel that a high percentage of the American public at large, between 80 and 90 percent, have this generally altruistic attitude.

The second quality of which some estimate was possible was intrinsic financial honesty. The word intrinsic is used here to differentiate these honest acts from those cases in which the individual may have wrongly believed his act of salvage to be legally defensible. It was found that at least 55 percent, and at most 70 percent, of the individuals tested were intrinsically honest about such a financial matter. It is our belief, from the analysis of the sources of loss in the experiments, that the lower figure is the more accurate.

It is an old question whether a person can be financially dishonest and still intellectually honest in other respects. The possibility can usually be proven by selected instances. It is possible that the 7 percent of letters returned opened indicates the extent to which this is true, if we exclude the likelihood of extreme curiosity in truly honest people.

SUMMARY

We conclude from the evidence presented that the public at large is very strikingly altruistic, manifesting obligingness, consideration, and responsibility. A sharp decline in the reliability of the public sets in under the effects of suggestion of financial gain. One third of the altruistically minded are converted to selfish behavior. It is probable that an even larger proportion of the public at large is unreliable in such a financial matter.

The success of these experiments indicates the possibility of their extension to more elaborate tests on the response of general and specialized groups. However, general disclosure of the method will in all probability destroy its effectiveness.

▽ ▽ ▽

ONE further example of situational testing in the field is cited because of its entertaining nature and also because it is an attempt to study a highly abstract personality trait—altruism. The situation presented is highly naturalistic, something few laboratory investigations can manage. One can therefore be certain that the behavior elicited is entirely spontaneous and that the situation has few, if any, of the demand characteristics known to operate with volunteers and in laboratories.

At the time of this study, Dr. Bryan and Miss Test were at Northwestern University. Dr. Bryan is currently a member of the Center for Psychological Studies at the Educational Testing Service in Princeton, New Jersey. The study is one of four experiments that appeared in the *Journal of Personality and Social Psychology* in 1967 under the general title, "Models and Helping: Naturalistic Studies in Aiding Behavior."

A LADY IN DISTRESS:
THE FLAT TIRE EXPERIMENT

James H. Bryan and Mary A. Test

Attention has been directed recently toward the study of altruistic behaviors, i.e., those acts entailing self-sacrifice for no apparent personal gain. While such actions have generally been ignored by the psychological community, perhaps because of this community's biological orientation, such behaviors have important practical and theoretical implications. At the very least such behaviors are useful to the survival of a variety of social institutions, man's included. Additionally, the study of such actions will further clarify the nature of reinforcement.

Several recent experiments have suggested that one important determinant of helping behaviors is the presence of models. Rosenhan and White (unpublished) have demonstrated that significantly more children will donate gift certificates, a highly valued secondary reinforcer, to a fictitious orphanage after having seen an adult model do so than will Ss who were not exposed to such models. While many of the studies on modeling effects have been based on children, several investigations have suggested that models might be effective in eliciting self-sacrificing behavior in adults. Rosenbaum and Blake (1955) found that college students exposed to a model who volunteered, upon the personal request of the *E,* to participate in an experiment would be more likely to consent than Ss not exposed to such a model or who observed a model refuse to cooperate. Pressures toward conformity in these experiments were great, however, as the request was made directly by the *E* and in the presence of a large number of other students. The present authors, under conditions designed to maintain *S* anonymity, but within a college laboratory, found that college students who were either helped or observed others being aided were more likely to offer help to a stooge than Ss who were provided with no model or a model who refused to help.

Investigations of modeling that employ adults as Ss and that demand self-sacrifice on the part of Ss are limited in number, exploit strong pressures toward conformity, and rely upon college students as Ss. The present experiment was designed to assess the impact of models upon subsequent spontaneous offers of help by using adults other than college students in an experimental setting other than a university.

METHOD

The standard condition consisted of an undergraduate female stationed by a 1964 Ford Mustang (control car) with a flat left rear tire. An inflated tire was leaned upon the left side of the auto. The girl and the flat and the inflated tires were conspicuous to the passing traffic.

In the model condition, a 1965 Oldsmobile was located approximately a quarter of a mile from the control car. The car was raised by jack under the left rear bumper, and a girl was watching a male changing the flat tire. Stooges played the same role throughout the experiment.

In the no-model condition, the model was absent; thus, only the control car was visible to the passing traffic.

The cars were located in a predominantly residential section in Los Angeles, California. They were placed in such a manner that no intersection separated the model from the control car. No turnoffs were thus available to the passing traffic. Further, opposite flows of traffic were divided by a separator such that the first U turn available to the traffic going in the opposite direction of the control car would be after exposure to the model condition.

The experiment was conducted on two successive Saturdays between the hours of 1:45 and 5:50 P.M. Each treatment condition lasted for the time required for 1000 vehicles to pass the control car. While private automobiles and trucks, motorscooters and motorcycles were tallied as vehicles, commercial trucks, taxis, and busses were not. Vehicle count was made by a fourth member of the experiment who stood approximately 100 feet from the control car hidden from the passing motorists. On the first Saturday, the model condition was run first and lasted from 1:45 to 3:15. In order to exploit changing traffic patterns and to keep the time intervals equal across treatment conditions, the control car was moved several blocks and placed on the opposite side of the street for the no-model condition. The time of the no-model treatment was 4:00 to 5:00 P.M. On the following Saturday, counterbalancing the order and the location of treatment conditions was accomplished. That is, the no-model condition was run initially and the control car was placed in the same location that it had been placed on the previous Saturday during the model condition. The time of the no-model condition was 2:00 to 3:30 P.M. For the model condition, the control car was placed in that locale where it had been previously during the no-model condition. The time of the model condition was 4:30 to 5:30 P.M.

Individuals who had stopped to offer help were told by the young lady that she had already phoned an auto club and that help was imminent. Those who nonetheless insisted on helping her were told the nature of the experiment.

RESULTS AND DISCUSSION

The dependent variable was the number of cars which stopped and from which at least one individual offered help to the stooge by the control car. Of the 4,000 passing vehicles, 93 stopped. With the model car being absent, 35 vehicles stopped; with the model present, 58 halted. The difference between the conditions was statistically significant.

. It should be noted that the time of day had little impact upon the offering of aid. Fifty vehicles stopped during the early part of the afternoon; 43, during the later hours. Likewise, differences in help offers were not great between successive Saturdays as 45 offers of aid were made on the first Saturday, 48 on the second Saturday.

The results of the present study support the hypothesis that helping behaviors can be significantly increased through the observation of others' helpfulness. The data further underscore the importance of modeling for the adult S. It is noteworthy that under conditions where conformity pressures are rather weak, that is, conditions where the direct confrontation with the requester can be easily avoided, where requests are not made directly, where the anonymity of the actor is so easily maintained, and where self-gain is so minimal, that adults are still affected by the presence of models.

While it is clear that the behavior of these motorists was not dictated by a variety of situational or social pressures usually associated with study of modeling in adults (Rosenbaum & Blake, 1955) or experiments in academic settings (Orne, 1962), the mechanisms underlying the model effects are not obvious. Berkowitz and Daniels, for example, have provided evidence that dependency states in others will elicit helping behavior from college students. They have argued for the existence of a "norm of social responsibility," a norm dictating the helping of dependent others. It is perhaps possible that the presence of a helping model served as a reminder of such a norm. If this were indeed the case, the model may not only serve to define normative behavior to adults, but also may serve to activate already internalized norms.

Whatever the mediating events, the present study does support the contention that models are important in eliciting helping behaviors under those conditions where nonconformity would produce no interpersonal consequences and conformity would produce very little personal gain in adults other than college students in situations other than academic settings. The findings thus lend support to the generality of laboratory findings regarding the impact of models upon behavior.

▽ ▽ ▽

SITUATIONAL tests have had much appeal to psychologists involved in the development and validation of selection batteries. Almost all such workers use the World War II work of the OSS Assessment staff as a base, as would be especially apt in selection of policemen when usually one wants to measure effective behavior under stress. Situational tests make possible the observation of personality characteristics that appear only infrequently. Dishonesty would be another example, as the previous report by Merritt and Fowler illustrates. It has also been pointed out that with tests of this type the subject's usually strong desire to do his best does not invalidate the results. The investigator is typically looking for a maximum performance on the part of the testee, and he is also trying to obtain this performance in the most naturalistic setting he can devise. However, the problem of long-range validity will always remain. Situational tests are typically rather short, and they tend to be fairly specific (i.e., measuring stress or frustration tolerance in a single and specific situation). How far one can generalize from such test situations is a critical issue. As the OSS staff found, the long-range validity of their own ingeniously devised situational tests was very modest.

The following report on situational testing for an urban police assessment is a condensed version of a more complete report that appeared in the *Journal of Criminal Law, Criminology and Police Science,* 1966. Dr. Mills, the senior author, is associate professor of psychology at the University of Cincinnati and Chief Psychologist, Division of Mental Health of the City of Cincinnati. Dr. McDevitt is a practicing psychiatrist in Cincinnati and, in addition, serves as a consulting psychiatrist to the city of Cincinnati's Division of Mental Health. He also teaches a course in psychiatry for the University of Cincinnati Medical School. At the time of this research, Miss Tonkin was a graduate assistant in the department of psychology at the University of Cincinnati.

SITUATIONAL TESTS IN METROPOLITAN POLICE RECRUIT SELECTION

Robert B. Mills, Robert J. McDevitt,
and Sandra Tonkin

The emerging profession of law enforcement, as it is perceived in municipal police departments, has started to place greater emphasis upon careful selection of recruits. Careful screening is required because of the complex demands upon a modern metropolitan officer, and a closer look at psychological selection procedures is in progress.

A recent survey of assessment procedures in 55 U.S. cities revealed that 85% use some type of "police aptitude" test, which in most cases was little more than an unstandardized intelligence test (Narrol & Levitt, 1963). While 16% utilized some psychiatric interviews, critical motivational-emotional-personality dimensions were largely untapped. Whether these deficiencies can be remedied by addition of standardized personality inventories to police selection test batteries is questionable. While standardized objective personality tests may be suited for preliminary rough screening, the police candidate seems quite guarded, and a questionable extrapolation from nonpolice norm groups must usually be attempted.

Even intelligence as measured in paper-and-pencil tests, may not always be translated into equally intelligent decision making in an emergency field situation. This quality of clearheaded use of intelligence under pressure was termed "effective" intelligence by the OSS staff during WW II (1948). A possible answer to the limitations of current police selection procedures may be use of situational-type tests.

METHOD

Three situational-type tests were designed for inclusion in an overall psychological selection program of Cincinnati police recruits. Situational tests, except for the Bull Session, did not enter into final ratings of candidates. Situational tests were administered in the course of an intensive five to six hour psychological evaluation conducted in small groups of eight to ten candidates. Intent of the situational tests was to create a microcosm of a "natural" field problem an officer might encounter and to observe closely the candidate's reaction and performance under stress.

Design of the testing tasks observed the following criteria:

1. The tasks should have a close relation to an activity in which an officer might commonly be engaged.
2. Tasks should present a standard stimulus situation to each candidate. Conditions should not vary, if possible.
3. Each task should have several alternate solutions.
4. Accomplishment of task should not require very specialized abilities, so no candidate would be handicapped by lack of experience.
5. Task should be complex and difficult enough to engage the candidate fully, and stressful enough to produce a variety of emotional reactions. It should differentiate between candidates' performances. Still, care should be exercised not to harm or alienate candidates, who were voluntarily presenting themselves as job applicants.
6. Some measure of group activity should be included.
7. A "debriefing" session should be provided in order to encourage a climate of high morale, encourage expression of anger or anxiety, and help to restore emotional equilibrium.
8. Staff observers should have ample opportunity to confer after completion of a testing session, in order to synthesize observations, reconcile differences, and arrive at final ratings on each candidate with a maximum of information.

Foot Patrol Observation Test. Candidates were instructed to proceed on foot, unaccompanied, over a prescribed route, having been advised to "observe everything closely" along the way. The route proceeded for six blocks through a busy, downtown, predominantly Negro business section to Police Headquarters. Upon arrival the elapsed time of their "patrol" was noted, and 25 multiple-choice questions of facts concerning number of intersections traversed, key stores, type of street paving, etc. were administered. Number of correct answers became their score. An open-end essay questionnaire was also administered in which candidates were asked to describe impressions of persons living in the neighborhood, unusual incidents they observed, and their feelings about "keeping the peace" in this district. Questions were designed to tap latent attitudes about law enforcement, minority groups, poor people, and motivation for a police career, as well as providing a written sample of grammar and self-expression.

Clues Test. This situational test was adapted from the "Belongings" test described in *Assessment of Men* (OSS, 1948). An area was roped off containing a desk, chair, and miscellaneous office equipment. Within this area a selected set of "clues" was planted which suggested hypotheses about the personality, habits, whereabouts, and possible flight of a hypothetical city employee. Racetrack sheets, Scotch bottles, tranquilizers, aspirins, "cold" checks, dunning letters from local department and jewelry stores, perfumed love letters, passport application, and a memo from the City Manager requesting audit of accounts were included.

Candidates were given ten minutes to "investigate" the mysterious disappearance of this hypothetical city employee, while a staff member working quietly in another part of the room observed the approach of the candidate to the task. Candidates then completed blank spaces in a questionnaire form requiring information ranging from simple factual data to hypotheses (more heavily weighted in scoring) regarding whereabouts, motives, probable mental state, and possible basis for prosecution. False leads and alternative hypotheses were possible. A final score from 0–60 points was derived.

Bull Session. The so-called "Bull Session" was a group diagnostic procedure which borrows heavily from the principles of group psychotherapy. Candidates from each testing session, eight to ten in number, were assembled around a large table in a conference room. Two group leaders and two observers, previously briefed on each candidate, formed the evaluation team. During the two-hour session group leaders initiated discussion by asking for introductions, present occupation, and reasons for choosing a police career. While discussion generally proceeded spontaneously, group leaders occasionally framed key issues of police work, called upon silent candidates, and pointed out the necessity for participation by each candidate. A typical session included discussion of use of force, handling of fears, use of alcohol and narcotics, mental illness, prostitution, homosexuality, administration of justice in the courts, minority groups, and use of authority. Questions were posed by group leaders in the form of concrete, practical situations.

No separate ratings were derived from the Bull Session; however, immediately after each diagnostic session the evaluation team met together to decide Overall Performance Predictions (OPP) for each candidate. Group participation was evaluated, together with earlier test results. Differences between team raters were discussed and reconciled, and final OPP ratings assigned as follows: 4 Superior; 3, Above Average; 2, Average; 1, Below Average; 0, High Risk. Only the High Risk category was recommended for rejection by the Civil Service Commission.

RESULTS

The situational tests, as part of a comprehensive selection program, were initially administered to a group of 62 Cincinnati police candidates. Of this group, 42 eventually completed recruit training in the Police Academy and were termed the "success" group; 20 did not accomplish police training and were termed the "failure" group (12 of the "failure" group were recommended for rejection by our evaluation team). Foot Patrol and Clues were not included in OPP ratings in order to test their value as independent predictors. The Army General Classification Test, Civilian Edition, was included as a reference measure, since its relationship to police performance has previously been demonstrated. Comparison of mean scores of the initial "success" and "failure" groups on Foot Patrol, Clues, and AGCT showed that the successful group had achieved higher mean scores than the unsuccessful group, but such differences did not reach statistical significance.

The 42 successful recruits were ranked according to their final standing in the Police Academy, which was a weighted measure based upon weekly examinations and notebooks during the three-month training period. Situational and AGCT test scores were then ranked for the group, and Spearman rank-order correlations computed. It was demonstrated that AGCT scores correlated .595 with final standing, which is significant at the .01 level. The Clues Test correlated .375 with final standing, which is significant at the .05 level. Since Clues and AGCT correlated only .105 with each other, it is possible that Clues represents a nonintellective test measure related to police performance, which tends to enhance the validity of the situational test rationale. No other correlations were significant between any measures.

In order to cross-validate results of the initial trial, an identical procedure was followed with a second group of 25 candidates. Fifteen candidates successfully completed Police Academy training, and ten did not accomplish this goal. Mean differences between the successful and unsuccessful group again failed to be significant. Following graduation from the Police Academy, rank-order correlations between final standing and test measures were again computed. AGCT correlated .708 with final standing, which is significant at the .01 level. Clues correlated .425 with final standing, which is significant at the .10 level (just misses .05 level). AGCT and Clues correlated .340 together, which is nonsignificant, so that findings from the initial group were substantially confirmed.

Bull Session evaluation must be indirect, since no separate measurement resulted; however, team members agreed that these diagnostic sessions were the single most valuable technique used in recruit selection and weighted Bull Session results heavily in their OPP ratings. The correlation between OPP ratings and Police Academy performance might, therefore, be used as an estimate of the efficiency of the Bull Session as a predictor. For this purpose, the Kendall rank-order correlation (*tau*) was used owing to the restricted ranks on the five-place OPP ratings. Results were converted to z scores and level of significance taken from a normal-probability table.

For the initial recruit group a Kendall rank-order correlation of .359 was obtained, which has a probability beyond the .0005 level. The second group correlated .473 between OPP and final Police Academy standing, which is significant at the .007 level of probability. It was concluded that the evaluation team's overall ratings were highly predictive of later recruit performance. By implication, the Bull Session accounted for a large proportion of this accurate prediction.

Unsuspected character traits and attitudes which had not been noted during previous tests and one-to-one interviewing sometimes emerged during the Bull Session. For example, a group leader proposed a hypothetical situation in which a patrolman, working alone in a "rough" neighborhood, encountered several men fighting in a cafe. The question was asked, "If you were that patrolman, what would you do?" As general discussion developed around this theme, a consensus was quickly reached that the lone officer should summon aid before committing himself to stopping the fight, even though it might mean walking away from the scene to summon assistance.

One candidate vociferously disagreed with this solution, insisting that "You'd never be able to show your face again on that beat if you walked away." When he was challenged by several candidates with previous Military Police experience, he became red in the face and sat glowering with clenched fists. Another group member finally offered the comment, "I'd never want to be on patrol with you, buddy, that would be a good way to get myself killed." At this point, the isolated candidate exploded, "I think all of you guys are a bunch of yellow-backs!" This explosive outburst was a valuable clue in establishing the poor judgment and emotional instability of this candidate under stress; the stubborn pseudomasculinity he displayed within the group was almost a promise of inappropriate behavior in police service.

On another occasion a candidate displayed very rigid and dogmatic attitudes on every issue and as the group began to warm up, he commenced to orate in an almost evangelical manner. This man, quietly referred to as "the preacher" by another group member, began to set everyone's teeth on edge, and they attempted to stop him by sarcasm and talking over him. However, this candidate, apparently insensitive to the reactions of the men around him, continued to rant about his pet religious beliefs, and to moralize about the duty of the policeman to correct moral injustices in the community. This candidate's reaction formation against his own unrecognized hostile impulses toward his fellow citizens would have made him an unreliable and sadistic officer, and the other candidates quickly sensed how difficult it would be to work alongside this fellow.

In some cases a candidate was encountered who appeared to be unable to organize his thoughts in any coherent fashion during the group sessions. Some of these men had previously performed adequately on paper-and-pencil tests, but in the Bull Session became disorganized, rambling, and circumstantial. They were unable to react in a realistic and appropriate fashion to the other group members, and displayed completely inadequate social judgment in their responses to questions about practical matters. The evaluation team suspected that these candidates were making a borderline psychotic social adjustment, and sought a police career to give themselves a firmer self-identity and to move toward a more assertive role in life.

These examples have been given to illustrate the usefulness of the Bull Session in confirming psychological test signs whose meaning may have been somewhat tenuous, and in ferreting out behavior not revealed by conventional methods.

DISCUSSION

It appears promising that a simple situational task (Clues) could be constructed on an a priori basis, and on its initial trials manage to correlate with a performance measure. The failure of the Clues Test to correlate with a standardized intelligence measure (AGCT) makes it reasonable to infer that situational tests may be sampling behavioral dimensions not present in paper-and-pencil intelligence tests but important to police field performance. It is premature to speculate on the behavioral constructs sampled by situational tests, since it is characteristic of these tests to require a broad spectrum of skills for this solution. In fact, their lifelike quality comes from this breadth. If situational measures can be devised within a setting of continuous cross checks with eventual police field performance, they can be a promising supplement to more conventional techniques of assessment.

The failure of the Foot Patrol Test to correlate with other measures may represent the narrow range of scores obtained or other inadequacies of test construction, and illustrates the pitfalls of attempting untried tests without reliability or validity checks. The selection process occurred with a highly homogeneous, preselected group from an original pool of more than 600 applicants, which places a severe task upon any unverified test instrument.

The limitations of using final grades in a Police Academy training program must also be recognized. It is not necessary to document here the disappointing patrol performance of some men who showed promise during the training period. And later, even the most painstaking rating system in the field is subject to multiple biases. For example, it is common practice to start "rookie" patrolmen with rather low ratings of efficiency, so that adequate differentiation between field performance of starting patrolmen becomes quite difficult. A weighted measure of activity level based upon systematic reports of arrests, citations, etc., is under study by the authors, and this activity field measure may ultimately vindicate the situational test approach to selection.

It may be important to note that, despite the rigor of the selection process, no candidate has yet withdrawn or failed to complete the psychological evaluation phase of selection. Candidates have reported that they enjoyed the lifelike quality of the situational tests, thought this type of test "made sense" to them, and apparently preferred the action-centered tests to the conventional paper-and-pencil approach. Some candidates have expressed the feeling that the careful evaluation reflected the importance of the position they were seeking, and that finalists must be a hand-picked "elite" group, which is true. The group spirit generated during the Bull Session, with its overtones of competition and camaraderie, tended to counteract any anger or anxiety caused by the protracted testing session. The teasing and joking with examiners was an emotional catharsis which seemed to be helpful in restoring emotional equilibrium.

A type of situational test that may strike the reader as unusual is the research using the College and University Environment Scales (CUES), whose antecedent was the College Characteristics Index (CCI). The CCI was developed over a period of years by Dr. C. Robert Pace in collaboration with Dr. George Stern at Syracuse University. The instrument in its present form (CUES) is composed of 150 statements about college life—campus features and facilities, campus rules and regulations, items concerning student life and extracurricular organizations—all of which help to pin down the intellectual-cultural-social climate of the campus. When students take the test, they merely indicate whether they feel the statements on the questionnaire are true or false about their own campuses. CUES is therefore a way of obtaining a description of the college from the students themselves. These are not new or entering students, as are those in the Astin (1965) research; rather, as recommended in the preliminary manual (Pace, 1963), students must fill out CUES from a position of real acquaintance. For this, ideally, the entire junior class might be used. Normative data are currently based on a total of 50 schools. Scores from CUES provide a measure of the college environment, along five dimensions developed by factor analysis. The dimensions are:

1. Practicality—the degree to which personal status and practical benefit are emphasized.
2. Community—the extent to which the campus may be said to be friendly, cohesive, group-oriented.
3. Awareness—how much emphasis is placed on self-understanding and personal identity, wide range of appreciations and a personal involvement with world problems.
4. Propriety—the degree to which politeness and protocol and consideration are stressed.
5. Scholarship—how much in evidence is competitively high academic achievement, shown by such things as concern for scholarship and intellectual discipline, interest in knowledge and ideas.

From these five factor scales, institutional patterns may then be constructed for individual colleges and universities, or even for smaller subdivisions within these organizations. What is done here is to take the early CCI scales (there were 30 of these) and then do a factor analysis based on the 50 colleges and universities. The 50 colleges now become the variables, and the CCI scale scores for each college become the number of observations. A factor analysis of this matrix will thus produce institutional patterns or clusters. This relatively small number of institutions obviously does not constitute a representative sample for all U.S. schools, and so the subtypes of institutional patterns cannot be delineated with much confidence. Pace feels, regardless of the tentative results, that even this small-scale search for pattern may be of some interest and might also stimulate new speculation.

The following report by Dr. Pace is a brief summary of these results, which are given in the CUES Preliminary Technical Manual (Pace, 1963, pp. 71–76). Dr. Pace, formerly a collaborator with Dr. Stern at Syracuse University, and for many years the director of the Psychological Research Center there, is now professor of higher education at the University of California at Los Angeles.

CUES INSTITUTIONAL PATTERNS

C. Robert Pace

From these analyses, one can tentatively group colleges and universities into six patterns. First, there is a group of very selective, private liberal arts colleges–scholarly, aware, somewhat more proper than rebellious, and unconcerned with practicality. Most similar to this group is a group of large academically oriented public universities which are also typically high in scholarship and awareness, generally low in practicality, but which differ from the selective liberal arts colleges in that they have uniformly low scores on the community scale and are generally lower than the liberal arts colleges on the propriety scale. Most dissimilar to the selective liberal arts colleges is a group of large nonselective universities, both public and private. A fourth group consists primarily of small strongly denominational colleges characterized by high scores on the practicality, community, and propriety scales and by low scores on awareness. The fifth pattern consists of universities with a strongly technical emphasis. Most of these schools have an average to strong emphasis on scholarship but very low scores on community and awareness and average to slightly below average scores on practicality. And the sixth pattern consists of moderately denominational colleges and a few teachers colleges. These are characterized by low scores on scholarship and awareness and by high scores on practicality and community.

ILLUSTRATIVE PROFILES

Although there are certain general institutional patterns described in the foregoing section, and although there are certain general correlations between various CUES scores, there are nevertheless some unique qualities in each institution and many significant exceptions to all general tendencies. For this reason, profiles are presented of specific institutions which are alike in certain ways, or which one might think would be alike, but which differ significantly in other ways.

The first set of profiles—for Antioch, Swarthmore and Reed in Figure 6 —shows all three schools to be high on scholarship and awareness but very low on practicality. Antioch shows a much higher score on community than Swarthmore or Reed and each college is noticeably unique on the propriety scale.

The second set (Figure 7) describes three large public institutions—Purdue, UCLA and San Francisco State College.[1] Purdue and UCLA scored relatively high on the scholarship scale. UCLA and San Francisco State

---

[1] A more detailed report on San Francisco State has been published by Pace (1962).

scored high on the awareness scale, but Purdue has a fairly low score. All three universities are rather low on the community scale, with San Francisco State and UCLA being particularly low. On the propriety scale San Francisco State is much higher than either of the other two. Purdue is uniquely high on the practicality scale. In this second set of profiles, it is evident that high scholarship and awareness are not always correlated and that high scholarship is not necessarily incompatible with high practicality.

FIGURE 6   FIGURE 7

THREE PRIVATE LIBERAL ARTS COLLEGE   INSTITUTIONAL PATTERNS OF THREE
INSTITUTIONAL PATTERNS   LARGE PUBLIC EDUCATIONAL
                                            ENTERPRISES

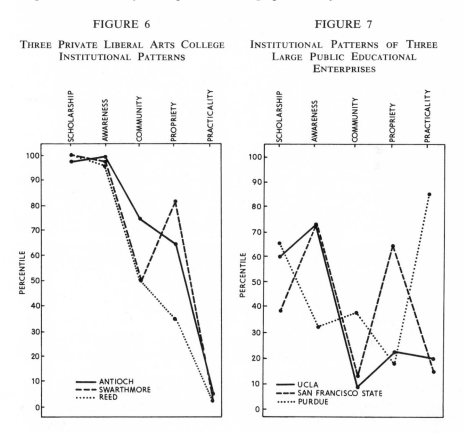

Certainly one generalization which clearly emerges from these studies of college environments is that it is risky to generalize. Many institutions of the same presumed type are, in fact, quite different from one another. Indeed, diversity of institutions is a characteristic of American higher education and this will remain true as long as it is a goal of American education to serve a diversity of students. It is partly for this reason that CUES are potentially useful both for the institution and for the prospective student. If colleges and universities are different from one another, with many being unique in significant ways, knowledge of the perceived atmosphere of a campus could lead to planned modification or planned preservation, whichever is wished by the faculty and administration, and to hopefully wiser choices on the part of selective students who are as eager to know more about the college as the college is insistent on knowing a lot about them.

Another and similar approach to arriving at a measure of college environments has been developed by Astin (1965). His method involves a set of 25 student attributes (typically, specific examples of nonacademic student achievement such as placing among the top three in a science contest, having a lead role in a play, being elected to one or more student offices) in the form of a simple questionnaire given to entering freshmen during orientation week at some 250 colleges and universities. In addition, the students were asked about their probable future major

FIGURE 8

MEDIAN INTELLECTUALISM SCORES (LEFT) AND AESTHETICISM SCORES (RIGHT)
OF STUDENT BODIES ENTERING 10 TYPES OF INSTITUTIONS
(Astin, 1965, p. 33)

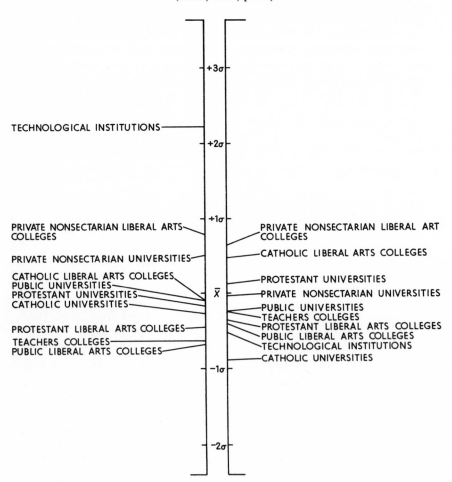

field and later occupation, the eventual college degree they planned to obtain, and father's occupation and educational level completed. Finished forms were obtained from over 127,000 students. From the replies to the open-ended questions concerning these last four items, students were classified according to Holland's (1963) occupational classification scheme, which corresponds to six basic personality types: realistic (as mechanic or tool designer); intellectual or scientific (botanist, anthropologist); social (speech therapist, foreign missionary); conventional (bank teller, statistician); enterprising (salesman, diplomat); and artistic (playwright, symphony conductor). These same six groupings may also be used to classify a student's major field. Thus, if a large proportion of entering freshmen reported they planned to become engineers, this student body would then receive a high rating on "realistic." (Astin comments on the remarkable variation among entering classes regarding future plans. For example, the percentage of first-year students eventually planning on graduate work varies from 6 to 98.) The questionnaire items answered by the students (52 input items made up the total) were factor analyzed into six factors—intellectualism, aestheticism, status, leadership, pragmatism, and masculinity. The result of all this made possible, then, the characterization of individual college environments in cookbook fashion. Figure 8 compares various college and university groupings on two of these factors obtained from the student input data—intellectualism and aestheticism. Astin specifically lists individual colleges by name and locale, followed by scores on all these variables. It is a very entertaining pastime for the reader to check scores of institutions with which he is well acquainted and compare these indexes with his own subjective impressions. Astin's handbook is a very useful compendium for both high school students and guidance counselors when involved with the proper selection of a collegiate institution.

PART NINE

Interests

OF the many kinds of psychological measurements, research has shown that the most valid, long-term results have been achieved with the Strong Vocational Interest Blank for males. Dr. E. K. Strong, Jr., has pioneered in this research for many years and has become famous for his persistent follow-up studies. It would be very difficult to find another psychological test or inventory about which so much long-range data are obtainable. This has, of course, made the SVIB one of the most useful counseling tools for college students.

The revised version of the blank for males was finished in 1966 and published by the Stanford University Press. Professor Strong, who had retired from Stanford in 1949, began thinking then about this now completed revision, since he wanted to eliminate some of the dated items and to incorporate certain psychometric improvement. At that time, he was totally involved in his large follow-up study of Stanford students of the 1930's (which eventually resulted in his 1955 volume, *Vocational Interests 18 Years After College*).

The job fell, eventually, to people at the University of Minnesota. In 1959, all of Strong's criterion data, consisting of about 40,000 completed interest inventories, were transferred to Minnesota and prepared for computer input and analysis. The Center for Interest Measurement Research was established, and Dr. David P. Campbell became the director. The research eventually involved two complete revisions of the inventory, plus the addition of a number of new scales (Campbell, 1966). The women's form is undergoing a similar revision, and plans are now formulated to make it available in the fall of 1968.

Strong (1951) published data on the permanence of interest scores for men ranging from 17 to 32 years of age, and for intervals of time from 3 weeks to 22 years. The coefficients of correlation were amazingly high for this test–retest data: .84 for 5 years, .83 for 10 years, .75 for 22 years. Campbell has continued this research, and, among the many reports issuing from the Center for Interest Measurement Research, has published data for a 30-year follow-up. This involved the Banker scale, and meant locating and retesting the original group which was tested in 1934. The Campbell study, condensed from its original version in the *Journal of Applied Psychology* in 1966, is also of interest because of the ingenious way of locating and constituting the 1964 group that would be involved in the retesting.

STABILITY OF INTERESTS WITHIN AN OCCUPATION OVER THIRTY YEARS

David P. Campbell

The Strong Vocational Interest Blank (SVIB) is one of the most widely used psychological measuring instruments. Its validity has been established in a variety of settings (see Berdie, 1960, for a review) and data collected over long periods of time have demonstrated the stability of measured interests over intervals as long as 22 years (Strong, 1955). The SVIB accomplishes this by providing an index of the similarity between an individual's likes and dislikes and those of successful men in a wide range of occupations. The results are particularly useful in guidance situations where counselors are trying to help young people plan their future.

The use of the SVIB, or any other empirically developed instrument, requires two assumptions of stability. The first is that the individual remains stable over time; the second is that the characteristics of the criterion groups remain constant. Specifically for the SVIB, the first assumption requires that the individual show some consistency over time in the activities that he finds interesting, thus allowing him to plan his future career on the basis of current likes and dislikes; the second requires that successful men in a specific occupation, say bankers, have the same interests today as did the bankers who were studied in 1934 to establish the SVIB Bankers Scale.

This study tests this second assumption.

The validity of the first assumption, that of consistency within the individual over time, has been well-established; data concerning this are extensively reported in the SVIB Manual (Strong & Campbell, 1966). The individual is consistent enough in his measured interests over several years, particularly if he is tested during his college days, to make this information useful in laying plans for a career several years in the future.

The second assumption mentioned above, that of constancy within a single occupation over several years, has received less attention. And it perhaps deserves less. Certainly any inventory successfully developed to distinguish between occupations is going to be useful for many years after its development because the membership of most occupations remains stable. Any inventory that distinguishes between a specific occupation and men-in-general in 1934 will certainly separate the two groups in 1935. The question under study here is whether it will do so 30 years later in 1964. This point is becoming more crucial as it has been over 3 decades since the original SVIB standardization data were collected and there is some concern as to whether the scales are still relevant.

Earlier studies of occupational constancy identified some mild but detectable differences between the original criterion group and groups from the same occupation collected several years later. It is not clear whether the differences were due to changes of interest within the occupation, or whether they could instead be explained by sampling differences.

What is needed is some method of holding the sampling technique constant over a substantial period of time. One possible procedure would be to study a group of individuals who today hold the identical positions held by the men in an occupational group studied years ago. This procedure has been used in this study with the group of bankers who were used to establish the SVIB Bankers Scale in 1934.

Essentially, this is a study of the interests of bankers who today hold the identical jobs held by the men in the banker criterion group 30 years ago.

METHOD

The group originally used to establish the Bankers Scale, collected in 1934, included 250 individuals. In the SVIB Manual, Strong described the group as follows:

> 172 were members of the Minneapolis Federal Reserve System; of these 172, 95 were bankers from state banks in Minnesota which opened immediately after the 1933 Bank Holiday and 77 were bankers from national banks and designated as "good bankers" by a qualified expert. The remaining blanks were obtained through The Psychological Corporation, New York, and from miscellaneous sources. Average age 45.5; Education 12.2 grade.

Using a 1935 bank directory, it was possible to identify the position held in 1934 by 189 individuals from the original criterion group. First, an attempt was made to locate and retest these men to determine the amount of change in interests within the individual over 30 years. Second, the individuals who held these 189 jobs in 1964 were approached and asked to fill in the SVIB.

Retesting the Original Group. The first phase of this study involved the follow-up study of the original criterion group. Table 16 reports the results of attempts to locate and retest these individuals.

As Table 16 indicates, most of the group—90%—were located or accounted for, but death and illness greatly reduced the potential sample size. The 48 usable respondents represented only about one fourth of the original group, though they constituted approximately two thirds of the current survivors.

TABLE 16

DISPOSITION OF ORIGINAL SAMPLE

	N	Percentage
Couldn't be located	20	10.6
Deceased	91	48.1
Seriously ill	6	3.2
Refused to participate	18	9.5
Filled out inventory incorrectly	6	3.2
Usable respondents	48	25.4
Total	189	100.0

Was this group of respondents a representative sample from the earlier group of 189? Certainly they were younger; one would expect a bias in age, simply because the older ones would die sooner. These respondents averaged 38 years old in 1934, compared with the average age of 46 of the entire criterion group. In 1964, their average age was 68, with a range from 54 to 81 and a median of 71.

However, this age difference should not affect the use of this sample to represent the interests of the total group as prior research has shown that interests are stable after about age 25. Further, a comparison of the average 1934 profile of this subgroup with the 1934 profile of the entire original criterion group showed virtually no differences between the measured interests of the two groups.

Testing the Current Bankers. The major part of this study involved the comparison of the SVIB profiles of the original 1934 sample of bankers with the matched profiles of the men who in 1964 held the identical jobs.

This job matching was accomplished by using Commercial West Bank Directories. The 1935 directory provided the job titles of the men in the original sample, and the 1964 directory provided the names of the men holding those positions currently.

This latter group was contacted and asked to fill in the SVIB. For example, if the President of the First State Bank of Duluth, Minnesota, was one of the original sample, the current president of that bank was asked to fill in the SVIB.

There were some problems with this matching. Occasionally the bank had changed names or organizational affiliation, and sometimes the job had been changed considerably. When in doubt, we erred in the direction of including the current individual in the sample even though it was not certain that he was working in precisely the same job as the earlier individual. But this was true in only a small percentage of the cases.

The results of the attempt to collect matchmates for each of the 1934 participants are summarized in Table 17.

TABLE 17

DISPOSITION OF MATCHED MATES OF BANKERS IN
ORIGINAL GROUP

	N	Percent-age
Bank had gone out of business	26	14
Woman held job in 1964	9	5
1934 individual still in same job in 1964 ..	13	7
1964 job-holder refused to participate	38	20
Usable respondents	103	54
Total	189	100

The total possible sample was 189. Disregarding those cases where the bank was no longer in business, where the job was today filled by a woman, and where the 1934 individual was still in the same job, the sample shrank to 141. Of these, 103 (or 72%) completed the Strong Blank.

RESULTS

The results of the retesting of the 48 subjects over an interval of 30 years show the same type of consistency that we have come to expect in interest measurement, though the median test–retest correlation of the occupational scales of .56 is lower than the .75 reported for college seniors over 22 years and the .72 for college freshmen over 19 years reported by Strong in his follow-up study (Strong, 1955). Though the characteristic interests of the group remained very stable, the individuals moved around somewhat in their rank orders. It is likely that these correlations were lowered slightly by the relative homogeneity of this group. Strong's data (1955, p. 68) indicate that the average retest standard deviation for 14 scales over 18 years was 11.7. For the retested bankers, the average standard deviation on the same 14 scales was 9.8.

The results of the comparison between the 1934 bankers and their matched mates in 1964 show that while the profiles were essentially similar, there were some differences, some of them as large as one standard deviation. No apparent pattern appeared in these differences; some of them were on scales where the 1964 bankers might be expected to score higher because of the generally increasing level of education—scales such as Psychologist, Physician, and Senior CPA. But other scales usually associated with technical, nonprofessional interests, such as Industrial Arts Teacher and Vocational Agriculture Teacher, also showed differences in favor of the 1964 bankers.[1]

In general, because the 1964 bankers scored lower on the Banker Scale than did the 1934 bankers (46 to 52, respectively) and slightly higher on most of the other 44 scales (on the average, 27 to 24), it appears that the Banker Scale is slightly less effective in differentiating bankers from men in other occupations than it was in 1934. However, some of this regression can be explained by cross-validation shrinkage as this comparison is essentially comparing the validation group with a cross-validation group collected 30 years later.

Although some shrinkage did occur, the most noteworthy result shows the SVIB Banker Scale is still valid 30 years later—current bankers score higher on it than on any other scale.

IMPLICATIONS

The results of this study indicated there was substantial similarity between the likes and dislikes of the bankers in the original SVIB criterion group and a group of bankers in identical jobs 30 years later. This finding clearly upheld the continued use of the SVIB Banker Scale for counseling purposes.

Can these results be generalized to other occupational scales of the SVIB? The answer to that question depends on whether the banking profession is more or less stable over time than other occupational groups, and this can only be conjecture. It would certainly seem that the changes in the banking business over the last 30 years have been as substantial as those in almost any other occupation. The original criterion group was collected in 1934, just after the banks reopened after the national bank holiday; in many ways, a new era began. Accounting procedures have evolved from hand-written records to the most elaborate electronic computer systems. To the

---

[1] The profiles for test–retest results over 30 years and for banker scores compared with their matched mates, contained in the original article, are not reproduced here. The 1966 SVIB Manual reproduces the first (p. 29) and also provides comparison profiles for the second (p. 32), but for only 93 rather than 103 bankers here. Both sets of profiles are visually very close.

naïve observer, it appears that the banking business has attempted to change its public image from that of a somber, staid old patriarch to that of an aggressive, hard-driving public servant. This is particularly reflected in the architecture of bank buildings; frequently the bank is the most modern building in the small midwestern town, the setting that most of these bankers were drawn from.

In spite of these many changes, considerable stability was found in the characteristic interests of bankers over 30 years. If the above speculations have any veracity at all, if the banking profession is changing at least as fast as other occupations, then it seems safe to generalize to the other SVIB scales and assume that they also remain appropriate for use today. It would, of course, be comforting to have comparable follow-up data on other scales to buttress this generalization.

The test–retest results from the 48 individuals over 30 years deserve brief comment. Strong has earlier said that interests remain very stable from age 25 until about age 55, the upper limit of the age of men in his follow-up studies (Strong, 1955). Based on the sample in this study, that is, men tested once at about age 40 and again at age 70, it seems safe to conclude that measured interests remain stable well into old age.

AN interesting sidelight on the predictive efficiency of the SVIB has emerged from the follow-up reports of the Study of Adult Development (formerly known as the Grant Study) at Harvard. Here the SVIB has been shown to work more effectively in one subculture than in another, and it is because of this new insight that the article by Dr. McArthur is presented here. What follows is a considerably condensed version of the original report, which appeared in the *Journal of Applied Psychology* in 1954. Dr. McArthur currently is psychologist at the Harvard University Health Service.

LONG-TERM VALIDITY OF THE STRONG
INTEREST TEST IN TWO SUBCULTURES

Charles McArthur

Surprisingly few long-term follow-ups have been made on the Strong Vocational Interest Blank, when one considers that the test has now been in use two decades.[1] Strong (1943) adduces support of four rather indirect propositions:

1. Men continuing in Occupation A obtain a higher interest score in A than in any other occupation.
2. Men continuing in Occupation A obtain a higher interest score in A than other men entering other occupations.
3. Men continuing in Occupation A obtain higher scores in A than men who change from A to another occupation.
4. Men changing from Occupation A to Occupation B score higher in B prior to the change than in any other occupation, including A.

A special 20-year follow-up by Strong (1952) dealt with medical interests only but was reported in a more direct manner. Of 108 Stanford alumni who were physicians 20 years after testing, Strong reports that 70 had A ratings on the physician scale in their undergraduate tests and 14 received a rating of B+. In all, then, 78 percent of these men who made careers as doctors had had a "high" physician score when tested in college.

PROCEDURE

The Sample. A series of 61 participants in the Study of Adult Development were given the Strong Vocational Interest Blank in the academic year 1939–1940. These young men were part of a longer series selected for interdisciplinary long-term study on the basis of their apparent "normality." All were sophomores at the time in Harvard College. We can now test the

---

[1] But see the previous Campbell article (ED.).

predictive power of the Strong over a fourteen-year interval from 1939 to 1953.

SVIB as a Predictor.   How well did the Strong taken in college predict the occupations of these men 14 years later? In Table 18 an assessment of the correctness of prediction is made in terms of "Good Hits," "Poor Hits," and "Clean Misses." The definitions of these terms are implicit in the claims made

TABLE 18

FOURTEEN-YEAR VALIDATION:
STRONG VOCATIONAL INTEREST BLANK

Validity	Direct	Indirect	Total
Good hit 22		5	27
Poor hit 7		5	12
Clean miss 14		7	21
Total 43		17	60

by Strong; he feels that a good hit may be counted when a man enters an occupation for which he scored A or which had the 1st, 2nd, or 3rd highest ranking score on his test. Less credence is given to a B+ score when it is outranked by many others, yet such scores are usually regarded as "worth some consideration" in counseling. They are here called "Poor Hits." Anything below these criteria is taken to be a "Clean Miss."

The table also specifies whether or not a scale offered a "Direct" or "Indirect" measure of interest. The indirect measures are often no fair test at all, yet a counselor might in practice be forced to make just this sort of inference (as using the Author-Journalist scale to assess the advisability of teaching drama) for lack of other evidence.

Sixty cases could be used for validation, one man being in an occupation for which no scoring scale seemed even indirectly pertinent. It becomes apparent by inspection of Table 18 that some accuracy is lost through the necessity of using indirect measures. The fairest evaluation of the Strong's predictive power may be had from the 43 men whose occupations can be directly tested. Of these, only one third are Clean Misses. Just half were hit well.

These figures are slightly lower than those given by Strong in his follow-up of medical interests. There, about one out of four tests turned out to be complete misses. Yet one must remain pleased with an instrument that under "blind conditions" (these tests were all unscored until 1952) predicts future behavior even half the time.

STRONG'S FIRST PROPOSITION

Had a counselor used these tests in 1939 to suggest to the boys their likeliest future vocation, he would have been downright misleading only once in every three attempts. Yet even the "good" tests would have presented him with a grave difficulty: the tests containing accurate predictions also contain too many "extraneous solutions." Like a mathematician solving a cubic equation, the counselor must enter the problem with the expectation that not all the answers offered will be real and pertinent.

Whatever its latter rating, the scale most pertinent to future choice of occupation ranked anywhere from 1st to 33rd highest out of the 44 scales for which each test was scored. The median rank of the most pertinent scale was 5th. That means that the counselor using these tests could have expected, on the average, four "extraneous solutions" with higher-ranking scores than the true solution. It is, of course, true that the "extraneous" quality of certain high scores is obvious: few would counsel a tone-deaf boy to be a musician.

Strong (1934) states that "a college student who continues ten years in the same occupation enters an occupation in which he ranks second or third best." Like our group as a whole, our men who continued in the same occupation (not considering interruption by the war) entered occupations in which, on the median, they had ranked fifth best. Once again, our figures are slightly less impressive than Strong's. It is certainly not true among our cases, men "continuing in Occupation A obtain a higher interest score in A than in any other occupation."

STRONG'S SECOND PROPOSITION

The proposition that men engaged in an occupation score higher on that occupational scale than all other men is well supported by our data. That is, doctors outscore controls on the physician scale, lawyers outscore controls on the law scale, etc. (Controls are simply all the rest of the 61 cases.) This is true for every directly scaled occupation that occurs more than once.

Strong's second proposition seems to be valid.

STRONG'S LAST TWO PROPOSITIONS

Seventeen of our 60 men have made changes in occupation other than shifts enforced by entering the armed services. Often, these men abandoned two or more vocations before settling on the job they are engaged in today. Strong's follow-up data showed that men who abandoned an occupation were likely to possess lower scores on that occupational scale than the scores made by men who continued on the job. Strong found that rule to hold "except for the records of two individuals," while we, except for one instance of tie, find it to be entirely so.

Another generalization Strong offers about men who change vocational fields is that they will proceed from a field in which they have a low score into a field in which they score high. That was true of nine of our changeable men, seven men going contrary to their tests and entering new jobs for which their test scores were lower. (One man changed between jobs with identical scores.) These figures run faintly in the right direction, probably looking even less convincing than the data from which Strong felt that Proposition 4 was "almost but not quite sustained."

CONTENTMENT IN OCCUPATION

As Strong has pointed out (1952), "the validity of an interest test should be measured in terms of satisfaction" but for this "there is no satisfactory measure." The Study of Adult Development has accumulated much data on expressed satisfaction and dissatisfaction with occupational choice, through the use of annual questionnaires.

The 1953 questionnaires were still coming in when this was written. Of the 60 men in whom we are interested, 37 had returned their questionnaires. There was, as a matter of fact, some tendency for the men engaged in occupations for which they possessed a favorable Strong score to return their questionnaires early! (Three quarters of them had done so, as against half the men with lower scores.) For this, Fisher's p comes out .09. This is not so trivial an indication as it may appear; the study staff has long been aware that among people who are hardest to hear from are those who have a sense of not having succeeded.

Several 1953 questions were pertinent to an inferrable sentiment of job satisfaction. There were 13 men, in all, who showed some evidence of discontent, in answer to one or another of the questions. These 13, who are "less than completely happy about their jobs, only three scored A on the Strong.

OTHER EVIDENCE

These findings, though not so favorable to the test as Strong's results, nonetheless suggest that the test has its usefulness. Furthermore, someone familiar with the study participants cannot help feel that, however inaccurate its predictions of behavior, the test is measuring interests. There is the evidence, for example, of the correlated pair of scores: lawyer and public administrator. Some men enter the law because they have politics in mind. Cases 20, 25, and 27 are examples. In Case 27, the public administrator score matches that for lawyer. In Case 25, the lawyer score is low; the choice of lawyer would seem to have been contraindicated. That would have been correct. Case 25 escapes being one of our dramatically unhappy group only because the practice of law is rationalized as a means to a political end. The Strong has measured the relative interest in law and politics quite accurately. Some indication of the injustice of "occupations entered" as a criterion of interest may be had from Case 20. This man is reported as a lawyer, and his low score on that scale makes him count in the validation as a "poor hit." Yet he, too, intends to use law as a steppingstone into politics, a fact that was not shown in the table, since circumstances have prevented his carrying out his plans. His score on public administrator is an A. That is also the scale on which he ranks first.

One is impressed by the logic underlying the relative efficiency of the test in predicting well or poorly certain occupational choices. Engineers, ministers, and teachers seem to be highly predictable; all three are likely to choose their vocation in response to an inner "call." By contrast, men who are in their own business the Strong simply does not predict. Another way of saying these facts would be to assume that the Strong tested interest and that the difference in prediction represented differences in the importance of interest as a factor in various sorts of career choice. The very patterning of the failures of the test therefore confirms its validity as a measure of interest.

PRIVATE AND PUBLIC SCHOOL RESULTS

Suppose we explore the consequences of postulating that the Strong does measure interests. We infer that the test will predict future job choices only for those men who (consciously or unconsciously) give weight to their own interests when they choose a career. For men who do not follow their interest, the test will not predict. We therefore expect the Strong's "validity" to vary between groups known to take their own interests more or less seriously. A major instance of such a prediction is provided by our tests from men who prepared for Harvard at public and private secondary schools.

The public school boy has usually been raised in the "American success culture," described by many anthropologists. His parents' efforts focused on preparing the boy for future vocational achievement. Job choice has been for him a vital matter; his future self-esteem will hinge on his job-title and on how well he does within his occupational field. As one study participant explained it, "I have satisfied myself as to my ability to compete successfully with most of my contemporaries."

The private school boy will often have been reared in a variant orientation, ably described by Kluckhohn (1950), where child-rearing was intended to perpetuate in him a "preferred personality." Occupational role will have been subordinated to family social patterns. In our 1953 questionnaires, eleven private school boys, but only three public school boys, put family interest or personal breadth ahead of achievement values when discussing their "personal future." As Kluckhohn so nicely phrased it, the contrast is between two subcultures, one emphasizing a "doing" and the other a "being" orientation.

One consequence of this subcultural contrast is a difference in the importance assigned to interests when men make their vocational choice. In the "success culture" a son is expected to surpass (therefore often bypass) his father's occupation. Choosing a job is for him a vital matter, the more so because the choice is so greatly "up to him." So much hinges on his making a "right" choice, calculated to yield maximal success, that he will often consult his own interest pattern, either introspectively or with formal aid from a vocational counselor. By contrast, the purest case of the upper class variant is a man whose permitted choices are limited to three: trustee, lawyer, or doctor. (The study has witnessed dramatic conflicts within upper-class men when personal "calls" gave way before the pressure of tradition.) While the average private school boy is not subjected to so focal a pressure, he will nevertheless possess values reinforcing the tangible demand that he join his father or uncle in "the business," and the intangible expectation that he will first of all be the "right sort." As one participant wrote, "As near as I can tell, I have those (personal) qualities in some small measure, so I think it foolish to spend time thinking about my future."

If all this is true, we arrive at the prediction that interests will matter less, and therefore the Strong will be less valid when applied to the behavior of private school boys. Table 19 shows this to be the case. Chi-square suggests p less than .05; if we combine cells (avoiding the low cell and isolating the relation between public school attendance and "Good Hits"), we can apply Fisher's formula and arrive at p below .01. Our proposition seems well validated.

If we translate Table 19 into percentage, we discover that three quarters of the public school tests gave some sort of "hit" on the occupation engaged in fourteen years after testing. That is exactly the figure reported by Strong

TABLE 19

VALIDITY OF STRONG TEST APPLIED TO PUBLIC AND PRIVATE
SCHOOL BOYS

Validity	Public	Private	Total
Good hit	19	8	27
Poor hit	4	8	12
Clean miss	8	13	21
Total	31	29	60

(1952) for his 20-year follow-up. If, on the other hand, we try to apply the test to private school boys, our predictions will be useless almost half the time.

Splitting out the public school cases, we can try revalidating Strong's four propositions. Proposition 1 fares better: men engaged in Occupation A still do not have "a higher interest score in A than in any other occupation" but the median rank of the pertinent scale is third, where formerly it was fifth. That is more consistent with Strong's claim, quoted earlier, that the occupation continued in will have ranked first, second, or third. Proposition 2 is no better for the public school group alone; that is because some occupations (engineer, chemist) attract high scores from public school, while others (lawyer, minister) attract higher scores from private school. At any rate, Proposition 2 was already verified sufficiently. Proposition 3 was already verified in every comparison, and so cannot be improved. There is one scale (public administrator) on which Proposition 3 is false for the private school group but true for the public school group. Proposition 4 is about equally valid in both groups.

DISCUSSION

This finding will raise various questions, some of which can be answered from our data. To forestall one, the "private school effect" cannot be explained in terms of income. It is true that the Strong is less accurate when applied to families receiving over $16,000 per year, but this figure marks only the upper quartile of our income statistics, while the "private school effect" is visible at all income levels. For example, in the second income quartile, with income held reasonably constant between four and six thousand dollars, public school tests score good hits 75 percent of the time, private school tests only 40 percent. In all income quartiles that are adequately represented by public school cases, the proportion of misleading tests remains about one in four; in all income quartiles that are adequately represented by private school cases, the proportion of misleading tests remains about one in two.

These figures suggest that it is the fact of having attended private school (or of being reared in a subculture from which one is sent to a private school), rather than income, and somewhat independently of social class that depressed the validity of the test. Several explanations suggest themselves. The most obvious would be that the Strong was validated against public school graduates. Next most obvious might be that attending private school is one of those "experiences affecting interests" that Super warns us have been too little studied.

SUMMARY AND CONCLUSIONS

A 14-year follow-up was made of Strong Vocational Interest Blanks administered in 1949 to participants in the Study of Adult Development. The validity of the test as a predictor of occupational choice at first appeared to be slightly lower than that reported by Strong. Of Strong's four validation propositions, two were confirmed, one (that lawyers outscore non-lawyers on the law scale, etc.) Strikingly, the other (that lawyers obtain one of their best scores on the law scale, etc.) less so. The median test offered four "extraneous" predictions.

It was possible to demonstrate a relation between conformity to choices commended by the test and future vocational happiness. Choosing a job for which one had (some years before) scored "A" also seemed to reduce the likelihood of developing fatigue, irritability or other symptoms of strain.

The proposition was offered that SVIB validly measured interests, but that failure to predict what job a man would choose could be explained in terms of his making the choice on some basis other than interest. Certain case histories supported this idea as did the apparent pattern in occupations which the test predicted accurately and which it did not.

As a corollary of this proposition it was predicted that the Strong would be applicable to boys who attended a public secondary school but less useful for boys who had prepared in a private preparatory institution. That was the case. The predictive validity of the test among the public school group was almost exactly that originally reported by Strong. Among private school boys, the test was inapplicable half of the time. Further, Strong's first validation proposition was improved in the public school group, the median test record offering only two extraneous predictions.

The import of this finding may be real in one of two ways. If we assume the anthropological theories about the American middle and upper classes to be true, then this is a demonstration that "invalidity" in the Strong arises because interests do not determine choice rather than from failure of the test to measure interests. On the other hand, the implication that there may be a distinct psychology of the upper class is also pointed out.

From all this may be drawn the following conclusions:

1. The Strong has at least the validity claimed for it as a measure of interests.

2. Its most rigorous validation criterion will be the prediction of actual behavior, but even that criterion is met at least 1 time in 2.

3. We may regard as critical for understanding the use of the test Strong's proposed "future calculations as to how much other factors, such as economic conditions, family pressures, etc., affect a man's occupational career." In this respect, attention should be called to upper class variants of the American personality.

Further study of: (*a*) the effects of environmental pressure in conflict with interests measured by the Strong, and (*b*) the differences between public and private school personalities will be made from Study of Adult Development data.

IN contrast to McArthur's rather select sample, the following article by Lipsman focuses attention on lower socioeconomic groups and their broader concerns with security needs. Occupational choices when predicted by interest measurement, as with the SVIB, emphasize intrinsic in contrast to extrinsic motivation. But it is just this extrinsic type of motivation that characterizes individuals in poverty groups. Here, then, the usual ways of measuring career interests are likely to fail.

In the following article, considerably abbreviated from its original form in the *Vocational Guidance Quarterly* for 1967, Dr. Lipsman addresses herself to this problem, centering her discussion around Maslow's hierarchy of needs. Considering the magnitude and importance of the individual problem of vocational choice, it is surprising how little research (until only recently) has been directed to this topic. Here is a suggested scheme by which basic needs can be fitted into career decision.

Dr. Lipsman is associated with the School of Education at the Catholic University of America. She is also a consultant to Vista, Office of Economic Opportunity, Washington, D.C.

MASLOW'S THEORY OF NEEDS IN RELATION TO VOCATIONAL CHOICE BY STUDENTS FROM LOWER SOCIO-ECONOMIC LEVELS

Claire K. Lipsman

The President's war on poverty, in focusing public attention on the poor and the disadvantaged, has pointed up the difficulties of planning remedial or preventive action for a phenomenon whose complex elements are not fully understood or agreed upon. The question of what distinguishes poverty from non-poverty is usually answered in terms of a cluster of statistical measures: family income level, type of housing, nutritional standards, extent of unemployment, dependence on transfer payments, and so on. In addition to these economic and financial indicators, poverty has been found to have certain psychosocial or cultural components equally powerful in their impact on the individual, but not readily susceptible to analysis. Controversy has arisen, for example, regarding the needs and values of the poor: are they middle class values manqué, or are they of a quite different character?

This general issue of the quantitative and qualitative differences between the poor and the upper classes is of particular relevance to vocational guidance because one of the original goals of vocational guidance was to mitigate the impact of society upon young people without extensive resources.

The war on poverty reminds us that the overall terms of the battle between the individual and society have really not changed; it appears so only because major theoretical interest has been confined to those individuals

—middle and upper class, brighter, better educated—in the most favorable position. But for the majority of young people, and not just the poor, the world of work still presents itself as a wall which they must somehow penetrate. As Roe (1956) and others have pointed out, their work per se is not likely to be intrinsically interesting or challenging, and their personal interests and capacities not so relevant to the job. In addition, non-college bound youngsters are operating in a labor market relatively more favorable to the buyer, and their individual interests and capacities are of less value to them in negotiating for a job.

If individual profiles are not the key factor in providing occupational satisfaction and successful integration in society for this group, what are some other major considerations? Seeking answers to this question, and paralleling the theoretical strategies developing in the war against poverty, vocational guidance is also moving beyond the cluster of statistical measures describing the individual, to consideration of broad cultural patterns, values, and motivation.

MASLOW'S THEORY OF MOTIVATION

In this connection, Maslow's theory of motivation has recently been receiving attention as a possible model for the way in which needs, both individually and culturally determined, interact with vocational development and vocational choice. This application of Maslow's theory was first suggested by Roe in 1956; a rather sporadic interest was evidenced subsequently in the literature, but in the last two or three years, with increasing attention to needs, values, and social patterns, Maslow's work has been more frequently and favorably cited.

Maslow's theory describes man as an integrated whole, reacting to drives as a whole, and impelled by ultimate goals or needs which may be conscious or unconscious. In relation to these needs or wants, Maslow believes ". . . first, that the human being is never satisfied, except in a relative or one-step-along-the-path fashion, and second, that wants seem to arrange themselves in some sort of hierarchy of prepotency" (1954). Within this hierarchy the prepotent needs are more urgent and insistent than the others, under conditions of equal deprivation, and until the prepotent needs are relatively satisfied, the others do not emerge as consistent motivators. The hierarchy of needs, ranging from greatest prepotency to least includes:

Physiological needs
Safety needs
Needs for belongingness and love
Needs for self-respect and esteem
Needs for self-actualization

Maslow observes that higher order, or later-emerging, needs require better environmental conditions—familial, economic, political, educational—to make them possible. This observation raises many questions. Does each individual go through the whole hierarchy of needs, or does he come to maturity at a more or less fixed point within the hierarchy based on early environment and socialization? Does the hierarchy unfold in chronological time, or only in psychological time? There is evidence in studies of deprivation and of concentration camp life that this schedule of needs can reel backward quite rapidly in situations of extreme stress, but how quickly will it move forward, how rapidly will higher order needs unfold, in favorable conditions? If higher order needs require better environmental conditions, do poorer environmental conditions restrict the capacity for individual development, or only the means?

Are there substantial differences in needs at different socio-economic levels? Is there evidence that successively higher socio-economic levels call out successively higher order needs? And, if so, what can we learn about the probability of success in moving from one level to another? If a poor boy gets a college scholarship, will going to college evoke higher order needs and satisfactions, or can he only be successful in college if his needs have already expanded upward?

RESEARCH APPLICATIONS OF MASLOW'S THEORY

Little research has been directed specifically to the testing of Maslow's ideas. There is, however, a considerable amount of research which throws light on the relationships of various needs to socio-economic level and occupational satisfaction or choice. This literature comes from two major sources: industry-oriented studies of worker needs and job satisfaction, and school-oriented studies of student needs and motivation in relation to vocational choice.

Industrial studies have provided the most ample evidence that there is a differing emphasis on needs at different socio-economic levels. A clear correlation between security needs and blue collar workers, on the one hand, and esteem needs and white collar workers, on the other, emerges from Herzberg's comprehensive survey (1957). The general picture in industrial research appears to bear out Roe's comment that in studies "particularly of morale and job satisfaction, there is much to support Maslow's views, and nothing to contradict them . . ."

Research in the school setting has not, for the most part, examined needs or motivation in a conceptual framework comparable to Maslow's. Popular research instruments for measuring needs or motivations in normal subjects are more oriented to areas of interest, as in the Allport-Vernon Study of Values, or to personality, as in the Edwards Personal Preference Scale.

However, a recent study of occupational values by Thompson (1966) defines values in terms similar to those of Maslow. Thompson's study of 2,000 California ninth and tenth grade students, relating their occupational values to a number of variables including socio-economic level, shows job security is much more important to students whose fathers are in low level occupations; leadership in the occupation is much more attractive to students whose fathers are in high level occupations.

THE DYNAMICS OF NEEDS, SOCIAL CLASS, AND VOCATIONAL CHOICE

The structure of relationships suggested by Maslow is buttressed by the research literature; the dynamics of his theory remain mostly speculative. Some insight into the dynamics of moving from need to need is offered by three studies, by Wilensky (1961), Grier (1963), and Miller (1956), which are of special interest because they combine, as a group, to suggest a tentative framework for relating needs to vocational choice and to vocational guidance.

Wilensky studies a group of 600 white male adults, ranging in age from 21 to 55, whom he describes as being in the middle class (i.e., at the upper-working and lower-middle class level), and analyze their work history in relation to their social participation. He defined the latter in terms which embrace a major aspect of Maslow's need for belongingness: participation in formal civic, religious, or business groups, and in leisure, recreational, or personal-social activities. Wilensky concluded that in this group orderly careers went with social participation, and that chaotic experience in the economic order fosters a retreat from both work and the larger communal life. He asserts a specific sequence of cause and effect, namely that an orderly career leads to social participation, on the basis of his findings that earlier socialization and environmental forces appeared not related to later work history.

Grier's study (1963) focuses on a small group of 46 Negro adult males, consisting of all the male graduates from one urban high school who could be located five years later. These boys came from families at a low socio-economic level, but actually or potentially upwardly mobile. The occupations of both fathers and mothers ranged from unskilled laborer or service worker to professional. Almost half the fathers were semiskilled or unskilled laborers (the majority of boys came from two-parent homes), and almost half the mothers were service workers. On the other hand, only 10 percent reported that neither parent had graduated from high school, and almost half had at least one parent with some college training. Twelve parents were employed professionally, the majority of them school teachers and women.

Of the 46 graduates, 32 entered four-year colleges. Five years later, only seven of these 32 had actually received bachelor's degrees. The most frequent explanation given by the students for leaving college is what Grier describes as the "floundering" phenomenon: their initial choice of a career wavered and sagged into uncertainty.

College had been urged on these boys primarily as a means to financial security. Grier argues that they were not prepared to go beyond this initial step upward because neither their own nor their parents' experience, nor that of other adults in their environment, offered any realistic information about a range of specific careers. This phenomenon may also be interpreted in Maslow's terms: these boys were not prepared to go beyond the lower-order need for security because it was still largely unsatisfied, and its salience prevented the emergence of drives for higher order satisfactions. They had perhaps assumed (as Maslow suggests) that in the future they would be perfectly happy if they could only satisfy this one need. The college experience, evoking a vista of higher order needs for belonging, esteem, and status, bewildered them because they had not anticipated it.

To a certain extent Grier's findings contradict those of Wilensky; the latter is arguing that occupational success leads to need satisfaction, and Grier that inadequate need satisfaction blocks occupational success. It may be that both are right, and that the causal relationship between need satisfaction and occupational choice or satisfaction is different for different needs. Miller's study (1956) of the relationship between need saliency and the presence or absence of vocational choice, in a group of college students, suggests this. He found that of students who valued security or prestige the most, about half had failed to make any career choice; whereas of those who valued belonging the most, only 20 percent had failed to make career choices.

FUTURE PROSPECTS

In the studies cited above, the restrictive effects of unsatisfied safety needs appear particularly frustrating to the vocational development of young people. They present a case for the proposition that young people from low socio-economic levels make their major response to vocational decision-points in terms of this need.

Maslow's theory suggests that significant differences between socio-economic levels, and between individuals within these levels, may be reflected in the relative positions these individuals occupy in the need hierarchy. If those at the bottom are to be successful in moving upward, they must be helped to find satisfaction for their security needs sufficient to permit the emergence of higher order needs.

Beyond the basic security level, as Wilensky has found, vocational choice and its attendant train of events may be critical in satisfying higher order needs. However, the particular occupation may be less important than the particular psychosocial characteristics of the job, characteristics which may be common to jobs in many different occupations.

Maslow's theory suggests a useful and parsimonious approach to vocational guidance which focuses on commonalities, rather than on individual differences. A critical evaluation, however, requires initially the development of psychological instruments to measure the relative strengths of these particular needs within the individual. Job analysis is already proceeding along similar lines, in the research on worker traits and temperament by the U.S.E.S. Within the job setting, industrial personnel specialists and management are also thinking in terms of common needs. In a review of research on motivation in work groups, Clark (1960) takes up the point of view of management, which is concerned with developing worker motivation in the direction of greater productivity. Clark reviews the position of those who feel that the application of Maslow's theory to industry is hopeless; that the administrator is faced by a random schedule of employee need schedules, and that as soon as he succeeds in satisfying any felt needs, a host of others arise. Clark contends that work studies show the possibility of making certain general responses to these needs within the work environment, and that external working conditions can be manipulated by management, either to release or constrain various motivations in members of industrial work groups. He combines the findings of a number of industrial and organizational studies to show the relationship of working conditions to need satisfaction: as external working conditions improve, higher order needs are progressively called out, productivity increases, and turnover and absenteeism go down. Clark concludes that an administrator can use this general way of thinking to predict, at least on a gross basis, that certain consequences are quite likely to follow from the "givens" in any situation.

Effective vocational guidance on a large scale—a prospect which automation and population growth, as well as the war on poverty, are bringing ever closer—may well utilize these broad psychosocial predictors along with more individualized techniques.

PART TEN

Achievement or Proficiency Testing

Sᴛᴀɴᴅᴀʀᴅɪᴢᴇᴅ achievement or proficiency testing is perhaps the oldest form of psychological examining. Various forms of civil service agencies have long made use of such tests, not only in the West but also in the East. The following historical piece by Dr. DuBois relates some of the procedures adopted by the Chinese as early as 2200 B.C. Later, these testing programs involved millions of men. As the author indicates, since the selection ratio was so small the issue of test validity was not a significant one. But the testing program became a very significant tool of the government. The United States and some European countries made use of this Chinese system when they began to construct their own civil service testing machinery.

Dr. DuBois is professor of psychology at Washington University in St. Louis, Missouri. His original paper appeared in the *Proceedings of the 1964 Invitational Conference on Testing Problems,* a conference sponsored by the Educational Testing Service. The article was reprinted in the Anastasi collection (1966) of representative papers from these conferences.

A TEST-DOMINATED SOCIETY:
CHINA, 1115 B.C.–1905 A.D.

Philip H. DuBois

Our negative enthusiasm for the present government in Peking should not lead us to a lack of appreciation for great Chinese achievements of the past. They have been many.

It is often said that the Chinese invented gunpowder and, quite humanely, used it to frighten, rather than to kill, their enemies.

Certainly they solved the problem of diverse languages with the remarkable invention of a common written language—a code by which peoples who could not communicate with one another orally were able to communicate freely by means of writing. This invention was so successful that the Chinese came to regard themselves as a single people.

They invented paper, which the West did not know how to make until some Chinese papermakers were captured by Arabs at Samarkand in 751 A.D. They invented printing. They developed the arts. But, more importantly for our purposes, they invented the psychological test, applying it to government, the very framework of their society, in such a manner that the test-makers, in effect, determined over many centuries much of the format of Chinese society.

The prolonged and intensive Chinese experience with testing seems to have been completely ignored by contemporary psychometricians. In none of the writings on psychometrics with which I am familiar is there any mention of some 3,000 years of examinations in the Chinese empire. This is rather surprising because in civil service procedures it is easy to trace the continuity of Eastern and Western methods. Continuity between Western educational and psychological examining methods on the one hand and Chinese civil service testing on the other is more difficult to demonstrate, but some influence is probable.

Even if Western psychometrics had been completely independent of Chinese testing, the Eastern experience would have been of great interest to us. It affords the one historical example of a society in which examining methods introduced to attain certain restricted objectives actually began to determine many characteristics of the society itself.

It should be noted that through the ages the Chinese empire, unlike the West, did not have a numerous hereditary aristocracy to constitute its governing class. The chief way to a political career was through passing a series of examinations in which competition was very severe. Moreover, China lacked another invention of the West: the university. The learned Chinese was one who had been successful in passing competitive examinations, and whose success brought changes in his attire and in his title as well as public recognition of his abilities, and employment in government service.

For long periods of time the system worked very well indeed. Only occasionally were examinations suspended, one notable period being the time in which the Mongol emperors ruled in Peking. (The accounts of Marco Polo, who spent a number of years in China during their rule, make no reference to the Chinese civil service examining procedures.)

The Chinese scholar seems to have been a reasonably successful public administrator. Public office was often distributed by lot among the mandarins who passed three successive sets of examinations.

Millions of men prepared for the tests, often for decades, and relatively few achieved final success. The selection ratio was so small that the tests themselves would not have had to be very valid in order to be useful. That they were useful is perhaps indicated by their long history and by the fact that for many centuries, with relatively few interruptions, the government of the Chinese empire preserved internal peace, provided security from many would-be invaders, and permitted a flowering of civilization that in many respects was far more advanced than that prevailing contemporaneously in the West.

The earliest development seems to have been a rudimentary form of proficiency testing. About the year 2200 B.C., the emperor of China is said to have examined his officials every third year. After three examinations, he either promoted or dismissed them from the service. There seems to be no record of the exact content nor of the methods of testing, but the precedent of periodic examinations was to continue for many generations.

A thousand years later in 1115 B.C., at the beginning of the Chan dynasty, formal examining procedures of candidates for office were established. Here the record is clear. Job sample tests were used requiring proficiency in the five basic arts: music, archery, horsemanship, writing, and arithmetic. Of the five, at least two, writing and arithmetic, still have validity for public office. Knowledge of a sixth art was also required—skill in the rites and ceremonies of public and social life.

It should be pointed out that this examining system, which was later to be centered upon the Confucian classics, was actually in existence long before the time of Confucius (551–478 B.C.).

While the procedures changed from time to time, and the sources to which I have had access are somewhat contradictory, a few dates seem to be clear. In 165 B.C., by which time Confucian ethics had become current, moral standards were introduced in the selection of competitors. District magistrates were required to send to the capital candidates who had acquired a reputation for filial piety and integrity. Those whose moral character had been sufficiently attested were then examined with respect to their intellectual qualifications. At this time, the test included not only measures of the six arts, but also familiarity with the geography of the empire, civil law, military matters, agriculture, and the administration of revenue.

After 622 A.D., open, competitive examinations took place at more or less regular intervals. By 1370 A.D., three levels of examinations were well established. The candidate who passed the examination in his district became eligible to take a test at the provincial capital, and those successful at the provincial capital were eligible for final examinations in Peking. For about 500 years the system was stable and a description by William A. P. Martin (1870) is pertinent.

. . . The candidates for office—those who are acknowledged as such, in consequence of sustaining the initial trial—are divided into the three grades of *siu-ts'ai, chu-jin,* and *tsin-shi*—"Budding Geniuses," "Promoted Scholars," and those who are "Ready for Office." The trials for the first are held in the chief city of each district. . . . They are conducted by a chancellor, whose jurisdiction extends over an entire province, containing, it may be, sixty or seventy such districts, each of which he is required to visit once a year, and each of which is provided with a resident sub-chancellor, whose duty it is to examine the scholars in the interval and to have them in readiness for the chancellor's arrival.

About two thousand competitors enter the lists, ranging in age from the precocious youth just entering his teens up to the venerable grandsire of seventy winters. Shut up for a night and a day, each in his narrow cell, they produce each a poem and one or two essays on themes assigned by the chancellor, and then return to their homes to await the bulletin announcing their place in the scale of merit. The chancellor, assisted by his clerks, occupies several days in sifting the heap of manuscripts, from which he picks out some twenty or more that are distinguished by beauty of penmanship and grace of diction. The authors of these are honored with the degree of "Budding Genius," and are entitled to wear the decorations in the lowest grade in the corporation of mandarins. The successful student wins no purse of gold and obtains no office, but he has gained a prize, which he deems a sufficient compensation for years of patient toil. He is the best of a hundred scholars, exempted from liability to corporal punishment, and raised above the vulgar herd. . . .

Once in three years these "Budding Geniuses," these picked men of the districts, repair to the provincial capital to engage in competition for the second degree—that of *chu-jin,* or "Promoted Scholar." The number of competitors amounts to ten thousand, more or less, and of these only one in every hundred can be admitted to the coveted degree. The trial is conducted by special examiners sent down from Peking and this examination takes a wider range than the preceding. No fewer than three sessions of nearly three days each are occupied instead of the single day for the first degree. Compositions in prose and verse are required, and themes are assigned with a special view to testing the extent of reading and depth of scholarship of the candidates. Penmanship is left out of the account—each production, marked with a cipher, being copied by an official scribe, that the examiners may have no clew to its author and no temptation to render a biased judgment.

The victor still receives neither office nor emolument; but the honor he achieves is scarcely less than that which was won by the victors in the Olympic games. Again, he is one of a hundred, each of whom was a picked man; and as a result of this second victory he goes forth an acknowledged superior among ten thousand contending scholars. He adorns his cap with the gilded button of a higher grade, erects a pair of lofty flag-staffs before the gate of his family residence, and places a tablet over his door to inform those who pass by that this is the abode of a literary prize-man. But our "Promoted Scholar" is not yet a mandarin, in the proper sense of the term. The distinction already attained only stimulates his desire for higher honors—honors which bring at last the solid recompense of an income.

In the spring of the following year he proceeds to Peking to seek the next higher degree, the attainment of which will prove a passport to office. This contest is still with his peers, that is, with other "Promoted Scholars," who like himself have come up from all the provinces of the empire. But the chances are this time more in his favor, as the number of prizes is now tripled, and if the gods are propitious his fortune is made. . . . If his name appears among the favored few, he not only wins himself a place in the front ranks of the lettered, but he plants his foot securely on the rounds of the official ladder by which, without the prestige of birth or the support of friends, it is possible to rise to a seat in the grand council of state or a place in the Imperial Cabinet. All this advancement presents itself in the distant prospect, while the office upon which he immediately enters is one of respectability, and it may be of profit. It is generally that of mayor or sub-mayor of a disrict city, or sub-chancellor in the district examinations—the vacant posts being distributed by lot, and therefore impartially, among those who have proved themselves to be "ready for office."

Before the drawing of lots, however, for the post of a magistrate among the people, our ambitious student has a chance of winning the more distinguished honor of a place in the Imperial Academy. With this view, the two or three hundred survivors of so many contests appear in the palace, where themes are assigned them by the Emperor himself, and the highest honor is paid to the pursuit of letters by the exercises being presided over by his Majesty in person. Penmanship reappears as an element in determining the result, and a score or more of those whose style is the most finished, whose scholarship the ripest, and whose handwriting the most elegant, are drafted into the college of Hanlin, the "forest of pencils," a kind of Imperial Institute, the members of which are recognized as standing at the head of the literary profession. These are constituted poets and historians to the Celestial Court, or deputed to act as chancellors and examiners in the several provinces.

But the diminishing series in this ascending scale has not yet reached its final term. The long succession of contests culminates in the designation by the Emperor of some individual whom he regards as the Chuang-Yuen or model scholar of the empire. . . . Provinces contend for the shining prize, and the town that gives the victor birth becomes noted forever. Swift heralds bear the tidings of his triumph, and the hearts of the people leap at their approach. We have seen them enter a humble cottage . . . and, amid the flaunting of banners and the blare of trumpets, announce to its startled inmates that one of their relations had been crowned by the Emperor as the laureate of the year. And so high was the estimation in which the people held the success of their fellow-townsman, that his wife was requested to visit the six gates of the city, and to scatter before each a handful of rice, that the whole population might share in the good fortune of her household. . . .

It is obvious that which excites so profoundly the interest of a whole nation must be productive of very decided results. That it leads to the selection of the best talents for the service of the public we have already seen; but beyond this— its primary object—it exercises a profound influence upon the education of the people and the stability of the government. It is all, in fact, that China has to show in the way of an educational system. She has no colleges or universities,— if we except one that is yet in embryo—and no national system of common schools; yet it may be confidently asserted that China gives to learning a more effective patronage than she could have done if each of her emperors were an Augustus and every premier a Maecenas. She says to all her sons, "Prosecute your studies by such means as you may be able to command, whether in public or in private, and when you are prepared, present yourselves in the examination hall. The government will judge of your proficiency and reward your attainments."

Nothing can exceed the ardor which this standing offer infuses into the minds of all who have the remotest prospect of sharing in the prizes. They study not merely while they have teachers to incite them to diligence, but continue their studies with unabated zeal long after they have left the schools; they study in solitude and poverty; they study amidst the cares of a family and the turmoil of business; and the shining goal is kept steadily in view until the eye grows dim. Some of the aspirants impose on themselves the task of writing a fresh essay every day; and they do not hesitate to enter the lists as often as the public examinations recur, resolved, if they fail, to continue trying, believing that perseverance has power to command success and encouraged by the legend of the man who, needing a sewing-needle, made one by grinding a crowbar on a piece of granite.

This quotation from Martin, describing and praising the Chinese testing system, is by no means unique. The use of competitive examinations for the selection of state officials was praised by many Western observers and writers, including Voltaire. In fact, it is clear that initially all civil service examining in Europe and in the United States used the Chinese system, directly or indirectly, as a model. Civil service testing was introduced in France as a 1791 reform, only to be abolished by Napoleon. In England the first competitive examinations in connection with public office were instituted for the selection of trainees for the civil service in India by men familiar with the Chinese system. Later, when the question of civil service examinations for Great Britain as a whole was debated in Parliament, the Chinese model was discussed with both favorable and unfavorable comments. As a part of an extensive study, Congressman Thomas A. Jenckes, one of the fathers of the United States Civil Service, wrote 12 pages on the civil service of China.

Westerners seem to have been particularly impressed with the fact that competition was open, that distinction came from merit, and that a highly literate and urbane group of public officials resulted from the examination system.

The great crisis in Chinese affairs came, of course, when the Chinese realized that they were militarily inferior to the West. They quickly discovered that equality in military power could not be achieved without modern science and technology. Accordingly, technological schools and universities were set up, but as long as the civil service examinations, which were largely literary in character, continued to be the way for an ambitious man to have a career, modern education was not sufficiently attractive. Consequently, in 1905, the Chinese examination system was abolished as a reform measure.

So much for a description and a bit of the history of an ancient Chinese venture in psychological examining as a tool of government. What can be said about their testing techniques from the point of view of the modern psychometrician? In the first place, I find no evidence to indicate that they invented either the multiple-choice format, the test-scoring machine, or item analysis. They did, however, recognize that a relatively short performance under carefully controlled conditions could yield an estimate of the ability to perform under less rigorously controlled conditions and for a longer period of time. I think there is no doubt that the procedure selected capable public servants.

They recognized the problem of objectivity, concealing candidates' names, and sometimes using a bureau of copyists to copy examination material before it was graded. In some cases, tests were read by two independent examiners who handed their sealed evaluations to a third examiner who reconciled any differences. Scores seem to have been in terms of rank order.

The need for uniformity in testing conditions was well recognized. Considerable attention was given to proctoring the examination halls, which were large and permanent installations consisting of hundreds of small cells. Sometimes candidates died during the rigors of the examinations, which went on day and night.

Now, when psychological tests are being used more and more extensively at critical points in the careers of all our citizens, we will do well to consider their effects on individuals, on specific institutions, and on society. The long Chinese experience is a pertinent case history. It is a plausible hypothesis that much of the great strength of the Chinese empire came from the intellectual vigor of men who were bright enough to compete in examinations requiring the writing of poems and "eight-legged essays."

Certainly the opportunities that were opened up by success in the examinations stimulated millions of individuals to long years of scholarship. Perhaps the greatest drawback was that the scholarship was not always pertinent. In the nineteenth century, China suddenly found herself surpassed in technology by the West. While Chinese civilization had been relatively static, Westerners invented the steam engine, the power loom, and the iron-clad. It was then that the Chinese, in order to preserve their country and their institutions, began to desire progress according to the Western model. At that time the age-old examining system was discovered to be a hindrance.

So far, with 60 years of experience, we Westerners have not found our psychological examining a hindrance. But it is becoming increasingly apparent that our test-makers, like those of ancient China, established goals for individuals and influence the shape of social institutions. Item writers as well as song writers mold the patterns of a culture.

SEVERAL objections to school reliance on achievement tests have been voiced—for example, they eventually will dictate the curriculum. Such objections also relate to teaching objectives. In the article that follows, Dr. Ebel discusses some of the common objections that have been raised and interprets the validity of these points.

The article is reproduced, in slightly abbreviated form, from the *National Elementary Principal* for 1961. It has also been reprinted in the collection of readings by Chase and Ludlow (1966). Dr. Ebel is professor of education at Michigan State University.

STANDARDIZED ACHIEVEMENT TESTS:
USES AND LIMITATIONS

Robert L. Ebel

Standardized tests of educational achievement are essential educational tools, especially in the elementary school. They can be used to improve the effectiveness of the competent teacher or school administrator. They can help motivate and reward the child. They can provide a basis for constructive cooperation between parents and teachers in guiding the child's educational development. They can help the school staff and the community it serves assess the effectiveness of the school program.

A demonstration of how standardized tests can focus public attention on an educational need occurred recently in New York City. Results of a citywide standardized reading test showed that the average reading ability of school children in New York was below the national average. A few years before, it had been above the national norm. While these findings were doubted, discounted, and rationalized by experts and spokesmen inside the schools and out, there was almost universal support for the vigorous action taken by the Board of Education to strengthen the program of reading instruction. Among other things, the number of specialists in remedial reading on the school staff was sharply increased.

This use of standardized tests as a basis for judging the effectiveness of a school program has been criticized by some educators. They point out that half the pupils or schools *have* to be below the norm and that remedial programs can never alter this situation. Further, they say, it is unreasonable and unfair to expect the same levels of achievement of all pupils and all schools. A pupil ranking well above average may, in fact, have less reason for self-satisfaction and complacency than a pupil ranking below average, if the high-ranking pupil had educational advantages the other lacked.

There is merit in both these criticisms, perhaps more in the second than in the first, but it would be dangerous to accept them completely. No pupil, no teacher, no schoolboard, no community should be continuously satisfied with their educational achievements, and few are. Information provided by standardized tests of achievement helps them focus their dissatisfactions more purposefully and take remedial action more constructively.

The second criticism is sometimes used in general terms as a rationalization for below-average performance. It contains enough truth to be a persuasive argument for unsound interpretations of test results and for inaction when action is needed. On the basis of intelligence tests and other measures, we know it is unreasonable to expect the same achievement of all pupils and all schools. Unfortunately, the usual effort to obtain a standard of reasonable expectancy of achievement from intelligence test scores is based, I think, on some misconceptions about intelligence, achievement, and the educational process.

The important point to remember is that most pupils and many schools could achieve considerably more than they have achieved. Further, it is probably true that the pupils and schools which are below average in achievement have both the greatest need and the greatest opportunity to improve.

Understanding the causes of inferior achievement is an important prelude to effective remedial action. No child's potential and no school's potential for educational achievement is unlimited. But this should never be used as an excuse for inaction.

If standardized tests are valuable tools, why do many schools lag in using them effectively? Lack of full awareness of the potential value of test information and lack of training in how to use that information may be partly responsible. But there are also three common misconceptions about educational testing which may account for much of the skepticism about the value of tests and the reluctance to use them more extensively.

IMPORTANCE OF TANGIBLE OUTCOMES

The first of these misconceptions is the belief that the most important outcomes of education are too subtle, too complex, too subjective to be measured effectively. Elementary school teachers are less guilty on this score than some college professors who take off on flights of fancy when discussing intangible but supposedly essential outcomes of education.

Teachers of young children know that the development of skills in the tool subjects and the establishment of solid foundations for understanding and interest in the major fields of human knowledge are concrete, specific, important objectives. But some of them may feel that tests, especially objective standardized tests, fail "to get at" the real essentials of achievement in these skill and foundation subjects. This mystical devotion to a hidden reality of achievement which is more essential than overt ability to perform has never satisfied the research worker. He wants to know the nature of this hidden reality and what evidence there is that it is important.

DANGER OF OVEREMPHASIS ON ADJUSTMENT

The second misconception about educational testing arises from over-concern with the child's immediate happiness and self-satisfaction. Extreme supporters of this view often regard testing as an unfriendly, threatening, anxiety-generating process. They would shield the child from its stress and possible pain. I demur, and call as the first witness the physician.

Most of us learn to adjust to the physician's prescriptions, whether they are bad-tasting medicines, disinfectants that sting, shots that hurt, or even surgery. There is some emotional stress and discomfort, but the end result is usually increased health. To do what must be done a doctor needs courage, but this implies no lack of sympathy. What it does imply is farsighted concern for the ultimate welfare of the patient.

I have been appalled by the lack of this far-sighted attitude among some advocates of child-centered education. They talk as if the teacher's primary responsibility were to guard the child's ego against any bruises whatsoever. Let him achieve as much as he can without strain, they say, but be careful not to ask too much of him. Their excess of concern for protection of the child's present "security" may, however, encourage neglect of needed small readjustments until they accumulate into a crisis of major proportions.

Take the case of Sharon which illustrates a problem all too many schools and families have become unhappily acquainted with in recent years. Sharon was the third of four children in an upper middle-class family. Her early years at school were uneventful. Periodic descriptive reports indicated that she was adjusting well and making progress. If any standardized tests were given, the significance of the results was not reported to the parents.

Midway through the third grade, trouble developed. Sharon began to say she hated school and to seek escape by feigning illness. Investigation showed the basic problem was that Sharon couldn't read, at least not nearly as well as her classmates. They were beginning to refer to her as "dumb." The parents proposed that Sharon attend the reading clinic of a nearby university and perhaps get special individual instruction. The school staff counseled against such a step arguing that they could provide all the special help needed, now that the problem had been identified. Further, they said, much harm could be done if too much attention were paid to the problem. Better to treat it as casually and quietly as possible, they said.

Despite some misgivings, Sharon's parents agreed. For a while, things seemed to improve. Sharon was happier in school. She brought home reports of small triumphs, of special recognition and opportunities. The school reports, still couched in general, unthreatening phrases, indicated generally satisfactory progress. Then, near the end of Sharon's eighth-grade year, trouble developed again. Her teacher recommended that she repeat the grade because of her serious reading disability. The special attention she had received had apparently taught her to learn by listening, but she had not learned effective self-direction in reading.

After some plain-speaking conferences between teacher and parents, Sharon did not fail. She did go to summer reading camps. She went on to high school and took five years to finish college instead of four.

If the school had had a systematic program of standardized testing and had reported the results regularly, Sharon's reading disability would probably have been identified before it was translated into an emotional and social problem. And once the difficulty was identified, if the school had been more concerned with Sharon's future welfare than her current happiness, the problem might well have been corrected before it affected her subsequent schooling. In education, as in medicine and justice, an excess of present sympathy can postpone or even defeat the procedures necessary for an individual's future welfare.

LIMITED VALUE OF PURELY LOCAL OBJECTIVES

The third misconception about standardized educational achievement tests results in their avoidance or de-emphasis on the ground that this teacher's objectives or that school's objectives are uniquely different from those for which the standardized test was presumably built.

We all recognize that it is desirable for both teachers and schools to have freedom to experiment with new materials and methods and that it is unwise for them to be bound tightly to a rigidly prescribed curriculum. It is good that they can capitalize on their own unique talents and opportunities. But it is also necessary that they recognize their responsibilities to develop the same basic skills and fundamental understandings which other teachers and other schools are seeking to develop.

What constitutes a good elementary education today in Bangor, Maine, is not radically different from what constitutes a good elementary education in Los Angeles, California. Even if the ideal elementary education in one locality should differ from the ideal in another, it would be unwise to build an educational program around only the local needs. For it is certainly true that many of those educated in one place will spend most of their lives in some other.

One of the essential values of a well-constructed standardized test is its reflection of expert consensus on nationwide objectives of achievement. Instead of asking how well the standardized test fits local objectives, the test selector should ask with how much competence the test constructors can speak concerning the common objectives of all schools. A teacher should not ask a standardized test to provide evidence on how well she has taught all the things she has tried to teach, but only on the things that all teachers ought to have taught! For those achievements which are truly and rightly unique to a particular school or teacher, locally constructed tests are the best answer.

WILL THE TEST–MAKERS DICTATE CURRICULUM?

Many of those who mistrust the nationally developed standardized tests of achievement frequently express fear that the test-makers will dictate the curriculum. There is some basis for this belief, but it should not be a source of anxiety. If the standardized test is taken seriously, it will certainly exert some influence on teaching. But if the test is constructed by competent experts, that influence should be more beneficial than harmful.

The content and emphasis of textbooks, courses of study, teaching methods, and tests of achievement should all be sanctioned by the same kind of authority—a consensus of expert judgments. If the test-makers try, as many of them do, to catch and reflect in their tests a consensus of the judgment of curriculum specialists, it seems unreasonable to charge them with attempting to dictate curriculum developments. If standardized tests of achievement are supplemented by locally constructed tests, there is slight danger that the use of standardized tests will result in undesirable uniformity in curricula.

EXPERT TEST CONSTRUCTION

A well-constructed standardized achievement test provides an independent, broadly based definition of *desirable goals* of achievement in *all* schools. This is one of its primary values. Two others are related to it. The first is expert, painstaking test construction. The second is independent, broadly based norms of achievement.

Those who prepare standardized tests, in consultation with subject-matter experts, usually are skilled in writing items. In addition, they pre-test the items to identify those which are too difficult or too easy or which fail to discriminate clearly between high and low achievers. Careful attention is also given to the balance of the test among content areas and item types.

The result of the expertness and care applied to the construction of a standard test of educational achievement is usually a technically better test than a local teacher or group would be likely to create. The task it presents are those the pupils should be able to handle. The scores it yields discriminate reliably different levels of achievement. It is usually convenient to administer and score and is efficient and economical in its yield of useful information.

The provision of national, regional, or statewide norms for score interpretation is a third valuable contribution of the standardized achievement test. To secure accurate norms for clearly defined and widely appropriate reference groups is not a simple matter. It is even more difficult to present these norms so that they will be easy to use and to interpret properly.

These norms enable the user of a standardized test to obtain an external, broadly based standard for judging the achievements of pupils. Norms are not universal standards. Nor are they self-interpreting. An oversimplified approach to test norms can rob them of much of their potential usefulness. After the comparison of local achievements with external norms has been made and the difference noted, one must still ask, "Is this good or bad?" and "Why do we seem to do so well, or poorly?" and "Under the circumstances, what should we do about the situation?" Standardized tests and their norms will not provide any automatic answers, but they can provide the basis for wise planning and for more reasonable decisions.

Schools exist to educate pupils, but it is the exceptional classroom teacher or school administrator who can report very precisely how much learning the pupils have acquired. Enrollment, attendance, and per-pupil cost can be specified accurately and in detail, but the acquisition of skills, knowledge, and attitudes is not readily stated in statistical terms. Educational achievement is not easy to measure, and existing tests leave much to be desired. But relatively few schools and teachers are obtaining and using even a small fraction of the information on educational achievement that existing tests could provide. I am persuaded that competent teachers and school systems can improve their effectiveness rapidly by making good use of existing standardized tests of educational achievement. Combined with other efforts, the systematic and skillful use of standardized tests should move any school toward higher levels of achievement.

A special and rather recent form of proficiency testing is that of readiness testing. Here the purpose is to ascertain how well an individual will profit from some subsequent course of training. Most such tests are used in educational settings and concern themselves, in particular, with programs in reading or mathematics. Their earliest use is typically at the entrance of a pupil into first grade, and it is this special use of readiness tests that Dr. Hildreth discusses in the following article.

The article is a digest of Chapter 4 of Dr. Hildreth's book, *Readiness for School Beginners* (1950), which was prepared for the series, *Test Service Notebook,* published by the Division of Test Research and Service of the World Book Company. Issue 10 of this series is reproduced here in its entirety. Dr. Hildreth is currently Visiting Professor of Education at American University in Beirut, Lebanon, and has long been noted for her writings and research in the field of child learning and reading.

USING READINESS TEST RESULTS[1]

Gertrude Hildreth

One of the important problems the first-grade teacher faces is that of adapting group methods of education to meet the needs of a number of individual children of widely diverse capacities, maturity, and backgrounds. The information provided by a good readiness test is one helpful basis for making necessary adjustments in the first-grade program.

These tests provide the first-grade teacher with evidence of the range of maturity of her pupils and indicate their particular learning problems. In schools that have a formal first-grade program, using basal textbooks early in the term, readiness tests help the teacher screen out at the beginning of the term those pupils who would almost certainly fail if they were to undertake the difficult work to come. In schools following a less traditional program, the purpose in giving readiness tests is to discover pupil traits early so that the school can provide the proper environment and training for the pupils. Kinds of training can be differentiated in harmony with the children's capacities, and the children can be grouped according to individual needs.

Obtaining readiness information early saves time and prevents costly errors by eliminating much of the guesswork in sizing up the class as a whole and in determining the abilities and limitations of individual pupils.

TYPES OF READINESS TESTS

Several different types of tests can be used to determine a beginning pupil's readiness status. They include:

---

[1] A digest of Chapter 4 of Dr. Hildreth's book *Readiness for School Beginners.* Copyright 1950 by World Book Company.

Mental ability or intelligence tests, both group and individual, which are used in determining the mental maturity of children.

General and composite readiness tests, such as *Metropolitan Readiness Tests,* which determine readiness for learning by measuring a number of different traits and skills contributing to success in schoolwork. They suggest limitations in pupils which proper schooling may overcome.

Specific readiness tests, used to measure readiness for instruction in specific subjects such as reading, number work, etc.

Intelligence Tests as Measures of Readiness. Although distinctions should be made among tests of reading readiness, general readiness, and intelligence or scholastic aptitude, the well-known intelligence tests for children may be classed as readiness tests because they throw light on the potentialities of beginners for learning at school. Reading readiness tests and intelligence tests measure much the same thing. Most investigations show a substantial correlation between intelligence test ratings and either general achievement or reading achievement at the end of one year and at the end of two years of schooling.

General Readiness Tests and Readiness Tests for Specific Skills. Some readiness tests measure various aspects of general readiness for school learning; others are chiefly tests of readiness for instruction in specific subjects, such as reading or arithmetic. Both types perform useful functions; the choice of one type or the other depends on local circumstances—purposes of testing, curricular emphases, other tests in use, etc.

Teachers are advised to focus their attention at the beginning of the year on overall readiness factors that affect learning in general, and not to be too much concerned about specific traits that indicate the child's readiness for reading, writing, or other particular subjects. General readiness tests will help to identify children of high or low general maturity and also will indicate those who are outstanding or relatively weak in such basic factors as vocabulary comprehension, perceptual discrimination, motor control, information, and so on. This broader type of measurement, appraisal, and evaluation is required as a basis for planning the best curriculum.

Metropolitan Readiness Tests are an example of such general readiness tests measuring a variety of traits and achievements of school beginners. The subtests that make up the battery have been selected on the basis of their proved validity for predicting success in first grade and for differentiating between pupils of greater and less maturity and between pupils of superior and inferior experiential backgrounds. Traits measured directly or indirectly by the tests include:

Linguistic maturity
Visual and auditory perception
Number knowledge and readiness
Information about common objects
Ability to pay attention and follow directions
Ability in handling paper and pencil
Ability to sustain interest in looking at pictures and responding to them.

The tests yield diagnostic information that is valuable to teachers in planning the program for beginners. Analysis of results of the various subtests is helpful in understanding the individual child's particular lacks and disabilities in specific traits. Detailed information on interpretaton and application of results is included in the *Directions for Administering and Key for Scoring* that accompany the test.

HOW TO CHOOSE A GOOD READINESS TEST

In selecting the most suitable readiness test to use for a particular purpose in a particular school system, many factors must be considered. In general, all good readiness tests have the following characteristics:

If they test general readiness, they contain a variety of materials that measure several different traits or skills closely related to success in first-grade work. There should be evidence of the test's validity.

If they purport to measure separate skills, they are long enough and have a wide enough range to test the skills accurately.

They are interesting to young children.

They can be scored objectively. Scores should be easily translated into letter ratings, percentile ranks, or other meaningful ratings.

They can be easily administered by the classroom teacher.

Normative Information. In selecting the readiness test, particular attention should be given the norms that accompany it. The normative data furnished with a good readiness test afford a means of making comparisons between the average readiness score for a given class or group and that of a larger normative population on which the test was standardized. This information is useful in determining the extent to which the individuals or groups deviate from the population of school beginners as a whole.

The value of making normative comparisons among first-grade groups depends somewhat upon the type of curriculum for beginners that prevails in the school. If teaching tends to conform to conventional practices, these comparisons with a national standardization group have considerable value.

Diagnostic Possibilities. An analysis of the results of readiness tests may disclose pupils' limitations that are likely to interfere with learning specific skills. While total score on a general readiness test is chiefly useful in grouping pupils, the separate scores on the subtests of certain of them are of more value as a guide to specific training needed to supply background or to overcome deficiencies.

Some group intelligence or readiness tests measure not only such specific traits as vocabulary, visual perception, and number knowledge, but also other more general traits needed for success in beginning schoolwork, such as the ability to listen to directions and follow them carefully, the ability to use crayons or pencils, the ability to find and keep the place indicated in a book, and the ability to give sustained attention for a short period. All these tests afford the teacher an opportunity to observe the behavior of pupils in reacting to uniform and comparable situations. The same feature permits comparisons to be made among individual pupils.

Readiness tests tend more than intelligence tests to reveal the extent of the learning the child derives from his background. Children with rich experiential backgrounds are able to work successfully with the tests earlier than those with limited backgrounds. First-grade intelligence tests, on the other hand, are more apt to be "culture free."

Non-language tests, which measure readiness traits independently of language knowledge and facility, will be required for children from foreign-speaking homes, unless the tests can be given in the children's native language. However, on the chance that some children will know more English than the teacher suspects, it may be desirable to include in the testing types of materials that require comprehension of English on a simple level, thus affording a check on English vocabulary and a rating of English usage.

Tests of copying geometric forms, such as the Copying Test of *Metropolitan Readiness Tests* and the Copying of Geometric Figures found in the *Gesell Developmental Schedules,* are useful because they do not require understanding or use of language, and also because they throw light on the child's spatial and visual perception and his oculo-motor coordination.

HOW TO USE READINESS TESTS

Normally, group readiness tests should be administered by the children's own teacher, since she is logically the one who will make most immediate use of the test results. Most group readiness tests in common use can be easily and effectively administered by the classroom teacher without previous special training.

The particular time during the first year when various tests are to be given depends on the type of tests to be used and the purposes the test is meant to serve. If test results are needed for prompt classification of pupils or for screening out pupils who are immature or linguistically retarded, tests should be given early in the term. General readiness tests are used most advantageously at the end of the kindergarten period or early in first grade.

Occasionally an objection is raised against the use of readiness tests this early, on the grounds that the children lack the experience needed in working successfully with paper-and-pencil tests or that they have widely dissimilar backgrounds. Since a good test requires little more skill than handling a crayon, the tests can be given effectively as soon as the children know how to mark or draw. Dissimilarity in background is precisely the thing that the more general types of readiness and intelligence tests are designed to measure.

Reading readiness tests should ordinarily be deferred until shortly before the teacher expects to undertake systematic instruction in reading. Some reading readiness tests would be discouraging to beginners because they re-

quire considerable discrimination between words, and the skills measured
are rather tedious to test adequately.

HOW TO UNDERSTAND RESULTS

Most group intelligence tests yield scores that are interpreted in terms of
mental ages, which can be converted into IQs. Readiness test scores, however, are usually interpreted in terms of percentile ranks, which indicate the
pupil's standing on the test in relation to all pupils in the group on which the
norms are based. These percentile ranks, in turn, are sometimes interpreted
in terms of probability of success or failure in first-grade work. The use of
percentile rank is generally satisfactory, as the teacher is chiefly concerned
at first with knowing how the child compares in maturity with the others of
his group.

Patterns of variability shown by class groups of beginners will differ
greatly, as will their average performance in relation to the norms for the
test. In some classes a large proportion of the pupils will rate below the
published norms for the test, showing that the class as a whole is comparatively backward; in other classes the reverse condition will prevail, with the
majority rating well above the norms; in still others the numbers of relatively
slow and relatively fast learners may be nearly equal. In each case, the
overall pattern of variability for the group is a strong indicator of the most
suitable type of first-grade program for that group.

Special attention should be given to all low-scoring pupils. Low scores
on a general readiness test are danger signals indicating possible failure
unless the first-grade program is modified in the direction of kindergarten
activities for the first few months of school. Any child who is fully six years
old and scores below 65 on the total *Metropolitan Readiness Tests* (*a*) may
be lacking in normal background of experience, (*b*) may be mentally immature for his age, or (*c*) may have a language handicap or physical defects
that interfere with full response to the test.

Similarly, though not for the same reasons, children who rate exceptionally high on initial tests should be observed with care. These children
may have latent talents and assets that need to be drawn out.

Caution should be exercised in interpreting the results of tests, since a
certain amount of error will be found in any test score or norm. Information
on the probable or standard error of a test is usually included in the descriptive or interpretative material that accompanies the test.

APPLYING TEST RESULTS

Teachers should not become unduly perturbed over results for low-scoring
pupils or berate the children for not having done better. Nor should they
convey to parents the impression that such children have "failed" on the

test or are not up to grade. Instead they should regard the results as indications of need for differentiated instruction and individual guidance.

Teachers are advised to have individual intelligence tests given to pupils who score extremely low on the readiness tests. They also should observe the behavior of such pupils especially closely during the weeks after testing in order to arrive at a reliable estimate of their capacities. If the initial test results are confirmed by subsequent testing and observation, then special types of training will be required in the beginning school years.

Superior children are frequently neglected for the time-consuming activities and individual attention needed for slow learners. However, their outstanding traits deserve to be discovered early so that suitable training for well-rounded development can be provided. Parents should be informed of the findings if the information is needed to help them understand the children better.

The results of readiness tests should be summarized on an individual pupil basis, as well as for the class as a whole. In *Metropolitan Readiness Tests,* spaces are provided on the cover page of the test booklet for recording scores on each subtest and for summarizing and interpreting the reading readiness, number readiness, and general readiness status of the pupil.

Some teachers take the time to summarize test findings and observations in the form of a brief paragraph report. Following is an illustration of such a report.

Child X, age 5 years, 10 months. (Class average age, 6 years, 3 months.)
Pintner-Cunningham Primary Test results: MA, 5–0; IQ, 86.
Metropolitan Readiness Tests results: Total score, 56. (Class average total score, 74.) Subtest scores: Word Meannig, 12; Sentences, 6; Information, 8; Matching, 13; Numbers, 12; Copying, 5.
Child has difficulty following directions and seems immature, particularly in language.
This child is shy in class, does not make friends easily with the other children, who tend to tease her. She talks little. The mother speaks a foreign language; the father speaks English. There are two other children in the family, one younger than X. Poor home conditions suggest low economic level. This child is somewhat underweight, appears to be poorly nourished. She responds slowly compared with the rest of the class and has difficulty following the teacher's directions.

A word of caution to teachers regarding the use of readiness tests: Do not use readiness tests primarily for the purpose of following up with intensive remedial drill to correct specific weaknesses disclosed. Rather, use the tests to rate children in terms of all-round maturity or general readiness for learning. Also, do not drill pupils on the specific test items they have failed, since this practice is not in harmony with good teaching practice and may well vitiate the results of later testing. Instead, give the pupil training in the type of experience in which the test shows him to be especially deficient, such as language and vocabulary, for example. Used diagnostically, the tests will have served their primary purpose, which is to guide the teacher in planning a curriculum that will meet the dominant needs of the group.

SUPPLEMENTING READINESS TEST RESULTS

Tests are by no means infallible. Paper-and-pencil readiness tests do not measure all the components of general readiness or readiness for specific skills, such as reading or arithmetic. A child's day-by-day behavior may give quite a different picture of his readiness for learning than that furnished by formal tests. A combination of these test results with the findings of teacher ratings, careful observation, and informal tests often furnishes a more reliable basis for determining readiness than do the tests alone.

Even though the tests may indicate a child's probable success in first-grade work, he may fail to make satisfactory progress because the methods of teaching are ill-adapted to his needs. He may develop antagonism toward schoolwork. Protracted absence may lessen his opportunities for experience and practice in different aspects of first-grade work. The child who has been overindulged at home, even though he is mature in the things the test measures, may be unsuccessful with first-grade learning on that account. Bright children from foreign-speaking homes may not advance unless they have additional language work. The type of curriculum, the morale of the group, and the length of the school day are also factors contributing to the success or failure of children in first-grade work.

SUMMARY

Good readiness tests, if employed properly, assist the teacher in evaluation of group and individual abilities and limitations. The information the tests provide is further extended by day-to-day observations and by home conferences. The test results can, however, play a major role in curriculum planning, in confirming teacher judgment of individual pupils, in grouping, and in prediction of probable success in first-grade learning.

A number of tests are available for determining level of mental ability, for estimating readiness for learning, and for evaluating progress in specific subject-matter areas. The teacher must clearly define the purposes of testing and then avail herself of the best possible materials.

▽ ▽ ▽

AN application for a position or an admissions blank for college entrance is not often thought of as a test, but by local research efforts such biographical inventories can take on many of the qualities of a validated measuring instrument. This is not surprising, since many such inventories contain items similar to personality measurements; in addition, they frequently ask for evidence of past achievements and interests. By doing an item analysis of all responses, by studying the extent to which these responses differentiate between a "success" and a "failure" group, by checking these data with a cross-validation group, one can then come up with a very good measuring instrument which has all the advantages of a standardized achievement test.

The earliest successful application of this technique was by the life insurance companies, who developed a weighted scoring system for certain items on a personal history blank which they found differentiated between their successful and unsuccessful salesmen. The Phoenix Mutual Life Insurance Company analyzed data for 500 men in the years 1919–21. It found that a mere 12 items differentiated the two groups, and the fantastic result was a reduction in their training failure rate from 90 to 30 percent (Russell & Cope, 1925). Goldsmith (1922) completed a similar research study for the Guardian Life Insurance Company, which after the establishment of a critical score eliminated 54 percent of the subsequent failures and retained 84 percent of the subsequent successes. The Aptitude Index, available only to members of the Life Insurance Agency Management Association, was first made available in 1938 and has undergone extensive cross-validation since then. It is basically a questionnaire about personal history data and also asks for self-ratings to which are applied weighted scores.

The technique has also been adapted, in a wide variety of settings, to concurrent validity situations. Kirchner and Dunnett (1957) used it to spot female office workers with long- versus short-term employment records; Lindemann et al. (1959) studied hospital clinical records and discovered five demographic variables which predicted long versus short stay in a neuropsychiatric hospital; Ehrle (1964) was able to quantify biographical data to predict vocational rehabilitation success; McGrath (1960), in an interesting study to identify unprofitable groups of customers (whose cars were later repossessed), found that a weighted application blank would discriminate between good and poor credit risks. Anastasi and her co-workers at Fordham University (1960) were able to develop a valid scoring key with a simple, factual biographical inventory that would predict college success. Criterion correlations as high as .548 were obtained in cross-validation study. To illustrate such a concurrent validity study, the following report from Standard Oil Company of Indiana, dealing with a high-ability group of subjects, is presented. Here the research competence and creativity, checked against three types of criteria, were assessed by means of personal history items. The report, slightly abbreviated from the original in the *Journal of Applied Psychology*, 1961, was a cooperative research effort on the part of Smith, Albright, and Glennon from the Employment Relations Research Office of Standard Oil, and Owens from the department of psychology, Purdue University.

THE PREDICTION OF RESEARCH COMPETENCE AND CREATIVITY FROM PERSONAL HISTORY

Wallace J. Smith, Lewis E. Albright,
J. R. Glennon and William A. Owens

Traditionally, two different research designs have been employed by investigators in their use of biographical data. These are directly analogous to the present-employee and follow-up methods of test validation. Exemplifying the latter are "weighted application blank" studies. In this approach, the pool of items for validation consists of those that appear on the employer's application form, filled out at the time of hiring by the criterion groups. Typically, the criterion used is job tenure, so that items are retained which discriminate the long and short tenure individuals. A validity coefficient based on the composite of surviving items would be a *predictive* validity estimate. The nature of the items retained, using this design, is almost always strictly demographic (age, marital status, number of dependents, etc.).

In the other design, which we will term the "personal history" approach, an instrument covering various background topics is administered to presently employed individuals who have been segregated into criterion groups. In contrast to the weighted application blank design, a diversity of criterion measures has been used; validity coefficients in these studies are *concurrent* validity estimates. Whereas, the weighted application blank is generally limited to factual items, the personal history questionnaire can include additionally items covering preferences, attitudes, and interpretation of experience.

The present study involves the attempt to validate an extensive personal history form with petroleum research scientists, using three different criteria of success in research work.

METHOD

Subjects. The Ss for this study were volunteer male employees at the Standard Oil Company's largest research laboratory. All of them were college graduates, the majority possessing advanced degrees. The most common areas of educational specialization were chemistry and chemical engineering with a few individuals having degrees in other technical areas such as mathematics, physics, etc. The length of service of the group ranged from less than 1 year to over 20 years, the heaviest single concentration (30%) occurring in the 1- to 5-year interval. Seventy-six percent were less than 40 years of age. The number of Ss varied from 331 to 198 because of missing predictor or criterion data.

Predictor. The personal history questionnaire used was tailor-made for this study and consisted of 484 multiple-choice items. The items were assembled from various sources. The content of the questionnaire included home and family background, various aspects of present and previous jobs, athletic interests, school and college activities, etc.

Criteria. The criterion which was used initially in the study was a rating of the researchers on overall job performance made by their supervisors. These ratings are made periodically for administrative purposes; they were not collected specifically for this investigation. The rating scheme used is a seven-step forced-distribution system, such that ratings of 1 and 7 represent the high and low ends of the distribution, respectively. The percentages of Ss at each point on the distribution are as follows: 1, 10%; 2, 15%; 3, 15%; 4, 20%; 5, 15%; 6, 15%; 7, 10%. For purposes of item analysis, the 20% with ratings of 4 were eliminated, leaving the high and low 40% as criterion groups. Some evidence for the reliability of this criterion is the fact that any man's rating is the product of the judgment of several different supervisors. Also, it is reported that relatively little shift in rating occurs from year to year for most people.

Some time after the project was underway, it became possible to collect ratings regarding the creativity of the Ss. The rating instrument used was the Check-List Rating Scale for Creativity: Form C-1, as developed by Taylor (1958). This is a Thurstone-type scale of 24 descriptive items. The rater checks only those items that apply to or describe the ratee. The statements range in favorableness from "He shows signs of being one of the most creative men in this work that I have known" to "He never has an idea of his own to suggest." The reliability of the scale is suggested by Taylor's correlations, which averaged .83, between the creativity checklist ratings and descriptive ratings of the same individuals made 4 to 5 months later on "originality." The form was scored by computing the algebraic sum of the scale values. On this basis, individuals with checklist scores of -160 to -10 made up the low criterion group and those whose scores ranged from $+50$ to $+180$, the high group.

The third criterion consisted of the number of patent disclosures filed by each man during the 5-year period 1954 to 1958 inclusive. (A patent disclosure is a document written by the technical man describing an idea which he regards as patentable. Before credit is received for the disclosure, it must be screened by an in-company patent advisory committee; after further processing it may eventually become a formal patent application.) This 5-year span was chosen after an examination of the distribution of disclosures showed that this period of time included sufficient data to be reasonably reliable. Only those Ss were included in this part of the study who had been employed prior to 1954. Those who had no patent disclosures during the period were classified as low criterion individuals, those having eight or more as the high criterion group.

Procedure. Because of the length of the personal history questionnaire, the items were grouped into five "units" of approximately equal length. The units were given to the volunteer participants at the rate of about one per week. Ss were allowed to complete the units during spare moments at their work places or to take them home if they wished. One unit was to be completed and returned before the next was given. Due to the voluntary nature of the project, normal turnover, travel schedules, etc. some attrition in numbers of Ss took place during the study.

For the item analysis, all criterion groups were subdivided randomly into validation and cross-validation samples. Ns ranged from, 25 to 68, but were approximately equal for high and low samples for a given criterion and content unit. Using a program developed for the IBM 705, the significance of the difference in response percentages of the high and low criterion groups was computed for every response, validation and cross-validation samples separately. A scoring key was developed for each criterion from those items which discriminated in both the validation and cross-validation samples at or beyond the .10 level, making a compound probability requirement of .05 or less. The keyed items were given weights of $+1$ or -1 in accordance with the direction of discrimination.

RESULTS

Representativeness of subjects. The fact that the Ss were volunteers raised a question as to their representativeness of the entire professional staff in the laboratory. A check of representativeness was made by testing the distribution of obtained overall performance ratings against that expected under the forced-distribution system. This was done for all five questionnaire units. None of the five values of X^2 was significant at the .05 level, indicating that the sample was not disproportionately weighted with Ss from one or another rating category. This test was also made for the 100 randomly selected Ss in the scoring sample, with nonsignificant results.

Intercorrelations of criteria. Table 20 presents the intercorrelations of the three criteria. These values are based on the total numbers of Ss for whom the criterion data were available, regardless of whether they filled out the personal history questionnaire. As might be expected, the two sets of ratings correlate more highly with each other than either does with the patent disclosure criterion. However, all three of the coefficients shown are significant at the .01 level.

Validity and reliability of scoring keys. The concurrent validity of the 37-item overall performance key was .613. Correspondingly, for the creativity and patent disclosure criteria the validities are .521 and .517, respectively, both based on 22 items. All of these coefficients far exceed the value required for significance at the .01 level.

The number of items indicated for each key may be somewhat misleading because the same item may discriminate on more than one criterion (although the same response is not necessarily scored each time). In fact, three items are included in all three keys. A total of 59 different items are scored.

An estimate of the reliability of some of these scored items was obtained when 25 researchers consented to retake two of the personal history units about 2 months after their original responses had been submitted. These two units contained 29 of the 59 discriminating items. The correlation of the 29-item scores obtained on the two administrations was .683. This value is similar in magnitude to those reported by other investigators with very large numbers of Ss.

TABLE 20

INTERCORRELATIONS OF CRITERIA

	2	3
1. Overall performance rating	.534 ($N = 362$)	.187 ($N = 285$)
2. Creativity rating		.200 ($N = 251$)
3. Patent disclosures		

DISCUSSION

The relatively high validities of the three scoring keys demonstrate the utility which the personal history technique can have with highly skilled individuals. As is often noted, aptitude and other types of tests which work well at lower ability levels may fail to discriminate in groups of this kind. Also, it would be difficult to find another instrument which would yield a better "rate of return" in predictive effectiveness per unit of testing time. For example, most applicants can easily complete the 59 keyed items in 30 minutes.

The only other studies in this general area of which the writers are aware are those by Mandell (1950), Stein (unpublished), and Taylor (1961). Mandell, using a 37-item inventory, was unable to discriminate chemists rated high and low on job performance by their superiors and colleagues. Taylor found that 20 out of 47 personal history items were significantly related to either or both of two criteria for 94 electronics engineers and scientists. The criteria were ratings of productivity and creativity. However, when he extended the scoring keys to a group of physicists, only chance relationships obtained. Stein reports a number of biographical variables which differentiate significantly between his groups of "more" and "less" creative industrial research chemists. There were 23 individuals in each group, the groups being determined by rankings and ratings from superiors, colleagues, and subordinates. No cross-validation data are reported.

Although some of our "personal history" items are similar in nature to those found in tests of personality, interests, and values, it is felt that they engender less hostility on the part of the applicant and are less subject to faking than is characteristic of many such tests. For one thing, they are presented in context with other items which do require responses of a strictly factual nature. Also, the applicant may do himself as much harm as good by trying to appear the "Organization Man," due to the empirical weighting procedure used.

A review of the discriminating items suggests that a "self-confidence" factor may be what these items assess. This interpretation is reinforced by the frequency with which the high criterion groups say that they (a) have more readily taken advantage of opportunities presented them, (b) consider their achievements thus far to be greater than those of others with the same education, (c) work more quickly than others, and (d) prefer to have many things "on the fire" simultaneously. Also the high groups tend to have more education than their colleagues, have obtained it on scholarships or fellowships, have worked as teachers or instructors, have published at least one technical paper and devote much time to reading—suggesting the presence additionally of an "academic orientation" factor.

SUMMARY

A personal history questionnaire was administered to a group of petroleum research scientists employed in a research laboratory of the Standard Oil Company. The questionnaire items were analyzed and cross-validated against three criteria of research effectiveness: ratings of overall performance, ratings specifically on creativity (both made by supervisors of the researchers), and objective records of the number of patent disclosures produced by each man during a 5-year period.

Three keys, totaling 59 items, were applied to a scoring sample of 100 randomly selected Ss. The concurrent validity estimates resulting were .613, .521, and .517 for overall performance ratings, creativity ratings, and patent disclosures, respectively. These results were interpreted as indicative of the value of the personal history technique with a highly select group.

A cautionary note should perhaps be appended to this presentation. Once the application blank items or the personal history data information has been studied, and scoring weights applied, it is unwise to allow such data to become old without reevaluation. Wernimont (1962), for example, found that the validity of a weighted application blank for female clerical workers declined for the period 1954–59. His recheck showed that only three items retained predictive validity over this time span. It would thus be wise to review, every three to five years, the scoring weights assigned to biographical items.

PART ELEVEN

Automation, Computers, and Multivariate Techniques

COMPUTERS more and more take over complex functions formerly managed by individuals. Large colleges and universities now are involved with extensive testing programs and prediction studies based on such test data. With the recent interest in over- and underachieving students—achievement, that is, measured by grade-point average and whether it is significantly above or below the earlier predicted grade-point average—computerized ways may now be found to provide feedback to individual students. With large college enrollments, extensive normative studies can be completed; multiple regression analyses come later. The counseling staff or faculty advisers formerly summarized entrance test data to students; now this task has been computerized. The following report is from Pennsylvania State University, where profile data plus predicted grade-point average, expressed in terms of probability, is succinctly presented to the individual student. The study originally appeared in *Educational and Psychological Measurement* for 1958. All three authors were at that time associated with Pennsylvania State University. Two are still there; Dr. Zeigler is now at the University of Illinois.

A NEW PROFILE FOR INTERPRETING ACADEMIC ABILITIES

Martin L. Zeigler, Robert G. Bernreuter,
and Donald H. Ford

A method of profiling and lucidly reporting a student's academic abilities was delivered at the Pennsylvania State University in early 1956 to meet the needs of a new comprehensive freshman counseling program introduced at that time. One of the shortcomings of the previous counseling program was the difficulty in communicating to students, parents, and faculty the student's relative class standing and his predicted achievement levels. Under the old system, the student's test results and predicted averages were reported on IBM cards. The predicted averages, however, could be reported on these cards only through a range of twelve intervals of one fourth of a grade point each, and there was no way to indicate the standard error of prediction. Under these conditions, the misconception often arose among the interviewees that the student could achieve neither better nor worse than the range predicted on the card. The new method attempted to ensure correct interpretation of the test results.

The new method also attempted to take into account the uncertainty of many entering freshmen concerning which curriculum they should pursue. To provide for this, multiple regression equations were formulated for two major curriculum groups—a "science" group (curriculums requiring mathematics beyond college trigonometry) and a "non-science" group (curriculums not requiring advanced mathematics). Depending upon the student's expressed interest in regard to these areas, his test scores were compared with those of other entering freshmen in that area and predictions were made of his probable academic attainment. In cases in which the student was more certain of his goals and evinced an interest in one of the specific colleges within the University, the counselor similarly had available to him the information necessary for comparison of his scores with those of other students showing an interest in that college and for prediction of his probable achievement within that college. An extensive manual was prepared for the counselor which contained—for all tests and subtests—the percentile ranks, means, standard deviations, sten scores (half standard deviation units from the mean), and beta weights multiplied by the test scores. These various measures were computed separately for each of the nine colleges. Accordingly, the counselor could plot on the profile the student's test scores as related to any specific college and portray for him how his performance compared with that of other freshmen entering that college. In addition, beta weights could be located and summed so that the student could be shown what his probability of success was within the particular college.

THE PROFILE

Figure 9 shows the complete profile developed for the counselors' use in the interview. For purposes of illustrating the way in which it appears in actual use, a fictitious case was set up on IBM and is printed on the profile. At the top of the profile appear the student's name, his student number, his high school rank reported in quintiles, the year in which the test was administered, sex, and the semester in which the student is enrolled.

The method for reporting test scores consists of using two curves: the smaller curve shows the distribution of academic ability scores of Pennsylvania State University students; the larger, distribution of scores that would be earned on the same test by persons in general. This technique communicates to the student how his overall and specific scores compare with other Penn State freshman students, and how they compare with the general population. Since the prospective freshman is almost always superior to the average member of the general population, this method can be reassuring for students and parents; especially is this true in the case of a student who scores in the fair or poor range of Penn State students. The profile does show, however, that such a student must expect to meet relatively keen competition and would have to work diligently to earn satisfactory grades.

The "SCI" appearing on the line of the profile opposite "University Aptitude Examination" means that the performance of the student is being compared with that of other students planning to enter one of the "science" curriculums; an "N SCI" would indicate comparison with students entering a "non-science" curriculum. The raw test scores beside each sub-test on the profile make it possible for the counselor, by referring to the manual, to

FIGURE 9

THE COMPLETE PROFILE USED IN COUNSELING WITH A FICTITIOUS
CASE ILLUSTRATION

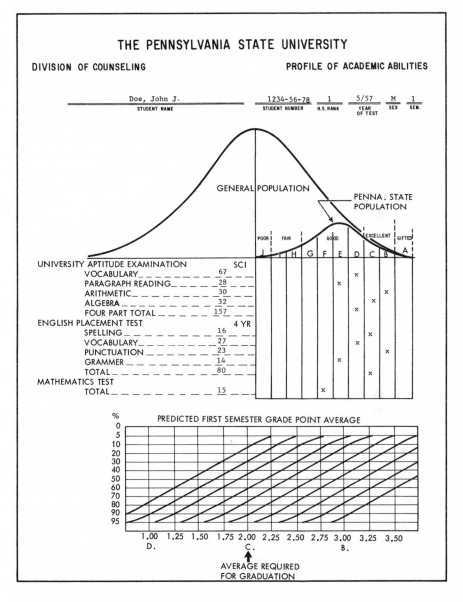

locate sten scores and make predictions of the student's achievement within
any college.

The second graph on the profile is an abac showing the predicted grade-
point averages. On the abscissa are intervals of grade-point averages from
1.00 (equal to a "D") through 3.50 (equal to a "B+"). A 4.00 (or "A")

does not appear on the graph since it cannot be predicted, because of regression, that any one will have a fifty-fifty chance of earning that average. On the ordinate are percentage values from zero to 100. The ogives plotted on the graph show the standard error of the predicted grade-point average for the middle ninety percent of the predictive range. The standard error has been presented in this way since extreme scores—the upper and lower five percent—tended to fluctuate widely and not in relationship to achieved grades.

Predicted averages were derived through multiple regression equations utilizing high school average and scores on the University aptitude examination. The abac was then constructed by plotting predicted averages against achieved first semester averages. This procedure was carried out on two separate groups; results obtained for both groups were very similar and both corresponded to the standard error of the coefficient of multiple correlation.

In order to determine the appropriate ogive for a particular student the multiple prediction was machine computed and the letter "X" printed on the slanted line within the appropriate predicted grade-point average interval. In all cases the "X" appears at the fifty percent level since the student has a fifty-fifty chance of exceeding or falling below that point.

An illustration will demonstrate how the abac is used. It can be seen from Figure 9 that an "X" identifies the ogive to be read for the particular student. The "X," in this illustration, is placed between the grade-point average values 2.25 to 2.50 and as always, at the fifty percent level. Thus it can be determined and explained to the student that fifty percent of the students whose predicted grade-point average falls between 2.25 and 2.50 may be expected to earn grade-point averages which fall within or *above* that cell, and fifty percent may be expected to earn grade-point averages which fall within or *below* that cell.

Similarly, any other probability may be determined and explained to the student. For example, by reading the same ogive at its top extreme it is seen that only five percent of students with a predicted grade-point average between 2.25 and 2.50 may be expected to exceed a grade-point average of 3.25, and that ninety-five percent will probably fall below that level. Or, it may be explained by referring to the required Penn State graduation average of 2.00 and reading upward to the same ogive and then across, that about seventy-five percent of students who scored in the interval of 2.25 to 2.50 may be expected to attain or exceed the graduation requirement.

The profile has been favorably received by students, counselors, and administration during its year of use. For all, it has appeared to provide a ready interpretation of test scores and an understanding of potentiality for achievement.

SUMMARY

A new method of illustrating and communicating test results by means of a profile has been reported. By this method it is possible to show a student how his academic abilities compare with those of his classmates, and how they compare with people in general. His relative abilities within two broad curriculum groups—a "science" and a "non-science" group—or within specific colleges of the University are also readily communicated to him. A more effective means of reporting predicted grade-point averages has also been presented.

The multiple regression technique here is clearly an advance. Still more sophisticated techniques are now coming to the fore, particularly multivariate procedures. The older ways of presenting a series of profiles to the student—say, one profile obtained from an aptitude test battery, such as the DAT, and then a second profile obtained from the Strong Vocational Interest Blank, and then perhaps a third profile obtained from, say, the Allport-Vernon-Lindzey Study of Values—only compound the statistical errors inherent in all these measurements, and they cause considerable confusion to the individual. As a recent paper by Sprinthall (1967) states, univariate or bivariate procedures for analysis of data are insufficient when it comes to dealing with complex issues. Discriminant function analysis, or multivariate procedures, where one simultaneously handles many variables, is the answer now proposed. Project TALENT is an excellent example of extensive use of such procedures (see pp. 292–304 of this book). Thus, when one wants to compare an individual's set of scores to the scores of people in a wide variety of groups—for example, the Strong Vocational Interest Inventory or the Pennsylvania State University method using various curricula—discriminant analysis is the appropriate technique. The result points up the similarities of the individual's scores to the group he most resembles. Aside from Project TALENT, the Harvard Studies in Career Development (see Sprinthall for a brief summary of these studies) have also made wide use of such analyses.

COMPUTERS can be made to do far more than mere clerical reporting or summarizing. Not only are regular class achievement tests now scored by machines; in addition, computers can now be programmed to do all the work in both reporting and evaluating guidance programs. Extensive test data—aptitude and achievement data of all sorts—pile up and are summarized on the cumulative record. Computers can be programmed to handle all this mass of data with great speed and efficiency.

In the past, many professional people expressed alarm at so much automation. At the Educational Testing Service's Invitational Conference on Testing, Traxler (1953) expressed concern over the presumed takeover of test scoring machines for psychological and educational testing, and the subsequent production of "the multiple-choice mind." Traxler was talking about what might now be labeled the Model-T version of scoring machines. Regardless, he is probably correct when he remarks that he believes many teachers have accepted objective measurement, "perhaps with quiet resignation," and are not at all comfortable with the thought that despite the skill and resourcefulness and imagination and stimulation they bring to their work, in the end the achievements of their students (and indirectly their own success) is to be evaluated by how well their students respond to a single type of test item.

Now with testing programs proliferating at a rapid rate, more extensive use of computer-based systems can now be made. But all too often the key people see such programs as simple automation of clerical tasks (such as reporting of scores). When at the Center for Research in Careers at Harvard University, Professor Cooley (now associate professor of psychology at the University of Pittsburgh) prepared the following paper dealing with a computer measurement system in which one could ask questions that would assist guidance people in interpreting the data at hand. Briefly, he proposed that we shift from the system of merely recording sets of numbers on student records to a procedure of "flashing red lights," which then indicate when a student seems to be in some special difficulty. Statistically, this means multivariate analysis. The paper is also of interest because it deals with the serious business of career decision and vocational choice. It is also one of the many reports emanating from Project TALENT.

The 1962 Fall issue of the *Harvard Educational Review* was entirely concerned with a critical and scholarly examination of guidance when the focus was on the search for theoretical models and substantiating evidence. This series of papers was later expanded (one of the additions was this paper by Cooley) into a special monograph edited by Mosher, Carle, and Kehas (1965). Dr. Cooley's original article appeared in the *Harvard Educational Review*, Fall, 1964.

A COMPUTER-MEASUREMENT SYSTEM FOR GUIDANCE

William W. Cooley

For some time psychologists have been convincing guidance workers that one test score alone is not sufficient evidence to conclude much of anything about a student. Their recommendation was to consider several test scores as a profile of the student. This resulted in the familiar "parallel stalks" model, each stalk standing for a test, with a line passing from stalk to stalk representing a particular student's score combination. Although this gives the impression that all the test score information available on a student is being considered simultaneously, anyone who has worked with this approach knows that it is only a slight graphical improvement over this same set of scores recorded in a cumulative record. *What has been needed is a summary of this test score evidence with respect to particular questions, questions with educational and career relevance for each student.*

I certainly do not visualize a system where the student's test scores are the input and prescribed curriculum and career are the output. Rather, the input consists of test scores, grades, biographical (including family) information, *and* the student's school and career plans. Output from the system would include, for example, certain information regarding students who appear to have high-risk plans. The actual form of this computer output could include explanatory paragraphs, if that seemed desirable. The task of the guidance program then, given this information, would be to plan experiences for such students which would give them more information about their plans, and about themselves in relation to those plans.

One key component of the output would be the probable success and satisfaction associated with a particular student plan. Most students seem quite willing and able to make plans and to discuss their plans in terms of probabilities. Interviews with the 700 boys of the *Scientific Careers Study,* a five-year study of career development, consistently found them talking in terms of their chances of doing this or that (Cooley, 1963). "Although I would rather be a doctor, I think I have a better chance of getting into a dental school." "With my grades, what are my chances of making it as a physicist?" "Do boys like me tend to go into law?" The students seemed to be continually searching for the type of data which a computer-measurement system could provide them.

Perhaps a specific example would help to clarify the points being made here. A case was drawn from the *Scientific Careers Study,* and it illustrates a frequent guidance problem. Selection of the case was quite simple. A brief inspection of computer output quickly identified several students with the characteristics needed. The files of that five-year study contained folders on each of the 700 boys, and each folder contained about 100 scale scores, 4 questionnaires and 2 interviews. Only with the aid of the computer can students with particular combinations of characteristics be identified quickly and easily from a file of data this extensive.

The Case of Robert S.   Bob S. was first contacted in the 8th grade. Our file contains his achievement data prior to 8th grade, as well as the data which were collected from grades 8 to 12 as part of the study.

Bob lives with his natural mother and stepfather. He has two younger brothers and no sisters. His father is a typewriter repairman and his mother does not work.

Ability and achievement information available on Bob when he was in 8th grade gave every indication that he had the potential for further schooling beyond 12th grade. A multivariate statistical summary of his ability and achievement profile indicated that about 83 percent of the boys with his particular combination of scores do enter some type of college.

Interest and temperament data available indicate that Bob "looks" very much like other boys who have entered careers in some field of science and technology. Of the boys with his pattern of interests, 73 percent enter some science-technical field. About one half of the boys who responded to the Temperament Survey as he did were pursuing careers in science-technology.

A summary of socio-economic data showed that 87 percent of the boys with Bob's family background do not go to college. These data include such variables as parents' education, father's occupational level, and the parents' expectations with respect to further schooling for the boy.

Notice that the numbers reported above tell something about Bob with respect to such questions as whether he is likely to go to college and/or become an engineer. Those percentages can be thought of as the probabilities associated with a particular type of prediction based upon a certain set of data. The data upon which these predictions are based were available when Bob was in 8th grade. Previously used techniques tend to report test results in terms like, "Bob did better on the mathematics test than did 50 percent of his classmates," or perhaps simply, "Bob received a score of 500 on the SCRAP mathematics test." It is difficult to decide what to think about such test scores. They are static. No implications are discernible.

Bob's career plans when first contacted in 8th grade were to enter the Coast Guard. He had an uncle and a cousin in the Coast Guard and felt "they had a good life." Otherwise, he might become an airline pilot. At grade 9, he was still talking about the Coast Guard but was also considering becoming a mechanic or engineer. He thought it might be a good idea to be a mechanic in the service because it is "more organized and less chance of business collapsing." In 10th grade he talked about "becoming a mechanical engineer because he liked to work on cars." This goal continued through 11th grade, but when he was last contacted in grade 12 he was planning to enter the service after high school graduation and become an airplane mechanic.

The point of this particular case is to illustrate a high risk in the sense that if Bob developed realistic college goals later during high school (as he did during grades 10 and 11), he would discover that his 8th and 9th grade behavior (e.g. course selection) was not consistent with those goals.

PROGRAMMED EXPERIENCES

By a systematic examination of several different types of data, a variety of potential problem cases can easily be uncovered today among a very large group of students. A computer-measurement system could allow the early identification of potential problems, soon enough to do something about it.

The problem then is what to do once a trouble spot has been observed. The recommendation here is to develop a system of *programmed experiences.*

In Bob's case, for example, general mechanical-technical orientation was quite clear. What was not clear was the level at which he might operate. A sequence of experiences could be designed to show the broad range of jobs open to boys like Bob, including the training required. For common problems, such as this one, films could be an excellent method. Included in these experiences would be some indication of the types of financial aid available to boys like Bob, so that college is not unrealistically discounted too early for financial reasons.

Included in his program of experiences would be a talk with a counselor. In fact, this might be the first experience in the sequence, to make sure that the established measurement-computer system did not miss something important, and to examine the prescribed sequence to see if it made sense. It is beyond the scope of this paper to consider other facets of the counseling interview. The plea here is that we do not rely so exclusively on such talks for either diagnosis or "treatment."

The concept of programming experiences perhaps needs further clarification, especially its difference from programmed instruction. Programmed instruction appears to be a very useful technique for teaching students many routine skills, such as arithmetic. Although some workers have attempted to adapt this stimulus-response technique to guidance, it might be more useful to adopt the concept of program, but broaden the units to be programmed. Instead of the sequences of separate one-sentence stimuli needed to take a student through the intricacies of arithmetic, programmed experiences would lead him through the types of experiences needed in order to develop a realistic concept of what a mechanical engineer does, what training he needs to have, what special abilities he has, the current and projected employment situation, etc. Such experiences might include work experience, meeting role models, visiting plants and laboratories, etc. Computer-measurement techniques are now developed to the point where they can be used to help the guidance programmer decide which students seem to need what types of experiences.

Additional Applications. At this point, it might be useful to survey other types of problems which a computer-measurement system could easily uncover.

The college placement function is a big consumer of counselor time. College finding services, for example, have demonstrated that much of this problem can be automated. Also, the computer-measurement system could identify trouble spots which, if acted upon immediately, the counselor could easily help remedy. If not identified early, the problem could grow until the student's situation required extensive remedial action.

One case occasionally observed is the student who is planning to apply to only two colleges and the chances of his being accepted at either one is something like one chance in one thousand. It would not be difficult to develop experiences which could point out to the student the desirability of *also* applying to a college for which he has a much higher probability of being admitted. Counselors are already using a type of intuitive estimate of such probabilities, so they should welcome assistance in this area.

The case just mentioned illustrates the problem of "over-aspiring," whereas Bob's problem, cited earlier, was a type of "under-aspiring." Both are frequent problems in educational and vocational planning, and if identified early, they might be remedied with suitable student experiences. The student may decide not to change his plans, but at least he will know he is pursuing a high-risk path. He may even decide to do something about some of the predictors (e.g., grades), thus changing his probability in that way. The main thing is that he have a rational basis for whatever plan he develops. As Kogan and Wallach (1964) have recently shown, the amount of risk a person is willing to take is a function of his personality, and this aspect could also be built into the computer-measurement system.

Another area in which an active computer-measurement system could accomplish much is in the analysis of student achievement. It is now possible for schools to develop a type of dynamic norm, which would make it possible to detect, for example, a student whose achievement-growth curve has suddenly slacked off. If this is done on a continuous basis, problems can be anticipated before they became serious, such as leading to another drop-out. The need for dynamic norms is considered in the next section.

A computer-measurement system could perform other very important diagnostic functions. Testing programs of the past have tended to assess "how much" the student knows, instead of asking what missing skills or concepts are interfering with his school progress. Perhaps a few weeks' review of fractions would help fill a gap which is currently giving some students trouble in shop work, for example.

THE NEED FOR DYNAMIC NORMS

Although there have been several factors which have limited the effective use of measurement in guidance, the problem of obtaining sufficient normative data has been one of the more serious problems. For one thing, norms have been allowed to get out of date. Funds are only now becoming available in the amounts needed to provide their continued updating. Another problem is that norms have been insufficiently developed, limiting the questions which can be asked. Norms are needed which are based upon multiple observations of the same students over time, and these need to be developed on a continuous basis. Also, counselors have not had the information needed for understanding the validity of test scores or the predictive implications of particular test score combinations.

Project TALENT (Flanagan *et al.,* 1962 and 1964) has shown that it is now possible to develop truly representative norms. These norms are also dynamic in the sense that they are based upon follow-up data which make it possible to ask questions about the subsequent educational or vocational implications of current behavioral and environmental observations, including the current plans of the student.

At regular intervals (say every three years), a five percent sample of schools could be selected for participation in a national "norming" study. The students would take a battery of tests which broadly sampled student behavior and determined their plans.

Periodic follow-up studies could then determine the pattern of events which followed the testing. The first follow-up might be conducted five years later, when most of the original group will have graduated from high school. This is more or less the current plan of Project TALENT, and so the feasibility of such an operation is now being demonstrated.

The computer-measurement system being proposed here is completely dependent upon obtaining such adequate normative data. The *Scientific Careers Study* (Cooley, 1963) has shown the potential utility and validity of the probability predictions for individual students based upon multivariate information, but only the *techniques* used there have generalizability. The actual prediction equations from that study are appropriate for a very restricted population (boys of above average ability in Eastern Massachusetts). Undertakings such as Project TALENT can now provide the type of normative data which has been lacking.

Not all applications of a computer-measurement system require national norms. In fact, "norming" can and should be frequently done on a regional basis. However, follow-up data must be made an aspect of this norming procedure if we expect to be able to utilize the test results in the manner described here.

This proposed, periodic, mass testing program may sound expensive. It certainly is when viewed in terms of the amount of money which has previously been spent on establishing norms and other validating information for tests. Yet it would cost only about $500,000 annually,[1] which is about what it would cost to add only 50 more counselors to the entire United States, a number which would not even make a dent in the current student–counselor ratio. If we really want to learn more about students from the millions of dollars annually spent on school testing programs, if we want to provide the type of information which students seem to want and need, then such undertakings seem necessary and feasible.

The skeptic may also claim that, although computers and multivariate methods are available today, they are out of the financial reach of most school systems. There are ways to solve this financial problem, however. Through establishment of regional data processing centers such as the New England Education Data Systems (NEEDS) project, a center computer facility is able to service many school systems, including the analysis of test scores for guidance purposes. In a few years each school could be directly connected

---

[1] Estimate based on approximate Project TALENT budget.

to a central computer by a remote typewriter-type terminal which would enable school personnel to ask questions of their school data stored at the central computer center.

THEORETICAL BASIS

The discussion thus far has been more or less exclusively about rather vague operations. By now the reader is probably concerned about the theoretical basis for this type of wild talk. Actually there are several bases, depending upon the area of application for the computer-measurement system. Perhaps it would be useful to examine the view of man which is behind the recommendations for applications in the area of student educational and vocational planning.

The basic proposition is that different plans are appropriate for different people. This proposition requires a taxonomy for plans and people, and a method for dealing with relationships between types of plans and kinds of people.

Factor theory provides a more operational basis for talking about people differences and their relationship to plans. In the factorial conceptualization of human behavior, personality has its locus in an m-dimensional space. An individual's personality is his unique location in this space, the location determined by the total pattern of the m behavioral measures which are available for that individual. In this context, personality encompasses all behavior, including intellectual functioning. People who have similar patterns of scores will occupy similar regions of this m-dimensional space. That is, people who behave similarly have similar personalities. Career planning and decision making is one aspect of behavior. People with similar personalities *tend* to make similar types of career decisions. Once the regions of the personality space occupied by people who have made particular types of career decisions are defined, the probability that another person will make a certain decision can be estimated.

Before this theoretical position can be further developed, it is necessary to explain that the test space concept, and the probability classification procedures which are the analytical techniques employed in the factor approach advocated here.

Say, for example, the task is to distinguish future scientists from non-scientists, Figure 10 represents a one-dimensional test space. An individual's location along axis X depends upon his score on test X. The height of the curve for the scientist group at some point, for example at x_1, is the frequency with which scientists receive that particular score on X. Knowing only the test score, you would predict that the person was a non-scientist if the score was low, and a scientist if the score was high. Knowing the heights of the two curves at score x_1, it is possible to compute the proportion of people receiving that score who are scientists, and the proportion who are non-scientists. With new test scores, from a person for whom the scientist–non-scientist designa-

FIGURE 10

A One-Dimensional Test Space

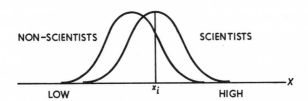

NON-SCIENTISTS   SCIENTISTS

LOW x_i HIGH

tion is unknown, the proportions became probabilities of group membership for that person.

For example, if one third of the people having a score of x_1 are non-scientists, and two thirds are scientists, then the probability that a person with score x_1 is a scientist is .67, and .33 is the probability of non-scientist. This assumes that the two categories exhaust the possibilities for the population under consideration. If the areas under the two curves are equal, this also assumes that the two groups exist in equal numbers within that population. These two conditions (that there are only two categories of people in the mixed population and that they are of equal frequency), are peculiar to this example and are not limitations of the technique.

Of course, a single test score yields inadequate information, so a method is needed for handling more than one test score. Consider the next most simple case, that of two tests. This results in a two-dimensional space similar to Figure 11. In this space, each individual can be represented as a point with a unique location depending upon his combination of scores on X_1 and X_2. This time questions can be asked about people receiving a *particular combination* of test scores: what proportion are scientists, and what proportion are non-scientists. These proportions are computed from the relative densities of "scientist points" and "non-scientist points" for a given score combination.

The importance of score combinations can be seen in this example. A score of x_1 on test X_1 could have different implications depending upon the score X_2. High scores on X_2 with x_1 on X_1 indicate the student is more like a non-scientist. Low scores on X_2 with a score of x_1 on X_1 indicate greater similarity to the scientist group. If a score on X_2 is viewed alone, nothing can be concluded about the student's resemblance to these two groups. Multivariate procedures make use of this combinational aspect of scores.

Consider another example. If a decision between two alternatives has been made by individuals located in the behavioral space, such as A college preparatory curriculum in high school, and B, non-college preparatory, the behavioral space will contain regions in which many individuals chose A over B, other regions in which choice B was preferred to A. There may be at least some A choosers in all regions of the personality space, but the A density varies from region to region. Comparison of the density of A choosers to B choosers at a particular point in the space determines the probability that choice A will be made by persons at or near that point. This scheme of analysis is generalizable to decision-making situations involving more than two alternatives and/or two variables. Each new variable adds a new axis to the system. The bivariate normal distributions for three groups on tests X_1 and X_2 are outlined in Figure 12. Once the means and dispersions of these three groups have been estimated, the probability that individual i is a member of group A, B, or C can also be estimated. The computations become rather extensive as the number of variables increases, but this is where the computer comes in.

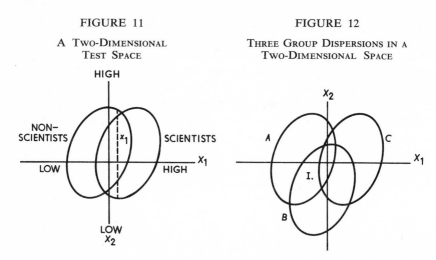

FIGURE 11

A TWO-DIMENSIONAL
TEST SPACE

FIGURE 12

THREE GROUP DISPERSIONS IN A
TWO-DIMENSIONAL SPACE

Mathematically the analytic task is handled by employing the algebra of matrices and vectors. A vector is a row or column of numbers. In a column vector of scores, each number represents a test score for someone. A row vector, if it contains m-scores, locates an individual in an m-dimensional space. If there are N such vectors, representing N people sampled from a population, the region of the test space occupied by that population can be estimated from the sample by assuming that the distribution of points in the population is multivariate normal. The center of the swarm of points is represented by the vector of sample means (called the centroid), and the dispersion of the points about the centroid is described by the variance-covariance matrix. This is the essence of multivariate analysis.

It is certainly not necessary for counselors to become familiar with the details of this type of multivariate analysis. The nature of these techniques was hinted at here for purposes of illustrating the type of thinking and analysis behind the computer output that would monitor student plans. To actually see how such techniques are applied in analysis of data, the reader might consult Cooley and Lohnes (1962) for computational details and Cooley (1963) for career research applications.

SUMMARY

As recently as 1960, participants at a conference on measurement and research (Traxler, 1961) have pleaded that counselors and teachers be taught how to interpret test scores in relation to all other data available on the same student. Although this is a noble goal, it is unrealistic. Even if they had the follow-up data which would make predictive interpretations possible, people are just not able to process that much information reliably.

It is possible to achieve this goal of sounder interpretation by use of the computer, methods of multivariate analysis, and results of continuous, normative, longitudinal studies. I do not mean to imply that such a system is ready to be installed tomorrow in any school that wants a computer-measurement system. The point is that, for the first time, the parts are all clearly discernible and feasible.

This paper and these arguments seem necessary because of the emphasis today on the counseling process. There seem to be too few people in guidance today who are concerned with the role of measurement in guidance and the ways in which new techniques might assist counselors in the task of helping our millions of students through school and into careers. The hope is that this type of article might stimulate renewed action along these lines.

HELM (1967) has proposed, in a similar vein, what he terms a "black box model" where computer programs are written to simulate the counseling process. He begins with the development of a special computer language to produce written evaluations of psychometric test data obtained from an extensive battery of ability and interest and personality measures. Working with clinical psychologists who were engaged in interpreting this complex battery, and with all test scores converted to a standard range of 0 to 9, Helm developed a list of rules to be fed into the computer. For example, if a score in the range of 6 to 9 on a measure of social responsibility is obtained plus a score between 5 to 7 on a scale measuring interest in supervisory tasks, then the following sentence would be produced: he appears to be willing to assume supervisory responsibilities. One application of this scheme involved a complex set of some 100 specifications or rules for the computer for a profile based on 70 test scores. The psychologist himself composes a paragraph of test interpretation and this is then compared with that produced by the computer. In some instances, the computer output is such as to simulate the psychologist's own performance in the clinical situation very well (for two examples, see Helm, 1967, pp. 50-51). Other applications of this type of work involve the performance of a counselor interacting with a ninth grade student in a guidance situation (Coulson and Cogswell, 1965) and a program which conducts a psychotherapy session at the console of a computer (Weizenbaum, 1966).

Mention has already been made of Project TALENT, probably the most ambitious longitudinal survey of aptitudes and abilities and plans that has ever been attempted. No volume on psychological testing would be complete without at least a summary presentation of this research under the general direction of John C. Flanagan. The project began auspiciously in 1957, when plans were made for two days of testing in a representative sample of approximately 1,000 high schools in the United States. Testing was commenced in 1960, when over 2,000 test and questionnaire items were administered to 400,000 grade 9 and grade 12 students. Long-range plans call for follow-ups 1, 5, 10, and 20 years after the expected date of the students' high school graduations. Because of the enormous size of this project, all data are handled by computers. The theoretical orientation of the research is that of classical trait and factor theory: certain traits are measured, the high school students are then followed up, and relationships are sought between the traits exhibited by these students in school and their subsequent vocational behavior. This criterion behavior includes their career plans and decisions, the degree of their job satisfaction and their job success. The study is another example of multivariate analysis, making possible consideration of patterns that occur in the data rather than analysis of only one trait at a time.

The following report concerns the sampling problems involved and the final test battery that was selected. It has been taken from the initial announcement about Project TALENT (Flanagan et al., 1962).

Dr. Flanagan, well known former director of the Army Air Force Aviation Psychology Research program (see pp. 103–10 of this volume), is now the director of Project TALENT, whose headquarters are in Palo Alto, California.

PROJECT TALENT SAMPLE

John C. Flanagan

We decided that a sample involving five percent of the high school enroll-ment, or between 400,000 and 500,000 students, would be large enough to provide a sturdy base for our contemplated research structure. Such a sample had the dimensions to satisfy many research needs of the present and future. For one thing, we knew that we would be studying many different groupings and sub-groupings of individuals and schools. To do this adequately, the initial size of the sample had to be large enough so that it could be divided, subdivided, then divided again and still yield substantial information. Later, as follow-up studies progressed, the original facts collected would be broken down for students who did and did not go to college; for those who did and did not finish college; for students who trained for many different professions and occupations; for those who succeeded and those who failed in their chosen field; for those who achieved high standing and renown—and, at the other end of the scale, for those who ran into trouble with society.

But there is still another reason the sample needed to be so large. We knew that a good percentage of this number would go into clerical jobs, sales work, mechanics; a smaller percentage would become lawyers, doctors, nurses, and teachers. But few indeed would become nuclear physicists, re-search chemists, or theoretical mathematicians. Yet, we would want to trace the factors in the career development of these future high-level specialists. Out of a half million students, probably no more than 2,000 would become Ph.D.s; of these there might be 100 mathematicians and 200 physicists. A large sample would be necessary if we were to draw these future specialists into our study.

Another question that had to be settled was whether to choose the sample on the basis of school systems, separate schools, or individual students. In many of the studies to be carried out with Project TALENT data, the schools would be the focus of concern. Student achievement and future success would be studied in relation to large and small schools, public and private schools, conventional and experimental curricula, and so on. For this reason—as well as for the sake of administrative efficiency—we established the school as the sampling unit.

How many schools would we need in order to draw a sample consisting of five percent of high school students? Five percent of the schools? Theoreti-cally, yes—and, as it turned out, we did give the tests in approximately one out of every twenty schools. But it wasn't as simple as that.

The sizes of public high schools differ radically—from less than a hundred students to more than 5,000. The small high schools dotting the rural countryside are far more numerous than very large city high schools.

To emphasize the contrast, the total enrollment of several dozen rural schools may fall far below the enrollment of one city school. To select one out of every 20 schools in the country without consideration of size differences would have resulted in so few large public high schools—and so very many small schools—that our later research on the effects of school size would have been inconclusive. The solution was to invite one out of every 20 medium-sized public high schools to participate in the study; one out of every 13 very large schools; and one out of 50 small schools. We invited one out of 20 private and parochial schools, regardless of size, to participate in Project TALENT.

To adjust for these variations, our statistical procedures called for "weighting" the schools in the analysis of the data obtained from them. Only by applying appropriate weights to the data can results be obtained which permit sound inferences about the total population of high schools or high school students.

The decisions made so far controlled the dimensions of the sample to be selected, but they did not control exactly which schools were to be included.

From various sources, primarily the U.S. Office of Education, we had obtained the names and addresses of all high schools in the United States—some 26,000 schools—along with their enrollment figures. It was from these official sources that we had to select approximately one out of every 20 schools. But which ones? We were face to face with the sampling problem.

In order to avoid biases, it is necessary to select the sample in a random manner. A characteristic of a simple random sample is that every member of an entire group has an equal chance of being in the sample. The laws of chance operate in such a way that a random sample will tend to be representative in all respects of the group as a whole.

Random sampling can be improved by a procedure known as stratified random sampling. This consists in dividing the entire group into smaller groups, according to one or more characteristics, and then using a strictly random selection method within each classification. To classify, or "stratify," the total group according to certain characteristics before drawing the random sample makes it more representative in certain respects and less representative in none. In view of this admirable feature, stratified random sampling was the method used in selecting schools to participate in Project TALENT.

There is a limit, of course, to the number of characteristics that can be singled out for such special handling, even in a survey as comprehensive as Project TALENT. We wanted to select only the most important characteristics and through stratifying, take out insurance, so to speak, that the sample would be truly representative in regard to these characteristics.

The first important characteristic to be singled out was an obvious one involving the type of school—public, parochial, or private. In our groupings we included all Roman Catholic high schools in the parochial classification. Other church-affiliated schools were put in the private school group.

We also wanted to be certain that we would have proper geographical representation. There is a big difference in schools because of differences in the economy of the region and the nature of the population. There are also differences in schools because the various state departments of education set different requirements for curricula, teacher certification, and graduation. Still another significant factor is whether the school is in a very large city or a relatively small community. For these reasons, we first grouped schools into broad geographical areas and then sub-grouped them by states, our basic geographic unit. Five cities, because of their large size were also considered as basic geographic units. These were New York, Chicago, Los Angeles, Philadelphia, and Detroit. Such treatment assured us of having proper large city representation.

We next took steps to insure that the sample would reflect the differences in school size. Size is certainly one of the most important variables among schools. For one thing, a small school cannot offer as varied a curriculum as a large school except at greater cost per pupil. We therefore divided the public high schools into the following four groups according to Grade 12 enrollment: (1) those with less than 25 seniors; (2) those with 25–99 seniors; (3) those with 100–399 seniors; (4) those with 400 or more seniors. One reason for this particular division was to set up two groups that would, and two that would not, meet the minimum size standards for schools recommended by educational authorities.

Another characteristic singled out for special attention among public high schools was the student-holding power of the schools. In some schools many students drop out before graduation; in others nearly all stay to graduate. Since we assume that there are major differences between schools with high and low holding power, we wanted to be sure we had proper representation of each type. This stratification was made by computing a retention ratio for each school. The ratio was the number of students who graduated in 1958 to the number of students in the 10th grade in 1959. This information provided a separation of schools into categories on the basis of whether (at one end of the scale) nearly all students graduate, or whether (at the other extreme) very few students graduate.

The machine that did the actual selection work (IBM–650) was given considerable human prompting on how to make a random choice from each category. For instance, the machine was instructed to take into account the different sampling ratios that had been set up for schools of different sizes. Instead of picking one in 20 as for medium-sized schools, the machine was programmed to pick out one out of 13 very large schools and one out of 50 very small schools.

Parochial and private schools were stratified (separately) into the 56 geographical units, but there were too few of these nonpublic schools to make it desirable to stratify them on school size and holding power, too.

The ninth-grader was, of course, an important individual in our study. But America's public secondary school organization sometimes places the ninth-grader in a four-year public high school and sometimes in a three-year junior high school. Not all graduates of a particular junior high school go to a particular senior high school, and not all tenth-graders in a senior high school come from the same junior high school. This gave rise to complications in obtaining a representative sample of ninth graders. However, a solution to the problem was found. Where junior high schools or groups of junior high schools were clearly and unambiguously associated with a senior high school that had been selected, the ninth-graders in those junior high schools were put in the sample. In communities where the situation was not so clear cut, the coordinators helped in deciding what junior high schools would include the maximum number of ninth-grade students who would go to the selected high school and the minimum number who would go to any other senior high school. A small supplementary sampling of the remaining junior high schools, together with a procedure for adjusting school weights, provided the means for mathematically correcting any minor inaccuracies that might have resulted from the approximation procedure described above for selecting the junior high schools.

One important phase of Project TALENT was to collect information on an entire age group, the 15-year-olds. This meant that the data had to be obtained not only for the 15-year-olds in high schools, but also for 15-year-olds still in Grade 8 or below, already in college, or not in school at all. We decided that the non-high-school 15-year-olds to be included in the study were to be residents of areas served by one-tenth of the public senior high schools selected in the sample. The schools selected in the sampling phase were divided into ten sub-samples which would be as close to equivalent in terms of the stratification variables as could reasonably be achieved. One of these ten sub-samples (designated "Sub-sample 0") was then selected to include the non-high-school 15-year-olds for study. These non-high-school 15-year-olds are not intended to be considered part of the regular sample, which consists entirely of high school students. However, they will supplement the 15-year-olds in the regular sample to provide a picture of the entire age group—the total group of 15-year-old Americans.

Two other special groups require mention at this point. The first consisted of two small groups of schools trying experimental courses in mathematics. The two experimental programs were developed by Dr. Max Beberman of the University of Illinois and Dr. E. G. Begle, formerly of Yale University. The performance of students in this new type of program will be compared with that of matched groups of students who take conventional mathematics courses.

Another special group are the schools in Knoxville, Tennessee, and in the surrounding county, Knox County. Two schools were drawn as part of the regular sample in this area, but as a result of the special interest of the school authorities there it was possible to arrange to test every student in every school—public, parochial, and private—in the entire Knoxville and Knox County area, not only in Grades 9 through 12, but also in Grade 8. This very comprehensive testing in a concentrated area, over a five-grade range, will make possible many special studies that could not otherwise be carried out.

A total of 23 tests, 3 inventories, 2 themes (5 minutes apiece for students to write on 2 topics—the meaning of high school and my view of an ideal occupation). The composition of the final battery is shown in Table 21.

TABLE 21

COMPOSITION OF THE FINAL PROJECT TALENT BATTERY

Aptitude and Achievement Tests

1. Information Test	12. Creativity
2. Memory for Sentences	13. Mechanical Reasoning
3. Memory for Words	14. Visualization in Two Dimensions
4. Disguised Words	15. Visualization in Three Dimensions
5. English: Spelling	16. Abstract Reasoning
6. Capitalization	17. Mathematics: Arithmetic Reasoning
7. Punctuation	18. Introductory
8. English Usage	19. Advanced
9. Effective Expression	20. Arithmetic Computation
10. Word Functions in Sentences	21. Table Reading
11. Reading Comprehension	22. Clerical Checking

23. Object Inspection

Miscellaneous	*Inventories*
Preference Test	Student Activities Inventory
Themes	Interest Inventory
	Student Information Blank

THE first one-year follow-up has now been published (Flanagan & Cooley, 1966) and certain implications for high school guidance programs are already very apparent. What follows is a summary of some of these findings, for both boys and girls, with data concerning the stability of their career plans. These data have been abstracted from Bulletin No. 5 (July, 1966), from the Project TALENT offices.

AFTER HIGH SCHOOL

During the four-year period of Project TALENT'S one-year follow-up studies, the percentage of young people reporting further education after high school increased from 57 to 68 percent. The first section of this bulletin concerns the relationships between data collected from these young people when they were in high school and their educational experiences after high school.

Comparisons of Students Attending Various Schools. The percentile scores on selected Project TALENT variables for various post high school educational groups are shown in Figures 13 and 14. Figure 13 presents the percentile scores of young men tested in 1960 as eleventh graders who later entered four-year colleges, junior colleges, technical schools, or trade schools. As indicated in Figure 13, the four-year college group scored highest on 13 of the 15 tests. Their score on Mechanical Information was equalled by the technical institute group, while their Table Reading score was below that obtained by the junior-college and technical institute groups. The young men attending trade school scored lowest on each of the tests.

FIGURE 13

Post High School Educational Groups
(Males)

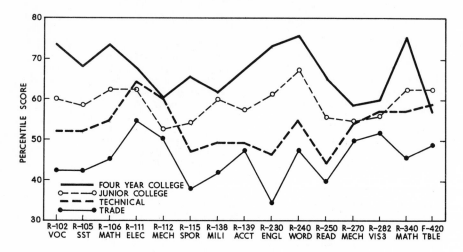

FIGURE 14

Post High School Educational Groups
(Females)

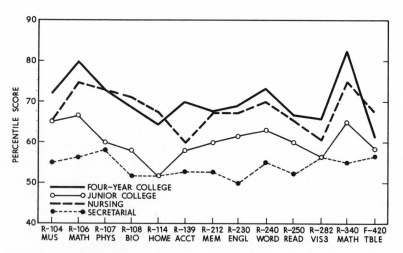

Figure 14 presents the percentile scores of the young woman from the same grade who entered four-year colleges, junior colleges, nursing, or secretarial schools. On eight of the 13 tests, the four-year college group had the highest percentile scores. The nursing-school students scored highest on Biological Science Information, Home Economics Information, and Table Reading.

Their scores on Physical Science Information and Memory for Words were the same as those obtained by the young women attending a four-year college. The percentile scores of the junior-college students were either the same as or lower than those of the nursing students. Below the junior-college group on most variables were the secretarial school students.

Probability of Entering a Four-Year College. Using general academic ability and socioeconomic level as predictor variables, Table 22 presents the probabilities that a grade 11 male will later enter a four-year college. These probabilities range from .06 for low socioeconomic and low ability scores to .87 for high socioeconomic and ability scores. Table 23 presents the probabilities of a grade 11 female attending college. As expected, these probabilities are generally lower than those for males. They range from .07 for low scores on both variables to .82 for high socioeconomic and ability scores.

TABLE 22

PROBABILITY OF A MALE ENTERING A
FOUR-YEAR COLLEGE

Ability Quarter	Socioeconomic Quarter			
	Low			High
	1	2	3	4
Low 1	.06	.12	.13	.26
2	.13	.15	.29	.36
3	.25	.34	.45	.65
High 4	.48	.70	.73	.87

TABLE 23

PROBABILITY OF A FEMALE ENTERING A
FOUR-YEAR COLLEGE

Ability Quarter	Socioeconomic Quarter			
	Low			High
	1	2	3	4
Low 1	.07	.07	.05	.20
2	.08	.09	.20	.33
3	.18	.23	.36	.55
High 4	.34	.67	.67	.82

As can be seen, a high socioeconomic score only partially compensates for a low ability score in predicting which students enter college. In other words, the ability score facilitates college entrance to a considerably greater degree than does socioeconomic level. For example, the probability of a young man with a high ability score and a low socioeconomic score entering college is .48. The college attendance probability of a young man with a low ability score and a high socioeconomic score is only .26.

JOBS AFTER HIGH SCHOOL

Young people who went directly to work after high school have also been a concern of Project TALENT. Of the noncollege high school graduates, approximately two thirds held full-time jobs one year after graduation. The greatest percentages of young men were employed as skilled or unskilled workers, while smaller percentages held jobs in clerical or sales occupations. Approximately 70 percent of the females were clerical or sales workers; 15 percent were employed as service workers.

Comparisons of Jobs Held by High School Graduates and Dropouts. Comparisons of the work experiences of high school graduates and dropouts have shown that the difference between the two groups is not in the percentages employed, but in the kinds of jobs held. For example, from both the ninth- and tenth-grade classes of 1960, the percentage of male dropouts with full-time jobs was the same as the percentage of employed male graduates not attending college.

However, of the young men from the class tested in tenth grade, more dropouts than graduates were protective, skilled, service, and unskilled workers; fewer dropouts than graduates held jobs in clerical or sales work. Of the young men from the ninth-grade class, the dropouts were more likely than the noncollege high school graduates to hold unskilled, outdoor, and protective jobs. However, fewer male dropouts than graduates were employed in skilled and clerical or sales work.

Of the young women from both classes, greater percentages of dropouts than graduates had skilled, service, and unskilled jobs. In contrast, female dropouts were less likely than the young women who completed high school to be clerical or sales workers. In fact, only 34 percent of the female dropouts from grade 10 held clerical or sales jobs compared to 72 percent of the graduates. From the class tested in ninth grade, 21 percent of the young women who dropped out of high school were clerical or sales workers, while 68 percent of the female graduates held similar jobs.

Holding Power of Jobs Varies. A study of 35 jobs held by young men, both graduates and dropouts from high school, has shown that occupations have different degrees of holding power. In other words, workers in some occupations are much more likely than those in other occupations to make careers of their present jobs.

For example, 63 to 88 percent of the barbers (percentages varied from class to class), 58 to 74 percent of the farmers and ranchers, 48 to 58 percent of the printers, and 39 to 59 percent of the photographers planned to remain in their present fields. These four groups had the highest stability of the 35 occupations studied.

Those employed in the crafts had slightly lower stability percentages— approximately 30 to 45 percent of the plumbers, carpenters, electricians, electronic technicians, machinists, and mechanics planned similar careers. Of those in business at the managerial level, 36 to 45 percent indicated they would remain in their present jobs. And 29 to 38 percent of the salesmen planned to continue careers in sales.

Among those with the lowest stability percentages were factory and assembly-line workers (5 to 9 percent), general clerical workers (4 to 5 percent), farm or ranch laborers (1 to 4 percent), and waiters or busboys (0 to 2 percent).

CAREER PLANS

Stability of Career Plans. One of the original goals of Project TALENT was to achieve a better understanding of the career plans made by young people. Through the 1960 testing and the four one-year follow-up studies, much progress has already been made toward this goal. One aspect of career plans—their stability from high school to one year after high school—will be discussed in this section of the bulletin using comparisons of the plans indicated by 15, 16, 17, and 18 year-old high school students and the plans indicated by these same young people on the one-year follow-up questionnaires. At the time of the follow-up studies, these young people were about 19 years of age.

The overall stability of career plans made in grades 9, 10, 11, and 12 is shown in Table 24.

TABLE 24

PERCENTAGES OF YOUNG PEOPLE HAVING CAREER
PLANS ONE YEAR AFTER HIGH SCHOOL SIMILAR TO
PLANS MADE IN GRADES 9, 10, 11, 12

	Males	Females
Grade 9	16.8	26.1
Grade 10	18.9	28.7
Grade 11	25.0	36.4
Grade 12	31.4	41.2

Some plans were more stable than others. For the boys, for example, careers as clergymen and physicians showed a high degree of stability. Of those twelfth-grade boys planning careers in these fields, over 50 percent had the same plans after high school. The twelfth-grade boys expecting to be teachers, writers, and farmers also showed better than average stability in their plans. Forty-four to 49 percent of these young men reported the same plans one year later. Career plans in engineering, dentistry, pharmacy, law, art or entertainment, and skilled occupations were between 30 and 40 percent stable from grade 12 to one year after high school.

As Table 24 has indicated, the overall stability of plans made by young men decreased from 31 percent (grade 12) to 17 percent (grade 9). For ninth-grade boys, only one career, businessman, was still planned by more than 30 percent of the boys who chose it in high school. Only 18 percent of the very large number of boys in the ninth grade planning careers as engineers still intended to work in this field four years later.

For the girls, teacher and housewife were the only career plans showing more than 50 percent stability from any grade level to one year after high school. Careers with more than 40 percent stability included office worker, nurse, beautician, and artist or entertainer.

This high degree of instability of the plans of boys and girls in ninth, tenth, eleventh, and twelfth grade raises the question as to whether the new career plans were closely related or generally unrelated to the initial career goals. Inspection of some of the plans of individuals initially in large groups such as those intending to be engineers has indicated quite clearly that there was no pattern to the new plans which could be predicted from the initial plans with better than chance success. This emphasizes the necessity of turning to more stable characteristics of the individual, such as those measured by the 1960 battery of tests, to predict his ultimate career plans rather than depending upon his initial selection to provide important clues. The following section of this bulletin will illustrate how 1960 data can aid in these predictions.

Predicting Career Plan Changes.   Using an individual's stated plans, his scores on the 1960 TALENT tests, and the techniques of multiple discriminant analysis and probability classification, Project TALENT has attempted to predict changes in career group membership. These changes come about when an individual perceives a discrepancy between what he thinks of himself and what he thinks of his plans for an occupation.

The most difficult aspect of this research has been determining the criterion to be predicted, since there is a seemingly infinite number of ways to classify career plans. Project TALENT's schemes for classifying plans have been developed by considering: (*a*) the test profile similarity of more specific career groups (i.e., boys planning either physics or chemistry were grouped into Physical Science because their 1960 TALENT profiles were similar), (*b*) the types of educational decisions students have to make as they move toward these various careers (there is no point in making finer distinctions in career planning earlier than required by the educational system), and (*c*) the types of back-and-forth changes which tend to be made in career planning.

One classification scheme used in our recent follow-up report makes two basic distinctions: (*a*) whether the career is science-technology or people oriented, and (*b*) whether or not a college education is necessary. The science-technology oriented careers requiring a college education are divided into Physical Science (mathematician, physical scientist, engineer, scientific aide) and Medicine-Biology (biological scientist, nurse, physician, pharmacist, dentist, medical technician). The people oriented careers which require college training include two groups—Humanities (social scientist, social worker, clergyman, teacher) and Business College (accountant, lawyer, businessman, government, salesman). The careers for which a college education is not necessary are divided into Technical (aviation, engineering aide, medical technician, skilled worker, structural worker) and Business Non-college (government, salesman, accountant, service worker, businessman, office worker).

One study conducted using this six-group criterion determined that the TALENT ability measures were more highly related to follow-up plans than to plans made in grade 9. That is, the later plans tended to be more consistent with ability profiles than were the earlier grade 9 plans.

Measures of vocational interests, on the other hand, tended to be more highly related to grade 9 plans than to follow-up plans. This is explained by the theory that both interest responses and stated plans are a function of the student's current self-concept and his current stereotypes of work and workers. As these change during high school, so will both stated plans and inventoried interests. We are currently exploring this question in greater detail using data available for a subsample of grade 9 students who were retested with the TALENT battery in grade 12.

These and other findings have demonstrated that the TALENT tests are relevant to the process of career development. It is also becoming quite clear that procedures based upon these results and the results of subsequent Project TALENT follow-up studies can aid in the development of a much improved system of school guidance.

IMPLICATIONS FOR GUIDANCE

The great number of career plan changes that take place during and immediately following high school suggest that plans formed in high school are unrealistic for one reason or another. This is an unfortunate phenomenon since educational decisions made during and immediately following high school are based upon these unrealistic (or at least unstable) plans.

There is really no concern if a boy changes his career goal from physics to mathematics between grade 10 and grade 12 because the high-school preparation of future physicists and future mathematicians is similar. On the other hand, if a tenth-grade boy planning to go into business later decides in twelfth grade to become an astronautical engineer, he will be rather set back if he has not taken the necessary mathematics options during high school.

These practical guidance considerations are based on the following principles: (a) there is no single high-school curriculum appropriate for all students, (b) the appropriateness of a curriculum depends in part upon career plans of the student, (c) different career plans are appropriate for different students, and (d) the appropriateness of a career plan depends upon the abilities and motives of the student and the projected supply and demand characteristics of the job market.

Because of the number of students to be served and the volume of information to be processed, at least partial automation of school guidance services is necessary if these principles are to be followed. One computer-measurement system of guidance has already been proposed by Cooley (see pp. 282–91). A major function of this system would be to give each student a good projection of his possible vocational future. Project TALENT would be useful in the development of such a system. First of all, the results of the follow-up studies described earlier have provided evidence of the predictive validity of the TALENT variables for membership in various post high school occupational, educational, and career-plan groups. A measurement system using these data could, for example, take a boy's test scores and return to him the probability of future membership in each of the six occupational categories discussed earlier. These probabilities would sum to one. A particular boy might get this set of probabilities:

1. Physical Science—.70
2. Medicine–Biology—.03
3. Humanities—.02
4. Business College—.04
5. Technical—.20
6. Business Noncollege—.01

This information does not tell the boy that he must become a physical scientist. It informs him that in a group of boys who share his measured characteristics, one year out of high school, most plan to be physical scientists, some intend to be technicians, and very few plan careers in the other four areas. He is not forced to react in any particular way, but he may choose to incorporate the information into his planning for his future.

Project TALENT can also aid in the development of a computerized system of guidance by providing a model for future career follow-ups. These follow-ups could be carried out by local school districts or by a central agency established by the Office of Education. Information obtained through these studies could then be systematically given to all local guidance programs.

Other TALENT contributions to a computer measurement system will include:

(1) the phrasing of a comprehensive, coherent trait-and-factory theory of adolescent personality
(2) the delineation of a measurement system related to that theory
(3) the packaging of computer programs for the data processing and analytical operations of a school measurement system
(4) an effort through content analysis of school courses, achievement tests, and vocational positions to synthesize the common element of curriculum and guidance sciences.

▽ ▽ ▽

PERHAPS even more remarkable is the imminence of computer grading of essay-type examinations. A preliminary report of this development was presented at the 1966 Invitational Conference on Testing Problems, sponsored by the Educational Testing Service. (And possibly even more ingenious was Stone's paper, presented at this same conference, in which he showed a computer playing the role of a psychotherapist). Because these yearly conferences offer interesting discussions, often of new techniques in only preliminary stages and not yet ready for final journal publication, listeners are provided with advance information concerning new testing developments and strategies. The conference proceedings are always published later in monograph form.

The following is an abbreviated version of a progress report by Dr. Ellis Page, presented by the author as "a description, clouded though it may be, of the view from where we stand." It is taken from the published conference proceedings (Page, 1967). Dr. Page is professor of educational psychology and director of the Bureau of Educational Research at the University of Connecticut. During 1966–67 he was on part-time leave as Visiting Scientist to the Massachusetts Institute of Technology Computation Center.

GRADING ESSAYS BY COMPUTER[1]

Ellis B. Page

It was a meeting at Harvard in late 1964[2] that started me tossing and turning and losing sleep about the whole field of essay grading by computer. *Why not?* I kept wondering, and little by little the necessary research design began to emerge. Once you ask the question *Why not?* and begin investigating this field, you might be astonished at how rich the background material is— and how much of it is virtually unknown to psychologists. You find yourself at a disciplinary interface, involving not only psychometrics and statistics, but also linguistics, English composition, computer science, educational psychology, natural-language analysis, curriculum, and more. This interdisciplinary aspect sometimes makes communication more complicated, since what will seem elementary to one segment of an audience will seem impossibly recondite to another.

The reactions to our effort have been fantastic. Our work has attracted a certain amount of attention in national news media, ranging from the favorable to the outraged. On one hand, there is the inevitable disbelief and dread of occupational replacement, and, perhaps, something still deeper.

[1] This work has been supported by the U.S. Office of Education (Research Branch), the College Entrance Examination Board, the National Science Foundation (through the Computing Center), the University of Connecticut, and the Massachusetts Institute of Technology.

[2] See Stone *et al., The General Inquirer* (1966).

My own favorite press reaction (possibly because I am a former English teacher) is one in a recent issue of a teachers' journal, which carried a drawing of this monster, an essay-grading machine. The machine was depicted at work with flailing arms (apparently losing some papers), glaring eyes, and thick sensual lips. The author of the accompanying article (Roby, 1966) wrote of a "cynical dehumanizing which, fully achieved, would reduce language to the terrifying 'duck-speak' of Orwell's nightmare world." He claimed that *human* essay grading is good *because* it is subjective—that is, because one teacher will not agree with another!

On the other hand, there have been many reactions to our work which were embarrassingly favorable, with such a wistful optimism about what we could do to help that some instructors at the University of Connecticut have called our bureau about grading their midterm exams!

The reality of our study, of course, lies somewhere between the impossible and the operational. We are not grading routing exams and will not be next year either. There are some good, hard problems on the way to this goal, but we feel the future is bright. Let us see whether, after having been brought up to date, you will share this optimism.

We may conceive our general problem as resembling Figure 15. As the column heads indicate, we are interested in *content* (what is said) and in *style* (the way it is said). Obviously, these columns are not mutually exclusive, but the simplification may be useful.

FIGURE 15
POSSIBLE DIMENSIONS OF ESSAY GRADING

	I Content	II Style
A. Rating Simulation	1 (A)	II (A)
B. Master Analysis	I (B)	II (B)

Similarly, the rows are not mutually exclusive either. But their general meaning must be mastered to understand what is being attempted. The first row refers to the simulation of the human product, without any great concern about the way this product was produced. It refers to actuarial optimization, a pragmatic approach to the simulation of the behavior of qualified judges. The bottom row, on the other hand, refers to the master analysis of the essay, to the sort of knowledgeable and detailed description of the essay, and of its various parts, which might emerge when competent judges apply advanced analytic skills.

We have coined two terms to describe this difference. Since the top row is concerned with ap*prox*imation, we speak of the computer variables employed as *proxes*. Since the bottom row is concerned with the true in*trins*ic variables of interest, we speak of such variables as *trins*.

A trin, then, is a variable of intrinsic interest to the human judge, for example, "aptness of word choice." Usually a trin is not directly measurable by present computer strategies. And a prox is any variable measured by the computer, as an approximation (or correlate) of some trin such as the proportion of uncommon words used by a student (where common words are discovered by a list look-up procedure in computer memory).

So far in our investigations, we have concentrated on the top row of Figure 15 looking for actuarial strategies, seeking out those proxes which would be of most immediate use in the simulation of the final human product. This does not mean that we have no interest in the trins. But many people have a misguided view of simulation. They imagine that a more microscopic strategy really does things in some "human" way. This is usually an illusion. The principal difference between strategies is often just in the size of bite, in the temporal scope of behavior chosen to be the target. For example, suppose we tried to imitate judges at a number of points along the behavioral continuum, picking up the essay, for example, then reading the title, and so on until we reach the eventual decision concerning overall grade. Suppose we imitated 10 such different choice points en route to this grade. That would perhaps seem a more accurate simulation of the process. Within each of these 10 behavioral blocks, however, we would still be using algorithms which had little to do with the "real" human procedures. In other words, *all* computer simulation of human behavior appears to be product simulation rather than process simulation. And the two fields of psychological simulation, on the one hand, and artificial intelligence, on the other, are not necessarily so very far apart as some would claim.

In adopting the overall, terminal strategy described here, we have not abandoned a goal of more refined analysis, nor of simulation closer to the human process itself. Indeed, we are pushing in much more deeply, as my later comments will suggest. But for the first attempts, we evolved a general research design, which we have more or less followed to date:

1. Samples of essays were judged by a number of independent experts. For our first trial, there were 276 essays written by students in grades 8 to 12 at the University of Wisconsin High School, and judged by at least four independent persons. These judgments of overall quality formed the trins.

2. Hypotheses were generated about the variables which might be associated with these judgments. If these variables were measurable by a computer, and feasible to program within the logistics of the study, they became the proxes of the study.

3. Computer routines were written to measure these proxes in the essays. These were written in FORTRAN IV, for the IBM 7040 computer, and are highly modular and mnemonic programs, fairly well documented.

4. Essays were prepared for computer input. In the present stage of data processing, this means that they were typed by clerical workers on an ordinary

key punch. They were punched into cards which served as input for the next stage.

5. The essays were passed through the computer under the control of the program which collected data about the proxes. Various counts (see Table 25) were made for the whole essay and were transcribed into scores, which then constituted the input for the final analysis.

6. These scores were then analyzed for their multivariate relationship to the human ratings, were weighted appropriately, and were used to maximize the prediction of the expert human ratings. This was all done by use of a standard multiple regression package.

The resulting data, summarized briefly in Table 25 for 272 students, suggest the nature and performance of some of the early proxes. Column A

TABLE 25

VARIABLES USED IN PROJECT ESSAY GRADE 1–A
FOR A CRITERION OF OVERALL QUALITY

A. Proxes	B. Corr. with Criterion	C. Beta wts.	D. Test-Ret. Rel. (Two essays)
Title present	.04	.09	.05
Av. sentence length	.04	−.13	.63
Number of paragraphs	.06	−.11	.42
Subject-verb openings	−.16	−.01	.20
Length of essay in words	.32	.32	.55
Number of parentheses	.04	−.01	.21
Number of apostrophes	−.23	−.06	.42
Number of commas	.34	.09	.61
Number of periods	−.05	−.05	.57
Number of underlined words	.01	.00	.22
Number of dashes	.22	.10	.44
No. colons	.02	−.03	.29
No. semicolons	.08	.06	.32
No. quotation marks	.11	.04	.27
No. exclamation marks	−.05	.09	.20
No. question marks	−.14	.01	.29
No. prepositions	.25	.10	.27
No. connective words	.18	−.02	.24
No. spelling errors	−.21	−.13	.23
No. relative pronouns	.11	.11	.17
No. subordinating conjs.	−.12	.06	.18
No. common words on Dale	−.48	−.07	.65
No. sents. end punc. pres.	−.01	−.08	.14
No. decl. sents. type A	.12	.14	.34
No. decl. sents. type B	.02	.02	.09
No. hyphens	.18	.07	.20
No. slashes	−.07	−.02	−.02
Aver. word length in ltrs.	.51	.12	.62
Stan. dev. of word length	.53	.30	.61
Stan. dev. of sent. length	−.07	.03	.48

gives the names of the proxes employed. Some were based upon careful analysis and hypothesis. Others (such as the less common punctuation marks) were recorded only because they were naturally produced by the computer programs. Column B shows their correlation with the criterion, the overall human judgment. Column C shows the beta weights for predicting the criterion, when all 30 proxes were employed. And Column D shows what could be called the "test-retest" reliability of the proxes. These coefficients in Column D are based on two different essays on different topics written about a month apart by the same high school students.

The overall accuracy of this beginning strategy was startling. The proxes achieved a multiple correlation coefficient of .71 for the first set of essays analyzed and, by chance, achieved the identical coefficient for the second set. Furthermore, and this is, of course, important, the beta weighings from one set of essays did a good job of predicting the human judgments for the second set of essays written by the same youngsters. All in all, the computer did a respectable "human-expert" job in grading essays, as is visible in Table 26.

TABLE 26

WHICH ONE IS THE COMPUTER?
Intercorrelation Matric Generated by the Cross-Validation
of the Computer Program

	Judges				
	A	*B*	*C*	*D*	*E*
A		51	51	44	57
B	51		53	56	61
C	51	53		48	49
D	44	56	48		59
E	57	61	49	59	

Here we see the results of a cross-validation. These are correlations between judgments of 138 essays done by five "judges," four of them human and one of them the computer. The computer judgments were the grades given by the regression weightings based on 138 *other* essays by *other* students. This cross-validation, then, is very conservative. Yet, from a practical point of view, the five judges are indistinguishable from one another. In eventual future trials, we expect the computer will correlate *better* with the human judges than will the other humans.

However useful such an overall rating might be, we of course still wish greater *detail* in our analysis. We have therefore broadened the analysis to five principal traits commonly believed important in essays. For our purpose they may be summarized as: *ideas, organization, style, mechanics,* and *creativity.* We had a particular interest in *creativity,* since some have from the beginning imagined that our study would founder on this kind of measure. "You might grade mechanics all right," someone will say, "but what about originality? What about the fellow who is really different? The machine can't handle him!"

Therefore, this summer we called together a group of 32 highly qualified English teachers from the schools of Connecticut to see how *they* would handle *creativity* and these other traits. Most had their master's degrees and extensive experience in teaching high school English, and all had the recommendation of their department chairmen. Each of 256 essays was rated on a five-point scale on each of these five important traits, by eight such expert judges, each acting independently of the other.[3] To investigate each of these five ratings, then, the same 30 proxes were again employed, with the results shown in Table 27.

In our rapidly growing knowledge, Table 27 may have the most to say to us about the computer analysis of important essay traits. Column A, of course, gives the titles of the five traits. Column B shows the rather low reliability of the group of eight human judges, computed by analysis of variance. This is the *practical* reliability of these pooled judgments. We get higher reliabilities when we subtract from the error term the variances attributable to period, session, and judge; but it would be misleading to do so in this present comparison, since these adjustments were not made preparatory to the machine grading regression analysis. Here in Column B it seems that *creativity* is less reliably judged by these human experts than are the other traits, even when eight judgments are pooled. And *mechanics* may be the most reliably graded of these five traits. Surely, then, *humans* seem to have a harder time with *creativity* than with *mechanics*.

Now what of the computer? Column C shows the raw multiple correlations of the proxes with these rather unreliable group judgments. These were the coefficients produced by the standard regression program. If a really fair comparison is to be made among the traits, however, the criterion's unreliability should be taken into account. And this results in the corrected multiple coefficients appearing in Column D. Here such difficult variables as *creativity* and *organization* no longer seem to suffer; the computer's difficulty is apparently in the criterion itself, and is therefore attributable to human limitations rather than to those of the machine or program. Column E simply shows the same coefficients after the necessary shrinking to avoid the capitalization on chance which is inherent with multiple predictors. Column E, then, exhibits what we might expect on cross-validation of a similar set of essays, if we were predicting a perfectly reliable set of human judgments.

Now there are standard beginning questions which people almost inevitably ask at this point if our subject is new to them: What about the input

---

[3] For a study of this size, the random assignment of essays to judges, to periods, and to sessions turned out to be a formidable task, and once again the computer was called in. This was our first experience of using the computer to *design* a study as well as analyze one. We discovered some interesting things in the process and recommend this idea to the consideration of others.

TABLE 27*

COMPUTER SIMULATION OF HUMAN JUDGMENTS
FOR FIVE ESSAY TRAITS
(30 PREDICTORS, 256 CASES)

A. Essay Traits	B. Hum.-Gp. Reliab.	C. Mult. R	D. Corr. (Atten.)	E. Shrunk. Multi. R
Ideas or Content	.75	.72	.78	.68
Organization	.75	.62	.64	.55
Style	.79	.73	.77	.69
Mechanics	.85	.69	.69	.64
Creativity	.72	.71	.78	.66

* Col. B represents the reliability of the human judgments of each trait, based upon the sum of eight independent ratings, August 1966.
Col. C represents the multiple regression coefficients found in predicting the pooled human ratings with 30 independent proxes found in the essays by the computer program of PEG–IA.
Col. D presents these same coefficients, corrected for the unreliability of the human groups. (Cf. McNemar, 1962, p. 153.)
Col. E presents these coefficients, both corrected for human unreliability and shrunken to eliminate capitalization on chance from the number of predictor variables. (Cf. McNemar, 1962, p. 184.)
Note: Cols. C, D, and E differ from the original text. Dr. Page reported a data-processing error to the editor and kindly supplied revised data. The conclusions of the article are not altered from the original.

problem? What about subject-matter grading? What about the student who tries to con the machine? What about detailed feedback to the student? And so on. These are all valid questions, and we have written our answers in the January issue of *Phi Delta Kappan* (Page, 1966). For most people these answers appear to be satisfactory.

But we are not presenting the results here as a terminal achievement against which to measure this sort of work. On the contrary, this is a temporary reading taken in the middle of the research stream. In the meantime, we go on with other strategies. Don Marcotte, for example, has recently developed an interesting phrase analyzer and has discovered that clichés, as usually listed, are pretty irrelevant in such essay grading. We have this summer studied some problems of style, parallelism, and certain semantic questions. We are exploring various dictionary and parsing options which lie before us. Recently we located what may be the most promising parsing program and used it to run certain essays. There are some fascinating studies done by people in artificial intelligence and information retrieval, which may have something different to offer in the near future. And we are interested in improving our statistical strategies as well. We are looking at the proxes themselves through factor analysis and stepwise regression. And then there is the question of extending the strategy to the humanities. One of the questions raised by scholars is whether it will handle various authors. A cartoon reflecting this question was printed in the *Phi Delta Kappan* and picked up by the *New York Times*. It is shown in Figure 16.

The machine is anthropomorphic and it seems embarrassed about "flunking Hemingway." Well, we are key-punching some passages from Hemingway and other standard authors to find out how the program handles them! In any case these present results are, as I pointed out above, the merest way station, but they may indicate to most of you, as they do to us, that workers in this field will not be wasting their time.

FIGURE 16

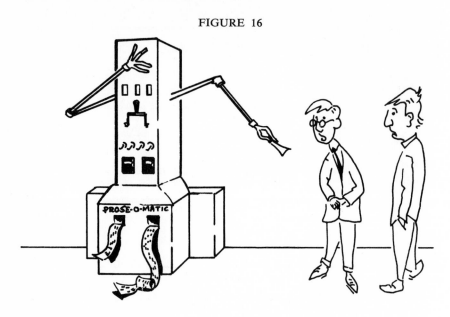

Great Scot! It's just flunked Hemingway.

Cartoon by Margaret McGarr reproduced by permission of *Phi Delta Kappan.*

There are many tantalizing problems in such research. One of the greatest is the effort toward psychologically deepening the work and making it more humanoid in process. Of considerable relevant interest to us, and to workers in related fields, is the possible verbal education of a computer. The solution will probably lie *not* in trying to *program* all the linguistic responses to be made by the computer. Rather, the solution may consist in programming only a certain set of quasi-psychological procedures, designed to enable the computer to learn on its own (i.e.—to gain literary *experience*) by reading in and correctly processing a great amount of appropriate text, making use of automated dictionaries and other aids while doing so. We dream of producing, in other words, the well-read computer. Part of our success to date has occurred through allowing the computer itself, in the multiple regression program, to determine which analytic weightings are valuable. What we hope is that somehow an expansion of this strategy of computer education can be undertaken. This is a very hard problem but a fascinating one and a number of people, in one field and another, are very interested in it.

And finally, a statement of present methodological bias: We believe that the work should not surrender to the purist on the one hand, who might claim that permanent improvement can be made only by a thorough mastery of theoretical concepts. Nor to the complete empiricist on the other, who may conceive that trial-and-error activities, with a poorly understood response surface, can lead to useful mastery of the underlying psychometric realities. No, a compromise would be more faithful to the professional history of my readers. Indeed, such a compromise between practical educational utility, on the one hand, and intriguing psychological and statistical depth, on the other, may be the very foundation on which our profession of measurement has flourished. In this new venture of grading essays by computer, competent measurement people, especially those with a love of language, should play an important role.

PART TWELVE

Psychological Testing in Relation to Public Policy and the Invasion of Privacy

THE November, 1965, and May, 1966, issues of *American Psychologist* were largely devoted to the broad controversy over psychological research and services. Congressional hearings were held; many newspaper stories were printed. The year 1965, at least among behavioral science people, is likely to be remembered as the year of Project Camelot. The furor over Camelot led both Congress and the White House to ask sharp questions concerning the conduct of social science research and measurement. The project was sponsored, to the tune of several million dollars, by the U.S. Army, and it involved those hot subjects of counterrevolution and counterinsurgency in Latin America. Senator Fulbright, chairman of the Foreign Relations Committee, registered his concern about such projects because of their "reactionary backward-looking policy opposed to change. Implicit in Camelot, as in the concept of counterinsurgency, is an assumption that revolutionary movements are dangerous to the interests of the United States and that the United States must be prepared to assist, if not actually to participate in, measures to repress them" (quoted by Horowitz, 1965).

Triggered by the adverse publicity over Project Camelot, hearings were held in July, 1965, before the House Subcommittee on International Organizations and Movements. The following summary description of Project Camelot is taken directly from these hearings, reprinted in *American Psychologist*, May, 1966, pp. 455–70.

PROJECT CAMELOT

During recent years, Communist support of "wars of national liberation," and U.S. commitments to aid the developing nations of the free world to meet this threat, propelled our Military Establishment into an expanding involvement in research relating to foreign areas and foreign populations. Noting the extent of this involvement, the Director of Defense Research and Engineering of the Department of Defense on April 24, 1964, requested the Defense Science Board to conduct a study of Defense research and development programs "relating to ethnic and other motivational factors involved in the causation and conduct of small wars. . . ." The report produced by that study disclosed various deficiencies in the behavioral sciences research program of the Department of Defense. Among others, the report cited the need to improve "the knowledge and understanding in depth of the internal cultural, economic and political conditions that generate conflicts between national groups," urged increased emphasis on the collection of initial primary data in overseas locations, and criticized the Military Establishment for "failure to organize appropriate multidisciplinary programs and to use the techniques of such related fields as operations research."

Prompted by these findings, the Department of the Army, having the responsibility for the administration of the military assistance program as well as for research, planning, and organization for counterinsurgency and

317

limited wars, embarked upon what became known as Project Camelot. Working through a contractor, the Special Operations Research Office (SORO) at American University, the Army began to prepare a project which sought to integrate many disparate research problems in pursuit of a single operational objective by attempting to develop a generalized model of a developing society. The purpose of this project was to produce a better understanding of how the processes of social change operate in the developing countries. On the one hand, Project Camelot was intended to assist in identifying the forerunners of social breakdown and the resultant opportunity for Communist penetration and possible takeover; on the other hand, it was also expected to produce basic information which would furnish some guidelines with respect to actions that might be taken by or with the indigenous governments to foster constructive change within a framework of relative order and stability.

The first phase of Project Camelot—the phase which was to be completed this past summer—was devoted to developing the research design, together with recommendations as to where the overseas fieldwork should be done. The primary proposals were then to be submitted for review by the Army Research Staff, by the Department of Defense, and by other Government agencies, including the Department of State. Subject to their recommendations and final approval, the actual research work was to commence either late this year or in 1966. However, Project Camelot never passed phase 1. While the preparatory work was going on, a representative of the contractor, traveling to Chile on personal business, attempted to ascertain the interest and resources available in that country in order to determine whether Chile should be included in the tentative program of research, or the research design. A distorted version of his activities and of the project appeared in a local newspaper, reported to be pro-Communist, and led to considerable adverse publicity in Chile, elsewhere abroad, and in the United States. The American Ambassador to Chile, having no previous knowledge of Project Camelot, protested to Washington and the resulting furor prompted the Army to cancel the project on August 2, 1965.

$$\nabla \ \nabla \ \nabla$$

MATTERS did not end here in 1965. Indeed, in certain respects this was only the beginning. Foreign universities and foreign scholars, especially in Latin America, became increasingly suspicious of contracts with U.S. universities and research teams because of the possibly hidden role of the CIA. In a June, 1967, issue of *Science*, this matter was thought of sufficient importance to merit an airing. Dr. Langer, a member of the editorial staff of *Science*, therefore made informal contacts with an unspecified number of social scientists who testified, albeit in general terms, to the discouragement of U.S. social science research abroad.

FOREIGN RESEARCH: CIA PLUS CAMELOT EQUALS TROUBLES FOR U.S. SCHOLARS

Elinor Langer

With social scientists now making their annual summer exodus to the foreign countries in which they conduct field work, many of them are discovering that their "laboratories" abroad have been metaphorically padlocked. In only a few instances have American schools been expelled or projects been subjected to abrupt cancellation. Nonetheless, inquiries by *Science* make it clear that following last winter's revelations about the involvement of the Central Intelligence Agency with the nation's universities—as well as earlier revelations about military sponsorship of social-research projects such as Camelot—a pattern is emerging of informal discouragement of the initiation or continuation of American social science research abroad.

This pattern is difficult to document with precision for two reasons. First, many of the scholars contacted are willing to discuss their experiences only in broad terms, evidently out of concern that naming names and institutions would only further threaten already fragile relations. More importantly, however, the process at work is a subtle one and difficult to pin down in any formal way. One scholar reports that in at least five Latin American countries American researchers are regarded with increasing suspicion. He told *Science* that feelers he had extended regarding the continuation of research in both Peru and Chile were discouraged by his Latin American associates, apparently out of fear that, whether or not the CIA was in fact involved, it would appear to have been. In these circumstances, collaboration with Americans involved great political risk to the collaborators. He also reported that, in the case of an international meeting that he was to have organized, the reaction of the scheduled participants was one of extreme suspicion about who would be paying the bills; plans for the meeting were canceled.

Another researcher, also in the Latin American field, told *Science* that, in addition to difficulties in arranging for institutional affiliations abroad, certain kinds of social research—particularly survey research—have become exceedingly difficult because of noncooperation by important sections of the population—the upper classes, the intellectuals, and the Left.

What it amounts to, according to one close observer, is that "You will not see a dramatic pattern of, for instance, 25 refusals of 100 proposed projects. The academic process isn't like this. The controls operate further back in the system, in the personal relationships between individuals and between institutions." There are also some official controls on foreign research. The State Department has been monitoring the federally financed portion of American projects since shortly after Camelot, and a number of foreign governments, especially in Africa, have begun to institute review procedures of their own. But by most accounts the barriers to research are those raised by individuals and institutions abroad who are no longer willing to play host to the Yankees.

One exception to the pattern of low-key discouragements is the direct withdrawal by a Brazilian group from a collaborative program with Cornell University, known as the Cornell-Brazil Project. The project was about to enter its 3rd year. In each of the last 2 years, about 20 American students, after substantial academic preparation and language training, have spent the summer studying the problems of development first-hand by working in poverty-ridden northeast Brazil in association with a group of Brazilian student leaders. Excerpts from a letter from the Brazilians to Cornell explaining the reasons for withdrawing from the project are printed in the box on p. 321. The letter is worth noting in detail, for it illuminates many of the complexities that currently affect American academic relations abroad.

The social scientists questioned by *Science* have discerned many of the same attitudes reflected in the letter from Brazil. They believe that the foreign academicians are not hostile to individual Americans so much as they are wary about the system in which the Americans appear to operate. Distinctions that may seem valid at close range—between an institution affiliated with the CIA and one not affiliated, between research sponsored by a military agency and research privately sponsored—are apt to look different from a distance. "It is not a question of mistrusting individuals," according to one researcher, "but a question of the public-relations impact on local institutions if they are discovered to be cooperating with Americans. Sometimes it happens even when the personal relationships are long-standing and secure. But, politically, they cannot afford to be cooperating with Americans anymore."

Another researcher believes that it is important to note that this pattern of rejection of U.S. ties, especially in Latin America, is by no means confined to the Left. He believes that while the desire to dissociate from America varies from country to country and, within each country, with particular classes, it is nonetheless an across-the-board phenomenon among those who are literate. In some places, he says, "The Right has been rejecting America for longer than the Left."

The following is excerpted from a letter to Cornell from a Brazilian group, explaining reasons for terminating the Brazil Project.

. . . There were two essential points of a general nature to be considered [regarding cancellation]. First there was a mobilization and radicalization without precedent in the Brazilian student movement. . . . The repudiation by the university student of American interference has produced demonstrations which were so strong that the Government came to the point of admitting a revision of the agreements between the Ministry of Education and USAID. In the second place, there is the pitiable incident of the involvement and interference of a security service of the American government in the academic community of your country. It is clear that in reality it is not possible, in this episode, to make a distinction between a university that was actually involved or disassociate one particular section of the university membership that is actually involved. In terms of work and of information, for the Brazilian student the entire North American academic community is involved with that agency of the government. This is the existing impression.

These two facts create a picture in which minute data or nuances lose meaning and from which it is impossible to escape. How can one maintain and justify a relationship with an institution—the university in the United States—which permits itself to be transformed into the instrument of a security agency which today is internationally known as the instigator of dictatorial coups.

We know perfectly well that you and all your friends at Cornell—both students and professors—are not to be associated with the unhappy discoveries of February. We also know that the Brazil Project did not receive money from foundations linked to the security service of the American government. And we know as well that those students chosen for this year are highly qualified, socially concerned, and "movement-oriented." *But the project is set up in the name of an institution called the University in America.* And as one of our mutual friends said in his letter, in this case, lamentably the just will pay for the sinners.

According to this scholar, as well as others, the notoriety given the CIA last winter only added to a preexisting tendency. Camelot isolated one particular way in which social scientists have used their disciplines in an exploitative fashion, and was important, he believes, in singling out American academicians as targets for the local politicians. But there seems to be a feeling that the social scientists are caught up in a general reaction against the United States, and that the role of researchers is only one component. With America situated on the profitable side of the "technology gap" and the "brain drain," resentment toward the U.S. is both inevitable and large, in the developed as well as the underdeveloped countries. But the underdeveloped countries add to this resentment a particular hostility toward American colonialism, and, while they share with the rest of the world a general dismay over the war in Vietnam, they have an additional fear that a similarly bloody form of American protection may be thrust on them next.

While the causes of hostility perhaps can be illuminated easily enough. The question remains: What can be done? Some of the professional associations and the area-studies associations are beginning to gather information about the extent of current problems, but no overall survey of their dimensions is underway, and there is no discernible movement to plan ways of reversing the trend. Among some social scientists there appears to be a hope that some salvation at least would derive from establishment of a National Social Science Foundation, such as is now being discussed. The belief is that such a clearly civilian umbrella for research funds would eradicate some of the doubts that have arisen abroad as a result of military financing. In other circles there appears to be a feeling that one way to remove the obstacles would be to scale down the nature of research projects—some of which have been extremely grandiose in both their use of resources and their objectives— to tone things down a bit and become generally less conspicuous. Others believe that the thing to do is to make sure that "our consciences are clear," that researchers are what they appear to be, that they are not undertaking research that will be used to manipulate the host country against its own conception of its own interests. A good many of those involved, themselves dismayed by some of the same aspects of American policy that trouble the underdeveloped countries, find themselves sympathizing with the reaction while distressed about the damage to their own professional interests. In these groups there appears to be a good deal of soul-searching about what the proper role of social researchers abroad should be.

Safeguards instituted by the professionals themselves may be of some help in restoring a climate more favorable to foreign research. But the research is also deeply affected by the political relations between the U.S. and foreign nations, and over these relations the researchers themselves have little control.

ALSO, in 1965 the Congress of the United States investigated the uses and abuses of psychological tests. Two different congressional committees were involved, and they mainly occupied themselves with personality inventories (specifically the MMPI) and issues related to the invasion of privacy. The American Psychological Association thought all this so significant that it devoted to these hearings the entire November, 1965, issue of the *American Psychologist* (Amrin, 1965). Pickets marched in front of the APA Washington headquarters. All the testimony, which ran to thousands of typescript pages, has been condensed in the journal referred to above. Aside from presenting statements from people both criticizing and defending test practices—and psychologists were represented on both sides of this controversy—important people outside psychology were also asked to give opinions.

Newspapers headlined all this activity with considerable glee. Art Buchwald wrote a piece for the *Washington Post* (June 20, 1965) with the caption "Psyching Out: you can't flunk this test but it tattles on your Id." Again, the *Post* (July 4, 1965) headlined an article by Willard Clopton, "Personality X-rays or Peeping Toms."

To the defense of psychological testing, and to the activities of professional psychologists engaged in testing and research, came Dr. Arthur Brayfield, executive officer of the American Psychological Association. The editor has abstracted and condensed his remarks before the Senate Subcommittee on Constitutional Rights of the Committee on the Judiciary (Amrin, 1965, pp. 888–94).

REMARKS TO SENATE SUBCOMMITTEE

Arthur H. Brayfield

The American Psychological Association is hopeful that this hearing and other action by this Constitutional Rights Subcommittee will assist in the further development and use of effective and responsible personnel procedures by Government agencies. Our members share your concern that such procedures shall give full recognition to the constitutional and human rights of present and prospective Government employees. . . . We would like to offer the services of our organization in any way in which they would be helpful to you. Most of our individual members are familiar with tests, and psychologists are quite concerned that the right tests be used for the right purposes in the right way.

Indeed, the Preamble to our Ethical Standards, which binds all of our members, clearly commits us to this interest and concern. I quote:

The psychologist believes in the dignity and worth of the individual human being. He is committed to increasing man's understanding of himself and others. While pursuing this endeavor, he protects the welfare of any person who may seek his service or of any subject, human or animal, that may be the object of his study. He does not use his professional position or relationships, nor does he knowingly permit his own services to be used by others, for purposes inconsistent with these values.

We hope that more and more persons in administration will come to an understanding of the capabilities and limitations of these instruments. We need that understanding, in addition to the proper use of psychological assessment materials by technically competent and responsible professional psychologists, before we can have a sound basis for personnel decisions arising in Government agencies.

These are not new issues to psychologists. The American Psychological Association has concerned itself with such scientific, technical, professional, and ethical problems and issues for the 70 years which have elapsed since the Association established its first Committee on Psychological Testing. And in recent years we have been particularly concerned that the possible abuses which psychologists repeatedly have warned against might become a reality— as the work of our present Committee on Psychological Assessment, recently reported in one of our journals and since submitted to your Subcommittee, indicates. We believe that yours is a justifiable and timely inquiry and that your deliberations and findings can be helpful wherever such procedures are applied. We believe that such inquiries as yours will help reduce any instances in which the wrong person or the wrong test or the wrong use of a test may do an injustice to some person.

We propose today to try (*a*) to put the use of psychological assessment procedures and materials in some appropriate perspective, (*b*) to discuss certain technical and professional considerations, (*c*) to inform you of our own efforts to improve our practice, and (*d*) to recommend a possible series of actions.

In our view, one of the major and crucial tests of the effective functioning of a democracy is the extent to which its citizens are able to use their skills, talents, and abilities in order to realize their own potentialities and to contribute to the common welfare.

A second test is the extent to which a democracy's social institutions, social structures, and specific organizational units function effectively to achieve their missions and goals and, in the process, enable individuals to realize their potentials and contribute to the common welfare.

In this view, a democratic society is concerned with the wise and humane use of its human resources.

It is in this context and perspective that psychological assessment procedures must be viewed and evaluated. The furtherance of these objectives of a democratic society has motivated much of the work on test development and is central to the professional use of assessment procedures. It is our hope that these tests have contributed to the wise use of human resources for productive purposes.

Undoubtedly the most rewarding application of psychological testing has been its very utility in the *discovery of unrecognized talent and under-*

developed personal resources. Tests have helped to identify the potentialities and unique personal qualities of the "sleepers," overlooked or neglected, and people in general.

The use of tests also, and very importantly, has demonstrated that many arbitrary barriers to employment such as age, sex, religion, race, and education requirements are responsible for a great waste of human resources. In many areas tests open to all have produced more democratic judgments for the greatest good of the greatest number. *I know of no other professional tool which has matched the effectiveness of psychological tests in assisting individuals to realize their civil and human rights.*

It is crucial to place the use of psychological tests in the appropriate context: It is a basic fact of life that judgments and decisions about other people are central in human affairs. All of us are subject to a continuing evaluation by others either formally or informally. We are assessed and evaluated daily and frequently there are designated judgment and decision points, as in hiring, performance review, and promotion. Assessment of human beings is going on every day throughout Government, at platoon level in the Marine Corps, in the Congress, and at Cabinet level—and in many different ways, including the judgment of witnesses, their testimony, and their experience when they testify to a Congressional committee. Men have always attempted to learn about and to assess the abilities, skills and competencies, interests and personalities of other men.

Such human judgments are, of course, subject to bias and to error. The variety of human errors in judgment making has been catalogued and described in many ways. In psychology we speak of the "halo" effect to describe the influence of general impressions, the "error of central tendency" to indicate judgments which hover around the average, the "error of leniency" which produces an overgenerous evaluation, and the "logical error" to describe judgments based on an assumed coherence of various traits irrespective of the individual being evaluated, i.e., when it is assumed that certain characteristics "go together."

Also, human judgment making is handicapped by the lack of objective standards of comparison, or, in measurement terminology, *norms.* We may be able to judge an accountant more formally than we judge a violinist or a lieutenant general.

In order to minimize error and to make judgments more accurate, the logic and methods of measurement have been introduced as an aid to judgment making. It is essential to recognize that *all* judgments take their point of departure from some reference point, usually an average for a known group. And judgments usually involve a statement of frequency of occurrence: For example, a judgment that an individual is observed to display "excellent emotional adjustment" is equivalent to saying, in measurement terms, that the individual is one sigma above the mean or at the eighty-fourth percentile.

From this logical analysis it is only a short step to the introduction of the concept of a psychological test which is defined as *an observation of a sample of human behavior made under standard, controlled conditions which results in a linear evaluation called a score.* That is, it is systematic refinement of the normal processes of observation and evaluation.

I should note here that the formal test is not the only way in which an effort has been made to introduce the logic and methods of measurement into personnel judgments and decisions. The interview itself has been made more objective, as has the application blank. In both instancs it has been demonstrated that these conventional personnel procedures can thus be made both more reliable and more valid for the purposes for which they are intended.

It is at this point that the unique contribution of the psychologist becomes apparent. for it is he who has insisted so vigorously that all personnel procedures *should be able to demonstrate their effectiveness.* That is, the psychologist requires evidence that the use of any given personnel procedure be demonstrated to have a relationship to the outcome of the employment process—to predict subsequent job performance.

This basic canon is illustrated by a classic personnel study made at the Scovill Manufacturing Company with the following results:

Over a 6-year period it was demonstrated that 61% of all employees selected by a conventional personnel interview were judged to be satisfactory.

Over the next 4 years, a mental alertness test was added to the interview and 83% of the employees so selected were judged to be satisfactory.

During the subsequent 7 years, two special aptitude tests were added to the mental alertness test and the interview, and it was found that 93% of the employees so selected were judged to be satisfactory.

The personnel procedures had demonstrated their effectiveness.

This study furnishes an excellent example of the *incremental* value of psychological tests. That is, the tests added something valuable to the use of the interview alone as a source of evaluation for judgment making. Their use improved the batting average of the personnel people.

This research report also serves to introduce a discussion of a central question: "What does a test score mean?" The rationale of the answer is straightforward, although the procedures for answering the question in any given instance may be complicated. In general, the relationship which has been observed to exist between one's relative standing on a test (e.g., scores) and some human performance (e.g., transcribing shorthand notes), or some status (e.g., success or failure in law school), or some mode of behaving (e.g., hypersensitivity, suspiciousness) tells what the test score means. That is, responses in the test situation are shown to be related to responses or behavior outside the test situation.

Let me illustrate by describing a rigorous "test of the tests" which was conducted in the Air Force during 1943–45.

A sample of more than 1,000 men was selected by representative Army

Air Force Examining Boards throughout the country *without reference to their test scores* (the test battery included tests of coordination and speed of decision, intellectual aptitudes and abilities, perception and visualization, and temperament and motivation, which were combined into a single score). All men who met the physical standards of the medical examination were accepted and sent into pilot training. Their test records were sent to Headquarters and were not made available to the training schools. These are the results (see pp. 103–10 for a more complete report).

Not one of the 125 men with the lowest combined aptitude score was successful in flying training.

Only 4% of the 391 men with low-aptitude scores were able to complete the full course of flying training.

Of the 468 men with medium-aptitude scores, 30% were graduated.

Of the 158 high-aptitude men, 65% were graduated.

It is clear from these data, which constitute a rigorous test of the tests, that important improvements in training efficiency resulted from the use of these objective selection procedures. The meaning of the scores on the test battery is reasonably clear. They were related to success in training. Incidentally, other studies demonstrated their relationship to bombing accuracy and to the accident rates.

This research investigation also illustrates that tests are not perfect but that they may lead to a marked improvement in personnel decisions over decisions made on the basis of conventional personnel procedures. In this instance, 25% of the entire group, selected by conventional methods, were graduated. If only men with high-aptitude scores had been selected, 65% would have graduated, representing a tremendous saving in time, materials, and money.

Obviously, I could also illustrate instances in which tests have *not* been effective. It is the responsibility of the test user to know from research what tests are effective for what purposes under what conditions.

This is sufficient background, I believe, to proceed to a discussion of the conditions under which personality tests may justifiably be used as an aid to personnel decisions.

Two basic considerations must obtain:

First, in most instances, such tests must be supervised by a qualified psychologist.

Second, in most instances, such test data must constitute only one of the sources of evaluative data. The test information must be integrated with other sources and types of data.

Given these conditions, it is appropriate to consider their use with all due caution, as follows:

First, to identify the potentially most effective members of an occupational group. Such use assumes that it has been empirically demonstrated that scores on a personality test are significantly related to some aspect of effective performance in the occupation. Example: inspectors in an electronics manufacturing company.

Second, to identify members of an occupational group where it has been empirically demonstrated that the personality characteristics of its members uniquely differentiate them from the members of other occupational groups or from people in general—i.e., when it has been established that the members of an occupational group have a distinctive personality profile. Example: telephone order clerks in a wholesale drug company.

Third, to identify persons suitable to perform in a given situation where an analysis of the job and its setting strongly suggests that its effective performance requires certain unique personality characteristics—or contraindicates certain unique personality characteristics—and there are available measures of such personality characteristics for which there is evidence that they do indeed measure such characteristics. Example: executive vice president in a medium-sized, family-owned hardware store chain.

Fourth, to identify individuals suitable to perform in a given situation where an analysis of the job and its setting specifies the nature of the performance and behavior required by the job. This further requires a well-qualified professional psychologist using a variety of sources of information, including personality tests, to formulate hypotheses regarding the potential functioning of individuals in the job and its setting. Example: the initial group of astronauts.

It should be obvious that these uses require increasing levels of competence on the part of the professional person as we go from the first to the fourth category. The last category puts a premium upon clinical judgment and professional skill and knowledge and requires the best available knowledge of the situation in which the individual applicant or employee is to perform. *The "costs" of a poor personnel decision must be demonstrably high to justify this approach.* However, it is in just such critical situations, where the hard data are most likely to be lacking or difficult of interpretation, that the need is greatest. In this circumstance, the ultimate decision maker must use the best available sources of evaluation, and I submit that one of these sources should be an assessment by a well-qualified psychologist thoroughly familiar with the hazards and difficulties of making such evaluations.

In our society, with its characteristic division of labor and specialization, the professional psychologist has emerged as the person whose education, training, and experience uniquely qualify him for this type of assessment responsibility. His profession has led in the development of assessment procedures, the establishment of standards of training and practice in their use, and the self-imposition of a Code of Ethics and a formal system for its administration. It is to these matters of ethics and professional responsibility that I now turn.

Throughout its history, our profession and our organization has pressed toward concrete definitions of professional responsibility in psychological work. At the beginning of this statement I quoted from our Code of Ethics, which describes the fundamental principle of professional responsibility, by pointing out that it includes other ideas which might be summarized as scientific integrity, technical competence, and a moral commitment to the welfare of society. Such general virtues are easy to admire from a distance, but of course it is quite another matter to make such ideals effective in an organization or as part of one's own way of life. We believe psychology attracts the kind of person who wants to help his fellow man, and we hope our training sharpens his judgment and disciplines this drive he already has.

Basic in our discipline is that psychologists must hold themselves to be familiar with the research regarding their procedures. In the field of psychological testing this commitment obligates a psychologist to study the technical literature regarding the devices he employs. If his own work leads him into research activity, the psychologist has an obligation to report his findings to his colleagues.

I would like now to direct this Committee's particular attention to the document titled *Technical Recommendations for Psychological Tests and Diagnostic Techniques,* published by our organization in 1954. Prepared by a joint committee of the American Psychological Association, the American Educational Research Association, and the National Council on Measurements Used in Education, this pamphlet has become the one standard reference regarding essential and desirable characteristics for psychological assessment devices. One of the major goals of this publication is to provide test users with a basic outline of technical requirements for these instruments in order to help them make better use of information about tests and of the tests themselves. The Subcommittee has been provided with copies of this document. Incidentally, I should perhaps note that our Association neither publishes nor distributes tests.

A revision of the above document has been published which takes account of 10 years of progress and helpful criticism by test publishers and users. The revised document (APA, 1966) carries the title *Standards for Educational and Psychological Tests and Manuals.*

Turning to standards of competence, I would like to note that members of the American Psychological Association and its affiliated state organizations have been leaders in the development of state laws related to the practice of psychology. At the present time, 27 states have either certification or licensing statutes that apply to psychological practice; 60% of our numbers are so covered. An additional 17 states have voluntary, nonstatutory certification programs operated by the psychological associations in those states; 32% of our members are so covered.

The American Psychological Association was instrumental in the establishment of the American Board of Examiners in Professional Psychology. This Board examines candidates who have had 5 years of experience beyond the Ph.D. in the specialties of clinical psychology, counseling psychology, and industrial psychology. The examination procedure involves a rigorous evaluation of the candidate's theoretical knowledge and technical skills in his area of specialization. The award of a diploma from this Board constitutes evidence of exceptional expertise in the chosen field.

Finally, in the matter of moral concern for others, our Association has had a written Code of Ethics enforced by a Committee empowered to receive and investigate complaints. A staff officer devotes one-half time to the work of the Ethics Commiteee. Additionally, each of our 50 state psychological associations maintains an active ethics program. A brief statement of our present Ethical Standards Code has been made available to the Subcommittee, and you will note that several paragraphs are devoted to the topic of psychological tests.

Even before our general Code of Ethics was formulated, our Committee on Ethical Standards developed some ethical guidelines for the distribution of psychological tests and diagnostic aids. A review of some of the principles embodied in these documents will help to make clear the nature of our concerns.

The following statements are representative:

Tests and diagnostic aids should be released only to persons who can demonstrate that they have the knowledge and skill necessary for their effective use and interpretation.

Psychologists assuming responsibility for testing programs or activities (including testing, supervising or sponsoring testing, and teaching courses in testing) obligate themselves to participate actively in the programs, either by actually carrying out the work or by planning, supervising, and checking it.

Test scores, like test materials, should be released only to persons who are qualified to interpret them and not indiscriminately or for self-evaluation.

Persons purchasing tests, assuming responsibility for testing programs, or distributing tests, should be governed by recognition of the fact that being qualified in one specialty does not necessarily result in being qualified in another specialty.

1. Being a trained psychologist does not automatically make one a qualified user of all types of psychological tests;
2. Being qualified as a user of tests in a specialty such as personnel selection, remedial reading, vocational and educational counseling, or psychodiagnosis, does not necessarily result in being qualified in any other specialty involving the use of tests. . . .

Finally, I should like to turn to your invitation to present our recommendations and views on the need for legislative action on these matters.

In our view, legislation may prescribe the roles and functions of psychologists in the Federal Government; it should not dictate the methods and procedures for carrying out these roles and functions. These methods and procedures are more properly reserved to professional judgments. Such a canon of professional autonomy does not, of course, preclude the use of common sense by the individuals concerned. Nor does it suggest an indifference to the important question of individual rights with which this Subcommittee is quite properly concerned—as are the members of our Association.

It does seem to us, however, that there are several ways in which the Government could strengthen its assessment procedures and safeguard the rights of individuals subject to them.

The underlying theme of our recommendations or suggestions is that professional competence should systematically be put at the service of the Government to develop guidelines for psychological assessment practices, to carry out such procedures, and to review such programs and procedures.

Specifically, the Government might act to:

1. Insure that all nonresearch test use and psychological assessment such as is not under the direct cognizance of the Civil Service Commission should be under the direction of highly qualified staff psychologists directly responsible to operating or line administrators.

2. Maintain a review or appeal procedure for personnel decisions in which psychological test data and psychological assessment have had an important part, perhaps with the possible use of an outside panel composed in part of psychologists.

3. Establish an interagency committee on assessment composed of representative agency psychologists. This committee would share experiences and formulate guidelines for sound practices.

4. Establish an advisory panel to such an interagency committee, composed of recognized psychologists from outside Government to periodically review agency assessment procedures and programs and to assist the committee in its activities.

5. Establish a task force under contract with the National Academy of Sciences–National Research Council (perhaps in conjunction with the Division of Behavioral Sciences of the NRC) to survey and evaluate current agency assessment procedures and practices and to make recommendations.

A task force, under the direction of an eminent psychologist and public figure such as, say, the present President of the Carnegie Corporation, the new Vice President of the Rockefeller Institute, the Executive Officer of the American Association for the Advancement of Science, or a recent National Medal of Science recipient, would bring superb scientific and professional resources to the task.

Such a task force would start with the advantage of having available to it the considerable preliminary work of this Subcommittee and its staff on these matters. One would hope that the final recommendations of this Subcommittee might be deferred until the findings of such a task force were reported to it.

6. Provide for continuing empirical research on the effectiveness of the personnel procedures used in those agencies where psychological assessment is an integral part of the procedures.

IT should be noted that certain of these suggestions are already well on the way to implementation. The 90th Congress, opening in 1967, held a variety of hearings of direct concern to the social and behavioral sciences. The entire November, 1967, issue of the *American Psychologist* (Brayfield, 1967) is given over to the general topic of Congress and social science. Senator Fred R. Harris of Oklahoma, together with 19 colleagues, has introduced bills to provide for the establishment of a National Foundation for the Social Sciences. Many other details of such legislative action are spelled out in this important A.P.A. journal.

By no means all psychologists would agree with Dr. Brayfield's statements just cited. The most highly critical, in the negative sense, of the entire area of psychological testing—especially when such tests are used to make decisions about people—was the testimony before this same subcommittee offered by Dr. Karl Smith, professor of industrial psychology at the University of Wisconsin. In effect, Dr. Smith says that the American public has been bamboozled. Dr. Smith's remarks, excerpted and condensed from this same issue of the *American Psychologist*, (Amrin, 1965, pp. 907–11), stress the "demand characteristics" inherent in testing programs—a topic now much researched even within the context of laboratory studies (see Orne, 1932; Rosenthal, 1963, 1964, 1967)—and also contain a protest against the "multiple-choice mind" that is formed in the process.

REMARKS TO SENATE SUBCOMMITTEE

Karl U. Smith

My reasons for preparing material for this Committee are that I represent a special scientific point of view in this field and have for many years. I have experimental evidence that testing at any level is not scientifically sound if it is . . . conceived as a generalized process of testing intelligence and so-called traits of personality.

My material consists of a report that embodies two special studies dealing with cybernetic analysis. This term "cybernetic" is used in this connection to mean system study, feedback study, study of the interactions, of tests and people, tests and institutions, the way in which the tester himself controls situations in order to arrive at what he considers predictions, the way in which the institution affects the testee and causes him to display certain characteristic forms of behavior . . . which may be set up as standards of performance for the development of the test. In other words, the term "cybernetic" here is used in its broadest sense as a systems interaction.

The scientific methods that I have just referred to, in our opinion, make it possible to bring certain new dimensions to the study of the testing movement, and our work possibly represents one of the first efforts to apply systems analysis procedures to broad psychological and personnel techniques in industry and in government. We have used these techniques in order to evaluate the psychological testing field and have done a number of studies over the last 20 years in the attempt to clarify our ideas about such procedures, and also about the testing movement as a part of the systems operation of industry and the Federal Government and education.

Among the various approaches that we have used we have analyzed industrial testing programs, not only from the standpoint of the validity of particular tests but from the standpoint of the meaning of the entire operation and its theoretical and scientific status. For example, I spent some six years as director and associate of a university-industrial bureau of psychology, in which my main task was to develop human quality measurement programs for industry, but which I used also to explore and develop some of these ideas about evaluating testing programs. A novel feature of this research was a determination of the ways in which a psychological tester himself could influence behavior he was supposed to predict in the industrial situation and in work situations in which he claimed he was predicting potentiality for development. A part of our program also was based upon my own direct participation as a test designer and test program director for the prison system in the State of Wisconsin. This was done on request.

We have also analyzed the feedback effects, that is to say, the interacting effects, the influence back of the tests or of institutional environments, particularly the prison and some industries, upon the characteristics of be- havior—what are called personality traits—upon the individual. This is one of the more important of our studies because we have found that the kind of things which tests predict or attempt to predict are often induced by the environment, the institutional environment itself, especially the prison or the custodial systems. After a few months or a year, it appears that these custodial systems impart much the same kind of behavior characteristics on everyone in the prison or in the institution, so that even the guards and the workers in the system come to display characteristics which are found in the inmates or the patients. This is one, I think, of our interesting findings in the prison system: that after a few months, a young man coming into the prison loses his characteristics as a person and begins to take on this peculiar suppressed, withdrawn, periodically aggressive feature of the prison personality or be- havior pattern.

We have analyzed test performances and learning functions. We have looked upon tests as an example of a learning situation and have drawn upon the facts in the science of learning to make deductions as to whether or not the test itself would be a predictable instrument if it were considered as a learning test. We have analyzed the test validity and reliability measures of all tests on which data are available relative to job design, the amount of con- straint that is put on the job, or the criteria or standards having different levels of relevance to performance situations.

Also, we have analyzed the control functions of the testing programs and testers, how the tester and the test program itself come to influence the design of the learning situation or the work situation. If the test program is involved, does the tester and does the program itself impart certain influences over the work situation and the job design and the work design, the supervision of the work, the personnel policies that make the test work? We have gone into that extensively.

Then we have gone into the whole matter of the scientific or research context of testing, not only in the history of psychology but in its current relationships with experimental psychology, and a number of the points that I am going to make for you here deal with just what the exact relationships are currently between experimental science and the testing movement in psychology. I shall give you a few of our conclusions from our studies.

1. The first major point has to do with some of the premises which we believe are followed by the people in the testing activity. Four major premises underlie the psychological testing field and testing movement today and in the past. The first is that testing is scientifically founded. The second is that intelligence and personality tests have predictive significance. The third is that personality tests have medical significance and can be used to specify the medical status of an individual. The fourth is that objective data can be assembled to substantiate the medical, educational, industrial, and governmental use of tests.

Our systems studies of testing, extending back over the past 20 years, have yielded evidence indicating that all of these basic premises are false.

2. Neither intelligence nor personality tests have a scientific basis or background. The tests themselves have been developed through crude procedures of item selection and the variables being measured can be identified and defined only in terms of the selected items.

The performance validity of both kinds of tests is related to the degree to which job performance and the worker or school performance and the student are routinized and constrained. In education, tests can be shown to have validity only in relation to those courses, usually in the beginning years of high school or college, oriented toward and emphasized in the taking of multiple-choice examinations.

Systematic study and analysis of the feedback dimensions and interactions between test movement and experimental science have led to these general conclusions: (a) psychological testing has no critical relations with experimental psychology or any other branch of experimental science and reflect none of the recent advances in scientific understanding of the mechanisms of behavior; (b) testing is based purely on estimating deviations from social norms and has no significant means within itself of dealing with the individual; (c) there are no objective scientific principles to guide test construction; (d) the criterion groups or population samples against which tests are originally validated by no means represent the population as a whole, that is to say, representative samples have never been used in this field; (e) test research in schools and industry is rarely objective and unbiased, and test validation programs have rarely been free of the influence of ongoing personnel and administrative operations. This has been particularly true in the Government uses of tests.

3. Various patterns of systematic cybernetic research on testing programs in prisons, welfare institutions, industries, and educational institutions have led us to reject the premise that tests have predictive significance in education and work. All results indicate that the limited correlations which are obtained between test scores and school grades can be accounted for in terms of the direct feedback effects of the test programs on personnel operations, administrative operations, grade assignments, and examination and classroom work in the school. The following points are supported by research findings:

a) Tests are widely used because they impart rigidity to the educational situation and give it a structure which is easy to control, to check on by administrators, to routinize, to subject to machine operations, to automate, and to standardize. A testing program enhances the importance of multiple-choice and true–false design in teaching and examining.

A few years back, for example, the Graduate Record Examination had no validity whatsoever in graduate school performance in universities in this country. Today, it can be shown to have some relevance and some correlation with first-year graduate performances in certain courses.

I would like the Committee to note, for example, that one of the massive corporations in this country which is best known for building computers and test-scoring machines, also is the sole owner of one of the major testing companies which sells both personality tests and so-called intelligence tests, some of the most widely so-called primary mental ability tests used for classifying students in grade school and high school in this country. This is the International Business Machines Corporation.

b) The apparent validity of tests is enhanced by an influence comparable to the Hawthorne Effect, an effect noted originally as an increase in work productivity brought about by the contextual influence on the worker of supervisory or administrative attitudes. In cybernetic analyses, we recognize this effect as a general phenomenon of control prompting, which may enhance any aspect of behavior in individuals on whom certain conditions of authority are imposed. We believe that phenomenon can account for the effects of placebos in medical practice and research, the initial acceptance by workers of work design and personnel programs in industry, and the acceptance of test programs. When a test program is adopted in a school, industrial, or governmental system, the administrative context of acceptance prompts congruent action in personnel administrators, supervisors, teachers, advisors, parents, students, workers, and everyone related to the institution. In schools, students are graded in courses not only on the basis of their performance in the classroom, but to some extent according to their IQ or achievement scores, which are known to their teachers. Students themselves are affected by the prompting. They wittingly or unwittingly conform to the pattern laid down by the multiple-choice and true–false items in tests and classroom examinations. There is no need to assume that some conspiracy goes on between testers and teachers in determining grades indicated by IQ ratings, because this comes about through any one of a dozen influences of an accepted program on both the teacher and the students.

In many of our schools today, for example, and certainly many of our industrial training programs, the adoption of a testing program leads within a very short time inevitably to the adoption of multiple-choice teaching-machine types of education which cohere exactly to the testing format.

c) Systematic surveys show that the validity of tests for predicting training or educational achievement is quite different from their validity for predicting performance in actual work. Generally speaking, we have no tests or test batteries which validly predict performance in areas of special talent or skill such as art, music, creative writing, medicine, engineering, executive ability, or scientific research. This has been found so many times in the history of the testing movement that there is no need to enlarge on this subject.

Personality testers themselves have proved beyond any shadow of doubt that their personality tests lack predictive significance in both medical and educational context. One of the most extensive research programs on tests ever carried out demonstrated that a group of outstanding clinical psychologists could not predict performance of their own graduate students by means of an elaborate set of tests, even when the tests were combined with a so-called depth interview. In this research, clinicians attempted to use tests and interviews to predict performance of their own students in both educational and clinical activities. None of their personality test predictions were statistically valid, and their interview predictions were even more random.

4. Systematic cybernetic analyses suggest that test-taking activities are no different from other forms of specific learning. The predictive validity of tests apparently is limited to the type of activity contained in their design: for example, performance on multiple-choice and true–false examinations. As with other specific learning materials, the generalization or transfer value of tests and their predictive significance are restricted to the particular task characteristics contained in them.

For over 20 years now, people working in the scientific study of learning have known that the variables that you can isolate and tag in a learning situation of any sort are heavily weighted in terms of the particular work or task situation that is involved, and that the degree of variance, as it is called— that is to say, the amount of actual data variation that you can ascribe to some general characteristic of people in that situation—is often most limited.

In other words, if we took an actual Government job and determined how much variance was due to the learning of the particular job, we might find that it was as much as 80 or 90% of the total variance that could be found in that situation, leaving, as it were, some 5 or 10% that might be used by a tester to predict generally in a situation.

The claims of psychometricians that the techniques of factor analysis enable them to isolate the variance due to individual traits or characteristics in a table of test intercorrelations cannot be substantiated. No statistical procedures of psychometric testing make it possible to isolate and thus identify the sources of variance in test performance due to individual characteristics, the effects of learning, and the specificity of task or performance situation. Accordingly, tests are not measures of so-called individual traits. At best, they are measures of limited situational performances and have no predictive significance beyond the specific questions and tasks included in the test.

5. The use of personality tests should be given special attention from the scientific point of view because of their special implications about the individual and individual behavior. The concept of personality has not been developed through scientific investigation, but has been derived gradually from prescientific views of mental life and from attempts to read temperament from limited characteristics of body makeup and behavior. Three types of

"character-reading" systems which persist in modern times are phrenology, which analyzes personality in terms of gross brain anatomy; body reading, or interpretation of constitutional types; and graphology, or handwriting analysis. Although graphology and the reading of body types have been converted into quantitative procedures which are said to provide detailed descriptions of character, the evidence is that neither can specify personality characteristics with any validity.

The ancient tradition of trying to classify individuals into neatly defined personality types is now carried on by the personality testing field in what is called the psychometric measurement of personality. Personality inventories and scales which have been based on concepts of deviate social adjustment include the Bell Adjustment Inventory, the Bernreuter Personality Inventory, and the Guilford-Martin personality tests. More clinical inventories are made up of questions which have been found to differentiate statistically between neuropsychiatric groups and so-called normal groups. The MMPI is one of the few personality inventories concerned with social adjustment or gross personality deviation which has been subjected to scientific study. Investigation of this test shows that the scores reflect the social environment of the testee rather than a pattern of innate traits.

There is no clear evidence that these tests accomplish either of the purposes for which they are intended in the first place: that is, reducing misrepresentation and faking of responses to the test situation. Research findings consistently show that these devices and procedures lack any kind of statistical and quantitative validity. The outstanding British critic of the testing field states categorically that the reported validity of both projective tests and paper-and-pencil personality tests is a direct function of the carelessness and inaccuracy of the studies done on the tests and the methods used. When used in conjunction with objective data, either from tests or from personal data, the results of projective tests more likely than not will dilute the validity of the objective observations. Their validity rests solely on their acceptance by clinicians as interview aids.

6. Cybernetic or feedback studies of personality testing in education, welfare institutions, industry, and government suggest that personality tests probe environmentally produced mood and stress reactions rather than persisting features of individual behavior organizations.

The field of personality testing is a hodgepodge of imprecise psychopathological terminology, of limited and biased procedures, and of poorly constructed test situations, designed to probe social nonconformity.

Personality testing is useful to industry not because it is scientifically valid nor because it represents enlightened human relations procedures. All of our experiences with personality tests in industry indicate that industries are interested only in quickie procedures of looking at people. They are not interested in careful, analytic, fairly long-term analysis of the individuality of the college student. We have college students today who go through as many as 12, 15, 20 quickie personality tests in carrying on their interviews for jobs during their senior year. The reason industry is interested in these procedures, we believe, is that the managements of the large industries have found in testing procedures, perhaps unwittingly, various techniques to crystallize and strengthen management authority over those individual workers and unions. The personality testing situation has provided the means for industrial management to achieve some quasi-medical authority over workers who are individualistic and assertive in social adjustment.

The only occupational area in which personality test methods have some semblance of predictive validity is in personal-contact selling. Evidence from our own item analysis of personality test variables in personal-contact selling indicates that vocational interest factors, and not emotional variables per se, determine the predictive significance of tests in this field. Thus, we believe that measures of vocational interest can serve in any area in which personality indicators are thought to forecast future job success. Such vocational measures at least are straightforward and positive in their design and are not derived from subjective judgments in the abnormalistic tradition in psychology.

7. Personality tests fail to give any real information about behavior and personality organization in the individual. Inasmuch as individual adaptation is always based on positive features and on the reserve and persistence of behavior organization in stress and change, the personality test score, based as it is on negative abnormalistic situational factors, in terms of which the tests are standardized, can never define the "positive potential developments" of health or achievement in the individual. This is theoretically very clear to us.

The concepts of psychological abnormality on which the criterion variables of personality tests are based are purely impressionistic and cannot be tested empirically from the scientific point of view. Further, they represent the operation of a social and emotional bias against persons in the lower economic sectors of society whose lives are most subject to decisions and judgments imposed by the professional and custodial levels of community life. Thus, personality testing may enhance and promote the disabling symptoms which it is supposed to correct.

Research findings regarding the behavioral factors measured by personality tests are fairly clear in showing that these factors consist of reactions to socially desirable situations, acquiescence to positive items, and lying when this is socially approved.

What this statement means is that a test like the MMPI probably most effectively picks out people who either know how to or are willing to carry on superficial lying in a situation where it is more or less socially approved. The application of such a test to the Peace Corps means that you probably have in the Peace Corps a great number of people whose prime trait is the ability to lie in a minor way in situations where it is socially approved. These results are not our own results, but the results of some of the best studies which have ever been done on the MMPI.[1]

---

[1] For a radically different view concerning the Peace Corps use of the MMPI, see the remarks by Dr. Carp, which follow this presentation by Dr. Smith.

8. The main finding of all of our systems studies of the testing field is that testers misunderstand and misrepresent their role as predictors of human behavior. Instead of being forecasters of performance, they act as controllers and manipulators of the very performances that they claim to predict. Psychological testing, aside from two or three examples, is not a field of scientific forecasting of human achievement, it is a nonscientific double-talk and double-dealing in using tests to classify, label, select, and pressure people in terms of dubious standards and fuzzy concepts of traits and human abnormality.

For the past 40 years testers have been engaged in a camouflaged game of proving that some unknown x equals the same unknown x.

9. The real social flaw in psychological tests is that they are nonscientific instruments, and therefore lend themselves to widespread misuse which may amount to illegal activity. I am not stating that as a legal authority, I am saying that the possibility exists. Because of the selective group performance standards on which the tests are based, testing inevitably discriminates against the underprivileged, the disadvantaged, the educationally disabled, the emotionally disturbed, the injured, those with a history of childhood illness, those from broken homes, the Negro, the foreign-born, and those individuals with unusual characteristics or atypical patterns of development.

10. The American people have been fooled into believing that a few simple-minded, true–false or multiple-choice questions can be used to forecast the careers of the children in school and in the university, and to predict their own careers in work, because of two influences: fear of the pseudo-quantitative mental-medical mumbo jumbo of the psychiatrist and clinical psychologist, and the misleading propaganda of organized psychology in claiming that guesswork and statistical shotgun procedures have medical and scientific significance.

Inasmuch as the tests do not have proven individual predictive significance, their use to determine the medical status of an individual is scientifically unwarranted and thus constitutes a form of medical quackery. We believe that it is time that the Congress demand standards of measurement in psychiatry and in applied medical procedures of psychology equal to those in other branches of medicine.

11. The source of positive scientific alternative to psychological testing procedures lies in a better scientific understanding of how the design of education and work processes determines individual behavior organization. Individuality or personality cannot be separated from the opportunities of individuals to develop their full psychological potential in positive human conditions.

▽ ▽ ▽

As the hearings progressed, more and more of the testimony narrowed down to the use of the MMPI in various governmental offices and bureaus, and to the specific issue of the invasion of privacy that might be involved. Fear was also expressed that such psychological data about a person, especially negative information, might become a part of his permanent file and so constitute, practically forever, damaging evidence against which the individual would have no defense. Because of the highly successful selection program inaugurated by the Peace Corps, and the extensive reliance made on clinical testing and observation, Dr. Al Carp's remarks about the MMPI and Peace Corps use are included here. Dr. Carp is now head of the Selection Program for this organization. He also participated in the development of the selection procedures by which the astronauts were chosen for service in the space program. These remarks have been excerpted from the published hearings (Amrin, 1965, pp. 916–18).

As an introduction to the testimony by Dr. Carp, Sargent Shriver spoke briefly about the history of Peace Corps selection procedures and also how successful these had been. (At the start of the Peace Corps, some people thought there might be a dropout as high as 50 percent in 18 months). Mr. Shriver also stressed that the tests given to trainees are only part of the entire selection process, since such selection occurs at the end of a three-month training program. In addition of psychological test data, the Peace Corps people also can make use of the actual experience of working with and observing trainees. There are also full field investigations by the Civil Service Commission and, in some instances, investigations by the FBI. Mr. Shriver felt that the record of performance of the Peace Corps Selection Division was extraordinary, since the return rate for both psychiatric and psychological reasons is only about 8 percent.

REMARKS TO SENATE SUBCOMMITTEE

Al Carp

In 1961, the Congress made clear in the Peace Corps Act its concern with the qualifications of Peace Corps volunteers. It directed that the Peace Corps make available to interested countries, "men and women of the United States qualified for service abroad and willing to serve, under conditions of hardship if necessary." The President was authorized to enroll in the Peace Corps only "qualified" citizens and nationals of the United States. In 1961, both the Senate and House Peace Corps Bill reports specified that Peace Corps volunteers should be "emotionally mature," and "in excellent mental health."

This concern is understandable. A Peace Corps volunteer does not live the life of the typical United States Government employee overseas. He must demonstrate his technical competence in what is often a technically primitive environment. Often, he must communicate in a new and difficult language. He must live with and work for people whose background, culture,

341

and way of life contrast dramatically with that to which he has been accustomed. Through all this, he must maintain his own physical and psychological well-being in essential isolation from his own culture. An emotionally immature and mentally unstable volunteer could do serious damage to the United States and the Peace Corps overseas.

But not only the United States' and the Peace Corps' interests are at stake. The individual volunteer has an obvious stake in his mental health. If the Peace Corps sent overseas a volunteer who was not qualified in this regard, it could be responsible for seriously and even permanently damaging his mental health.

The selection of people is a young science. No one selection tool even begins to approach perfection. That is why Peace Corps selection is deliberately structured to bring to bear many different selection tools. No one element of this process is determinative but each makes a definite and distinctive contribution to the process. In our judgment, the Peace Corps would be derelict in its responsibilities if its selection process deliberately failed to employ any one element of that process, including personality inventories properly used by qualified persons. Indeed, in 1961, the House Foreign Affairs Committee specified that during Peace Corps training each applicant will receive "psychological and psychiatric tests."

Each Peace Corps training contract requires the training institution, usually an American college or university, to appoint at least one experienced and qualified psychologist to be what we call a Field Assessment Officer. He is responsible for gathering psychological data throughout training. The only personality inventory he is asked to give all trainees is the Minnesota Multiphasic Personality Inventory, although the Field Assessment Officer may decide in consultation with the Peace Corps Field Selection Officer to give either generally or individually other personality inventories.

In our judgment, the MMPI is the only objective personality inventory which helps identify persons who may have or develop serious personality disorders. It has been extensively used for more than 20 years. More data has been accumulated about it than any other similar inventory, and much of it is relevant to the Peace Corps' selection process.

In my opinion, a good alternative to use of the MMPI does not now exist. Many persons who have potentially serious personality disorders are readily identifiable. Many are not. It is of critical importance that the Peace Corps' selection process make the best effort possible to identify those who are not readily identifiable.

Clinically, potentially serious personality disorders are identified through individual psychiatric interviews. But it is simply not humanly possible to have a qualified psychiatrist interview each of the approximately 10,000 persons who enter Peace Corps training each year.

In other words, if the Peace Corps did not use the MMPI, more volunteers sent overseas would fail to complete their Peace Corps service for psychiatric reasons. This would not be in either the United States' or the Peace

Corps' interests or, perhaps most important, in those volunteers' own interest.

The test contributes to selection-in decisions as well as to selection-out. A normal MMPI profile can help counterbalance negative data from other elements of the selection process. Moreover, trainees with abnormal MMPI profiles are not automatically selected out. Special attention is paid to them. As a result more data accumulates about them than usually accumulates about another trainee. This has resulted in selection-in decisions notwithstanding the abnormal MMPI profile.

Many MMPI items relate to attitudes toward sex, one's body, religion, one's parents, and other personal matters. This is because, as most of us know from common experience, personality disorders often express themselves in relation to these matters. What is significant is not an individual's particular response to a particular item, but whether or not his aggregate score on the MMPI's scales is similar to that of persons with serious personality disorders.

Because the MMPI involves personal matters it is only given by the Field Assessment Officer. He is, as we have seen, always a qualified and experienced psychologist. He is trained to respect the confidentiality of an individual's MMPI profile. Only two other persons have access to that profile—the Peace Corps' Field Selection Officer, who is also a highly qualified and experienced psychologist, and if the evaluation suggests that a psychiatric interview is warranted, a medical doctor trained in psychiatry.

After the end of the training program, all MMPI test data and any other personality inventory data will be destroyed. Our inquiry into the use of personality inventories during Peace Corps training has indicated that the Peace Corps has not had a consistent policy on this in the past. This was a serious error, and I assure you it has been corrected.

The Peace Corps is obviously equally interested in an applicant's mental and physical health. Properly evaluating either requires a highly professional examination. In both cases, failure to conduct the examination runs the risk of serious harm to the United States, to the Peace Corps, and to the applicant. But certain aspects of both kinds of examinations are quite personal, and as many of us know, some are not only personal but unpleasant as well. This does not mean that these examinations should not be given. But this does mean that they should only be given by qualified and experienced professionals who are trained to respect the individual's privacy.

▽ ▽ ▽

THERE is no question that invasion of privacy is a significant issue, especially when personnel selection situations are involved. This was an issue of some real concern before any congressional hearings—mostly with lay critics of psychological testing. One of the first to raise his voice against such practices was William H. Whyte, Jr., when he was an editor of *Fortune*, when the following article originally appeared (September, 1954). An expanded version of this article later appeared in the appendix to his book, *The Organization Man* (1956), under the title, "How to Cheat on Personality Tests." Reproduced here is a considerably abbreviated version of the original *Fortune* article.

Mr. Whyte is one of the most apt of the critics of personality testing, especially concerning its use for industrial assessments. He rightly gives credit to the psychologists themselves, who have not stood aside and unprotestingly allowed these practices to go undetected. A more recent and more angry protest, but in the exposé journalist tradition, is the book by Martin Gross (1962) with the loaded title *The Brain Watchers*. The fire here is directed most at the use of projective tests for industrial evaluations, but the typical paper-and-pencil type of personality inventory also comes in for heavy criticism. Unlike Mr. Whyte, Mr. Gross only occasionally refers to the efforts of the psychologists themselves to right some of these wrongs. Curious readers may also want to consult the appendix to the Gross book, where the author presents his "Corporate Adjustment Inventory" which, he states, is based on current "question-and-answer personality test theories" *(sic)* and which he has developed solely as illustrative material for the testee. Self-scoring directions are provided, and some interpretative suggestions are given for the guidance of a hypothetical personnel man who has the decision of whether or not to hire.

THE FALLACIES OF "PERSONALITY" TESTING

William H. Whyte, Jr.

Business is being tantalized by a fascinating possibility. After a long experimentation period with school schildren, college students, and inmates of institutions, applied psychologists are becoming more and more confident that with "personality" tests they can come close to answering the hitherto elusive question of who will succeed and who won't.

At first there were only rough measures—such as how introverted and neurotic a man is—but there are now in regular business use tests that tell a man's superiors his degree of radicalism versus conservatism, his practical judgment, social judgment, degree of perseverance, stability, contentment, hostility to society, and latent homosexuality. Some psychologists are tinkering with a test of sense of humor. To probe even deeper, testers are also applying the "projective" techniques like the Rorschach Ink Blot Test, which lead the subject into x-raying himself for latent feelings and psychoses.

America's secondary-school educators were the first to seize upon these tests, but business is catching up very quickly indeed. Two years ago only about a third of U.S. corporations used personality testing; since then the proportion has been climbing—of the 63 corporations checked by *Fortune,* 60 percent are using personality tests, and these include such bellwether firms as Sears, General Electric, and Westinghouse. While there are still some executives vigorously opposed to personality testing, all the signs point to a further increase.

But the really significant development is in personality testing. In perhaps 25 percent of the country's corporations, the tests are used not merely to help screen out those who shouldn't get into the organization, but to check up on people who are already in it. And the people being checked on, furthermore, are not workers so much as management itself. Some of these companies don't bother to give personality tests to workers at all; aside from the fact that testing can be very expensive, they feel that the limited number of psychologists available should concentrate on the more crucial questions.

HOW NEUROTIC ARE EXECUTIVES?

Should Jones be promoted or put on the shelf? Just about the time an executive reaches 45 or 50 and begins to get butterflies in his stomach wondering what it has all added up to and whether the long sought prize is to be his after all, the company is probably wondering, too. Where once the man's superiors would have threshed this out among themselves, in some companies they now check first with the psychologists to find out what the tests say. At Sears, for example, for the last ten years no one has been promoted in the upper brackets until the board chairman has consulted the tests. At Sears, as elsewhere, the formal decision is, of course, based on other factors also, but the weight now being given test reports makes it clear that for many a potential executive, the most critical day he spends in his life will be the one he spends taking tests.

One result has been the rise of a considerable industry. In the last five years the number of test blanks sold has risen 300 percent. The growth of psychological consulting firms has paralleled the rise; in addition to such established firms as the Psychological Corporation, literally hundreds of consultants are setting up shop. Science Research Associates of Chicago, a leading test supplier, reports that within twelve months, 700 new consultants have asked to be put on its approved list of customers. Colleges are also getting into the business; through research centers like Rensselaer Polytechnic's Personality Testing Laboratory, they have become directly competitive with leading commercial firms.

The types of service offered vary greatly. Some firms will do the entire operation by mail; for example, the Klein Institute for Aptitude Testing, Inc., of New York, within 48 hours of getting the completed test back will have an analysis on its way to the company. Usually, however, the job is done on the premises. Sometimes the consultant group, like the Activity Vector Analysts, will process the entire management group at one crack. More usually the analysts, very often a group of professors in mufti, will come in and study the organization in order to find the personality "profiles" best suited for particular jobs. They will then tailor a battery of tests and master profiles. Though the analysts may help out with the machinery of testing, the company's personnel department generally handles the rest of the job.

A dynamic would appear to be at work. The more people that are tested, the more test results there are to correlate, and the more correlations, the surer are many testers of predicting success or failure, and thus the more reason there is for more organizations to test more and more people. At Westinghouse Electric, for example, 10,000 management men have already been coded onto IBM cards that contain, in addition to vital statistics and work records, the men's personality-test ratings. What with the schools already doing much the same thing, with electronics making mass testing increasingly easy, there seems no barrier to the building of such inventories for every organization—except common sense. For a large question remains: leaving aside for the moment the matter of invasion of privacy, have the tests themselves been really tested?

WHO FLUNKED?

In an effort to find out, *Fortune* did some extensive testing of its own. What was under investigation, let it be made plain, was not the use of tests as guides in clinical work, or their use in counseling when the individual himself seeks the counseling. Neither was it the problem of ethics raised by the work of some practitioners in the field, interesting as this bypath is. What we have addressed ourselves to is the validity of "personality" tests as a standardized way of rating and slotting people. Question: do the tests really discriminate the man of promise from the run of the mill—or do they discriminate against him?

What would happen if the presidents of our largest corporations took the same tests that future executives are being judged by? What would happen if the tests were applied to a group of scientists, not just average scientists, but a group of the most productive ones in the world? Would they be rated as good risks? Would their scores jibe with their achievements? By actually giving tests to 60 exceptional persons, we found out. Conclusion: if the tests were rigorously applied across the board today, half of the most dynamic men in business would be out walking the streets for a job.

The effects of the day-to-day use of tests are less spectacular, but they are nonetheless far reaching. For the tests, *Fortune* submits, do not do what they are supposed to do. They do not do what they are supposed to do because, for one thing, they are not scientific. Neither in the questions nor in the evaluation are they neutral; they are, instead, loaded with debatable assumptions and questions of values. The result, deliberate or not, is a set of yardsticks that reward the conformist, the pedestrian, the unimaginative—at the expense of the exceptional individual whom management most needs to attract.

WHAT IS "PERSONALITY"?

To a large degree the growing acceptance of personality tests rests on prestige by association, for these tests at first glance seem no more than an extension of the established methods of aptitude testing. The difference, however, is crucial. What is being measured in aptitude and intelligence testing are responses that can be rated objectively—such as the correctness of the answers to 2 + 2 or the number of triangles in a bisected rectangle. The conclusions drawn from these aptitude and intelligence scores are, furthermore, limited to the relatively modest prediction of a man's minimum ability to do the same sort of thing he is asked to do on the tests. If the tests indicate that a man has only 5,000 words in his vocabulary, it is a reasonable assumption that he won't do particularly well in a job requiring 50,000 words. If he is all thumbs when he puts wiggly blocks together, he won't be very good at a job requiring enough manual dexterity to put things like wiggly blocks together.

To jump from aptitude testing to personality testing, however, is to jump from the measurable to the immeasurable. The mathematics is impeccable—and thus entrapping. Because "percentiles" and "coefficients" and "standard deviations" are of themselves neutral (and impressive sounding), the sheer methodology of using them can convince people that they are translating uncertainty, the subjective into the objective, and eliminating utterly the bugbear of value judgments. But the mathematics does not eliminate values, it only obscures them. No matter how objective testers try to be, even in the phrasing of their questions they are inevitably influenced by the customs and values of their particular world.

Questions designed to find your degree of sociability are an example. In some groups the reading of a book is an unsocial act, and the person who confesses he has at times preferred books to companions might have to be quite introverted to do such a thing. But the question is relative; applied to someone in a climate where reading is normal—indeed, the source of much social talk—the hidden "value judgment" built into the test can give a totally unobjective result. People are not always social in the same terms; a person who would earn himself an unsocial score by saying he would prefer bridge to bowling with the gang is not necessarily unsocial, and he might even be a strong extrovert. It could be that he just doesn't like bowling.

If the layman gags at the phrasing of a question, testers reply, sometimes with a chuckle, this is merely a matter of "face validity." They concede that it is better if the questions seem to make sense, but they claim that the question itself is not so important as the way large numbers of people have answered it over a period of time. To put it in another way, if 100 contented supervisors overwhelmingly answer a particular question in a certain way, this means something, and thus no matter whether the question is nonsensical or not, it has produced a meaningful correlation coefficient.

LOGROLLING WITH STATISTICS

Meaning what? This is not the place to go into a lengthy dissertation on statistics, but two points should be made about the impressive test charts and tables that so often paralyze executives' common sense. A large proportion of the mathematics is purely internal; that is, different parts of the tests are compared with each other rather than with external evidence. Second, the external evidence used in many "validation" studies will be found on closer examination to consist of the scores persons made on similar personality tests rather than such untidy matters as how they actually performed on the job. That there should be a correlation between test scores is hardly surprising; test authors are forever borrowing questions from each other (some questions have been reincarnated in as many as ten or twelve different tests) and what the correlations largely prove is how incestuous tests can be.

But how much have scores been related to individual behavior? Among themselves psychologists raise the same question, and for muted savagery there is nothing to match the critiques they make of each other's tests. The Bernreuter Personality Inventory is a particular case in point. This is by far the most widely used test in business (1953 sales by Stanford University Press, one of several distributors: one million copies). Yet a reading of the professional journals shows a long succession of negative results; when psychologists independently checked Bernreuter scores against other, more objective evidence of what the people tested were like, they found no significant relationships and sometimes reverse correlations.

As top psychologists point out, a really rigorous validation would demand that a firm hire all comers for a period of time, test them, seal away the tests so that the scores would not prejudice superiors, and then, several years later, unseal the scores and match them against the actual performance of the individuals involved. This has rarely been even attempted. To be sure, a good bit of work on the performance of groups has been done; for example, a group considered more productive has an average score on a test higher than another group. The average of a group, however, tells us very little about the individuals involved, for some of the "best" people will have lower test scores than some of the "poor" ones.

Testers evade this abyss by relying on a whole battery of tests rather than on just one or two. But no matter how many variables you add you cannot make a constant of them. If a man has a high "contentment index" and at the same time a very high "irritability index," does the one good cancel the other bad? Frequently the tester finds himself right back where he started from. If he is a perceptive man he may make a very accurate prognosis, but when, several years later, the prognosis turns out to be true, this is adduced as evidence of the amazing accuracy of test scores.

And there is the matter of the "profile." Testers collate in chart form personality scores for groups of people in different occupations to show how they compare with other adults on several personality traits. This is generally expressed as a "percentile" rating; if 30 salesclerks' sociability scores average somewhere around the 80th percentile, for example, this indicates that the average salesclerk is more sociable than 79 out of 100 adults. Thus a man being considered for a particular kind of job can be matched against the master profile of the ground. If the shoe fits, he is Cinderella.

Profiles are also worked up for jobs in individual companies. At Sears, Roebuck, there are charts that diagram the optimum balance of qualities required. Here is the one on executive values:

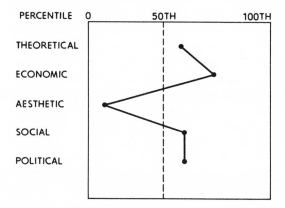

A man does not have to match this profile exactly, but it won't help him at all if his line zigs where the chart zags. Take a man who scores considerably higher than the 10th percentile on aesthetic values, for example; such people, Sears notes, "accept artistic beauty and taste as a fundamental standard of life. This is not a factor which makes for executive success. . . . Generally, cultural considerations are not important to Sears executives, and there is evidence that such interests are detrimental to success."

THE ECHO

Sears has every right to de-emphasize certain qualities and emphasize others; and in hewing to this type, it should be noted, Sears has built up one of the most alert management groups in the country. But the profile is not to be confused with science. When they are used as selection devices, tests are not a neutral tool; they become a large factor in the very equation they purport to solve. For one thing, the tests tend to screen out—or repel—those who would upset the correlation. If a man can't get into the company in the first place because he isn't the company type, he can't very well get to be an executive in it and be tested in a study to find out what kind of profile subsequent executives should match. Long before personality tests were invented, of course, plenty of companies had proved that if you hire only people of a certain type, then all your successful men will be people of that type. But no one confused this with the immutable laws of science.

Bias, in short, is no longer personalized; now it's institutionalized. For the profile is self-confirming. When it doesn't screen out those who fail to match it, it will mask the amount of deviance in the people who do pass. Few test takers can believe the flagrantly silly statement in the preamble to many tests that there are "no right or wrong answers." There wouldn't be much point in the company's giving the test if some answers weren't regarded as better than others. "Do you daydream frequently?" In many companies a man either so honest or so stupid as to answer "yes" would be well advised to look elsewhere for employment.

THE COMPANY "TYPE"

Even when the man who should have looked elsewhere slips through, the profile will be self-confirming. For the profile molds as well as chooses; it is, as Sears puts it, a statement of "the kind of behavior we have found to be desirable." Several years of give and take, and the organization will smooth the man out. Thus when the psychologists do their "validating," or re-checking, later, he will score near enough to the median to show them how right they were all along.

Up to a point the company "type" has some virtue; any first-rate organization must have an *espirit de corps,* and this implies a certain degree of homogeneity. But the pitfalls are many, for while a self-confirming profile makes for a comfortable organization, it eventually can make for a static one. Even the largest corporations must respond to changes in the environment; a settled company may have its very existence threatened by technological advances unless it makes a bold shift to a new type of market. What, then, of the pruning and molding that adapted it so beautifully to its original environment? The dinosaur was a formidable animal.

THE FIGHT AGAINST TALENT

Are the people who don't score well necessarily the misfits? Almost by definition the dynamic person is an exception—and where aptitude tests reward, personality tests often punish him. Look at the profiles and test scoring keys, and you will find that you will come closer to a high score if you observe two rules:

1. When asked for word associations or comments about the world, give the most conventional, run-of-the-mill, pedestrian answer possible.

2. When in doubt about the most beneficial answer to any question, repeat to yourself:

I loved my father and my mother, but my father a little bit more.

I was a happy, normal American boy and everybody liked me.

I like things pretty much as they are.

I never worry about anything.
I love my wife and children.
I don't let them get in the way of company work.
I don't care for books or music much.

CHOOSE (A), (B), (C), (D)

The sheer mechanics of the tests also punish the exceptional man. A test with prefabricated answers is precisely the kind of test that people with superior intelligence find hardest to answer. How big was that fire in the basement of the theatre? This is not a quibble; it is the kind of question that occurs to the intelligent mind, and the ability to see shadings, to posit alternatives, is virtually indispensable to judgment, practical or otherwise.

We now come to *Fortune's* experiment. With the stipulation by *Fortune* that their individual scores should not be identified, 14 corporation presidents and board chairmen agreed to take a battery of tests including Personal Audit, Thurstone Temperament, and the Test of Practical Judgment. Next, 12 of the country's most brilliant scientists (previously studied in connection with "The Young Scientists," *Fortune,* June, 1954) agreed to do the same. As a further check, 29 rising middle-management men who had been picked to attend an advanced-management school took the Thurstone and Practical Judgment tests.

Here are the highlights of the test results.

1. Not one corporation president had a profile that fell completely within the usual "acceptable" range, and two failed to meet the minimum profile for foremen. On the How Supervise? questions, presidents on the average got only half the answers right, thus putting them well down in the lower percentiles. They did particularly badly on the questions concerning company-employee-relations policies. Only three presidents answered more than half of these questions correctly.

2. The scientists' Personal Audit profile were more even than the presidents'—if anything, they scored as too contented, firm, and consistent. They did, however, show up as extremely misanthropic, over half falling under the 20th percentile for sociability.

3. The middle-management executives scored well on stability and sociability, but on practical judgment only three were at or over the mean indicated for executive work.

4. The range of scores was so great as to make a median figure relatively meaningless. On the Thurstone "S" score for sociability, for example, only eight of the 43 management men fell between the 40th and the 60th percentiles, the remainder being grouped at either extreme.

5. Internally, the scores were highly contradictory. Many of the same people who got high "steadiness" scores on the Personal Audit scored very badly for "stability" on the Thurstone test. Similarly, many who scored high on "contentment" had very low "tranquility" scores.

THE ABNORMAL NORMS

One explanation for this great variance between results and the standard norms would be that the men in the sample were answering frankly and thus their scores could not be properly compared with the standard norms given. But if this is true, then we must conclude that the norms themselves embody slanted answers. Another explanation of their showing would be that they scored low because they were in fact neurotic or maladjusted, as the tests said. But this leaves us with a further anomaly. If people with an outstanding record of achievement show up as less well "adjusted" than the run-of-the-mill, then how important a yardstick is adjustment? *Fortune's* sample, of course, is small. So is the supply of outstanding talented people.

The study of a man's past performance, the gauging of him in the personal interview, are uncertain guides; executives are right to use them with humility. But they are still the key, and the need is not to displace them, but to become more skilled with them. The question of who will be best in a critical situation cannot be determined scientifically before the event. No matter how much information we may amass, we must rely on judgment, on intuition, on the particulars of the situation—and the more crucial the situation, the less certain can we be of prediction. It is an immensely difficult task, perhaps the most difficult one that any management faces. But the question cannot be fed into a computer, nor can it be turned over by proxy for someone else to decide. Any management that so evades its most vital function needs some analysis of its own.

THE RIGHT TO PRIVACY

And doesn't the individual have some rights in this matter, too? Our society has taught him to submit to many things; thousands of civilians who went into the military meekly stood naked in long lines waiting for their numbered turn in the mass physical examinations. Many civilians who have been asked to work on government projects have submitted to being fingerprinted and to the certainty that government agents would soon be puzzling their friends and neighbors with questions about their backgrounds. In these cases a man can console himself that there is a reason; that if he is to enjoy the benefits of collective efforts he must also pay some price.

But there is a line. How much must a man testify against himself? The bill of rights should not stop at the corporation's edge. In return for the salary the organization gives the individual, it can ask for superlative work from him, but it should not ask for his psyche as well. Here and there, we are happy to report, some declarations of independence have been made. Last year the executives of a large and well-known New England corporation were subjected by the management to psychological examination by an outside consultant. Whether it was because of the consultant's manner or because of the New England character, the executives at length revolted. Let them be judged, they said, for their work. As for their inner feelings—that, as one man said who was almost fired for saying so, that was no one's damn business but their own.

As a postscript to Whyte's article, the reader may be interested in learning that his suggested "rules" have been put to experimental test by Shaw (1962).

Ninety-four upperclassmen, majors in business administration at the University of Florida, took the Bernreuter Personality Inventory. They were told to imagine themselves as applicants for a supervisory position in a manufacturing plant, to assume they really wanted the job, and that as a part of the application procedure they were requested to take this test. One half of the group knew Whyte's rules and were requested to fill out the inventory on this basis; the other half were asked to complete the blank honestly. The resulting profiles were then submitted to seven personnel supervisors, representing four industrial organizations that currently used the Bernreuter as part of their selection procedures. Each supervisor was requested to indicate which "person" he would prefer (and each supervisor was free to accept or reject both). As expected, the "honesty" scores differed significantly from the "dishonest" ones; yet, the dishonest were chosen significantly more often by the personnel people. Furthermore, 52 percent of the profile pairs were checked "would hire neither." Shaw concluded that following Whyte's rules offers no great advantage in a situation of this type.

To conclude the discussion on this significant ethical issue, the editor has chosen to present the views of a professional psychologist who is writing both after the lay critics have spoken and after the congressional hearings. In a closely reasoned paper, Dr. Lovell argues for clear restrictions on the personnel selection functions, especially where tests of character have been employed. He asks that we take the respondent clearly into our confidence and that we make an explicit contract with him. In effect, he proposes a new ethical standard that will restrict some of the activities of the personnel psychologist—and possibly some activities of the research psychologist—but will, he feels, protect the integrity of other kinds of psychological services.

Dr. Lovell is research associate at the Counseling and Testing Center at Stanford University. The following is a somewhat abbreviated version of the original paper, which appeared in the *American Psychologist,* May, 1967.

THE HUMAN USE OF PERSONALITY TESTS:
A DISSENTING VIEW

Victor R. Lovell

During the past 10 years, public resentment of personality testing has become increasingly evident. Testimony has been given on the abuse of personality tests before Senate and House subcommittees. It seems evident that unless psychologists concerned with personality assessment voluntarily restrict their own activities in some fashion, they will soon be subject to legal restrictions.

The response of psychologists to this outcry has usually been to attribute it to public ignorance or political extremism. I think we have been somewhat fatuous in this matter. In my opinion, the protests we have heard, however ill informed and inarticulate they have been, are directed at misuses of psychology which are quite real and very serious, to which our vested interests have blinded us.

Fundamentally, I think the issue is one of reconciling three divergent interests: (*a*) the public's right to privacy; (*b*) the social scientist's freedom of inquiry; and (*c*) the personnel worker's right to determine fitness for employment. Solutions, insofar as they have been proposed, have usually taken the direction of *restricting test content.* I do not think this tack can ever lead to any resolution of the basic conflicts involved.

The problem with restricting content is twofold. First, as is always the case with censorship, one does not know how to go about laying down concrete guidelines. Second, to do so will not offer adequate protection to the public, nor to the social scientist, nor to the personnel worker. Even if items dealing with sex, politics, and religion are deleted from personality inventories, the respondent's private thoughts are still likely to be probed. *Any* restriction of content is clearly an incursion on freedom of inquiry. Finally, determination of job qualifications may require the use of threatening stimuli, as, for example, when candidates for work in hospitals are given concept-formation tests involving pictures of horrible wounds.

An alternative to restricting content is to *restrict function*. Specifically, I am going to propose that certain kinds of tests should not be used in certain ways. I will lay down concrete guidelines for this proposal by arguing that certain kinds of "contracts" between assessors and respondents should be outlawed.

Basically, personality testing is used for two very different purposes, which I shall call the *personnel function* and the *client function*. I define the former as applying to situations where there is a potential conflict of interest between assessor and respondent, and the latter as applying to situations where there is not. The personnel function usually involves decisions about hiring, promotion, and termination. The client function usually involves providing services to the respondent. There are, however, important exceptions to these generalizations.

Where testing is purely for research purposes, we have the client function, except in situations where research subjects are coerced, deceived, or when their test results are not considered to be confidential, in which case we have the personnel function. The latter would include all research enterprises where participation by subjects is not voluntary. Testing serves a personnel function in all service situations where the respondent is not free to accept or reject services (as when he is committed to a mental hospital), or where he must qualify for them in some way other than by being able to pay for them (as when he is applying for welfare benefits).

THREE TEST CONTRACTS

Whether a particular assessment situation involves the client function or the personnel function becomes apparent when we examine the test contract involved. By "test contract," I mean whatever is understood between assessor and respondent. This involves some extension of the sense of "contract," since the term is usually restricted to voluntary agreements, and assessment often involves involuntary elements.

Suppose we should administer a personality inventory to a group of incoming freshmen at a college or university, and suppose the following message were to appear printed on the first inside page of the booklet which contains the test items:

To the Respondent:
We are asking you these questions because we really want to know what you

think, and how you feel, and because we are convinced that it will contribute to your education in some small way for you to ask them of yourself.

The information we are asking you to give will be used in one or both of two ways. First, it may contribute to our research on the process of higher education and the character of youth in our contemporary world. Second, it may be used to help provide you with psychological services during your college career, if you should decide that you require them. It will not be used by others to make decisions about you, although it may contribute to helping you make your own decisions more effectively.

If you take this inventory, the information you give us will be held in the strictest confidence. It will not be made available without your express permission (written, signed, and in our judgment uncoerced) to administrators, faculty members, parents, prospective employers, or anyone else except those on your campus whose primary obligation is to provide you with mental health or counseling services, or to do unbiased research in the social sciences.

When you take the inventory, we would like you to enter into a contract with us: *You don't try to fool us and we don't try to fool you.* The appropriate response to an item in this inventory is the one which you feel in your heart to be honest; the inappropriate one is the one which you know is not. If you do not feel that you can accept these terms, we would prefer that you did not take the inventory, for without this contract you will be wasting both your time and ours.

Since the inventory contains material which is personal and controversial, you should think carefully before deciding to take it. If you should decide not to, we shall understand and respect your decision.

If you decide to take the inventory, we wish you a pleasant and provocative exercise in self-discovery. We hope that this experience will move you a little closer to that intimate self-knowledge which has always been one of the primary goals of higher education.

Good luck!

Signed,
(the test authors)

We shall call this message the *client contract.*

Now suppose instead this message appears:

To the Respondent:

Because of the complexity of the technical considerations involved, and the limited space available here, it is not possible for us to explain to you the nature of this psychological assessment. We assure you that it is being done for sound reasons, and that nothing is being demanded of you capriciously.

The information you give us will be used in many very important ways. It will become a part of your permanent academic record. It may influence critical decisions which others will have to make about your career. It will be made available in various forms to administrators, faculty members, parents, prospective employers, and others who have a vital interest in your character and your welfare.

Make your test response as honestly as you can. It will not be in your best interest to do otherwise. If you should try to slant your answers so as to make a more favorable impression than is justified, this will become apparent to us when we score your test, and will reflect badly upon you.

Be conscientious and be careful!

Signed,
(the test authors)

We shall call this message the *strong personnel contract*.

Finally, consider a third message:

To the Respondent:

Because of the complexity of the technical considerations involved, the limited space available here, and the uses to which the material is to be put, it is not possible for us to explain to you the nature of this psychological assessment. We assure you that it is being done for sound reasons, and that nothing is being demanded of you capriciously.

The information which we will gain from this test will be used in many very important ways. It will become a part of your permanent academic record. It may influence critical decisions which others will have to make about your career. It will be made available in various forms to administrators, faculty members, prospective employers, parents, and others who have a vital interest in your character and your welfare.

You may try to slant your test answers so as to create a favorable impression. We will take this into consideration when we score your test. Your ability to create a favorable impression is of great interest to us, for it is likely to contribute much to your success or failure in a great many life situations. If you don't want to play this game with us, you can probably get away with refusing to take this test, if you really want to push it. We will try to make it as hard as possible for you to do so, because our boss wants you tested, and we work for him, and not for you.

We have to live too!

Signed,
(the test authors)

We shall call this message the *weak personnel contract*.

TEST CONTRACTS AND TEST STANDARDIZATION

The three examples given above represent the major alternatives available to the psychologist when he administers a personality assessment program. For the sake of brevity, the research contract and the counseling contract have been fused into one. It should be clear that current practice seldom involves making the nature of the situation explicit to the respondent. Typically, in the kind of situation alluded to above, the freshman class would be herded into an auditorium at some time during a crowded "orientation week," handed the test materials, and told to follow the simple instructions printed thereon. If someone should object, it is likely to be communicated to him that he is a trouble maker who has no business questioning the wisdom of professional people who obviously have only his best interests at heart.

The first point I should like to make is that, both as individuals involved in the administration of assessment programs, and I am convinced, eventually as a profession, we must choose between the alternatives suggested above, and we must make them explicit to the respondent. If we do not, we shall not be able to validate our assessment instruments in any very broad and profound fashion, because we shall not be able to maintain standard and uniform testing conditions. No matter what validation data we may have about our hypothetical personality inventory, if these data have been gathered under the client contract, we shall have difficulty making valid inferences about the meaning of test scores acquired under conditions where a personnel contract was involved. Further, if the testing actually serves a personnel function, the effect of personnel decisions will probably be a feeding back of information into the respondent population, which will alter the relationship of test variables with critical nontest variables; that is to say, people will become test wise and validity will vanish.

It has traditionally been argued that where the message making explicit the testing contract (or lack of such) is withheld, the respondent will make his own idiosyncratic interpretation of the situation, and that this interpretation, as manifested in his responses, will be indicative of broad and enduring traits of character in which the assessor is interested. While this argument is based on what is perhaps one of the most profound ideas in psychological assessment, its specific application to the *assessment contract* is naïve and wrongheaded. This is because most situations in which personality tests are administered are in fact highly structured. The respondent may be expected to infer the rules and goals of the game from the context in which it is played, even if they are not articulated by the assessors. In other words, variance due to interpretation of the test contract is probably mostly situational, rather than individual, in its determination.

If a man is applying for a job, and we give him a test, he does not need to be told that the success of his application is contingent on his responses (although present ethical standards state that he should be). He reasonably assumes that we would not do it if it were not good business, and he knows that the task at hand is to decide whether or not to hire him. If we in fact tested the job applicant for some other purpose, such as to decide where in the organization he might best be placed, we would run some danger of defeating ourselves, for our validity data would probably be based on the responses of men already placed, rather than on job applicants.

In the freshman testing situation described above, the respondent has spent a good deal of time during the past weeks providing information for various administrative records. Further, he has just spent the past year providing information to admissions officers, on the basis of which various critical decisions about his life have been made. It is unlikely to make much difference if a client contract is in fact the intention of the assessors. Even if independent psychological services exist on the campus, he will not come to the conclusion that they do, and he will infer a personnel contract.

I hold that eventually we must choose among the client contract, the strong personnel contract, and the weak personnel contract, not only for specific instruments and specific assessment programs, but also as a profession, for all "personality tests." This is because each time any one of us administers a personality test, he is participating in the creation of a cultural institution. Which test contract is understood by the respondent depends not only upon what cues are present in the testing situation, nor upon the immediate institutional context which surrounds it, but also upon the respondent's general understanding of the legitimate functions of personality assessment in his society. If one looks at what is said about personality tests, one gets the impression that, outside the private practice of psychology, with individual clients, the weak personnel contract is fast becoming normative, both from the point of view of the lay public, and from the point of view of professional psychologists. If we do not make the decision, it will be made for us as a result of the institutional processes in which we are involved. I am concerned lest it be already too late for a rational and considered choice to be possible.

If the reader has followed the argument thus far, three questions are likely to come to mind. First, what sort of contract with the respondent is most consistent with the ethical practice of psychology? Second, what sort of contract is most likely to lead in the long run to the valid measurement of personality? And third, what contract will allow us to offer the community the broadest range of psychological services? In the remainder of this essay, I shall argue for a client contract on all three counts.

TEST CONTRACTS AND ETHICS

In its public manifestos, the profession of psychology is firmly committed to political democracy, civil liberties, and the dignity of the individual. In practice, we sometimes violate these commitments, on behalf of bureaucratic or commercial interests. I do not believe that the strong personnel contract has any place in a free society, and I think that its occasional appearance is psychology's unique contribution to creeping totalitarianism in our times.

The strong personnel contract flatly denies the respondent's right to privacy. It proposes that kind of total surveillance of the individual which is characteristic of police states. Further, the strong personnel contract reeks with paternalism. It suggests total supervision as well as total surveillance. Finally, it creates the conditions for mutual suspicion and distrust among men. It invokes the possibility that deceit, if successful, may be richly rewarded, while at the same time threatening dire consequences if it is not.

The weak personnel contract might be considered ethically marginal. It is not a clear-cut invasion of privacy. It neither demands truth, nor threatens falsehood. Surveillance is more limited to that which is directly relevant, for to the degree to which the goal of the respondent's task is made clear, the test could be considered a work sample. Like the strong personnel contract, however, it is paternalistic (perhaps "maternalistic" would be more exact). It implies that those in positions of authority need not account to the public for their actions, and that their decisions must be taken on faith. Finally, the weak personnel contract, if received sufficiently often, will contribute in some small part to undermining the foundations of democratic process, for the efficacy of that process depends upon the authentic confrontation by the citizenry of each other, in order that their collective will may be determined. Since the weak personnel contract promises to reward conformity, it may discourage the articulation of loyal opposition, if it is true that what is learned in social situations is widely generalized.

The client contract protects the right to privacy, for it guarantees confidentiality, specifies the limits of confidence, and invites the respondent to decline to take the test if this is not satisfactory. It leaves him in a good position to make his decision, since it states the nature of the assessment and indicates the possible benefits of making the choice to participate. Finally, it attempts to promote the kind of human relationships which contribute to harmonious living in a free and open community.

PRIVACY AND DUPLICITY

Two related ethical themes arise when the proper use of personality tests is considered: *privacy* and *duplicity*. If the assessor is bound by no constraints in his invasions of the former, then the respondent is sure to react with the latter, and the assessor must outwit him by the use of *counter-duplicity*. This is a particularly messy business, because the respondent is not typically asked to testify as to objective matters of fact, but rather to the status of his attitudes, impulses, memories, emotions, and so forth. Because of this, his testimony cannot be independently corroborated. It may be examined for its internal consistency, but this is not relevant in the way that it would be, say in a legal situation, because consistency is not necessarily a property of attitudes, impulses, memories, emotions, etc.

It is sometimes suggested that this impasse may be resolved scientifically, rather than ethically. We need only investigate duplicity as a behavioral phenomenon, and when we have come to understand it, our subjects will not be able to deceive us. This line of thought springs from the notion that social science can function outside the social contract, without reference to moral concepts. All experimenters have moral commitments, however, just as all experimenters are either male or female, and I think it reasonable to expect the former to be as much involved in determining the behavior of subjects as the latter.

Once the respondent and the assessor have entered into a contract which permits them to deceive each other, it is difficult to see how any operational meaning can be given to the notion of duplicity. In order to investigate duplicity, the assessor must have some way of determining its presence or absence, but this requires that the declarations of the respondent be in some way corroborated, and we have seen that it is not clear how this is to be done. Even if the responses of the subject are recorded under conditions where it is believed that he is not aware of being observed, the authenticity of his behavior will be hard to establish, because this belief may be mistaken, and the observer is involved in a social game which leaves him no way to check up on himself.

However, even though duplicity is neither observed nor understood, administration of personality tests accompanied by a personnel contract might make it possible to validly predict some very critical events in which someone had a legitimate interest. The question of whether it is likely that this *can* be done will be taken up at a later point. The question at hand is whether it *should* be done.

Those who think it should often espouse what might be called the "hired-gun ethic." Duplicity in human relations, particularly in the presentation of one's own character to others, seems to be a common and pervasive characteristic of human society in general and personnel situations in particular. As long as this sort of thing is going to go on, the game might as well be played as well as possible by all concerned. It is not the business of professional psychologists either to rebel against the human condition, or to make policy for their employers. A similar defense is usually given by scientists and technicians involved in the design and production of war machines intended for the destruction of human property and human life.

Another kind of cold war could result. Some psychologists will make it their business to devise ever more complex and subtle ways of tricking their unwilling victims into revealing themselves. Others will offer their services as coaches to the respondent, to help him outwit the assessor. It is difficult to see how the enterprise of measuring individual differences could survive such a social holocaust, or how the individual would retain a voice in the conduct of his society. Actually, the orthodox version of the hired-gun ethic usually assumes that it is ethical for the psychologist to help the personnel worker to deceive the respondent, but not vice versa. The reasons for this bias are commercial, not ethical. So far, respondent coaching has been by nonpsychologists (Whyte, 1956, see also pp. 350–51).

In a nation where private enterprise is the dominant form of economic organization, it may be argued that while public agencies may be restricted, private institutions should be allowed to handle their personnel problems as they see fit, and therefore that professional psychologists who are employed by them should feel free to help them do so. A little thought should convince one that this is not so. Under our present system, hiring and firing practices are regulated by ethics and by legislation, just as working conditions are. To deny that this is as it should be would be to argue, for example, that personnel workers should be able to tap the telephone lines of job applicants, or inject them with truth serums.

ETHICS, PREJUDICE, AND PATERNALISM

It is sometimes argued that the use of personality tests in selection is equalitarian in effect, if not libertarian in method. The advent of abilities tests as selection devices contributed a great deal to the leveling of barriers to social mobility in our society. It tended to make advancement more dependent on merit, and less on privilege. It has been claimed that personality tests, if used in the same fashion, may do the same. I think it is more likely that they will have the opposite effect. The correlation between personality traits and demographic variables such as social class, caste, and religious persuasion is well known.

Suppose a personality inventory contained the following item:

I am a Negro.   (T)   (F)

As social scientists, we know that this item would be a valid predictor of all sorts of critical social outcomes in which the personnel worker has a legitimate interest, such as whether or not the respondent's conduct is likely to be criminal. However, we also know that the validity of the item would depend upon the operation of social forces the existence of which most of us deplore. Few of us would use this item if we could, because we would recognize that to do so would help perpetuate those social forces. Our prediction would be self-fulfilling, and contribute to the maintenance of barriers to social mobility. Yet it is probable that whenever we use personality tests in selection, we capitalize upon, and perpetuate, all sorts of prejudices, more subtle, less well understood, and perhaps more profound and in the very long run even more destructive than those regarding race. No matter how inclined we might be to use brute empiricism with our prediction problems, Federal law would prohibit us from using the item above. However, for the most part, the choice of what test content to use for what assessment purpose is presently left to our own discretion, as well as the use we make of such. I suggest that we should exercise discretion, before this choice is taken away from us by a justifiably resentful public.

It is often pointed out that effective selection may protect the respondent from being put in a situation where he will fail, or where he will be uncomfortable. If the information necessary to do this must be extracted from him without his consent, is it not doing him a service to extract it? The trouble with this view is that it presupposes a paternalistic view of society which seems hardly compatible with the democratic values to which we are committed. In order to afford the respondent this kind of "protection," someone else has to decide what is good for him. In some areas, it makes sense to do this. A doctor does not usually feel the need to ask permission to save a patient's life; he assumes that the patient wants to live. But in the area of physical well-being there are norms with which it can be safely assumed that almost everyone will agree. In the area of emotional well-being there are no such norms.

TEST CONTRACTS AND TEST VALIDITY

Our grandiosity in assuming that we can measure people who we can safely assume do not wish to be measured barely concealed our manifest failure, at least up to now, to measure nonintellective personality traits at all. I suspect that there is some kind of connection between the two. Would a physiologist attempt to measure basal metabolism without the cooperation of his subject? Why should we think we can do better?

The public seems well informed of the basic principles underlying the use of personality tests in personnel work, including the rather crude devices presently in existence for the detection of faking. This has been true for some time now (Whyte, 1956). I think it likely, as Whyte suggests, that the general nature of the game is understood intuitively even by unsophisticated respondents. The vast body of "hard data" in existence on dissimulation is probably irrelevant here, since almost all of it has been collected in totally artificial situations.

What is ethical is usually what is practical when one takes a broad view of things. We guarantee complete confidentiality to our clients in psychotherapy because we know that if we do not do so, they would not trust us and we would not obtain the kind of communication from them which we require in order to effectively provide this service. I believe that something of this sort applies to the relationship between validity and contract in personality testing.

What kind of test contract will tend to maximize overall validity? This, of course, is an "empirical question," but if it is approached in the hammer-and-tongs fashion which the term often implies when used by psychologists, the results could well be disastrous. If we gave our hypothetical personality inventory to three different groups of freshmen from the same class, each with a different one of our three contracts printed in the test booklet, we might then proceed to examine its validity under the three conditions, relative to various prediction problems. However, even if our consciences permitted us to conduct such an experiment, and we were able to obtain administrative approval for it, we might run some danger of precipitating a student revolt. In any case, we would create an atmosphere on the campus which would make validity data collected there subsequently somewhat difficult to interpret.

I believe that there are good empirical grounds for choosing the client contract in order to facilitate the development of valid procedures for personality assessment. All of our psychological theories contain propositions, well supported by empirical evidence, to the effect that when an organism is in danger, its behavior becomes less variable and less complex. Such behavior may not lend itself to the enterprise of differentiating between organisms.

Learning theory tells us that when organisms are placed on a reinforcement schedule their behavior becomes less variable. Cognitive theory informs us that when an organism is exposed to the threat of punishment or to induced conflict, dedifferentiation of the cognitive structure and isolation of its components is the result. Social psychology tells us that when the status of human beings is in jeopardy, their behavior will be characterized by rigid and pervasive conformity to norms which are perceived as associated with its maintenance. Psychoanalytic theory holds that the threat of ego damage evokes anxiety, and that anxiety produces repression and constriction, which prevent expression and articulation of the whole personality. All of these propositions seem to suggest that the threat and coercion involved in personnel contracts will tend to mitigate against the measurement of individual differences, where honesty is required of the subject.

Good psychological theory therefore, would seem to predict that under many conditions, with many variables, the effect of test administration involving personnel contracts will be to restrict the dispersion of the test variables, while at the same time increasing their intercorrelation, an effect which we would expect in general to render them less useful in the prediction of external criteria. To specify for which test variables, which criterion variables, and under exactly what conditions this will be so is the task of the theorist. Because this task is part of a process which is never complete, the issue at hand can never be summarily "settled" empirically, although it may always be further investigated, if other considerations do not dictate otherwise.

In terms of common sense, what is being suggested here is that we will obtain more information from people if we trust them and they trust us. This thesis is in good accord with the accumulated wisdom of the Judeo-Christian heritage. To hold that it will be true for all people, all situations, and all kinds of information would indeed be naïve. It is both normative and descriptive in intent, for as a prediction, it is likely to be self-fulfilling. I do not think it naïve to suggest that, for our profession, there is a presumption that it is the most viable game, both scientifically and socially.

Those who do personality research are often concerned lest, if the option to refuse to take a personality test is made explicit and available, and is as a result often accepted, the generality of their findings will suffer. Potential respondents who decline to be tested will surely be different from those who do not, in ways that are important to us as scientists. I do not think that the truth of this can be disputed, but I think that it is often felt to have implications which it does not, namely, that opportunity for empirical inquiry is seriously diminished. Offering potential respondents the option of refusing to be tested will enable us to record and search for correlates of this behavior.

An imaginative investigator who has a clear understanding of the theoretical questions and practical applications to which he has addressed himself will be able to use the data to achieve his goals. The loss involved in making the population tested more highly selected may not seem so great when we recall that most of the populations we test are already highly selected. Furthermore, we will now administer an additional "test," namely the acceptance or rejection of the assessment itself. We psychologists sometimes involve ourselves in an interesting paradox: On one hand we claim that our understanding of human nature will contribute to the "control" of human behavior, while on the other we demand that the control of human behavior be handed over to us in order that we may accomplish our ends.

A NEW ETHICAL STANDARD

It should be clear from what has already been said that I am proposing a considerable restriction of the uses to which certain kinds of mental tests may be put. The client contract is clearly appropriate to different assessment goals from those of the personnel contract. What will be the effect of this restriction on our capacity to provide psychological services? In order to discuss this question it is necessary to specify exactly what restrictions I advocate.

Up to now I have used the term "personality test." Although this more or less accords with popular usage, it is a misnomer, because all mental tests are, properly speaking, tests of personality. The kinds of tests I mean this discussion to refer to might best be called tests of character, virtue, psychopathology, and the like. The kinds of tests I do not mean to include under this rubric are tests of ability, aptitude, achievement, proficiency, and their ilk, where what is assessed is a work capacity of a work sample. In the remainder of this paper, I shall refer to the former as *tests of character,* and to the latter as *tests of capacity.*

A test of capacity is one for which there are criteria for deciding which responses are correct and which responses are incorrect, which are independent of the respondent, and of which the respondent is properly informed. By "correct responses" I mean those which will be rewarded; by "incorrect responses" those which will be punished. In testing for capacity, the respondent is told that he is to be evaluated, given an understanding of what is to constitute success and what failure, and success and failure are determined by norms which are external to him, be they subjective, as in an essay examination, or objective, as in an intelligence test. A test of character is one for which there are no criteria for deciding which responses are correct and which responses are not, or one for which the criteria of "correctness" are norms which are relative to the respondent, i.e., when the respondent is told that the "correct" answer is the "honest" one. Tests of character involve the recording of behavior under conditions where the assessor has not defined success and failure for the respondent, or under conditions where the assessor has defined success and failure for the respondent only in terms of the authenticity of self-report.

Personality inventories and projective techniques usually involve tests of character. Tests of capacity are most often concerned with ability, skills, problem solving, learning, the production of specified mechanical outputs, and so forth. But none of this is necessarily so, because the definition given above is independent of the nature of the test stimuli. A personality inventory becomes a test of capacity if the respondent is instructed to give the responses which will make a good impression on some particular class of people, and his protocol is scored for its correspondence with some reasonable determination of what responses do in fact make a good impression on this class. An intelligence test becomes a test of character if the respondent is asked not to solve problems but rather to indicate which kinds of problems he prefers and which he does not. It is still a test of character if the respondent is asked to solve problems, but his protocol is scored for his style of problem solving, rather than for the merit of his solutions. A person perception test is a test of capacity if it is scored for accuracy; if it is scored in terms of preferences for certain response categories, regardless of the appropriateness of these categories to actual persons, it is a test of character. Whether a test involves character or capacity depends upon what the respondent is told to do, and upon how response categories are defined by the assessor when he scores the test protocol.

One may determine whether a test is one of character or of capacity by asking if the respondent can "fake good." The notion of representing oneself as *better than one is* is never applicable to tests of capacity, but always applicable to tests of character. The latter are motivationally labile in a way that the former are not.

A moment's reflection should reveal that this distinction is independent not only of test content, but also of the construct which is measured. If intelligence is measured by the success of problem-solving activity, as it usually is, we have a test of capacity. But if it is measured, as it occasionally is, by the tendency to claim attitudes characteristic of successful problem solvers, then we have a test of character. If flexibility is measured by some kind of self-report device, then it is measured by a test of character. But if it is measured by success in a problem-solving situation, then it is measured by a test of capacity.

If the administration of a personality inventory involves the client contract or the strong personnel contract, as given earlier, the inventory is a test of character, because the respondent is asked to give an honest self-report. The interesting thing about the weak personnel contract is that it is a mixed bag. In terms of the distinction between character and capacity it is neither fish nor fowl. The question of whether a correct response is to be defined in terms of internal or external norms is left ambiguous. The accused is properly informed that what he says may be used against him, but he does not know how. If the task assigned the respondent were solely to make a good impression, and the persons to be impressed were indicated, and the scoring of the test were based in some way on the actual attitudes of these persons toward the test items, then we would have a *pure* test of capacity; otherwise we would not.

It may be objected that the categories of character and capacity may not be mutually exclusive. The weak personnel contract may make the inventory *both* a test of character and of capacity, since it is suggested that a correct response may be defined either with reference to internal or to external norms. The nature of the situation where the categories seem to overlap is perplexing, because the distinction involves what the respondent is asked to do, and it is not clear what he is being asked to do when he is told that his responses will be evaluated in terms of potentially conflicting norms. My inclination is to argue that under such conditions, we have a test of character, rather than of capacity, because if it is not clear what the respondent has been asked to do, then he has not been asked to do anything in particular.

The distinction between tests of character and tests of capacity is similar to that made by Cronbach (1960) between *tests of typical performance* and *tests of maximal performance,* and to that made by Wallace (1966) between *response predisposition* and *response capability.* The principle difference is that the categories used here are based solely on the nature of the test instructions and the test scoring, while those used by Cronbach and Wallace have reference also to theoretical constructs.

My position is that tests of character should never be used for any kind of personnel function, whether it be selection or placement. They should be used only for unbiased research, subject to the restrictions implicit in the client function, and to provide psychological services in situations where the assessor's first professional loyalty is to the respondent. I have argued this position on ethical grounds and on scientific grounds. I shall now consider what effect its implementation might have on the marketing of psychological services.

ETHICS AND PSYCHOLOGICAL SERVICES

I should first like to reemphasize a point which has already been made. Our capacity to provide assessment services cannot be discussed independently of the validity, present and future, of our assessment procedures, nor of the ethical standards which are to be applied to these procedures. We cannot provide services with invalid instruments. It is likely that we shall not be allowed to offer services if our ethics offend the public. Bills to restrict the activity of psychological testing have been appearing in our state legislatures for some time. They appeal to a variety of political groups for a variety of reasons, and are capable of attracting widespread support.

I have tried to define the sort of assessment procedure which must be restricted as narrowly as possible. In principle, the personnel psychologist is not to be enjoined from measuring any construct, nor from using any kind of test content. Essentially, all that must be given up is the demand for a certain kind of contract with the respondent, one which I doubt that much sense can be made of anyway, either in a legalistic or a scientific way. In practice, the personnel psychologist will not be able to measure constructs involving the notions of self-report or spontaneous behavior. I doubt that this is a real limitation; I think that the logic of such constructs dictates that they cannot be measured in personnel settings anyway, because of the likelihood that spontaneous or authentic behavior may be penalized. Many writers on the subject have reached similar conclusions.

My position is that the only way to escape from this dilemma is to make it clear in our testing contracts whether or not we intend to reward and punish, and if we do so intend, to indicate which response classes are to be rewarded and which punished, and then to try to the best of our ability to keep the contract, and that the only way to do this is to uniformly confront our potential respondents as a profession with some simple and broad ethical commitment. I think that if we do this we can become involved with constructs in which the concept of authenticity plays a part, while if we do not we shall of necessity close off many possible areas of research and service. I do not mean that we can produce interpersonal processes in which self-deception and the need to deceive others will not play a part; dynamic psychology dictates otherwise. I mean that we can only give operational value to such notions as authenticity and honest self-examination by creating situations where the integrity of interpersonal processes is protected by a particular kind of ethical structure, such as we have with regard to the processes of counseling and psychotherapy.

By restricting the activities of the personnel psychologist and in some cases those of the research psychologist, I believe we will act to protect the integrity of a variety of other psychological services, such as counseling and psychodiagnosis. These enterprises are simpler and more profound if we have the trust of our clients. Service-oriented research will also be facilitated if psychological assessors are trusted by their subjects. The counseling service might even be extended. Institutions which formerly depended only upon the personnel process to assign persons to places might employ private counseling psychologists who would report only to the candidate, and who would guarantee complete confidentiality to him. Self-selection and self-placement could then contribute to personnel decisions at the option of the candidate.

$$\triangledown \; \triangledown \; \triangledown$$

Bibliography

BIBLIOGRAPHY

AMERICAN PSYCHOLOGICAL ASSOCIATION. *Technical Recommendations for Psychological and Diagnostic Techniques.* Washington, D.C.: American Psychological Association, 1954.

AMERICAN PSYCHOLOGICAL ASSOCIATION. *Standards for Educational and Psychological Tests and Measurements.* Washington, D.C.: American Psychological Association, 1966.

AMRINE, M. (Ed.). Testing and public policy. *Amer. Psychologist,* 1965, **20,** 857–993.

ANASTASI, A. (Ed.). *Testing Problems in Perspective.* Washington, D.C.: American Council on Education, 1966.

ANASTASI, A., MEADE, M. J., & SCHNEIDERS, A. A. *The Validation of a Biographical Inventory as a Predictor of College Success.* Princeton, N.J.: Educational Testing Service, 1960.

ASCH, M. J. Negative response bias and personality adjustment. *J. counsel. Psychol.,* 1958, **5,** 206–10.

ASTIN, A. W. *Who Goes Where to College?* Chicago: Science Research Associates, 1965.

BARNES, E. H. The relationship of biased test responses to psychopathology. *J. abnorm. soc. Psychol.,* 1955, **51,** 286–90.

BARNES, E. H. Response bias and the MMPI. *J. consult. Psychol.,* 1956, **20,** 371–74.

BECHTOLDT, H. P. Construct validity: a critique. *Amer. Psychologist,* 1959, **14,** 619–29.

BECKER, S., LERNER, M., & CARROLL, J. Conformity as a function of birth order, payoff, and type of group pressure. *J. abnorm. soc. Psychol.,* 1964, **69,** 318–23.

BERDIE, R. F. Validities of the Strong Vocational Interest Blank. In W. L. Layton (Ed.), *The Strong Vocational Interest Blank: Research and Uses.* Minneapolis: University of Minnesota Press, 1960, pp. 18–61.

BERG, I. A. Deviant responses and deviant people: the formulation of the deviation hypothesis. *J. counsel. Psychol.,* 1957, **4,** 154–60.

BERKOWITZ, L. *Aggression, a Social Psychological Analysis.* New York: McGraw-Hill, 1962.

BERKOWITZ, L., & DANIELS, L. Responsibility and dependency. *J. abnorm. soc. Psychol.,* 1963, **66,** 429–36.

BETTLEHEIM, B. H. A study in rehabilitation. *J. abnorm. soc. Psychol.,* 1949, **44,** 231–65.

BLOCK, J. *The Challenge of Response Sets.* New York: Appleton-Century-Crofts, 1965.

BORING, E. G. *Sensation and Perception in the History of Experimental Psychology.* New York: Appleton-Century-Crofts, 1942.

BORING, E. G. The role of theory in experimental psychology. *Amer. J. Psychol.,* 1953, **69,** 169–84.

371

BOYLE, D. J., & HAGIN, W. V. The light plane as a pre-primary selection and training device: I. Analysis of operational data. *USAF Human Resources Research Center Technical Report*, 1953, No. 53-33.

BRAYFIELD, A. H. Remarks to the Senate subcommittee. *Amer. Psychologist*, 1965, **20**, 888–94.

BRAYFIELD, A. H. Congress and social science. *Amer. Psychologist*, 1967, **22**, 877–1041.

BREUER, J., & FREUD, S. *Case Histories* (original publication 1895; English translation by J. Strachey.) In J. Strachey (Ed.), *The Standard Edition of the Complete Psychological Works of Sigmund Freud*. Vol. 2. London: Hogarth Press, 1955, pp. 19–181.

BRIDGMAN, P. W. *The Logic of Modern Physics*. New York: Macmillan, 1927.

BRUNER, J. S. On perceptual readiness. *Psychol. Rev.*, 1957, **64**, 123–52.

BRUNER, J. S., & TAJFEL, H. Cognitive risk and environmental change. *J. abnorm. soc. Psychol.*, 1961, **62**, 230–41.

BRYAN, J. H. & TEST, M. A. Models and helping: naturalistic studies in aiding behavior. *J. pers. soc. Psychol.*, 1967, **16**, 400–407.

BRYAN, W. L., & HARTER, N. Studies on the telegraphic language: the acquisition of a hierarchy of habits. *Psychol. Rev.*, 1899, **6**, 345–75.

BRYDEN, M. P. A non-parametric method of item and test scaling, *Educ. psychol. Measmt.*, 1960, **20**, 311–15.

BURTT, H. E. An experimental study of early childhood memory. *J. genet. Psychol.*, 1932, **40**, 287–95.

BURTT, H. E. An experimental study of early childhood memory: final report. *J. genet. Psychol.*, 1941, **58**, 435–39.

BYRD, R. E. *Alone*. New York: Putnam's, 1938.

CAMPBELL, D. P. The 1966 revision of the Strong Vocational Interest Blank. *Personnel & guidance J.*, 1966, **45**, 744–49.

CAMPBELL, D. P. Stability of interests within an occupation over thirty years. *J. appl. Psychol.*, 1966, **50**, 51–56.

CAMPBELL, D. T. Recommendations for APA test standards regarding construct, trait, or discriminant validity. *Amer. Psychologist*, 1960, **15**, 546–53.

CAMPBELL, D. T., KRUSKAL, W. H., & WALLACE, W. P. Seating aggregation as an index of attitude. *Sociometry*, 1966, **29**, 1–15.

CANNON, W. B., & WASHBURN, A. L. An explanation of hunger. *Amer. J. Psychol.*, 1912, **29**, 441–54.

CAPLOW, T. *The Sociology of Work*. Minneapolis: University of Minnesota Press, 1954.

CARKHUFF, R. R., & BERENSON, B. G. *Beyond Counseling and Therapy*. New York: Holt, Rinehart & Winston, 1967.

CARP, A. Remarks to Senate subcommittee. *Amer. Psychologist*, 1965, **20**, 916–18.

CATTELL, R. B. *Personality and Motivation Structure and Measurement*. Yonkers-on-Hudson, N.Y.: World Book Company, 1957.

CATTELL, R. B. What is "objective" in "objective personality tests"? *J. counsel. Psychol.*, 1958, **5**, 285–89.

CATTELL, R. B. *The Scientific Analysis of Personality*. Baltimore, Md.: Penguin Books, 1965.

CATTELL, R. B., SAUNDERS, D. R., & STIC, G. *Handbook for the 16 PF Questionnaire*. Champaign, Ill.: Institute for Personality and Ability Testing, 1957.

CHASE, C. I., & LUDLOW, H. G. (Eds.) *Readings in Educational and Psychological Measurement*. New York: Houghton Mifflin, 1966.

CLARK, J. V. Motivation in work groups: a tentative view. *Human Organization*, 1960, **19,** 199–208.

CLARK, W. W., & TIEGS, E. W. *Technical Report on the California Achievement Tests, 1957 Edition*. Los Angeles: California Test Bureau, 1958.

COHEN, L. D., KIPNIS, D., KUNKLE, E. C., & KUBZANSKY, P. E. Observations of a person with congenital insensitivity to pain. *J. abnorm. soc. Psychol.*, 1955, **51,** 333–38.

COMREY, A. L. An operational approach to some problems in psychological measurement. *Psychol. Rev.*, 1950, **57,** 217–28.

COMREY, A. L. Mental testing and the logic of measurement. *Educ. psychol. Measmt.*, 1951, **11,** 323–34.

COOKE, M. K., & KIESLER, D. J. Prediction of college students who later require personal counseling. *J. counsel. Psychol.*, 1967, **14,** 346–49.

COOLEY, W. W. *Career Development of Scientists*. Cambridge, Mass.: Harvard Graduate School of Education, 1963.

COOLEY, W. W. A computer-measurement system for guidance. *Harvard educ. Rev.*, 1964, **34,** 559–72.

COOLEY, W. W., & LOHNES, P. R. *Multivariate Procedures for the Behavioral Sciences*. New York: Wiley, 1962.

COUCH, A., & KENISTON, K. Yeasayers and naysayers: agreeing response set as a personality variable. *J. abnorm. soc. Psychol.*, 1960, **60,** 151–74.

COULSON, J. E., & COGSWELL, J. F. Effects of individualized instruction on testing. *J. educ. Measmt.*, 1965, **1,** 59–64.

CRITES, J. O. The California Psychological Inventory: I. As a measure of the normal personality. *J. counsel. Psychol.*, 1964, **11,** 197–202.

CRITES, J. O. The California Psychological Inventory: II. As a measure of client personalities. *J. counsel. Psychol.*, 1964, **11,** 299–306.

CRONBACH, L. J. Response sets and test validity. *Educ. psychol. Measmt.*, 1946, **6,** 475–94.

CRONBACH, L. J. Further evidence on response sets and test design. *Educ. psychol. Measmt.*, 1950, **10,** 3–31.

CRONBACH, L. J. *Essentials of Psychological Testing*. New York: Harpers, 1949.

CRONBACH, L. J. Assessment of individual differences. *Annu. Rev. Psychol.*, 1956, **7,** 173–96.

CULLER, E., & METTLER, F. A. Conditioned behavior in a decorticate dog. *J. comp. Psychol.*, 1934, **18,** 291–303.

CURETON, E. E. Validity, reliability, and baloney. *Educ. psychol. Measmt.*, 1950, **10,** 94–96.

DANET, B. N. Prediction of mental illness in college students on the basis of "nonpsychiatric" MMPI profiles. *J. consult. Psychol.*, 1965, **29,** 577–80.

DATEL, W. E. Socialization scale norms on military samples. *Military Med.*, 1962, **127,** 740–44.

DeCHARMS, R., & MOELLER, G. Values expressed in American children's readers: 1800–1950. *J. abnorm. soc. Psychol.*, 1962, **64,** 136–42.

DINGLE, H. Book review of *Measurement: Definitions and Theories,* edited by C. W. Churchman and P. Ratoosh. *Scientific Amer.,* 1960, **202,** 189–92.

DRAKE, L. E. Interpretation of MMPI profiles in counseling male clients. *J. counsel. Psychol.,* 1956, **3,** 83–88.

DRAKE, L. E. MMPI patterns predictive of underachievement. *J. counsel. Psychol.,* 1962, **9,** 164–67.

DRAKE, L. E., & OETTING, E. R. An MMPI pattern and a suppressor variable predictive of academic achievement. *J. counsel. Psychol.,* 1957, **4,** 245–47.

DRASGOW, J., & BARNETTE, W. L., JR. $F-K$ in a motivated group. *J. consult. Psychol.,* 1957, **21,** 399–401.

DREGER, R. M., & MILLER, K. S. Comparative psychological studies of Negroes and whites in the United States. *Psychol. Bull.,* 1960, **57,** 361–402.

DuBois, P. H. A test-dominated society: China, 1115 B.C.–1905 A.D. *Proceedings of the 1964 Invitational Conference on Testing Problems.* Princeton, N.J.: Educational Testing Service, 1965, pp. 3–11.

DUKES, W. F. $N = 1$. *Psychol. Bull.,* 1965, **64,** 74–79.

DVORAK, B. J. Differential occupational ability patterns. *Bull. emplyt. stabilization res. Inst.,* 1935, **3,** (8). Minneapolis: University of Minnesota Press.

DVORAK, B. J. The general aptitude test battery. *Personnel & guidance J.,* 1956, **35,** 145–52.

EBBINGHAUS, H. *Uber das Gedächtnis.* Leipzig: Duncker & Humblot, 1885. (*Memory: A Contribution to Experimental Psychology.* English translation by H. A. Ruger and C. E. Bussenius. New York: Teachers College, Columbia University, 1913.)

EBEL, R. L. Standardized achievement tests: uses and limitations. *National Elementary Principal,* 1961, **40,** 29–32.

EHRLE, R. A. Quantification of biographical data for predicting vocational rehabilitation success. *J. appl. Psychol.,* 1964, **48,** 171–74.

EHRLICH, M. *The Selective Role of Aggression in Concept Formation.* Unpublished Ph.D. thesis, New York University, 1961.

EISEN, N. H. Some effects of early sensory deprivation on later behavior: the quondam hard-of-hearing child. *J. abnorm. soc. Psychol.,* 1962, **65,** 338–42.

ENGLISH, H. B., & ENGLISH, A. *A Comprehensive Dictionary of Psychological and Psychoanalytical Terms.* New York: Longmans, Green, 1958.

EVANS, J. Miller. *J. abnorm. soc. Psychol.,* 1950, **45,** 359–79.

FLANAGAN, J. C. The experimental evaluation of a selection procedure. *Educ. psychol. Measmt.,* 1946, **6,** 445–66.

FLANAGAN, J. C., & COOLEY, W. W. *Project TALENT One-Year Followup Studies.* University of Pittsburgh, School of Education, 1966.

FLANAGAN, J. C., DAILEY, J. T., SHAYCOFT, M. F., GORHAM, W. A., ORR, D. B., & GOLDBERG, I. *Design for a Study of American Youth.* Boston: Houghton Mifflin, 1962.

FLANAGAN, J. C., DAILEY, J. T., SHAYCOFT, M. F., GORHAM, W. A., ORR, D. B., GOLDBERG, I., & NEYMAN, C. A. *The American High-School Student.* Pittsburgh: Project TALENT Office, 1964.

FLYNN, J. T. & GARBER, H. (Eds.) *Assessing Behavior: Readings in Educational and Psychological Measurement.* Reading, Mass.: Addison-Wesley, 1967.

GALTON, F. *Hereditary Genius*. New York: Appleton, 1870.

GARFIELD, S. L., & AFFLECK, D. C. A study of individuals committed to a state home for the retarded who were later released as not mentally defective. *Amer. J. ment. Defic.*, 1960, **64,** 907–15.

GEISSER, S. A note on McQuitty's index of concomitance. *Educ. psychol. Measmt.*, 1958, **18,** 125–28.

GHISELLI, E. E. *The Validity of Occupational Aptitude Tests*. New York: Wiley, 1966.

GOLD, R. Janitors versus tenants: a status-income dilemma, *Amer. J. Sociology,* 1952, **58,** 486–93.

GOLDMAN, M., HORWITZ, M., & LEE, F. L. Alternative classroom standards concerning management of hostility and effects on student learning. *ONR Technical Report,* Washington, D.C.: Office of Naval Research, 1954.

GOLDSMITH, D. B. The use of personal history blanks as a salesmanship test. *J. appl. Psychol.*, 1922, **6,** 149–55.

GOUGH, H. G. The *F* minus *K* dissimulation index for the Minnesota Multiphasic Personality Inventory. *J. consult. Psychol.*, 1950, **14,** 408–13.

GOUGH, H. G. Theory and measurement of socialization. *J. consult. Psychol.,* 1960, **24,** 23–30.

GOUGH, H. G. Cross-cultural validation of a measure of asocial behavior. *Psychol. Rep.,* 1965, **17,** 379–87.

GOUGH, H. G. A cross-cultural analysis of the CPI femininity scale. *J. consult. Psychol.,* 1966, **30,** 136–41.

GOUGH, H. G. Appraisal of social maturity by means of the CPI. *J. abnorm. Psychol.,* 1966, **71,** 189–95.

GOUGH, H. G., & SANDHU, H. S. Validation of the CPI socialization scale in India. *J. abnorm. soc. Psychol.,* 1964, **68,** 544–47.

GRIER, E. S. *In Search of a Future*. Washington, D.C.: Washington Center for Metropolitan Studies, 1963.

GRIGG, A. E., & THORPE, J. S. Deviant responses in college adjustment clients: a test of Berg's Deviation Hypothesis. *J. consult. Psychol.,* 1960, **24,** 92–94.

GROSS, M. *The Brain Watchers*. New York: Random House, 1962.

GUION, R. M. Personnel selection. *Annu. Rev. Psychol.,* 1967, **18,** 191–216.

HAGGARD, E. A. Isolation and personality. In P. Worchel & D. Byrne (Eds.), *Personality Change*. New York: Wiley, 1964, pp. 433–69.

HARRIS, F. R. National Social Science Foundation: proposed Congressional mandate for the social sciences. *Amer. Psychologist,* 1967, **22,** 904–10.

HARTSHORN, H., & MAY, M. A. *Studies in Deceit*. New York: Macmillan, 1928.

HARTSHORN, H., & MAY, M. A. *Studies in Service and Self Control*. New York: Macmillan, 1929.

HARTSHORN, H., & MAY, M. A. *Studies in the Organization of Character*. New York: Macmillan, 1930.

HATHAWAY, S. R. A coding system for MMPI profiles. *J. consult. Psychol.,* 1947, **11,** 334–47.

HATHAWAY, S. R., & MONACHESI, E. D. *Analyzing and Predicting Juvenile Delinquency with the MMPI*. Minneapolis: University of Minnesota Press, 1953.

HAYES, K. J., & HAYES, C. Imitation in a home-raised chimpanzee, *J. comp. physiol. Psychol.*, 1952, **45**, 450–59.

HEINEMANN, E. G. Photographic measurement of the retinal image. *Amer. J. Psychol.*, 1961, **74**, 440–45.

HELLER, K., MYERS, R. A., & KLINE, L. V. Interviewer behavior as a function of standardized client roles. *J. consult. Psychol.*, 1963, **27**, 117–22.

HELM, C. Computer simulation techniques for research on guidance problems. *Personnel & guidance J.*, 1967, **46**, 47–52.

HERZBERG, F., MAUSNER, B., PETERSON, R. O., & CAPWELL, D. F. *Job Attitudes: Review of Research and Opinion*. Pittsburgh: Psychological Service of Pittsburgh, 1957.

HILDRETH, G. Using readiness test results. *Test Service Notebook #10*. Yonkers-on-Hudson, N.Y.: World Book Company (undated).

HOFFMANN, B. *The Tyranny of Testing*. New York: Crowell-Collier, 1962.

HOLLAND, J. L. Explorations of a theory of vocational choice and achievement: II. A four-year prediction study. *Psychol. Rep.*, 1963, **15**, 547–94.

HOROWITZ, I. L. The life and death of Project Camelot. *Trans-action*, 1965, **3**, 3–7, 44–47.

HUNT, H. F. The effect of deliberate deception on the Minnesota Multiphasic Personality Inventory. *J. consult. Psychol.*, 1948, **12**, 396–402.

JACKSON, D. N. Book review of Block's *Challenge of Response Sets*. *Educ. psychol. Measmt.*, 1967, **27**, 207–10, 502–7.

JACOBSON, E. Electrical measurements of neuromuscular states during mental activities: VI. A note on mental activities concerning an amputated limb. *Amer. J. Physiol.*, 1931, **96**, 122–25.

JENNINGS, E. E. The motivation factor in testing supervisors. *J. appl. Psychol.*, 1953, **37**, 168–69.

JENSEN, M. B. Mental deterioration following carbon monoxide poisoning. *J. abnorm. soc. Psychol.*, 1950, **45**, 146–53.

JONES, M. C. A laboratory study of fear: the case of Peter. *J. genet. Psychol.*, 1924, **31**, 308–15.

KATZ, I., ROBERTS, O. S., & ROBINSON, J. M. Effects of difficulty, race of administrator, and instructions on Negro digit-symbol performance. *ONR Technical Report*, Washington, D.C.: Office of Naval Research, 1963.

KATZ, I., ROBINSON, J. M., EPPS, E. G., & WALY, P. The influence of race of the experimenter and instructions upon the expression of hostility by Negro boys. *J. soc. Issues*, 1964, **20**, 54–59.

KAY, B. R. The use of critical incidents in a forced-choice scale. *J. appl. Psychol.*, 1959, **43**, 269–70.

KELLOGG, W. N., & KELLOGG, L. *The Ape and the Child*. New York: McGraw-Hill, 1933.

KIRCHNER, W. K., & DUNNETTE, M. D. Applying the weighted application blank technique to a variety of office jobs. *J. appl. Psychol.*, 1957, **41**, 206–208.

KLEIN, G. S., BARR, H. L., & WOLITSKY, D. L. Personality. *Annu. Rev. Psychol.*, 1967, **18**, 467–560.

KLEINMUNTZ, B. MMPI decision rules for the identification of college maladjustment: a digital computer approach, *Psychol. Monogr.*, 1963, **77,** (Whole No. 577).

KLUCKHOLM, F. R. Dominant and substitutive profiles of cultural orientations: their significance for the analysis of social stratification. *Soc. Forces,* 1950, **28,** 376–93.

KOGAN, N., & WALLACH, M. A. *Risk-Taking: A Study in Cognition and Personality.* New York: Holt, Rinehart & Winston, 1964.

KRUMBOLTZ, J. D., & CHRISTAL, R. E. Relative pilot aptitude and success in primary pilot training. *J. appl. Psychol.,* 1957, **41,** 409–13.

LANGER, E. Foreign research: CIA plus Camelot equals troubles for U.S. scholars. *Science,* 1967, **156,** 1583–84.

LENNEBERG, E. H. Understanding language without ability to speak: a case report. *J. abnorm. soc. Psychol.,* 1962, **65,** 419–25.

LEVINE, A. S. After the Samoans come of age. *Amer. Psychologist,* 1957, **5,** 259–63.

LINDEMANN, J. E., FAIRWEATHER, G. W., STONE, G. B., SMITH, R. S., & LONDON, I. T. The use of demographic characteristics in predicting length of neuropsychiatric hospital stay. *J. consult. Psychol.,* 1959, **23,** 85–89.

LIPSMAN, C. K. Maslow's theory of needs in relation to vocational choice by students from lower socioeconomic levels. *Voc. Guidance Quart.,* 1967, **15,** 283–88.

LORGE, I. Gen-like: halo or reality. *Psychol. Bull.,* 1937, **34,** 545–46.

LOVELL, V. R. The human use of personality tests: a dissenting view. *Amer. Psychologist,* 1967, **22,** 383–93.

MAAS, J. B. Patterned scales expectation interview: reliability studies on a new technique. *J. appl. Psychol.,* 1965, **49,** 431–33.

MACMEEKAN, A. M. *The Intelligence of a Representative Group of Scottish Children.* London: University of London Press, 1940.

MANDELL, M. Selecting chemists for the federal government. *Personnel Psychol.,* 1957; **41,** 206–8.

MARTIN, W. A. P. Competitive examinations in China. *N. Amer. Rev.,* 1870, **111,** 62–77.

MASLING, J. The effects of warm and cold interaction on the interpretation of a projective protocol. *J. proj. Tech.,* 1957, **21,** 377–83.

MASLING, J. The effects of warm and cold interaction on the administration and scoring of an intelligence test. *J. consult. Psychol.,* 1959, **25,** 336–41.

MASLOW, A. H. *Motivation and Personality.* New York: Harpers, 1954.

MAYFIELD, E. C. The selection interview—a re-evaluation of published research. *Personnel Psychol.,* 1964, **17,** 239–60.

McARTHUR, C. Long-term validity of the Strong Interest Test in two subcultures. *J. appl. Psychol.,* 1954, **38,** 346–53.

McCURDY, H. G. La belle dame sans merci. *Charact. & Pers.,* 1944, **13,** 166–77.

McGEE, R. K. Response style as a personality variable: by what criterion? *Psychol. Bull.,* 1962, **59,** 284–95.

McGRATH, J. J. Improving credit evaluation with a weighted application blank. *J. appl. Psychol.,* 1960, **44,** 325–26.

McNemar, Q.   Sampling in psychological research. *Psychol. Bull.*, 1940, **37,** 331–65.

McNemar, Q.   More on the Wilson test. *Psychol. Bull.*, 1958, **55,** 334–35.

McNemar, Q.   *Psychological Statistics* (3d ed.). New York: Wiley, 1962.

McNemar, Q.   Lost: our intelligence: Why? *Amer. Psychologist*, 1964, **19,** 871–82.

Meehl, P. E.   *Clinical versus Statistical Prediction.* Minneapolis: University of Minnesota Press, 1954.

Meehl, P. E.   When shall we use our heads instead of the formula? *J. consult. Psychol.*, 1957, **4,** 268–73.

Megargee, E. I. (Ed.).   *Research in Clinical Assessment.* New York: Harper & Row, 1966.

Mehrens, W. A., & Ebel, R. L.   *Principles of Educational and Psychological Measurement.* Chicago: Rand McNally, 1967.

Merritt, C. B., & Fowler, R. G.   The pecuniary honesty of the public at large. *J. abnorm. soc. Psychol.*, 1948, **43,** 90–93.

Metfessel, N. S., & Sax, G.   Systematic biases in the keying of correct responses on certain standardized tests. *Educ. psychol. Measmt.*, 1958, **18,** 787–90.

Miller, C. H.   Occupational choice and values. *Personnel & guidance J.*, 1956, **35,** 244–46.

Mills, R. B., McDevitt, R. J., & Tonkin, S.   Situational tests in metropolitan police recruit selection. *J. crim. Law, Criminology & Police Sci.*, 1966, **57,** 99–106.

Mosher, R. I., Carle, R. F., & Kehas, C. D.   *Guidance: An Examination.* New York: Harcourt, Brace, 1965.

Murphy, G.   *Historical Introduction to Modern Psychology.* New York: Harcourt, Brace, 1949.

Narrol, H. H., & Levitt, E. E.   Formal assessment procedures in police selection. *Psychol. Rep.*, 1963, **12,** 691–94.

Norman, W. T.   Relative importance of test item content. *J. consult. Psychol.*, 1963, **27,** 166–74.

Orne, M. T.   On the social psychology of the psychological experiment: with particular reference to demand characteristics and their implications. *Amer. Psychologist*, 1962, **17,** 776–83.

Oseas, L.   "Give the first natural answer." *J. counsel. Psychol.*, 1966, **13,** 454–58.

OSS Assessment Staff.   *Assessment of Men.* New York: Rinehart, 1948.

Pace, C. R.   Methods of describing college cultures. *Teach. Coll. Rec.*, 1962, **63,** 267–77.

Pace, C. R.   *Preliminary Technical Manual for CUES: College & University Environment Scales.* Princeton, N.J.: Educational Testing Service, 1963.

Page, E. B.   The imminence of grading essays by computer. *Phi Delta Kappan*, 1966, **47,** 238–43.

Page, E. B.   Grading essays by computer: progress report. *Proceedings of the 1966 Invitational Conference on Testing Problems.* Princeton, N.J.: Educational Testing Service, 1967, pp. 87–100.

PIERCE, R. C. Note on testing conditions. *J. consult. Psychol.,* 1963, **27,** 536–37.

PRINCE, M. *The Dissociation of a Personality.* New York: Longmans, Green, 1905.

RICHARDSON, M. W. The relation between the difficulty and the differential validity of a test. *Psychometrika,* 1936, **1,** 33–49.

ROBY, K. E. A voice against computer correction of themes. *The Maine Teacher,* 1966, **27,** 19–20.

ROE, A. *The Psychology of Occupations.* New York: Wiley, 1956.

ROHRER, J. H. *Human Adjustment to Antarctic Isolation.* Arlington, Va.: Armed Services Technical Information Agency Publication AD 246610, 1960.

RORER, L. G. The great response-style myth. *Psychol. Bull.,* 1965, **65,** 129–56.

ROSEN, E. George X: the self-analysis of an avowed fascist. *J. abnorm. soc. Psychol.,* 1949, **44,** 528–40.

ROSENBAUM, M., & BLAKE, R. Volunteering as a function of field structure. *J. abnorm. soc. Psychol.,* 1955, **50,** 193–96.

ROSENTHAL, R. Experimenter attributes as determinants of subjects' responses. *J. proj. Tech.,* 1963, **27,** 324–31.

ROSENTHAL, R. Experimenter outcome-orientation and the results of the psychological experiment. *Psychol. Bull.,* 1964, **61,** 405–12.

ROSENTHAL, R. Covert communication in the psychological experiment. *Psychol. Bull.,* 1967, **67,** 356–67.

ROSENWALD, G. C. The assessment of anxiety in psychological experiments. *J. abnorm. soc. Psychol.,* 1961, **63,** 666–73.

ROWE, P. M. Individual differences in selection decisions. *J. appl. Psychol.,* 1963, **47,** 304–307.

RUCH, F. L. A technique for detecting attempts to fake performance on the self-inventory type of personality test. In Q. McNemar and M. A. Merril (Eds.), *Sudies in Personality.* New York: McGraw-Hill, 1942, pp. 229–34.

RUCH, F. L., & RUCH, W. W. The *K* factor as a (validity) suppressor variable in predicting success in selling. *J. appl. Psychol.,* 1967, **51,** 201–4.

RUCH, G. M. Recent developments in statistical procedures. *Rev. educ. Res.,* 1933, **3,** 39–40.

RUNDQUIST, E. A. Item and response characteristics in attitude and personality measurement: a reaction to Rorer's "Great Response-style Myth." *Psychol. Bull.,* 1966, **66,** 166–77.

RUSSELL, W., & COPE, G. V. Method of rating the history of achievements of applicants. *Publ. Personnel Stud.,* 1925, **3,** 202–19.

SARASON, S. B., DAVIDSON, K. S., LIGHTHALL, F. F., WAITE, R. R., & RUEBUSH, B. K. *Anxiety in Elementary School Children.* New York: Wiley, 1960.

SATTLER, J. M., & THEYE, F. Procedural, situational and interpersonal variables in individual intelligence testing. *Psychol. Bull.,* 1967, **68,** 347–60.

SAWYER, J. Measurement and prediction, clinical and statistical. *Psychol. Bull.,* 1966, **66,** 178–200.

SCHWARZ, P. A. Adapting tests to the cultural setting. *Educ. psychol. Measmt.,* 1963, **23,** 673–86.

SECHREST, L. Incremental validity: a recommendation. *Educ. psychol. Measmt.*, 1963, **23,** 153–58.

SECHREST, L., & JACKSON, D. N. Deviant response tendencies: their measurement and interpretation. *Educ. psychol. Measmt.*, 1963, **23,** 33–53.

SELLS, S. B. Structured measurement of personality and motivation: a review of contributions of Raymond B. Cattell. *J. clin. Psychol.*, 1959, **15,** 3–21.

SELLS, S. B. A model for the social system for the multiman extended duration space ship. *NASA Report No. NGR 44-009-008* (undated).

SHAW, M. E. The effectiveness of Whyte's rules: "How to cheat on personality tests." *J. appl. Psychol.*, 1962, **46,** 21–25.

SMITH, E. E. Obtaining subjects for research. *Amer. Psychologist,* 1962, **17,** 577–78.

SMITH, K. U. Remarks to Senate subcommittee. *Amer. Psychologist,* 1965, **20,** 907–11.

SMITH, P. C., & KENDALL, L. M. Retranslation of expectations: an approach to the construction of unambiguous anchors for rating scales. *J. appl. Psychol.,* 1963, **47,** 149–55.

SMITH, W. J., ALBRIGHT, L. W., GLENNON, J. R., & OWENS, W. A. The prediction of research competence and creativity from personal history. *J. appl. Psychol.,* 1961, **45,** 59–62.

SOCIETY FOR PSYCHOLOGICAL STUDY OF SOCIAL ISSUES. Guidelines for testing minority group children. *J. social Issues,* 1964, **20,** 127–45.

SORENSON, W. W. Test of mechanical principles as a suppressor variable for the prediction of effectiveness on a mechanical repair job. *J. appl. Psychol.,* 1966, **50,** 348–53.

SPRINTHALL, N. A. Test interpretation: some problems and a proposal. *Voc. Guidance Quart.,* 1967, **15,** 248–56.

STONE, P. J. An interactive inquirer. *Proceedings of the 1965 Invitational Conference on Testing Problems.* Princeton, N.J.: Educational Testing Service, 1967, pp. 63–79.

STONE, P. J., DUNPHY, D. C., SMITH, M. S., & OGILVIE, D. M. *The General Inquirer: A Computer Approach to Content Analysis.* Cambridge, Mass. M. I. T. Press, 1966.

STRATTON, G. M. Vision without inversion of the retinal image. *Psychol. Rev.,* 1897, **4,** 341–60, 463–81.

STRONG, E. K., JR. *Vocational Interests of Men and Women.* Stanford, Calif.: Stanford University Press, 1943.

STRONG, E. K., JR. Twenty-year follow-up of medical interests. In L. L. Thurstone (Ed.), *Applications of Psychology.* New York: Harper & Brothers, 1952, pp. 111–30.

STRONG, E. K., JR. *Vocational Interests 18 Years after College.* Minneapolis: University of Minnesota Press, 1955.

STRONG, E. K., JR., & CAMPBELL, D. P. *Manual for Strong Vocational Interest Blanks.* Stanford, Calif.: Stanford University Press, 1966.

STRONG, E. K., & TUCKER, A. C. Use of vocational interest scales in planning a medical career, *Psychol. Monog.,* 1952, **66,** (Whole No. 341).

SUPER, D. E. *Appraising Vocational Fitness.* New York: Harper, 1949.

SUPER, D. E. The use of multifactor test batteries in guidance. *Personnel & guidance J.,* 1956, **25,** 2–8.

TANNER, J. M. *The Physique of the Olympic Athlete.* London: Allen & Unwin, 1964.

TAYLOR, D. W. Variables related to creativity and productivity among men in two research laboratories. In C. W. Taylor and F. Barron (Eds.), *Scientific Creativity.* New York: Wiley, 1963, pp. 228–50.

TERMAN, L. M. The intelligence quotients of Francis Galton in childhood. *Amer. J. Psychol.,* 1917, **28,** 209–45.

TERMAN, L. M., & MERRILL, M. A. *Measuring Intelligence.* New York: Houghton, Mifflin, 1937.

TESKA, P. T. The mentality of hydrocephalics and a description of an interesting case. *J. Psychol.,* 1947, **23,** 197–203.

THIGPEN, C. H., & CLECKLEY, H. A case of multiple personality. *J. abnorm. soc. Psychol.,* 1954, **49,** 135–51.

THOMPSON, O. E. Occupational values of high school students. *Personnel & guidance J.,* 1966, **44,** 850–53.

TRAXLER, A. E. Impact of machines and devices on developments in testing and related fields. *Proceedings of the 1953 Invitational Conference on Testing Problems.* Princeton, N.J.: Educational Testing Service, 1954, pp. 139–46.

TRAXLER, A. E. (Ed.). *Measurement and Research in Today's Schools.* Washington, D.C.: American Council on Education, 1961.

U. S. DEPARTMENT OF LABOR, BUREAU OF EMPLOYMENT SECURITY. *Guide to the Use of the General Aptitude Test Battery.* Washington, D.C.: Government Printing Office, 1958.

U. S. DEPARTMENT OF LABOR, BUREAU OF EMPLOYMENT SECURITY. *GATB Norms for Ninth and Tenth Grades.* Washington, D.C.: Government Printing Office, 1959.

VINCENT, C. *Unmarried Mothers.* New York: Free Press, 1961.

WALLACE, J. An abilities conception of personality: some implications for personality measurement. *Amer. Psychologist,* 1966, **21,** 132–38.

WATSON, J. B., & RAYNER, R. Conditioned emotional reactions. *J. exp. Psychol.,* 1920, **3,** 1–4.

WEBB, E. J. Unconventionality, triangulation and inference. *Proceedings of the 1966 Invitational Conference on Testing Problems.* Princeton, N.J.: Educational Testing Service, 1967, pp. 34–43.

WEBSTER, E. C. *Decision Making in the Employment Interview.* Montreal: Industrial Relations Centre, McGill University, 1964.

WEIZENBAUM, J. ELIZA—a computer program for the study of natural language communication between man and machine. *Communications of the ACM* (Association for Computing Machinery), 1966, **1,** 36–45.

WERNIMONT, P. F. Re-evaluation of a weighted application blank for office personnel. *J. appl. Psychol.,* 1962, **46,** 417–19.

WHYTE, W. H., JR. The fallacies of personality testing. *Fortune,* 1954, **50** (No. 3), 117–19, 204–8.

WHYTEN, W. H., JR. *The Organizational Man.* New York: Simon & Schuster, 1956.

WICKERT, F. R.   An adventure in psychological testing abroad. *Amer. Psychologist,* 1957, **5,** 86–88.

WILENSKY, H. L.   Orderly careers and social participation: the impact of work history on social integration in the middle mass. *Amer. sociological Rev.,* 1961, **26,** 521–39.

WILSON, K. V.   A distribution–free test of analysis of variance hypotheses. *Psychol. Bull.,* 1956, **53,** 96–101.

YATES, A. J.   The application of learning theory to the treatment of tics. *J. abnorm. soc. Psychol.,* 1958, **56,** 175–82.

YERKES, R. M.   The mind of a gorilla. *Genet. Psychol. Monogr.,* 1927, **2,** 1–193.

ZEIGLER, M. L., BERNREUTER, R. G., & FORD, D. H.   A new profile for interpreting academic abilities. *Educ. psychol. Measmt.,* 1958, **18,** 583–88.

ZUBIN, J.   Clinical versus actuarial prediction: a pseudo-problem. In A. Anastasi (Ed.), *Testing Problems in Perspective.* Washington, D.C.: American Council of Education, 1966, pp. 625–37.

Indexes

Author Index

385

Subject Index

This book has been set in 10 and 9 point Times Roman, leaded 2 points. Part titles and numbers are in 18 point News Gothic Bold 93J. Reading titles are in 12 point Trade Gothic Bold. The size of the type page is 27 x 46½ picas.